$1,250

GATEWAY TO THE PROMISED LAND

Ethnic Cultures on New York's Lower East Side

D0876891

GATEWAY TO THE PROMISED LAND
Ethnic Cultures on New York's Lower East Side

Mario Maffi

NEW YORK UNIVERSITY PRESS
New York and London

NEW YORK UNIVERSITY PRESS
New York and London

Library of Congress Cataloging-in-Publication Data
Maffi, Mario, 1947–
Gateway to the promised land : ethnic cultures on New York's Lower
East Side / Mario Maffi.
p.   cm.
Includes bibliographical references (p.)
ISBN 0-8147-5509-7 (cloth : acid-free paper). — ISBN
0-8147-5508-9 (pbk. : acid-free paper)
1. Ethnology — New York (N.Y.)   2. Immigrants — New York (N.Y.) —
History.   3. Lower East Side (New York, N.Y.) — Social conditions.
4. Lower East Side (New York, N.Y.) — Emigration and immigration —
History.   5. New York (N.Y.) — Social conditions.   6. New York
(N.Y.) — Emigration and immigration — History.   I. Title.
F128.9.A1M34   1995
305.8'009747'1 — dc20   94-43556
CIP

Manufactured in the United States of America

New York University Press books are printed on acid-free paper,
and their binding materials are chosen for strength and durability.

10 9 8 7 6 5 4 3 2 1

CONTENTS

The beauty of the Lower East Side escapes all easy definitions. It is a beauty shaped by the desperate will to survive, a beauty of form and content so tightly interwoven that warp and woof, by now, are one.

Leo Lionni, "An Irresistible Urge To Make Things" (Commencement Address, Cooper Union, 29/5/1991)

PREFACE

I made my first acquaintance with the Lower East Side (the area of Manhattan bordered by East 14th Street, the East River, the access to the Brooklyn Bridge, and Lafayette Street-Fourth Avenue) on a bright November day in 1975. At that time, little did I know of its past and present. I was familiar with some of Abraham Cahan's writings and Jacob A. Riis's photos, and with the fact that the neighborhood had been and still was an immigrant quarter, an 'inner city'. That was almost all. But the person I went to see on that November day, after repeated warnings not to do so 'after dark', lived (an almost premonitory coincidence) on a crucial corner on East 9th Street and Avenue B, just across from the tall tower which would later become a controversial symbol of gentrification and from the huge school building which would soon be turned into one of the area's most active community centers.

In the years that followed, I went back to the Lower East Side time and again, both before and after dark. And, as I spent ever longer periods on East 13th Street and Avenue A, on Avenue A and St. Mark's Place, on East 7th Street and Avenue D, on East 4th Street and Avenue C, an intense relationship developed between me and the neighborhood — one which was based upon fascination and respect for a past I was slowly discovering and for a present I saw unfolding before my eyes. Out of this relationship, among other things, the present book was born, the result of some ten years' study and research, involvement and experience — *not* a history of the Lower East Side as such, but an analysis, in terms of multi-ethnic and cross-cultural experiences, of two key-periods: the years between 1880 and 1930 and the last three decades.

To an outsider like me, the Lower East Side taught several lessons. As a socio-cultural microcosm, it introduced me to a territory ripe with dramatic if overlooked creative energies. As a socio-cultural laboratory, it provided me with a clearer insight into the mechanisms of ethnicity, multi-culturalism, Americanization, class and gender relations, 'high' and 'low' culture. Let me briefly dwell upon some of these topics, which I find of great importance. The common notion of 'Americanization' (the 'melting-pot theory', with all its variations) is that of a one-way process through which immigrants from different parts of the world eventually shed their specific traits and, once turned into molten metal, are poured into the new mould to be reborn Americans. An inevitable corollary to

7

this notion is that such quarters as the Lower East Side are but stages of a journey which has basically *two* stations: that of departure and that of arrival. They become no man's lands, extensions of Ellis Island, the pots where immigrants are melted and cleansed. True, such a purely assimilationist view was recently counterbalanced by an opposite (though specular) one which rediscovers and celebrates ethnicity as a separate, strong identity, focuses upon continuity and permanence of original traits, and approaches immigrant neighborhoods as territories where the past is strenuously safeguarded and stubbornly recreated. But, to be sure, even this view is partial, interaction with America almost becoming a phenomenon which takes place only once immigrants have left their quarter.

The Lower East Side experience shows on the contrary (and I hope this book will sufficiently prove it) that the process is rather more complex than a one-way one and that such neighborhoods play a crucial rôle in it. Both socially and culturally, in fact, immigrant communities are living organisms. They are class structured, and they are gender oriented. They contain the past, and they entertain a continuous, osmotic relationship with the present. They give birth to new traits, and they remould old ones. They stimulate creative inner ferments, and they exercise a powerful attraction on the outside. And they express socio-cultural forms which are often as distant from traditional mores as from mainstream values. From the beginning, in the streets, tenements, sweatshops, meeting places of the Lower East Side, a multiform tension developed — within each immigrant group and within the quarter at large, between each group and America and between the quarter and America. The Lower East Side as a whole made up of different parts thus entered into a peculiar relationship with the rest of the country — *one which, while shaping and reshaping immigrant cultures, also shaped and reshaped mainstream culture.* As Waldo Frank wrote in *Our America* (1920): 'We go forth all to seek America. And in the seeking we create her'.

Such a dramatic experience went on for more than a century and still goes on today, and gave (gives) the neighborhood its peculiar character of laboratory ever at work, ever defying and denying too easy assumptions about culture and society. After witnessing how this laboratory functioned, I became increasingly aware of the fact that American culture is *not* the end product of a smooth and linear process through which different cultures are melted and, once purified, are poured into a pre-determined mould; or are uplifted by contact with a higher model, thus discarding impurities. What I saw (the neighborhood's daily life, its resistance to poverty and disintegration, its creative energies) and what I discovered (in books and archives, or in the oldtimers' vivid recollections) gave me the sense of a lively, ever-going dialectics between different fields of force — a dialectics which was and is at the very heart of cultural production.

These are some of the lessons the Lower East Side taught me, and for them I am infinitely grateful to it. The pages that follow are also an attempt on my part to give something in return[1].

***

No book is a separate world, but is inscribed in a complex system of stimulating references and cross-fertilizations. And, although this book charts several almost unexplored lands, its debts are many. First of all, to those 'classics' which, by exploring the *old* Lower East Side, formed the solid basis for my research — Moses Rischin's *The Promised City* (1962), Allon Schoener's *Portal to America* (1967), Ronald Sanders's *The Downtown Jews* (1969), Irving Howe's *World of Our Fathers* (1976), Elizabeth Ewen's *Immigrant Women in the Land of Dollars* (1985). Then, to a few seminal books which, by providing the necessary theoretical nourishment, helped to focus themes and problems — Alan Trachtenberg's *The Incorporation of America* (1982), Marshall Berman's *All That Is Solid Melts Into Air* (1982), Werner Sollors's *Beyond Ethnicity* (1986), not to speak of Walter Benjamin's and Siegfried Kracauer's work. Needless to say, the responsibility for the use I made of them all (and for the conclusions I drew) lies entirely with myself.

But the debts I contracted go well beyond books and their authors, however important they might have been. These other debts are often the most difficult to pay, because they are the less obvious to the reader. The present book, in fact, is not only the outcome of long, solitary hours spent in libraries and archives. It owes perhaps as much to the fecund interplay I enjoyed with the people of the Lower East Side — with the anonymous inhabitants who walked by in the streets, sat near me in theatres and cafés, spoke to me in shops and community centers, at rallies and on park benches; who, little by little, made me feel less an outsider and more an insider, and thus helped me to reach a better understanding of a variegated, difficult reality. And it owes a lot to a veritable cohort of generous persons who, from within as well as from without the neighborhood, helped me in all possible ways. To name them all (and perhaps to write a few words for each of them, as one is tempted to do when almost all is done and one's mind is free to flow back across time) would mean to add a whole new chapter to an already massive book[2].

9

For their timely and attentive coöperation, I am then most grateful to the directors and staff of the New York Chinatown History Museum, the Chinese Staff and Workers Association, the Community Service Society of New York, the Albizu Campos Community Center, Pueblo Nuevo, the Cooper Square Committee, Charas, the Henry Street Settlement, the Grand Street Settlement, the University Settlement Society, the Department of Puerto Rican Studies at the Brooklyn College of the City University, the Tenement Museum, the Museum of the City of New York, the New-York Historical Society, the New York Public Library (of its Manuscript and Archives Division and of its Seward Park and Tompkins Square Park branches), the Poetry Project at St. Mark's Church, the East Sixth Street Community Center, the Elmer Bobst Library and the Tamiment Library at New York University, the Columbia University Library, the YIVO Institute for Jewish Research, the American Italian Historical Association (Staten Island), the American Jewish Historical Society (Waltham, Mass.), the Brooklyn Museum, the Whitney Museum of American Art, the Metropolitan Museum of Art, the Library of Congress (Washington), the Los Angeles County Museum of Art, the Detroit Institute of Arts, the Corcoran Gallery (Washington), the Brown Brothers Photo Archives (Sterling, Pa.), *The Americas Review* (Houston), the British Library (London), the Centre de Documentation "B. Franklin" (Paris), the USIS Office in Milan, and the Centro di Studi Americani in Rome.

Some debts of gratitude I wish to pay in greater detail. Without the enthusiastic support of Eric Homberger, of the University of East Anglia (Norwich), and his patience and meticulousness in reading and criticizing each successive draft, it would have been difficult for this book to be born. My friends at Pennsylvania State University, Sandra Stelts and Ronald Filippelli, offered precious help by discussing the book each time we met, by answering all my requests for xeroxes and documents, and by never ceasing to send clippings and articles that 'might be of interest'. In Milan, Dennis Marino gave the finishing touches to my English, by painstakingly reading page after page and never failing to hope that, sooner or later, I would remember to write 'capable of', instead of 'capable to'. Finally, Werner Sollors of Harvard University, Maurizio Vandagna of the University of Turin and Rob Kroes of the University of Amsterdam definitely wanted to see the book published in the language it had originally been written in, and Fred van der Zee at Rodopi and Niko Pfund at the New York University Press (together with Laura Grandi and Victoria Satlow, my agents in Milan), made it possible.

After books and people, a third element concurred to the gestation and birth of this book. And it was places, all those places on the Lower East

10

Side that functioned as decompression chambers to me, where I stopped after a day's field work (or where I started it or broke it), to gather ideas and to scribble notes, to let impressions settle and to absorb atmospheres from all around — the Café Orlin, the Life Café, Christine's, the Leshko Café, the Odessa Restaurant, the Bo Ky Restaurant, the Sidewalk Café, Casa Adela, the Nuyorican Poets' Café, Yonah Shimmel's Bakery, McSorley's Old Ale House, and innumerable others which I now recall with nostalgia.

Through it all, Mariella and Alice, my father Bruno and my friends were much more than passive observers — surely the uneasiest task of all.

Mario Maffi
Milano, July 1993

The book was also made possible by some funds granted by the Italian Ministero per l'Università e la Ricerca Scientifica e Tecnologica (MURST) and the Centro Nazionale delle Ricerche (CNR).

Bibliographical note

In order to make reading easier, I decided to place between square brackets the author's name, the date of original publication (followed if necessary by the date of reprint), and the page number (which *always* refers to the edition shown by the last date), and to gather the whole bibliography, alphabetically, at the end of the volume.

Notes

1. This book has a rather uncommon history. Written directly in English, several vicissitudes delayed its publication, till it was translated into Italian by its author, and published in Milan by Feltrinelli, in the fall 1992. Now, three years after its completion, it finally sees the light in the language in which it had been originally written. Meanwhile, I have updated it and rewritten some parts — a kind of "work in progress" which, in a way, is very much "Lower-East-Side".

A few sad words are also needed here. Late in May 1992, as I was completing the Italian edition, the news reached me of the sudden death in New York of Bimbo Rivas, poet and activist, *genius loci* of the Lower East Side and dear friend of mine.

I remember him here, with emotion and affection, regretting that he (like other dear friends who passed away in the meantime: Ewan MacColl, Eugenio Battisti) will not be able to see what is also the result of so many hours spent together.

2. But I need to mention at least Janet Abu-Lughod, Moe and Mary Albanese, Miguel Algarín, John Auchard, Eva Banchelli, George Barteneff, the late Eugenio Battisti, Rosie Begun, William Boelhower, David Boyle, Jorge Brandon, Howard Brandstein, Carla Cappetti, Bruno Cartosio, Jules Chametzky, Michael Chandler, Fay Chew, Fay Chiang, Peter Cramer, Giuseppe Gadda Conti, Esther and the late Sam Dolgoff, María Dominguez, Francesco Durante, Sandra María Esteves, David Finn, Olean For, Paolo Gallerani, Chino Garcia, Allen Ginsberg, Diana Giossi, Frances Goldin, John Hausdorff, Kurt Hollander, Bob Holman, Irving Howe, Betsy Hulton, Paula Hyman, Yuri Kapralov, Tuli Kupferberg, Marvin Jones, the late Joe Juliano, Frank Ilchuk, Charlie Lai, Daniela Leoni, Nora, Leo and Mannie Lionni, Mary McCarthy, the late Ewan MacColl, Greg Mantsios, Martino Marazzi, Franco Minganti, Tom McKitterick, Marlis Momber, Antonello Negri, Hugh and Marilyn Nissenson, Daniela Noé, Lizzie Olesker, Al Orensanz, Francesca Orestano, Val Orselli, Jane Osmers, Pedro Pietri, Giampiero Piretto, Alison Prete, Moses Rischin, Bimbo Rivas, Joel Rose, Paula Rothenberg, Emily Rubin, Beppe Sacchi, the late Ronald Sanders, Peter Schumann, Jack Scully, Peggy Seeger, Greg Sholette, Joan Micklin Silver, Werner Sollors, Ellen Stewart, Cathy Taylor, Catherine Texier, Arthur Tobier, the late Esther Unger, Pegi Vail, Alberto Valentini, Benedetta Villa, Mark Waren, Jack Waters, Eve Weiner, Laura Zelasnick, Steven "Pepe" Zwaryczuk. I also wish to thank my students and former students Myriam Bait, Laura Cicognani, Stefania Lazzaroni, Fabio Malgaretti, Danila Silvestri, Patrizia Villani, for helping me in the often difficult task of transcribing tapes and reordering files.

Ill. 1
Map 1: The Lower East Side Today

13

INTRODUCTION

What I see before my eyes are layers of darkness encircling me, wrapping around me. Yet, darkness cannot bury me away. In darkness, I refuse to be intimidated. I struggle. I fight back to break open a way for my search of brightness.

Xiandai Yugong, "My Awakening" (1940)

I.

The walker in the city who takes St. Mark's Place at Third Avenue and from there heads east, crossing first the numbered and then the lettered avenues, and from Avenue D proceeds to the knot of streets below East Houston Street, discovers one of New York's most complex realities. The scene is shocking and fascinating at the same time. On the one hand, the city's physical aspect and social fabric gradually deteriorate. After the first rather bohemian blocks, a kind of no-man's land opens up beyond Avenue A (two bars in the vicinity carry the eloquent names of "Downtown Beirut" and "Downtown Beirut II"): the towering shells of empty tenements that stand as if bombed in some unheard-of war, the layers of debris scattered on the abandoned lots, the discarded furniture and household appliances cluttering the sidewalks, the hydrants turned open, feeding muddy puddles, and everywhere the hieroglyphs of signs, posters, graffiti. On the other hand, the city's skin seems to change, while a new territory is entered — a land of faces, words, and scenarios radically different from the glossy images of so many slick magazines or Hollywood movies.

Here are the *new* 'huddled masses' ["The New Colossus", in Lazarus 1883, p.203], the Other America which seems ever to accompany Mainstream America as its *alter ego*, dramatically linked to it in a life-and-death relationship that implies tragedy at the same time that it expresses potentialities — the vast expanse inhabited by the *Latino* population with their *bodegas* and *carnicerias* (on and around Avenues B, C, D, and between East Houston and Grand Street), the rapidly growing area of Chinatown teeming with the ant-like bustle of its crowds (on Canal, Mulberry, Mott, Bayard, Doyers streets, East Broadway), and those 'pockets of old, [...] pockets of time'[1] where survivors from

15

another epoch of immigration to the "golden land" still cling together (Orthodox Jews along Essex Street and East Broadway, Italians on First Avenue and Elizabeth Street, Slavs along Second Avenue and around Tompkins Square Park). On the map and in common usage, the neighborhood often receives different names. Some cut out the portion between the Bowery and Tompkins Square, south of East 14th Street and north of East Houston, and term it "East Village"[2]. Some choose the quadrilateral formed by the lettered avenues, and name it "Alphabet City". Others speak generically of the "East Side" [See Map 1]. All are somewhat improper definitions, each containing specific synecdochical implications and socio-cultural approaches. As W. H. Auden, long-time resident at 77 St. Mark's Place, once wrote, 'to me, it will always be the *Lower East Side*, never the *East Village*' [Auden 1972].

In this geography of urban wilderness, the walker in the city unearths rich signs of cross-cultural life and creativity. On Lafayette Street, East 4th and East 3rd streets, three mythical theatres show all-Shakespeare bills or Reinaldo Povod's "La Puta Vida Trilogy" (the late Joe Papp's Public Theatre), Dario D'Ambrosi's "Altra Italia" Festival and Wallace Shawn's "The Fever", plus a dense bill of plays, one-night performances, dance, poetry and art (Ellen Stewart's La Mama E.T.C.), Jean Genet's "The Maids" and William Hasenclever's "Humanity" (Judith Malina's Living Theatre). In the former retail market building on First Avenue and in the empty lot on East 8th Street between Avenue C and Avenue D, George Barteneff's and Crystal Field's Theatre for the New City stages its collective productions, "Homecoming" and "The Coney Island Kid". On First Avenue, Performance Space 122 hosts Mabou Mines and Spalding Grey, Betsy Hulton's dance performances and Pedro Pietri's "spaghetti dinner" poetry reading. On Second Avenue, the Orpheum Theatre presents Eric Bogosian in "Sex, Drugs & Rock 'n' Roll". A few blocks away, the Bouwerie Lane Theatre shows Robert Patrick's "Judas" and Mark Waren's "Mexico". Other theatres enliven the area — the Fourth Wall Political Theater, the New Theater, the Elysium Theater Company, the Pyramid Club, the Playground Theater, the CSC Repertory, the WOW Café, the New Federal Theater, the House of Candles, the NADA, the Jewish Repertory Theatre, several others. Poetry readings are held in the epochal St. Mark's Church at East 10th Street and Second Avenue, at MosaicBooks on Avenue B and East 10th Street, amid the fantastic scrap metal sculptures of the Gas Station on Avenue B and East 2nd Street, at the Nuyorican Poets' Café on East 3rd Street (Pedro Pietri and Bob Holman hosting the "Poets in the Bar" program), in the Knitting Factory's Knot Room on East Houston between a concert of the Lounge Lizards and a cabaret performance of Vince

16

Ill. 2
A Nuyorican Poets' Café Play-bill

Katz's The Throbbers, at the Life Café at the corner of East 10th Street and Avenue B, at ABC No Rio on Rivington Street, in bars, theatres, and cafés everywhere. At Charas-El Bohio, on East 9th Street, Bimbo Rivas's *bombas* are staged, movies by D. W. Griffith, Paul Morrissey, Morris Engel, Rudy Burckhardt are shown, paintings by Latino artists are exhibited, dance parties are held on the *Terraza*. Music is played at the CBGB on the Bowery, at the Knitting Factory, at the Gas Station, at the Nuyorican Poets' Café, at the Pyramid Club, at El Bohio, in tens of other places.

The walker in the city can also enjoy a fascinating plunge in a century-old past by sitting down in the Café Orlin on St. Mark's Place and in McSorley's Old Ale House on East 7th Street, or taste ethnic food at the Indian and Pakistani restaurants on and around East 6th Street, at the Ukrainian Veselka on Second Avenue, Leshko Café and Odessa Restaurant on Avenue A at Tompkins Square Park, at the Polish Christine's on First Avenue, at the Caribbean Casa Adela's on Avenue C, at the various Mexican and Latin American eating places on Clinton and Rivington streets, at the Italian Lanza's and De Robertis's on First Avenue and Veniero's on East 11th Street (and in a by-now rather touristic Little Italy), at the Chinese *kosher* Bernstein on Essex Street and at the innumerable large and small restaurants in Chinatown's Mott, Baxter, Doyers streets, at Sammy's Roumanian Steakhouse on Chrystie Street, at the Jewish Katz's Deli and Yonah Shimmel's Bakery on East Houston Street, and Ratner's on Delancey Street.

S/he can visit the library of the Chinatown History Project, use the archives of the University Settlement on Eldridge Street, attend the socio-cultural activities organized by the Henry Street Settlement on Grand Street and by the Educational Alliance on East Broadway, stroll down Mulberry Street during the San Gennaro Feast, down Clinton Street during the Immigrants' Fair (the Willie Colon Band playing to a large crowd), down Second Avenue and East 9th Street during the Ukrainian Festival, and among the stalls of Chassidic Jews at the corner of Essex, Division, and Canal streets at the time of the High Holy Days. And s/he can run into street demonstrations of the Lower East Siders Against the War or into pickets organized by the Chinese Staff and Workers Association in front of the Chinese-American Planning Council, or attend meetings of the Lower East Side Joint Planning Council at the East 6th Street Community Center or at Community Access on Avenue C, and discuss strategies against displacement at the Cooper Square Committee on East 4th Street and at Pueblo Nuevo on Pitt Street...

II.

This impressive mixture of decay and vitality is the product of the past fifty years' continuous change on the Lower East Side. Its great era as an immigrant quarter had come to an end by the 1930s. The war and the immigration legislation that accompanied and followed it had reduced the flow of foreigners to a small trickle[3]. At the same time, a kind of diaspora had been triggered by the previous half century of socio-economic developments — improved living standards won after decades of union activity, relocation of plants to other parts of Manhattan in order to comply with health and security provisions and to follow the city's commercial and manufacturing northern shift, better job opportunities opening midtown and uptown New York, further development of mass transportation...Second- and third-generation immigrants began to leave the Lower East Side in large numbers, heading for Brooklyn, the Bronx, the suburbs, in order to find more comfortable quarters, more room and air, and thus to celebrate a newly acquired social status. As population dropped from over 540,000 to 205,000 (-62%) between 1910 and 1940 [Grebler 1952, p.106], most immigrant enclaves shrank to a small nucleus — people who had not managed to climb the social ladder, old-timers reluctant to move due to age, language, religious affiliations and related jobs.

The physical aspect of the Lower East Side also changed more than it ever had in the past. Between 1903 and 1948, the dwelling units demolished in the quarter accounted for 27% of the units of the same kind in Manhattan and for 21% in New York City. As part of the New Deal's public-works programs, whole tenement blocks were razed. The Sara D. Roosevelt Parkway was opened by tearing down the eastern side of Chrystie Street and the western side of Forsyth Street. Allen, Essex and East Houston streets were enlarged in the same way. The early low-income housing projects began to appear, such as the Vladeck Houses. The trend continued after the war, on the basis of a strategy which a close look at Map 1 makes apparent. With the only exceptions of the Village View Houses, of the First Houses, and of the Seward Park Houses, the big projects (from the Alfred E. Smith Houses on the southern end to the Jacob Riis Houses on the north-eastern end) border the Lower East Side on its eastern edge, along the river. The vast inner part — so close to Wall Street and to Broadway, i.e. to the financial and commercial heart of the metropolis — offers itself as a tempting land of conquest for real estate speculation. As a matter of fact, a plan to gentrify the area existed from the 1930s[4]. But it came to a sudden if provisional halt during the post-war boom years, because it contradicted what was emerging as one of the major social phenomena of the period — the middle-class move to the suburbs. With the complete development of the rapid transit systems and the prospect of an independent house in New Jersey or upstate, complete with a lawn in front, a garage aside, and a pool behind, who would choose to live in a gentrified Lower East Side?

The neighborhood thus became 'an area in transition' [Grebler 1952, p.5; also Jacobs 1961, and Harrington 1962], 'a kind of waste land' [Tobier, interview, 1987]. Plagued by higher vacancy ratios than in Manhattan and New York City, it was still inhabited by a hard-core of old-timers. Mainly Jews, but Italians as well, non-Jewish East Europeans, and Chinese, they catered to, and so helped to retain at least partially, those business enterprises that in the past had been a typical feature of the neighborhood — ethnic food shops and restaurants, religious articles supplies, garment retail centers, markets, pushcarts. At the same time, absentee ownership began to rule the Lower East Side. Landlords, many of them former immigrants who had moved out of the quarter, abandoned buildings to time and decay, offering as justification the unprofitable rent-control regime. The material consequences were quick to be noted — worsening of the framework, malfunctioning of pipes and plumbing, collapse of staircases, rusting of fire escapes, stoppage of heating...More and more buildings were boarded up and storefronts closed, while the malpractice of "suspicious fires" (relieving the owner of a burden and allowing him to collect the insurance premium) was sadly inaugurated [Grebler 1952]. The area was now ready for new, deep social changes, and these came when its high vacancy ratio began to attract again a composite population.

The middle-class suburban shift was in fact paralleled by an opposite trend. Enticed by its opportunities, demobilized soldiers preferred to settle in the city rather than go back to smalltown dreariness, soon joined by country boys and girls. At the same time, low-income families rediscovered the Lower East Side's abandoned buildings and started to reopen them, side by side with a post-war disaffected youth highly charged with an emotional sense of social, existential, and cultural displacement [Cartosio 1992]. It was a somewhat explosive combination, variously captured by such works as Michael V. Gazzo's "A Hatful of Rain" (1955), Allen Ginsberg's "Howl" (1956), Galway Kinnell's "The Avenue Bearing the Initial of Christ into the New World" (1960), Edward Adler's *Notes from a Dark Street* (1962), or by such independent movies as Morris Engel's *Weddings and Babies* (1956), Lionel Rogosin's *On the Bowery* (1956), Rudy Burckhardt's *What Mozart Saw on Mulberry Street* (1959).

20

Above all, deep subterranean shifts were taking place in the neighborhood's ethnic composition, of the utmost importance for the future. While in fact the definition of 'area in transition' held true — and the dispersal of most immigrant enclaves undoubtedly led to 'a diluting of the ethnic composition of the Lower East Side population' [Grebler 1952, p.147] —, still the quarter retained a basically multi-ethnic aspect. In the post-war years, the survivors of the old immigrant communities were in fact joined by new groups of Ukrainians and Poles, who — as "displaced persons" — often had political views other than those of former, more radical, settlements from the same areas[5]. Blacks also began to arrive — although in very small numbers (from 185 in 1910 to 1,372 in 1940), Harlem always being their main destination in the city —, and an important foothold was established in the 1950s, when a group of black artists (poets Leroi Jones and Ted Joans, painters Bob Thompson, Benny Andrews, and Willima White, jazz musician Marion Brown) turned a non-descript Bowery bar on Cooper Square (the Five Spot) into a lively crossroads of poetry, jazz, and Black liberation[6]. But the two, new major phenomena in the never-ending saga of immigration to the Lower East Side were the growth of Chinatown and the birth of Loisaida, as the Puerto Rican area soon came to be known[7].

III.

An isolated, almost besieged community on the material as well as cultural/psychological level[8], Chinatown first underwent important changes in the 1930s. Such grassroots organizations as the Chinese Unemployed Council, the Chinese Hand Laundry Alliance, the Chinese Youth Club, and the Chinese seamen's unions, began to challenge the community's traditional power hierarchy — the pyramid composed of the merchant-dominated Chinese Consolidated Benevolent Association (CCBA), the feudal village, surname, district and speech-pattern associations, the semi-legal *tongs* often functioning as the CCBA's strong-arm, and the Nationalist Party, or Kuomintang. In so doing, they also tried to reach out to the larger American labor movement in a delicate and often difficult balance between China's internal developments (and their effects upon the New York's community) and the American reaction to them [Kwong 1979]. But the real breakthrough took place in 1943 when the Chinese Exclusion Act was repealed, and two years later, when the War Brides Act was passed. Other acts then followed, in 1948, 1953, 1957, 1962 — all of them rather dependent upon the shifts in the United States government's relationship with China. Finally, in 1965, the 1924 quota system was abolished and a new quota of 20,000 immigrants per year assigned to each country outside the Western Hemisphere[9]. For the first time in Chinatown's history, the foundations of a normal life were laid and the community was thus revitalized.

The effects were many. Chinese women started to arrive at a time in which the city's labor market was experiencing important transformations. The economic boom following the brief post-war recession, the reduced availability of the traditional immigrant workforce, and the new developments in a by now international fashion world were in fact pushing the garment industry downtown again, in search of new, cheap labor. The large inflow of Chinese women thus proved a blessing, as the case had been some seventy years before with the Jewish and Italian immigrants. Their entrance into the garment industry also started a chain reaction. Still based on the central figure of the contractor (the ethnic middle-man who spoke the workers' language, knew the community's labor market from the inside, and thus could distribute orders and settle conflicts), the industry became a vital economic factor in the community. It bred a new entrepreneur class who could in time turn into factory-owners (the 8 Chinese garment factories active in the area in 1960 became 34 in 1965, 209 in 1974, and 500 in 1984, with some 20,000 workers). The accumulated capital could then be (and was) reinvested in other economic sectors, mainly in restaurants (some 450 today, employing 20,000 persons) and in real estate, which in turn led to the community's economic take-off in the early 1980s and to the ensuing, massive inflow of foreign capital, above all from Taiwan and Hong Kong.

At the same time, such sweeping developments deepened (and clearly brought to the surface) Chinatown's class stratification — a reality which, in the community's separation from the larger American world and in the peculiar situation of the "bachelor society", tended to be overlooked, if not played down or denied in the name of ethnic solidarity. More Asian immigrants arrived in the 1970s and 1980s, and the original six-block area soon burst at its seams spreading out into all directions. Not without strong resistance, it extended up Mulberry Street in Little Italy and entered such Jewish strongholds as Orchard and Essex streets and East Broadway — two eloquent signs being the opening of a Chinese *kosher* restaurant, "Bernstein-on-Essex", and the purchase of the *Jewish Daily Forward* building, an East Broadway historical landmark. So, while Fukienese settled on Division Street, Burmese Chinese on Henry Street, Chinese from Taiwan on Centre Street and Vietnamese on East Broadway, a large working class developed, ruthlessly exploited in restaurants, sweatshops, and in a growing underground economy. And this in turn led to new harsh confrontations with the traditional power structure[10].

It was inevitable that such drastic changes on an enclave that had remained frozen for more than half a century should have deep effects on the cultural level as well. And in fact, precisely in the 1940s, a literary movement developed[11]. On the pages of the *Xin Sheng* ("New Life") supplement to *Hua-ch'iao jih-pao* (*China Daily News*), a lively newspaper which took courageous progressive positions and was finally gagged by the House Un-American Activities Committee, sketches, poems, short-stories began to appear, which provided dramatic insights into Chinatown's earlier experience and the inevitable problems its gradual opening up was creating. Lao Mei (pen-name of Eugene Moy, the newspaper's editor), Xiandai Yugong, Lao Zhu and Wei Ling, most of them obscure labourers, voiced the loneliness of sojourners drudging away in laundries and restaurants, the longings bred by the cruel separation from wives and families, the dreams and frustrations, yearnings and self-hatred produced by the "bachelor society", the generational rifts and the early challenges to traditional gender rôles — but also the intriguing awe inspired by New York and the stubborn response to racism and isolation[12]. Of course, these works addressed themselves to an inside audience, much as had been with several turn-of-the-century Italian and Yiddish literary efforts. But, as with them, they ultimately paved the way for future developments that, while rooted in the Chinatown experience, would reach out, to confront America, its culture, and its stereotyped views of Chinese immigrants.

Some ten years passed, and the appearance, in 1961, of Louis Chu's novel, *Eat a Bowl of Tea* (recently turned into a movie by director Wayne Wang), was a real turning point. Written in English, it showed the neighborhood in its everyday life, "warts and all", avoiding the traps of the sensational or saccharine. The story of long-time friends, Wah Gay and Lee Gong, who arrange a marriage between their respective son, Ben Loy, and daughter, Mei Oi, is set at the time when the old "bachelor society" was giving way (amid tensions and contradictions) to normal life and family rhythms. Against this backdrop, portrayed with bitter-sweet attention, three worlds collide and finally come to terms. Wah Gay's and Lee Gong's is the old, isolated, all-male world, scarred by the need to control and redirect lives and emotions. Ben Loy's is a no-man's land between his father's past (so alien, so burdening) and his own present of a married man emotionally disturbed to the point of sexual impotence. Mei Loi's is the world of a young country girl, suddenly thrown from her small village into the complexities and anomies of the big American metropolis ('To Mei Oi the novelty of New York soon wore off.

23

Chinatown turned out to be less glamorous than she had pictured it. Buildings are buildings everywhere. New York lacked the intimacy of a rural village. She could not go over to Lane Four to borrow a porcelain dish for her cooking...') [Chu 1979, p.79]. As she accepts the courtship of disreputable Ah Song and bears him a child — in what ultimately amounts to an act of vengeance against traditional allegiances *and* modern gender rôles —, the whole microcosm verges on tragedy. Written with a masterful attention for places and ear for spoken language (no pidgin English, but the translation into English of the colourful Sze Yup dialect), Chu's novel signalled the real coming-of-age of literary Chinatown and ushered in a decisive decade in terms of the search for a socio-cultural identity. The fact itself that no whites are present in the story, unless very marginally, has perhaps the most far-reaching implications — almost as if that was the only way, at that time, to keep at a distance any possible stereotype.

But it was during the 1960s, with their widespread social and political ferment, that the neighborhood initiated a rediscovery of its own history. Second-generation Chinese joined Blacks and other minorities in the effort to wring their own past from generalized amnesia and tried to break isolation and self-withdrawal by confronting the traditional power structure [Chiang, interview, 1987; Lai, interview, 1987; Kochiyama 1981; Chiang 1987 and 1987-88]. The experience of the Black Panthers was thus paralleled by the emergence of such Chinatown groups as the I Wor Kuen ("Righteous and Harmonious Fists") and the Workers' Viewpoint, and of the front organizations they set up in order to root themselves in the community (the Progressive Chinese People's Association, the Asian Americans for Equality). Particularly significant was the experience of the Basement Workshop, founded in 1970 by some 30 artists and militants (second-generation Chinese, third-generation Japanese, foreign-born from Hong Kong and Taiwan, and Chinatown residents), directed for a long time by Fay Chiang and originally located at 54 Elizabeth Street, but soon to spread to several different locations on Lafayette and Catherine streets [Chiang 1986; L. Lippard 1984 and 1990; "Two Voices" 1987-88; Wasserman 1987-88]. In the span of a fifteen-year, often turbulent history, it developed a most rare Asian American Resource Center, the lively *Bridge Magazine*, and several activities, from the Amerasia Creative Arts Workshop to the Community Planning Workshop, from the Neighborhood Youth Corps to the Visual Arts, Performance, Literature, Folk Arts, and Children's programs. Together with other groups active in the quarter — Charas, the Lower East Side Printshop, Cityarts Workshop, the Children's Art Workshop, El Teatro Ambulante, and the Fourth Street "i" —, the Basement was also a member of Seven Loaves, a key organization on the Lower East Side which provided training in fund raising and management. It thus functioned as a forge of future talents in all fields of creative arts and community organization, the structure and venue through which new (or different) generations could come together on the political and cultural level and spread across the city and America at large.

From its very beginnings, the Basement was a *multi-ethnic, cross-cultural* project and laboratory, acknowledging and expressing, in its varied activities, Chinatown's and the Lower East Side's complexity. It was in fact increasingly clear that the term "Chinatown" — while it surely expressed the numerically dominant presence of Chinese from China, Hong Kong and Taiwan — had rather curtailing implications. With the 1965 Act, a new flow of immigrants had began to arrive from most Far East countries, due to increase in future years. As Filipinos, Hawaiians, Koreans, Vietnamese came and settled in the city, Chinatown itself grew more and more *Asian-American* than simply *Chinese* [Kessner and Caroli 1982; Bogen 1987; N. Foner 1987]. At the same time, the internationalist approach of most minority organizations led to a fruitful exchange of experiences. So, it was not surprising to find, among the Basement's "graduates" and collaborators, Puerto Rican, Filipino, Hawaiian, Black, Japanese, and American poets, painters, community activists, performing artists. Fay Chiang's poetry and Jessica Hagedorn's performances offer perhaps the best insights into this development.

Chiang's collections *In the City of Contradictions* (1979) and *Miwa's Song* (1982), and her works-in-progress, the narrative poem "Chinatown" and the play "Laundryman", all revolve around the theme of the past — of a personal and collective past to be recaptured by following again, in reality and metaphor, the paths opened by the ancestors in their isolated existence, and now buried in microcosm and macrocosm, in Chinatown and New York City. The poet-activist thus has the task of discovering and reopening them up[13]. But this past isn't simply the *old* past. It is also *a more recent one*, represented by the younger generations' struggle for self-identity — a past of Lower East Side militancy that embraces Chinese as well as Puerto Rican (and other nationalities') poet-activists, in the humbly proud feeling that 'in the city of contradictions/ we are among the survivors' ["in the city of contradictions", in Chiang 1979, p.vi]. Jessica Hagedorn came to the Basement via the West Coast and a personal interpretation of rock music as a multi-media experience, a field which continues to be her main interest. Out of this came the piece "Tenement Lover: no palm trees/ in new york city" (1981, music composed and performed by herself & The Gangster Choir and by "Butch" Morris, a Lower East Side Black artist), centered on the theme of solitude and displacement, racism and homesickness, otherness and identity. In one of the letters which form the piece's guiding thread, central character Bongbong writes: 'I think I may come back to Manila soon, but somehow I feel I'm being trapped into staying here...' ["Tenement Lover", in Berson, ed., 1990, p.86; also see Hagedorn 1987] — and this is a bitter but crystal-clear definition of the immigrant's (the other's) material and psychological condition. Hagedorn's most recent productions, especially those done with the group Thought Music formed with two other important Lower East Side artists and activists, Black Laurie Carlos and Robbie McCauley [Hagedorn, Carlos, McCauley, 1990], insist on these themes, on a multi-ethnic perspective, and on racism and sexism, with a growing toughness and a more aggressive personal/political involvement.

The birth of what is today one of the neighborhood's most significant experiences was also connected to the Basement. In 1978, two of its members, Charlie Lai and John Kuo Wei Tchen, organized an exhibition called "Images from a Neglected Past: The Work and Culture of Chinese in America". The old-timers' enthusiastic response convinced the two Basement activists of the need to pursue that road. The New York's Chinatown History Project (70 Mulberry Street, renamed Chinatown History Museum in 1991) was thus born in 1980, as a cultural center engaged in reconstructing the past in order to compensate for the 'loss of memory' [Lai, interview, 1987; also see Lai and Tchen 1984] produced by the "bachelor society" experience. In ten years, with its exhibits and cultural programs, with its *Bu Gao Ban* bulletin and oral history programs, with its library and archives, the History Project has proved a crucial enterprise, not of Chinatown alone, but of the Lower East Side itself. As such exhibitions as "Puerto Rican Women in the Garment Industry" (1986) and "Between Mott and Mulberry: Views of Italians and Chinese in New York City" (1990) show, the center in fact, while firmly rooted in its own ethnic community, operates in a dimension which — as with most recent Asian-American activities — is openly multi-ethnic, and socially and politically progressive. So, while the Chinese neighborhood expanded and its contradictions became more apparent, the rôle of the New York Chinatown History Project, as well as of such organizations as the Asian Americans for Equality (176-180 Eldridge Street) and the Chinese Staff and Workers Association (15 Catherine Street), resulted increasingly vital.

Ill. 3
Poster of an Exhibition at the Chinatown History Museum

IV.

Although a veritable *mass* migration from Puerto Rico took place only after World War II, small Puerto Rican enclaves had existed in New York since mid-19th century, mainly made up of political exiles engaged in revolutionary activities in the Antilles. After the island's annexation in 1898, a new wave of immigrants (or, perhaps better, "in-migrants") joined them. Carpenters, bricklayers, house painters, type-setters, and above all cigarmakers were in fact being "pushed" to America by the structural changes occurring in *la isla*'s central productive sectors (tobacco, sugar, coffee) and, as a consequence, in its labor market — changes which had created a large, marginal work-force. Then, during World War I and after the new immigrant legislation of the 1920s, it was the needs of America's own changing labor market that "pulled" these available workers who, as a consequence of the 1917 Jones Act, now came as *citizens*, although the relationship that linked them to the mainland continued to be perceived as being semi-colonial[14].

New enclaves developed in Brooklyn, South Central Harlem, and principally in East Harlem, soon to be known as Spanish Harlem, or *El Barrio*. Contrary to some scholars' assumptions, a dense weave of coping institutions was created, that would play an important rôle when immigration began to increase[15]. Unions, such as La Internacional and La Unión Internacional de Tabaqueros, were founded by the cigarworkers of the 500 Hispanic-owned cigar-factories on the Lower East Side and in Chelsea[16]. Mutual aid societies, such as La Aurora or the Porto Rican Brotherhood of America, were born, as well as "hometown clubs" similar to contemporary Jewish and Italian *landsmanshaftn* and *società di mutua assistenza*. Cultural organizations with socialist or anarcho-syndicalist tendencies (the Ateneo Obrero, the Francisco Ferrer y Guardia School) offered busy schedules of evening or Sunday-afternoon lectures[17]. And there were more directly political organizations, often entertaining complex relationships with the island's political parties (the Puerto Rican Committee of the Socialist Party, El Corserio). Newspapers, like the anarchist *Cultura Proletaria*, the general-interest *El Heraldo*, and the most famous one, *La Prensa*, served as important links within the community. A crucial experience was that of the *Gráfico* (edited for some time by Vega), whose mainly working-class circulation and wide range of articles — union news, advice columns, community issues, fiction, general essays, movie reviews — made it a sort of Puerto Rican *Jewish Daily Forward* [Iglesias, ed., 1984; Rodríguez, Korrol, Alers, eds., 1980; Korrol 1983; Rodríguez 1989]. The community could then boast such charismatic *politicos* as Arturo Alfonso Schomburg,

Bernardo Vega, Jesus Colon, Luis Muñoz Marín, and pivotal cultural figures as poetess Lola Rodríguez de Tío (author of the Puerto Rican revolutionary anthem) and folklorist Pura Belpre (storyteller at the Madison House, at the Educational Alliance, and at the Seward Park Branch of the New York Public Library, all important cultural institutions on the Lower East Side).

As the immigrants slowly mastered the metropolis's new rhythms and spaces, an informal community system also developed. Barbershops, *bodegas* selling *plátanos* (fruit of the plantain tree) and *yautía* (root vegetables), *botánicas* specialized in plants and religious articles, small restaurants serving *mofongo* (an appetizer) and *arroz con gandules verdes* (rice and pigeon peas) became crucial meeting places where news, information, and advice were exchanged, before taking the way of stoops, rooftops, and backyards. The traditions of *compadrazgo* (which linked in a ritual kinship the natural parents of a child to his/her godparents) and of *hijos de crianza* (foster children), the "family intelligence network" based upon home work, shopping at the *marqueta*, and childcare, the *jaranas* and *veladas* (evening parties) where *conjuntos* played *merengue, bombas*, and *plenas*, helped to hold together the ethnic group confronted by an often hostile environment. Popular street figures such as *el piraguero*, who sold ice sweetened with syrup, and *el bolitero*, who ran numbers, also served to aggregate individuals and disseminate information.

If, up to the 1940s, all this took place *mainly* outside of the Lower East Side, pockets were already growing there — on East 1st, 3rd, 13th, 14th streets, along First Avenue and Avenue C. The situation changed when Caribbean immigration peaked as a consequence of wartime labor shortage and, afterwards, when "Operation Bootstrap" — a kind of forced industrialization — further upset Puerto Rico's social and economic situation[18]. Original Puerto Rican enclaves got congested and recent immigrants began to search for new neighborhoods. As an "area in transition", the Lower East Side was a suitable destination, and changes soon became apparent in its streets while a new Hispanic population settled side by side with the remains of older immigrant communities[19]. It was at that very time that a literary movement took form, whose early, most significant products were José Luis González's *El hombre de la calle* (1948), René Marqués's "La carreta" (1952), Pedro Juan Soto's *Spiks* (1956), and Jesus Colon's *A Puerto Rican in New York and Other Sketches* (1961). With his novel, González was among the first to explore the impact of immigration upon individuals thrown, in the span of a brief and convulsive experience, from the island's luxuriant interior, first to San Juan's city atmosphere and then to New York's metropolitan chaos. The same progression was central to Marqués's drama, which followed a family's hardships as it leaves the land, faces humiliation in San Juan and death in New York, and finally goes back to the land and its healing power. The real turning point came with Soto and Colon. First of all, they wrote mainly in English and in so doing inaugurated the complex reflection/operation upon language which would bear so much fruit in the future [Algarín, in Algarín and Piñero 1975; Algarín, in de Laguna 1987; Aparicio, in Fabre 1988; Benmayor 1989; Flores 1993]. Secondarily, they rendered big-city life with an immediacy and bitterness, and at the same time with a sympathy and warmth, that placed their sketches alongside the best works of contemporary city writing. Lastly, they presented life in New York as more than simply a parenthetical experience. Underneath the indifferent city's steel and concrete, paths were being opened and roots laid, although fluctuation and instability would continue to affect Puerto Rican settlements, giving rise to many economic, socio-cultural, and psychological problems. In 1967, a new stage was reached with the publication of Piri Thomas's *Down These Mean Streets* (Bernardo Vega's memoirs would appear only a decade later). Angry, hurt, outspoken, in terms of the search for an identity the book was almost as crucial as *The Autobiography of Malcolm X* (1965) and belied many surfacing stereotypes as regards life in the modern ethnic ghetto (Robert Wise's movie *West Side Story*, 1961, being a good example, with its Hollywood temptations and strong sentimental appeal)[20].

Meanwhile, another spontaneous form of aggregation was developing. With their tight hierarchy, paramilitary structure, precise codes of honour and rituals of combat, and a male *and* female membership that could reach as high as 2,000 people, such youth gangs as, in New York, the Assassins, the Dragons, the Sportsmen, the Unknowns, the Latin Crowns, the Bapin Balerinos, the Jaguars, the Robins, the Counts, came to fill a dramatic socio-cultural vacuum in the lives of many teen-agers. Often as young as thirteen, kids came together to defend "their" turf (a project, a block, a street, a park), generally organizing along ethnic or color lines[21]. Turf wars raged — from minor scuffles to pitched battles like the one which occurred in Central Park in May 1960 (and possibly inspired Sol Yurick's 1964 novel *The Warriors* and Walter Hill's subsequent movie version). Two of New York's most feared gangs were the Chelsea-based Assassins, led by teen-age Carlos "Chino" Garcia, and the Lower East Side-based Dragons, led by teen-age Angelo Gonzales. In the early 1960s, at a critical point in their private lives and the ghetto youth scene, these two charismatic leaders came together and began to rethink the whole gang experience, with the aim to redirect its enormous human potential towards constructive goals. At the time, several events throughout the country were moving in that direction. Large sectors of ghetto youth were turning away from the gangs' dead-end, towards forms of more direct political involvement. In Chicago, a Puerto Rican street gang followed the Black Panthers' example and founded the Young Lords Organization, which soon opened chapters in New York. In the Lower East Side, it had a branch at 256 East 3rd Street, held educational courses at St. Brigid's Church on Avenue B between East 7th and 8th streets, offered free breakfasts to ghetto children at 930 E.4th Walk, and shared with the Panthers and other radical organizations the sixteen-storey Christodora building at the corner of East 9th Street and Avenue B[22].

Out of "Chino"'s and Angelo's rethinking, the Real Great Society (a spoof on president Johnson's catch-phrase) was born, a community group which started to deal with the neighborhood's major issues — housing, jobs, education, youth gangs, drugs. In a few years, the small nucleus, originally based in a loft at the corner of Avenue B and East 6th Street, grew in numbers and importance and soon attracted city-wide attention. By late 1969, a new step was taken with the foundation of Charas (an acrostic from the six founders' names), godfathered by such an epochal figure as R. Buckminster Fuller, the inventor of geodesic domes [Garcia, interviews, 1984, 1986, 1991][23]. Since then, from El Bohio — its new, larger quarters in an abandoned school building at 605 East 9th Street —, Charas has been playing a fundamental rôle of aggregation and resistance, search for a socio-cultural identity and community work. It has opened a gallery, a theatre, and a cinemathèque, and has organized a series of stable programs, which go from music, murals, and cabaret to dance, martial arts, and capoeira. It has shown Ed Montgomery's and Robbie McCauley's Sedition Ensemble performances, and plays by the Bread & Puppet Theatre, the Living Theatre, and by local artists Bimbo Rivas ("The Winos", "Coco Baile", "Benito Vasconpique"), Tee Saralegui ("How Would You Handle a Rent Strike?"), Emily Rubin and Luis Guzman ("We Don't Want Cheese, We Want Apartments Please"). It has sponsored art exhibits, Maria Dominguez's and John Weber's mural workshops, the yearly Loisaida International Festival, and such local group as A Band Called Loisaida. And it has been involved in major housing activities. In the face of many external pressures (gentrification, displacement, drugs, decay), which have often caused individual break-ups, collective disillusionment, or internal strife, Charas has remained a true bulwark in Loisaida[24].

Those were surely fertile years. On August 28, 1970, for instance, the Young Lords' newspaper, *Palante*, published "Puerto Rican Obituary", by Pedro Pietri. It was a long, powerful and moving poem-monologue, which explored and laid bare the dreams and realities of the New York *colonia* and the devastating effects of supine assimilation[25]. Pietri was hailed as a new bard by a Puerto Rican community that now stretched from San Juan and Ponce to the Lower East Side, El Barrio, and the South Bronx. While his writing grew in satirical and visionary intensity (the plays: "LewLulu", 1975; "The Livingroom", 1975; "No More Bingo at the Wake", 1982; "The Masses Are Asses", 1984; "Happy Birthday MF", 1990; the poems of *Traffic Violations*, 1983), his themes continued to be the loss of identity in the pursuit of the American dream, the vulgarity of the middle-class search for social status, the tragedy of self-hatred [Pietri 1973, 1983, 1992][26]. To Pietri, and to Miguel Algarín, Sandra María Esteves, Tato Laviera, the late Miguel Piñero, to this generation of poets and playwrights who looked at street poet Jorge Brandon (*el coco que habla*, "the talking coconut" and founder of El Teatro Ambulante) as 'the sacred father-testament' ["don luís muñoz marín", in Laviera 1985, p.87; Brandon, interview, 1991] and tried to follow him as bards and troubadours, New York and Puerto Rico were gradually (if painfully) blending into a novel dimension — physical, cultural, and psychological —, finely captured by the name they gave themselves, *Nuyorican* poets[27]. When Algarín, Piñero and others opened the Nuyorican Poets' Café at 505 East 6th Street, it immediately became the vital crossroads and catalyst of a developing multi-ethnic socio-cultural scene.

Algarín, the most articulate writer of the group, has since published a *corpus* of poetry, which, beyond its Caribbean horizon, also bears witness to an intense relationship with American and European poetry (*Mongo Affair*, 1978; *On Call*, 1980; *Body Bee Calling from the 21st Century*, 1982; *Time's Now. Ya es tiempo*, 1985). Harsh and loving, brutal and tender, Manhattan and Puerto Rico, it fully explores the complex reality of "Nuyoricanity", the rootless search for roots in the city and in the island: 'there are no more Puerto Ricans/ in Borinquen/ I am the minority everywhere/ I am among the few in all societies/ I belong to a tribe of nomads/ who roam the world without/ a place to call a home,/ there is no place that is ALL MINE/ there is no place that I can/ call mi casa' ["Mongo Affair", in Algarín 1978, p.89][28]. Piñero, a tragic figure of poet-bandit who died 42 in 1988, wrote some of the last two decades' most interesting off-off Broadway plays, from the powerful and much-awarded "Short Eyes" (1974, a hard-hitting jail drama) to the bitter "The Sun Always Shines for the Cool", "A Midnight Moon at the Greasy Spoon", and "Eulogy for a Small Time Thief" (all 1984) and the one-act plays of the 1986 *Outrageous* collection. The world of his theatre

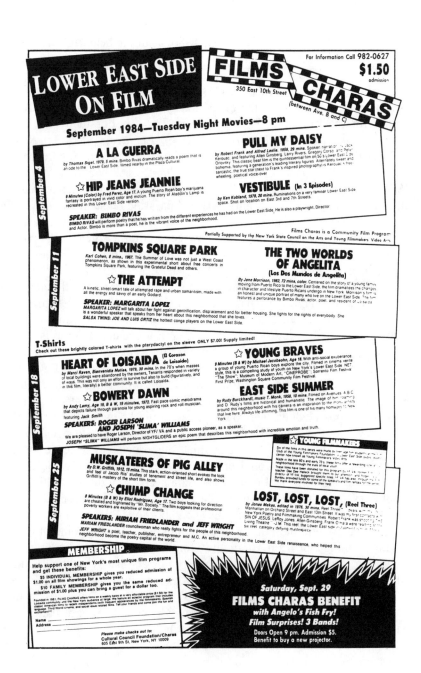

Ill. 4
A Films Charas Program

and poetry (*La bodega sold dreams*, 1980, with the beautiful "A Lower East Side Poem") is the ghetto underworld, its ruthless codes and, at the same time, its deep human yearnings — a place where 'it's all dragged out, no holds barred. Kick...punch...scratch...spitting...screaming. Fight. [...] because on the street the game is staying alive' ["The Sun Always Shines for the Cool", in Piñero 1984, p.33, 44]. For their part, Tato Laviera (*La carreta made a U-turn*, 1979; *Enclave*, 1981; *AmeRícan*, 1985; *Etica dominante. Mainstream Ethics*, 1988) and Sandra María Esteves (*Yerba Buena*, 1981; *Tropical Rains: A Bilingual Downpour*, 1984; *Bluestown Mockingbird Mambo*, 1990) search for and recreate a cultural and linguistic continuity between past and present, life *en la isla* and metropolitan pressures, Caribbean heritage and American reality. Sings Laviera: 'we gave birth to a new generation,/ AmeRícan, broader than lost gold/ never touched, hidden inside the/ puerto rican mountains' ["AmeRícan", in Laviera 1985, p.94], and echoes Esteves: 'What new paintings will be created on whose walls?/ Whose names will emerge in which new brilliant journals?/ What melodies will evolve from our mixings?/ In whose gardens will we water our visions?/ I want to know/ who will decide our fate?/ You, or I, or WE together?' ["Who Is Going To Tell Me?", in Esteves 1990, pp.58-59]. Reinaldo Povod (with his successful plays: "Cuba and His Teddy Bear", 1986; "La Puta Vida Trilogy", 1987), Nicholasa Mohr (*In Nueva York*, 1977; *Nilda*, 1986), Bimbo Rivas ("A Job", 1975), Lucky CienFuegos, and many others have in time variously added their own voices to the "Nuyorican" scene.

And while it may be true that not all of them are specifically *from* the Lower East Side, it is also true that the crucial experience of the Nuyorican Poets' Café would probably have been inconceivable in any other place than in the Lower East Side's cross-cultural, multi-ethnic laboratory. As with "Chinatown", the concept itself of "Loisaida", while it surely indicates a part of the neighborhood, is taking on new implications, while the Puerto Rican community is being joined by ever greater contingents from Haiti, the Dominican Republic, El Salvador, Columbia, Ecuador (partly illegal immigrants and partly political exiles, with all the many ensuing problems) [Kessner and Caroli 1982; Foner, ed., 1987]. At the same time, Loisaida more and more absorbs former East European and Italian enclaves around Tompkins Square Park, and, on Delancey Street, almost meets Chinatown in its northward thrust. In 1990, the reopening of the Café at 236 East 3rd Street, after several years' inactivity, has made this complexity even more apparent. In its huge bar-and-hall, the Café brings together Black musicians Butch Morris and Jemeel Moondoc, "Fred Ho & the Afro-Asian Music Ensemble", Pietri's "Happy Birthday MF", Ishmael Reed's "Savage Wilds", and

34

Emily Rubin's "Her Minding Eyes", poets Bob Holman and Robert Creeley, Amiri Baraka and Lois Griffith, Bimbo Rivas and Jorge Brandon, Adrienne Su and Bob Rosenthal, performers Jessica Hagedorn, Robbie McCauley, Laurie Carlos, the "All of Us Band" and Sekou Sundiata & the "DAHDADOODAHDA BAND", in a fascinating crucible of voices and cultures, talents and experiences.

For the past fifteen years, this lively scene of resistance to decay has been poetically recorded by German photographer and long-time resident in the area Marlis Momber. Her works (published in many community magazines, calendars, and fliers, and often exhibited in the United States and abroad) are devoid of any mystifying, sensational, or local-color temptation, in favor of a view of the neighborhood (even in its darker aspects) which exalts its more communal dimension, its stubborn will to create with the raw materials of experience and in the face of so many adversities [Momber 1984; Momber, interview, 1987; see Tables 21-28]. The same feeling runs through other expressions of the neighborhood, which Marlis Momber has frequently portrayed — its fascinating gardens and murals. With the support of organizations such as the Lower East Side Garden Coalition or the Green Guerillas, and thanks to the unflinching enthusiasm of local activists Liz Christy, Olean For, and Carmen Pabón, during the late 1970s and early 1980s, debris-ridden and drug-infested empty lots were turned into luxuriant gardens, where flowers and plants alternated with drawings and sculptures, objects and installations, to compose a wonderland of fantasy and creativity, of which Adam Purple's Garden of Eden on Eldridge Street, with its huge yin-yan symbol designed with neighborhood detritus, was perhaps the most famous example. And while many of them have been in time abandoned again, some still remain as testimony of potentialities within the city and its ghettoes [For, interview, 1991][29].

The same is true of the murals. Starting in the early 1970s, CityArts, an organization engaged in art projects all over Manhattan, has been responsible for an intense activity in the neighborhood. Eva Cockcroft, John Weber, and other painters got in touch with community people — kids and such local artists as James Jannuzzi, Susan Caruso-Green, Tomie Arai, Alfredo Hernandez, Alan Okada, Maria Dominguez, Tabo Toral, Lee Quinones, Chico —, and out of a relationship based upon cultural interaction came some of the city's most beautiful murals — "Afro-Latin Coalition" (1973), on East 4th Street and Avenue C; "New Birth" (1974), on the parking lot on Rivington and Chrystie streets; "The Wall of Respect for Women" (1974), on the outside wall of the Garden Cafeteria (165 East Broadway); "Chi Lai/Arriba/Rise Up!" (1974), at 191 Madison Street; "Art as an Alternative to Violence" (1974), on

35

'A festa 'e tutte 'e ffeste

55.ma • GRANDIOSA FESTA ANNUALE • 55.ma

IN OMAGGIO AL NOSTRO MIRACOLOSO

SAN GENNARO

che avra luogo nei giorni

10-11-12-13-14-15-16-17-18-19-20 SETTEMBRE 1981

IN MULBERRY STREET • NEW YORK CITY

Program   *Programma*

THURSDAY, SEPTEMBER 10
6:00 P.M. — Grand Opening
The Band will play through the street.

FRIDAY, SEPTEMBER 11
Entertainment.

SATURDAY, SEPTEMBER 12
3:00 P.M. — Procession with the Statue of the Miraculous St. Gennaro through the streets of Little Italy
8:00 P.M. — Entertainment
10:00 P.M. — Scholarship awards ceremony.

SUNDAY, SEPTEMBER 13
2:00 P.M. — Spectacular parade with colorful Floats, Bands and Noted Personalities.

MONDAY, SEPTEMBER 14
Entertainment.

TUESDAY, SEPTEMBER 15
Entertainment

WEDNESDAY, SEPTEMBER 16
Entertainment.

THURSDAY, SEPTEMBER 17
Entertainment.

FRIDAY, SEPTEMBER 18
Entertainment.

SATURDAY, SEPTEMBER 19
San Gennaro's Feast Day
4:00 P.M. — Solemn High Mass will be celebrated by the Bishop at Most Precious Blood Church, 113 Baxter Street, followed by Veneration and Procession with the Relic of St. Gennaro.

SUNDAY, SEPTEMBER 20
3:00 P.M. — Entertainment.
8:00 P.M. — Entertainment.
11:00 P.M. — Drawing: 1st Prize Solid Gold Jackpot plus 10 other Prizes.

SAN GENNARO

GIOVEDI 10 SETTEMBRE
6:00 P.M. — Grandiosa apertura della festa.
La banda suonera' per le strade del rione.

VENERDI 11 SETTEMBRE
Trattenimenti.

SABATO 12 SETTEMBRE
3:00 P.M. — Grande processione con la Statua del Miracoloso San Gennaro che girera' per le strade del rione.
8:00 P.M. — Trattenimenti.
10:00 P.M. — Cerimonia della consegna delle "Borse di Studio."

DOMENICA 13 SETTEMBRE
2:00 P.M. — Sfilata con carri allegorici e bande con l'intervento di Note Personalita'.

LUNEDI 14 SETTEMBRE
Trattenimenti.

MARTEDI 15 SETTEMBRE
Trattenimenti.

MERCOLEDI 16 SETTEMBRE
Trattenimenti.

GIOVEDI 17 SETTEMBRE
Trattenimenti.

VENERDI 20 SETTEMBRE
Trattenimenti.

SABATO 19 SETTEMBRE
4:00 P.M. — Messa solenna che verra' celebrata dal Vescovo nella Chiesa "The Most Precious Blood," 113 Baxter Street, fara' seguito la venerazione e processione con le Reliquie di San Gennaro.

DOMENICA 20 SETTEMBRE
3:00 P.M. — Trattenimenti.
8:00 P.M. — Trattenimenti.
11:00 P.M. — Grande Riffa lo Premio Sorteggio in Oro piu altri 10 Premi di Consolazione.

NOTICE	AVVISO
In case of rain on	In caso di pioggia
SEPTEMBER 12	il 12 SETTEMBRE
The Procession	la processione
will be held	verra' fatta
SEPTEMBER 19	il 19 SETTEMBRE
at 3:00 P.M.	alle ore 3:00 P.M.

PROGRAMS
ARE SUBJECT TO CHANGE

FOR INFORMATION CALL OR WRITE: **SOCIETA' SAN GENNARO, NAPOLI E DINTORNI**
140 MULBERRY STREET — NEW YORK 10013 — TEL. CAnal 6-9546
Any visual or audio reproduction of this Festival, other than News Media, is Strictly Forbidden without the written permission of the Society of San Gennaro, Napoli e Dintorni, Inc.

M.A. LUPO, New York City 431-9755

Ill. 5
The San Gennaro Feast

Allen and Delancey streets; "Seeds for Progressive Change" (1975), at the corner of Delancey and Forsyth streets; "Women Hold Up Half the Sky" (1975), on a wall of P.S.63, on East 3rd Street; "Crear Una Sociedad Nueva" (1976), on East Houston Street, east of Second Avenue; "Arise from Oppression" (1978), on Pitt Street at the corner of Grand Street; and many more, some of them now either obliterated or seriously damaged [Shapiro-Kiok, in Cockcroft, Weber, Cockcroft, eds., 1977; Pockock and Battcock 1980; Glickman 1984; Cockcroft 1984; L. Lippard 1984]. Maria Dominguez, in particular, one of the most accomplished and exhibited artists of the Puerto Rican community, has been an active muralist in the Loisaida area. She has conducted several Charas-sponsored workshops with kids and local artists, and has worked at such noteworthy murals as "Baile Bomba" (1983; on Clinton Street), "Homenaje a Don Pedro" (1985; Albizu Campos Community Center, on East 13th Street), and "La Lucha Continua" (1986; on La Plaza Cultural, at the corner of Avenue C and East 9th Street), all of them celebrating the vibrant Caribbean heritage and a positive approach to life, creativity, and struggle in the ghetto [Dominguez, interview, 1991].

In such a lively scene, a process emerges which is ever clearer. While minority artists are engaged in rediscovering and proclaiming their own ethnic roots and identity, they increasingly relate to each other well beyond ethnic boundaries, in a fruitful dialectics that will eventually touch and reshape (as in part it is already happening) American culture. Martin Wong's "Attorney Street: Handball Court With Autobiographical Poem by Piñero" (1982-84), for instance, is the end product of the collaboration between a Chinese American painter and the late Nuyorican poet Miguel Piñero: by weaving together Chinatown and Puerto Rico, words and images (part of the painting is devoted to the deaf sign translation of a sentence), it really celebrates the Lower East Side's cross-cultural, multi-ethnic dimension, based upon all that is 'hybrid and relational' [Yau 1988, p.9; also see Urquhart 1988; L. Lippard 1990; Maffi, in Bak, ed., 1993; also see Table 29][30].

IV.

Starting with the late 1940s, the neighborhood also became the destination of 'a movement of people East, away from the West Village with its high rents and older bohemians' [Jones/Baraka 1984, p.175], a "gathering of the avant-garde"[31] which renewed the turn-of-the-century artists' flight from genteel America's stifling atmosphere. Following the trail of Jackson Pollock, action painters Willem and Elaine de Kooning, Franz Kline, Philip Guston, Philip Pavia, Alfred Leslie, Francisco Sainz,

Larry Rivers, Joan Mitchell, and others, settled in the neighborhood and, on and around East 10th Street, turned abandoned lofts, storefronts, and basements into studios and cooperative galleries (the Hansa, the Tanager, the Area, the Brata, the March, the Nonogan, the Phoenix)[32]. They were followed by pop-artists Robert Rauschenberg, Jasper Johns, Claes Oldenburg, Allan Kaprow, Jim Dine, Red Grooms, who, by exploring the pictorial/theatrical implications of Pollock's gestural approach, were already moving towards mixed forms of expression[33]. Soon, the beat scene too began to move from the West Side, as Allen Ginsberg, Peter Orlovsky, Jack Kerouac, Gregory Corso, Diane Di Prima found their "Paradise Alleys" in the quarter and began to knot new, peculiar threads in its ethnic warp. And, in the early 1960s, a series of bars and coffeehouses (the Tenth Street Coffeehouse, the Café Les Deux Megots on E. 7th Street, the Café Le Metro on Second Avenue) became the site of a new phenomenon[34]. "Poetry readings" multiplied and new names became familiar — Carol Bergé, Paul Blackburn, Joel Oppenheimer, Jerome Rothenberg, Ron Padgett, David Ignatow, Denise Levertov. The fact that readings were attended by such fountain-heads as Walter Lowenfels, Frank O'Hara, Charles Reznikoff, Muriel Rukeyser, Louis Zukofsky, was itself a sign of continuity with a recent past *and* with a tradition of poetry on the Lower East Side which dated back to the turn-of-the-century heated discussions on literature, theatre and the arts in the cafés of East Broadway, Grand Street, Second Avenue. The whole East Village, as the area north of East Houston Street came to be known, soon blossomed with socio-cultural activities, and when the poetry scene shifted again, from Le Metro to St. Mark's Church and Ann Waldman's Poetry Project, an entire period came full circle[35].

By the mid-1960s, this scene formed the basis for a mass phenomenon — the generational flight from middle-class white America, in search of alternative lifestyles. As thousands of kids flocked to the East Village, in a not always easy relationship with older and more recent residents, the "gathering of the avant-garde" turned into a "gathering of the tribes". New scenes developed, new places were opened, a new socio-cultural map was drawn, and soon narrated in Ronald Sukenick's *Up* (1968), Bill Amidon's *Charge!...* (1971), Emmett Grogan's *Ringolevio* (1972), Robert Patrick's "Kennedy's Children" (1973), Yuri Kapralov's *Once There Was a Village* (1974), William Kotzwinkle's *The Fan Man* (1974), Ed Sanders's *Tales of Beatnik Glory* (1975), Abbie Hoffman's *Soon To Be a Major Motion Picture* (1980)[36]. What took place afterwards, between the mid-1970s and the mid-1980s, represented a kind of extreme continuation of these ferments. Still another spillover from the West Side (mainly from the SoHo area, made rich and then devitalized by an

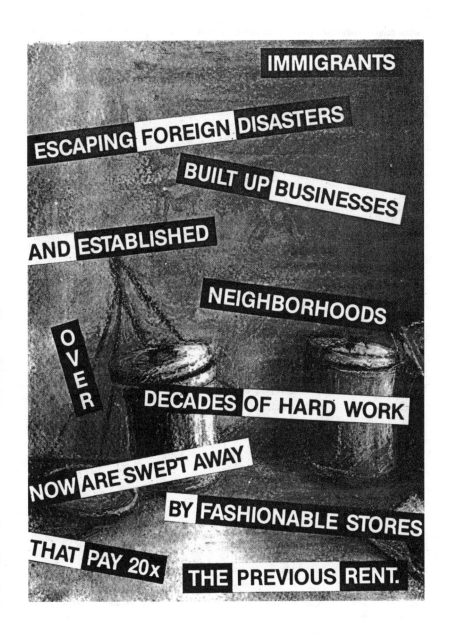

Ill. 6
A Drawing by Beatrice Schafroth for *World War 3*

international art market which had singled out New York as its capital), it was also the expression of two seemingly contrasting, but deeply related, phenomena — the city's bankruptcy, which opened a new phase of alienation and decay, violence and heavy drugs in the neighborhood, and the emergence of a new generation of *nouveaux riches* steeped in Reaganomics, with headquarters just round the corner, on Wall Street. The Punk, New Wave, No Wave culture reworked typical 1960s alternative lifestyles with a more disillusioned approach, a parodistic revival of 1950s American pop culture (TV serials, B-movies, dresses, images), and a conscious re-using of Dada and Bauhaus motifs, without forgetting such Lower East Side traditions as vaudeville and street culture.

The new movement was rooted in the Bowery rock club CBGB (which launched such seminal artists as Patti Smith, Iggy Pop, Mink DeVille, Television, the Voidoids, the Ramones, the Talking Heads, the B52s), in the East 3rd Street community of performing artists (Patti Astor, Tina L'Hotsky, David McDermott, Eric Mitchell), in Klaus Nomi's and Ann Magnuson's New Wave Vaudeville, in films by Amos Poe, Jim Jarmush, Eric Mitchell, Lech Kowalski, Paul Morrissey, Susan Seidelman, Jonathan Demme, in music by John Lurie, John Zorn, Laurie Anderson, Elliott Sharp, in works by graffiti artists Keith Haring, Jean-Michel Basquiat, Kenny Scharf, in Jenny Holzer's aggressive street stickers, Eric Bogosian's scathing monologues, Beth Lapides's, Holly Hughes's, Lenora Champagne's, Karen Finley's, and Ethyl Eichelberger's performances, in novels by Kathy Acker and Tama Janowitz, in such places as the Mudd Club, the Club 57, the Pyramid Club, the WOW Café, the Limbo Lounge, the 8BC, the Darinka Performance Studio, the P.S. 122, the Club Chandalier, the Shuttle, the Life Café, and in the fifty or more small galleries which came to dot the area, from Patti Astor's archetypical FUN Gallery to Piezo Electric, Gracie Mansion, Oggi Domani, Pat Hearn, P.P.O.W., Civilian Warfare, Nature Morte[37]. It was a fervid and convulsive scene, not without a decadent and self-destructive edge, frequently plagued by drug abuse and, after 1981-82, increasingly scarred by AIDS — a scene that started as a reaction to the West Side's sell-out and often ended by supplying Hollywood and the big art world with a long string of actors, musicians, designers, and painters. And by helping gentrification run wild throughout the Lower East Side.

In many ways, the East Village functioned in fact as real estate's inroads to the neighborhood. After surviving the state of abandonment of the 1950s and 1960s (itself an early stage in the gentrification process), the quarter began to confront phase two in the mid-1970s. Side by side

Ill. 7
A Drawing by Cosmo for *Squatter Comics*

with the new rock clubs and art galleries, fancy restaurants and chic boutiques multiplied around Tompkins Square Park, attracting a varied midtown and uptown clientele. At the same time, suspicious fires turned more frequent, old tenements were left to rot, entire areas became drug-infested, various forms of displacement pressures and tenant harassment were resorted to. By 1980, the process was well under way, and had made the neighborhood a '"hot" gentrifying housing market' [DeGiovanni 1987, p.27][38]. Whole buildings were sold and resold, their value rising each time. Others were razed, leaving empty lots whose land value also continued to rise. Still others were made into luxury condos, as was the case of the Christodora Building or of the northern side of East Houston Street at Avenue A, presently known as "Red Square". Steps were taken to get rid of the homeless (a critical issue in the neighborhood as in the whole city), squatters were repeatedly evicted by police, and the renovation itself of Tompkins Square Park seemed to obey military strategy[39]. In 1984, Operation Pressure Point, with its quasi-militarization of the quarter under the pretext of getting rid of drugs, climaxed the strategy of making the Lower East Side safe for an upper middle class eager to come back to the city from the suburbs. After the West Side, SoHo and Tribeca, the Lower East Side had been discovered as a very profitable area for gentrification.

The neighborhood's response was stubborn. A varied group of organizations began to wage a daily battle of resistance, which could rely on a long tradition of community mobilization[40]. The oldest and most famous group was the Cooper Square Committee (61 East 4th Street), born in 1959 to resist developer Robert Moses's plan to tear down the blocks between Delancey and East 9th streets from Second Avenue to the Bowery, and ever since a major force in the area devoted to organizing tenants, building low-income housing, and negotiating with developers and the city administration quotas of local residents in any new plan[41]. Founded in 1970, Pueblo Nuevo Housing and Development Association (125 Pitt Street) became active in the Clinton Street area, where it has built new apartments for low-income residents, managed several neglected or abandoned buildings, and sponsored murals and fairs (the important Annual Clinton Street Immigrants Festival was inaugurated in 1985)[42]. Another group, Interfaith Adopt-A-Building, Inc. (73-75 Avenue C), has been advocating affordable housing in the Loisaida area and giving assistance to community gardens and grassroots organizations. The Good Old Lower East Side (525 East 6th Street) and, more recently, the Lower East Side Local Enforcement Unit (31 Avenue A) have been providing legal services to tenants, while Chinatown's quick growth and ensuing tensions have been taken care of by the Asian Americans for

Equality (176-180 Eldridge Street). A widespread homesteading movement also developed in the 1980s. Groups formed by local activists and residents took possession of abandoned buildings and, with the help of R.A.I.N. (Rehabilitation in Action to Improve Neighborhoods), the Lower East Side Catholic Area Conference, the East 6th Street Community Center, and other agencies, several of the neighborhood's most depressed areas were revitalized by working on the concept of "sweat equity" (the acquisition of the right to inhabit, manage, and own a building cooperatively, by paying through physical labor instead of capital, i.e. by rebuilding or renovating it)[43].

Coupled with the cultural vitality of the more recent ethnic enclaves, this scene of daily resistance was instrumental in the radicalization of a few artists who came to view themselves as *part of the Lower East Side* rather than simply as *East Villagers*. Their discovery of the neighborhood (or rediscovery, since by settling there some actually went back to their own family roots) was an acknowledgement of its laboratory-like character, of its dense historical texture, of the contiguity and overlapping of cultures and mores in its streets. To them, this cross-cultural, multi-ethnic world ceased to be just another exotic, romantic, or decadent ingredient, and became again a *community* carrying on a century-old experience. The figures of Jorge Brandon, with his Teatro Ambulante and the oral tradition he represented, and of Miguel Piñero, with his poignant plays and intense ghetto life, served as direct sources of inspiration, as epitomes of a quest that had always gone on in its streets. So, around Joel Rose's and Catherine Texier's magazine, *Between C & D*, a group of authors emerged in the years of New York's most blatant transformation and decay — Patrick McGrath, Lisa Blaushild, Peter Cherches, John Farris, Lynne Tillman, Ron Kolm (with his short stories and editorship of several downtown magazines) and David Wojnarowicz (with his multi-media activity and dramatic battle on several levels, all of them Lower East Side-related — gentrification and art, censorship and funding, AIDS and racism). Texier's *Love Me Tender* (1987) and Rose's *Kill the Poor* (1988), in particular, were two significant and telling accomplishments, as were the collections *Between C & D. New Writing from the Lower East Side Fiction Magazine* (1988) and *A Day in the Life. Tales from the Lower East. An Anthology of Writings from the Lower East Side, 1940-1990* (1990) and Wojnarowicz's *Close to the Knives. A Memoir of Disintegration* (1991). In all of them, a direct, raw-edged, often ironic and oneiric, capture of inner-city life stands out, along with a vivid, physical sense of place and an embittered rethinking of traditional mores and values confronted with social and cultural fragmentation, the AIDS

43

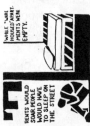

III. 8

A Leaflet with a Cartoon by Seth Tobocman

44

crisis, the gentrifications's process and the East Village's rôle in it, and an increasingly conservative political atmosphere [Rose, interview, 1987; Charyn 1986; Siegle 1989]. On its part, Kurt Hollander's and Alison Prete's magazine, *The Portable Lower East Side*, provides still another example of self-expression, which carefully links the neighborhood's past and present[44].

The urgency of a more radical foundation in the artistic approach to the Lower East Side also led to the birth of such groups and galleries as Collaborative Projects, Group Material, PADD, Avant, Attack Art, the Kenkeleba House, the P.A.C.A. Gallery. Most significant was the experience of ABC No Rio (156 Rivington Street). With its varied activities and important exhibitions ("Real Estate Show", "Internationalist Art", "Not For Sale", "Artists Call Against U.S. Intervention in Central America"), this club/gallery, at the junction of Loisaida and Chinatown, was founded in 1979 and functioned as the spearhead of a new, engaged scene which also geographically set itself apart from the East Village [Cramer and Waters, interview, 1988; Moore and Miller, eds., 1985; "Not For Sale" 1984; L. Lippard 1990][45]. Through the years, such newspapers as the *East Villager*, the *Quality of Life in Loisaida*, and *Downtown* also contributed to this daily battle for identity [Scully, interview, 1987; McCarthy, interview, 1987]. On the pages of *World War 3 Illustrated* and *Squatter Comics*, cartoonists Lawrence Van Abbema, "Cosmo", and above all Seth Tobocman and Eric Drooker have offered a more aggressive (often darker and even nightmarish) interpretation of the gentrification process, thus writing a vivid chapter in visual arts, which seems consciously to work in the tradition of the early XX-century avant-garde or of the Belgian artist Frans Masereel [Tobocman 1990; Drooker 1992]. The St. Mark's Bookshop, Books 'n' Things, Embargo Books, The Bridge Bookshop, Chapter II, Reborn 14th Street Books, MosaicBooks, and several other small and often ephemeral bookstores were and are as many precious venues for literature and the arts and meeting places for residents and artists, as were or continued to be the Life Café, the Gas Station, the Knitting Factory, the St. Mark's Church, La Mama E.T.C., the Theatre for the New City, the Living Theatre, Joe Papp's Public Theatre, P.S. 122, the Fourth Wall Political Theatre, and several others, in the ever shifting geography of places and groups, individuals and organizations, that remains one of the most stimulating aspects of the neighborhood.

VI.

All this is recent history. But fascination with the Lower East Side is strongly rooted in its remote past as well. In a warmly self-ironic tale,

Ills. 9 and 10
Two Drawings from Eric Drooker's *Home*

Ed Sanders has old-timer Rose Snyder go back to the Ludlow Street flat where she was born in 1894 and which is now occupied by a typical mid-1960s hippie commune. What follows, as Rose uncovers her own private and the Lower East Side's collective past (and Sanders's writing moves from fiction to poetry and to history, also graphically incorporating turn-of-the-century images), is a kind of archaeological dig. At the end, Rose's past as a Socialist "firebrand" flows into her new hippie friends' present, as they get ready to join an anti-nuclear demonstration ["Farbrente Rose", in Sanders 1990; also see Sanders 1984].

The theme of the 'usable past' runs through some of the quarter's most significant and fascinating socio-cultural experiences. Its historical texture — the fact that, notwithstanding the daily erosion of time, an immigrant hard core has managed to stand its ground — has produced a veritable *territory of memory* which, in a culture so often plagued by amnesia, acquires an ever stronger meaning. Such different novels as Budd Schulberg's *What Makes Sammy Run?* (1941), Isaac Bashevis Singer's "Sonim, di Geshichte fun a Liebe" (1966; *Enemies, a Love Story*, 1972), E. L. Doctorow's *Ragtime* (1975), Hugh Nissenson's *My Own Ground* (1976), and Meredith Tax's *Rivington Street* (1982) and *Union Square* (1988), are exemplary in this regard. In Schulberg's novel, for instance, it is to the 'belly of Rivington Street', to 'all Rivington Streets of all nationalities' [Schulberg 1941, 1978, p.194, 203], that one has to revert in order to find the answer to the title question — a *bleak* Rivington Street that stands for all the suffering and dejection, physical brutality and emotional trouble marking the immigrant experience, and finally amounts to a sort of gigantic and collective Id^{46}. Written so close to the end of the neighborhood's first great era but, as it were, *from the outside*, the novel thus insists on *one* side of the Lower East Side experience, the dark and tragic one. Changes are already apparent in Singer's novel (recently adapted for the screen by Paul Mazursky). Here, the Lower East Side is charged with other, even ambiguous, implications. It is the collective past of the original Jewish settlement, increasingly altered by the arrival of new immigrants. It is the more recent and private past of Herman Broder, who now leads a schizoid life in Brooklyn, torn between two women. And it becomes a more complex and painful past intruding into the present, when Herman's first wife (whom he thought dead in a *lager*) suddenly reappers there. Singer's view of the Lower East Side is in some way steeped in the gradual rediscovery of the neighborhood as the "world of our fathers" that was taking place in the mid-1960s, with all the overt and not so overt implications (even psychological ones) it inevitably contained.

The increasingly metaphorical dimension the Lower East Side was acquiring in the 1970s is also clear in Nissenson's and Doctorow's novels. In *My Own Ground*, the turn-of-the-century past, recreated with the precision of the historian but also with a painter's eye, becomes a key place in the search of one's own identity (both the main character's *and* the writer's), the context for a physical and philosophical quest and rite of passage: and this sets the novel firmly in such a tradition as that of Henry Roth's *Call It Sleep* — but with an intriguing historical distance. In *Ragtime*, the same turn-of-the-century Lower East Side, once more accurately reconstructed with the help of a precise historical documentation, becomes one of the socio-cultural forces that help bring about the gradual disintegration of old, well-ordered and well-mannered, genteel America, represented by the figure of Father. Tax's novels *Rivington Street* and *Union Square* also recreate the past, but to paint a canvas onto which different disciplines — social history, women's studies, labor studies, material culture — converge in a rather convincing way. In their diverse approaches and representations, these novels — and such others as J. R. Schwartz's *Orchard Street* (1960), Norman Fruchter's *Coat Upon a Stick* (1962), Jerome Weidman's *Fourth Street. A Novel of How It Was* (1970) — show how dense and shifting the image of the Lower East Side has become over the past decades, gaining in complexity and depth and finally becoming a sort of large metaphor of America itself — of the way in which it grew and changed, and still grows and changes, and of the way in which immigrant cultures from all the world joined in that dialectical process[47].

This usable past, filtered through memory's mythopoeic eye, is also at the core of such autobiographical works as Samuel Chotzinoff's *A Lost Paradise. Early Reminiscences* (1956), Harry Roskolenko's *The Time That Was Then. The Lower East Side, 1900-1914. An Intimate Chronicle* (1971), and above all of many pages in the long work-in-progress, *Mercy of a Rude Stream* (a "novel in memoir-form"), which Henry Roth is writing after so many decades of almost complete silence[48] — each of them tinged with a particular brand of nostalgia that, far from anaesthetizing the harsh realities of everyday survival, also voices a deep-hearted regret for the loss of a communal dimension. While retrospective looks have always been part of the neighborhood's experience, at least ever since the late 1910s, it was mainly around the late 1950s and early 1960s that they became a discernible trend. Under the spur of diverse phenomena such as the movement back to the quarter on part of many old-timers' sons and daughters and the generalized search for (cultural, ethnic, class, gender) identity, the Lower East Side has thus become a place ever to go back to in order to unearth one's private/collective, social/cultural, material/symbolic roots, the area *par excellence*, not only for writers, playwrights, and movie directors, but for urban and labor historians as well, and social scientists, town planners, scholars in the fields of ethnicity, women's, immigrants', labor studies, arts and literature — its complex history literally haunting its inhabitants as well as its visitors, and reclaiming never-ending care and attention.

In the past twenty years, an even subtler rediscovery has also taken place from *within* the neighborhood itself. The 1965 exhibition organized by Allon Schoener for the Jewish Museum (and subsequently transformed into a precious book) [Schoener, ed., 1967] was one of the first attempts in the direction of a detailed reconstruction of the neighborhood's past, and a sort of grassroots movement of local historians soon developed which in time managed to create its own venues. Attentive to physical sites and material culture, to the individuals' paths of survival and places of aggregations, the enterprises of such local historians have nothing of the varnished polish that characterizes such dubious experiments as, for instance, the touristy South Street Sea Port area. A *political* sense of the past (of a continuity in the history of a neighborhood which remains at its core working-class and immigrant) has guided, for instance, Arthur Tobier's activities with the Community Documentation Workshop, started in the mid-1970s at the St. Mark's Church and originally aimed at rescuing disaffected neighborhood kids. Tobier, an immigrants' son, free-lance journalist and long-time resident in the area, collected a series of "oral histories" which formed a first, precious reconstruction of life on the Lower East Side through the eyes and memories of old timers. He then enlarged the scope of the oral history program by staging a series of exhibitions which documented the area's past and present history with rare photographs and maps, paintings and drawings, documents and letters [Tobier, ed., 1978; "*Community Histories*" 1984][49].

A similar urgency has also animated many of the events organized by the settlement houses still active on the Lower East Side, themselves living proofs of an uninterrupted history. Beyond their usual programs of youth and senior workshops, evening schools and professional development courses, theatre and art classes, the Henry Street Settlement (265 Henry Street), the University Settlement (184 Eldridge Street), the Educational Alliance (197 East Broadway), the Grand Street Settlement (80 Pitt Street), have variously contributed to the reclaiming of the neighborhood's experience — an intense activity, which can be best exemplified by the two festivals organized in 1987 and 1988 by the Louis

Abrons Arts for Living Center of the Henry Street Settlement at 466 Grand Street[50]. Their archives, so full of memorabilia from the past (documents, letters, books, surveys, bulletins of a by-now century-old history), also represent a real treasure of information to the historian. For its part, the Chinatown History Project (now Museum) was born precisely with the aim to foster a search for identity within the community, by rediscovering and celebrating its past. The exhibits it has been organizing have always been a powerful tool to this end, philologically precise works-in-progress which grew upon the audience response and brought to light a wealth of objects, often adventurously redeemed from oblivion and decay in basements and flats[51]. This attention to material culture is at the heart of another Lower East Side enterprise, the Tenement Museum (97 Orchard Street). Opened in 1988 by the Lower East Side Historic Conservancy, the Museum is located in a tenement building which has been *ad hoc* renovated, with the idea of showing exactly how life was one hundred years ago. Flats were restored with particular attention to their spaces and furniture and attributed to the original inhabitants, so that by walking up the staircases one directly experiences the neighborhood's ethnic variety. Beside this enticing "physical" dimension, the Museum offers walking tours, theatre performances, forums and lectures, a publication called *Tenement Times*, and a series of impressive photo exhibits featuring the work of WPA photographer Arnold Eagle and such historical reconstructions as "Out of the Ashes: The Triangle Shirtwaist Fire of 1911" and "Meddling With Peddling: The Pushcart Wars, 1906-1941". The Tompkins Square, Chatham Square, and Seward Park branches of the New York Public Library also house important archives and have repeatedly organized interesting exhibits, while Seward Park High School teachers Jessica Siegel and Bruce P. Baskind have organized an oral history program, "Our Neighborhood: The Lower East Side Experience", which resulted in two lively mimeographed collections, *From the Kitchens of the Lower East Side. Recipes and Remembrances* (1985) and *Our Lives, Our Stories, Our Neighborhood* (1985). A.R.T.S. (Art Resources for Teachers and Students, Inc., 32 Market Street) has also been active in the field, especially for what concerns the reconstruction of recent immigrants' past, through the periodical exhibition "Waves" centered on family celebrations, traditional remedies, religious beliefs from the Chinese, Hispanic, and Jewish communities of the Chinatown area, the study project "Waves: People and Culture on the Lower East Side", the production of music tapes in Chinese and Spanish, and such useful publications as the *Trictionary*, a dictionary in Chinese, Spanish and English compiled by immigrant youth.

***

This proud fascination with a past extending into the present is thus the real *leit-motiv* at the heart of so many enterprises in the neighborhood, of so many ways of being and of cultural creation. We catch it in the words with which Yuri Kapralov, in a 1980 paper ("The House That Jack Built"), told the story of the Lower East Side through the story of a building and of its inhabitants; or in the re-use by such artists as Hale Garland and Angel Orensanz of the Warschauer Synagogue on Rivington Street and of the Norfolk Street Synagogue, to turn them into museums and artists' studios; or in the opening of the March-April 1992 issue of *The Quality of Life in Loisaida*:

> Loisaida is one of the most ethnically diverse neighborhood in Manhattan, and possibly in all of New York City. The composition of its ethnicity changes, but the ethnic diversity seems to be a permanent feature of its nature. Nevertheless, our neighborhood is an example of how people from different background can unite in the struggle for a decent quality of life. [...] The proud history of multi-ethnic activism in our community resulted in great victories.

It is this subtle fascination with the past that the walker in the city vividly experiences while taking a rest in McSorley's Old Ale House on East 7th Street, with its walls covered with yellowed memorabilia, or in the old Café Orlin on St.Mark's Place. Or passing in front of the Russian & Turkish Baths ("Since 1892") on East 10th Street, of the old synagogue on East 6th now turned into the East 6th Street Community Center, of Lou the Pickleman's stand on Essex Street, of Ratner's dairy restaurant on Delancey Street, of Schapiro's *kosher* wines on Rivington Street, of Katz's Delicatessen and Yonah Shimmel's *Knish* Bakery ("Original, Since 1910") on East Houston, of Veniero's pastry-shop (1894), Russo's cheese shop (1908), Lanza Restaurant (1908), on and off First Avenue. Or strolling down the East 4th Street block between the Bowery and Second Avenue, where historical sites follow one after the other — the building where once was the Labor Lyceum, the other one built in 1889 with a most unusual winding fire-escape, the next one that housed the Industrial Workers of the World's New York headquarters, the one that once was the Turn Hall where the first Yiddish play was staged in America in 1882, and finally the "concert hall" with the heads of Beethoven, Wagner, and Mozart...

What is then this Lower East Side past that ever keeps surfacing and in so doing subtly lays out a warp and a woof, a mental and physical pattern which holds together — in the face of so many adversities — experiences personal and collective?

Notes

1. Ken Jacobs, interviewed in *New York Framed* (produced by Simon Field and Keith Griffiths for Channel Four, England, 1987).
2. The name "East Village" was coined in the 1960s by real estate broker D. D. Stein, as a way to lure east rich Greenwich Village residents.
3. According to the 1924 Immigration Act, each country was allowed an annual quota calculated upon the national origins of the American population in 1890. 94% of immigration quotas were thus given countries of Northern and Western Europe. "Alien" nationalities, deemed ineligible for citizenship (Chinese and Japanese, for instance), were excluded.
4. Author's conversation with Val Orselli, director of the Cooper Square Committee (New York, Jan.27, 1991). "Gentrification" means 'the physical renovation and social-class upgrading of inner-city neighborhoods' [Kerstein 1990, p.620], accompanied by displacement of former low-income residents.
5. Of the 30,000 Ukrainians living in New York City, some 10,000 came as a consequence of the Displaced Persons Act. In the 1950s, the Lower East Side hosted all Ukrainian institutions in the city: four churches (on East 4th, 7th, and 13th streets), a bookstore, a daily, a Democratic club, a reception center, a labor home. The split within the community was also graphically represented by the fact that nationalist Ukrainians settled mainly along Second Avenue, while left-wing Ukrainians had their meeting point at the corner of East 4th Street [Ilchuk, interview, 1987; Goldin, interview, 1987; Tobier, interview, 1987]. There were also sixteen Polish institutions in the 1950s, mostly on St.Mark's Place. On the ethnic transformations in the neighborhood during the period 1930-50, see Grebler 1952; Wakefield, 1959; Kapralov, 1974 and 1980; Saroff, 1983; Gajdycz 1984.
6. An as yet unknown Archie Shepp played there, as did Sonny Murray, Cecil Taylor, Charlie Mingus, Ornette Coleman, Don Cherry, Charlie Haden — a procession of jazz innovators and creators that climaxed when Thelonious Monk played with John Coltrane. Charlie "Bird" Parker also lived on Tompkins Square (at Avenue B) for some time. Around Leroi Jones — "the king of the Lower East Side", according to the *Herald Tribune*, at the time of his successful play "Dutchman" —, who afterwards changed his name to Amiri Baraka, a multi-ethnic avant-garde came into prominence. The Totem Press and such magazines as *Yugen*, *The Floating Bear, Kulchur, Zazen, The Drifting Deer* (some of them co-founded by Jones with poetess Diane di Prima) attracted a group of important young poets and activists — Ishmael Reed, David Henderson, Calvin Hernton, Steve Cannon, who soon formed the *Umbra* group and magazine. Baraka quotes racial tensions as one of the reasons why many black artists moved from the Greenwich Village area to the Lower East Side, especially if they had relationships with white women [Jones/Baraka 1984].
7. Poet-activist Bimbo Rivas wrote the poem "Loisaida" in 1974 ('En mi mente, mi amada,/ yo te llamo, Loisaida'), while working with "Chino" Garcia at the film

script "Don Quixote de Loisaida". The term defined a socio-cultural area, a concept of community work, and a "state of mind", and was formally adopted in 1975 (Avenue C is now also called Loisaida Avenue). It also contains a reference to Loiza, a Taíno (i.e., Puerto Rican Indian) woman and chief, who died in the defense of a rainforest on the island, considered a holy place [Hernandez 1987; "Loisaida" 1990; and Otero 1991].

8. See below, Chapter Two: "Who Is My Neighbor?"

9. The 1882 Chinese Exclusion Act, and its subsequent extensions and additions, made Chinese ineligible for naturalization, barred the immigration of skilled and unskilled Chinese labourers, and forbade entrance into the United States of the wives of those labourers already in the country, allowing only teachers, students, merchants, tourists, and diplomatic personnel (and their spouses) to enter. In so doing, it gave rise to what came to be known as the "bachelor society" (a community almost of males only, most of whom had wives or fiancées overseas) and to the widespread and dramatic phenomenon of the "paper sons" (through an illegal slot system, firmly controlled by merchants and thus clearly class-oriented, thousands of persons tried to enter the United States through false papers attesting they were sons of people already residing in the country). As for the War Brides Act, it finally allowed wives and fiancées of men in the American army to enter the United States. Between 1945 and 1947, 80% of all Chinese immigrants were women, and by 1947 some 9,000 Chinese women had entered the United States. By 1950, the ratio was 1.89 males to 1 female [Kwong 1987, p.32].

10. In 1980, Asian *residents* in Chinatown amounted to some 27,000 persons, or 16% of the Lower East Side population ["Advisory"]. On immigrants, sweatshops and contractors in New York's modern garment industry, see Hirschman and Wong 1984; Waldinger 1986; Noble 1988; Bagli 1988. On unionization in Chinatown and the several episodes of class struggle in the 1980s, see Kwong 1987, which also details the growth of a Chinese mafia out of the economic boom of the early 1980s.

11. As a matter of fact, existence of a Chinese Writers' Society in the 1920s was recorded by Puerto Rican activist Bernardo Vega, who recalls that, on February 19, 1928, one of its members, H. C. Wu, was among the speakers at a protest rally against U.S. invasion of Nicaragua held at the Labor Temple at East 14th Street and Second Avenue [Iglesias, ed., 1984, p.153].

12. 'Toiling in a laundry:/ Just keep on ironing, keep on washing!/ Eighteen hours a day;/ Not enough time for any decent sleep!/ Not enough time for any decent sleep;/ Illness will come and you'll be besieged./ You lie in a hospital; no one comes to visit./ How lonely can a person be?' [Yang 1945, 1988].

13. 'You haunt me:/ Those smells and the images/ of men reading Chinese newspapers/ in noodle shops, coffee shops,/ playing mah jong in the backrooms,/ carting merchandise and food/ on handtrucks, two baskets/ suspended from a pole,/ cleavers cutting roast duck/ and biting the wood block/ of women carrying babies/ tied to their backs,/ delivering or picking up/ piecework, shopping and/ haggling over fruit and/ vegetables, meat/ piecing together a meal/ These images still live on/ in your streets/ I pace them/ their names imprinted/ in my heart/ Bayard, Mott, Pell,/ Doyer, Bowery, Mulberry,/ Canal, Division,/ East Broadway, Henry,/ Catherine/ All hours of the day and night/ I have coursed these streets/ like the memories/ coursing through my veins/ holding onto them/ like charms — / a child's

54

wish — / that someday they/ would make sense' ["Chinatown" 1987, courtesy of Fay Chiang]. In a personal conversation with the author (New York, Jan.25, 1991), Chiang explained the difficulties most Chinese-American authors, especially male, still encounter in dealing with Chinatown's past and the "bachelor society" in particular — something that almost amounts to a writer's block. It is significant that it is mainly women writers who seem able to surmount it. On Fay Chiang's poetry, also see Maffi 1988; Maffi and Minganti 1990.

14. According to the Porto [sic] Rican Brotherhood of America, by 1926 Puerto Rican residents in New York City amounted to some 100,000, mainly concentrated in Manhattan. The 1925 Census showed that the great majority were employed in the private sector (production, commerce, and services), while another large portion was defined as "housewives" (most of them possibly also engaged in piece work and childcare). On the economic background of the early Puerto Rican migration, on its socio-cultural consequences, on the "push and pull" factors, and on the occupational situation in New York, see Cordasco and Bucchioni, eds., 1973; Wagenheim 1975; Maldonado-Denis 1976; Wagenheim 1983; Korrol 1983; Morales 1986; Rodríguez 1989. On the difficult relationship between Puerto Ricans and America, also see Sutton and Chaney, eds., 1987; Flores 1993.

15. In recent years, Glazer and Moynihan's classic study [1963] has come under attack on many sides, but especially for its refusal to acknowledge the extent of this early net. For Glazer and Moynihan, no real Puerto Rican community existed in New York, because no real community-building process had ever taken place on the island (see pp.86-136). For a specific answer to this view, see Korrol 1983; Rodríguez 1974 and 1989.

16. Cigarworkers were the most sizeable, combative, and articulated sector in the immigrant Puerto Rican labor. Back in the island, they had already been involved in union activity and created the particular institution of the *lectura* — i.e., a worker was paid by his fellow workers to read while they chose leaves and rolled cigars (generally, newspapers in the morning and novels and essays in the afternoon, followed by regular discussions in the evenings, in the village square). While the figure was also common among American cigarmakers, in Puerto Rico the "reader" was invested by an even more charismatic community rôle. He was a union agitator, a troubadour, and a *commedia dell'arte* actor, capable of reciting by heart whole passages from *Don Quixote* or *Les Misérables* or of composing *impromptu* poems on daily events ["A Voice Through the Window", in Colon 1961]. Popular poets, like the ones competing in the *juegos florales* (beauty contests during which dramatic or poetic competitions took place) or such nationally renowned bards as Jorge Brandon, developed from this very tradition. Later on, when New-York cigar-factories began to attract a female workforce as well, many of these readers would be women. A Círculo de Tabaqueros also existed, 'part cultural center and part social club. People would come to play chess, checkers, and dominos. The canteen, where they sold coffee and cigars, was open every night and on holidays. No gambling was allowed, and they did not hold dances. There were frequent lectures and cultural events' [Iglesias, ed., 1984, p.34]. An educational organization of tobacco workers was also active in the 1920s, the Trabajadores Amalgamado de la Industria del Tobacco, which published the newspaper *The Tobacco Worker* and had a widely multi-ethnic membership. When cigarmaking declined in the 1920s,

due to mechanization and the advent of cigarettes, Puerto Ricans in New York were increasingly absorbed by the garment industry, which could not count any more upon the steady influx from Italy and Eastern Europe. As a consequence, Local 22 of the International Ladies Garment Workers Union took its place among Hispanic unions in the city.

17. '[O]ne Sunday afternoon there was a forum conducted by internationally renowned anarchist intellectuals. On the day I am thinking of, Carlos [sic] Tresca, who was chief editor of the newspaper *Il Martelo* [sic], spoke in Italian about anarchism and the theories of Darwin; Elizabeth Gurley Flynn spoke in English about free communities and liberated relations among human beings; Pedro Esteves held forth in Spanish about war, peace, and the situation of the proletariat; and, finally, the Catholic anarchist Frank Kelly gave another talk in Spanish about Jesus Christ, the "first Communist"' [Iglesias, ed., 1984, p.34]. Vega also recalls that attendance at such forums — often lasting five or more hours — was rather numerous. The audience, made up of women as well, was patient and attentive, and always ready to engage in long discussions after the lectures. Other socio-cultural clubs were La Liga Antillana (made up of working-class women), the Puerto Rican Literario, La Liga Puertorriqueña e Hispana, and, later on, La Confederación de Sociedades Puertorriqueñas, the Sociedad de Mujeres Puertorriqueñas, the Club Artes y Letras, and many others.

18. The resurgence of activities on part of the Puerto Rican movements for independence also had great effects on the New York community, which became a pivotal center of operation on the mainland [Iglesias, ed., 1984]. Increasingly cheaper air fares then made communications between *la isla* and *la urbe* easier and more frequent. By 1970, according to the Census of that year, there were some 811,000 Puerto Ricans living in New York City [Wagenheim 1975, p.104].

19. Wrote Galway Kinnell in his poem "The Avenue Bearing the Initial of Christ into the New World": 'From the Station House/ Under demolishment on Houston/ To the Power Station on 14th,/ Jews, Negroes, Puerto Ricans/ Walk in the spring sunlight' [Kinnell 1974, p.107]. And Isaac Bashevis Singer in his novel *Enemies, a Love Story*: 'The neighborhood had changed since his arrival in America. Now many Puerto Ricans lived there. Whole blocks of buildings had been torn down. Nevertheless, one still occasionally saw a sign in Yiddish and, here and there, a synagogue, a yeshiva, a home for the aged' [Singer 1972, 1989, p.66].

20. Among the many books that variously (and even contradictorily) contributed to that process, see Padilla 1958; Wakefield 1959; Lewis 1965; Senior 1965; Steiner 1974. On the early stages of Puerto Rican literature in the mainland, see E. Mohr 1982.

21. With significant exceptions: given the wide range of color shades in their community — white, black, mulatto —, the Puerto Ricans' relationship to the "color line" was for instance rather looser.

22. The Christodora House (147 Avenue B) was built in 1928 on the site of a previous settlement house, where fifteen-year-old East Sider George Gershwin had given the first public concert of his own work in 1914. In more recent years, the building has been at the center of a completely different story, becoming a true symbol first of radicalism and then of gentrification [Gordon 1973; Sanders and

Gillon 1979; Wickenhaver 1989; Garcia, interview, 1984; Rivas, interview, 1987; Abu-Lughod, ed., 1993].

23. Between September 1972 and January 1973, under the direction of Fuller and architect Michael Ben-Eli, a series of geodesic domes was built by Charas on the Lower East Side. The story of this experience, as well as of The Real Great Society and Charas, is told in Mottel 1990; see also McNamara 1966; "Real Great Society" 1967; Vaughan 1967.

24. The Taller Latinoamericano (originally at 63 East 2nd Street) is also an important community center catering to the broader Latin-American population of New York. Other vital organizations struggling for a cultural and social identity and resisting Loisaida's progressive decay are C.U.A.N.D.O. (Cultural Understanding and Neighborhood Development Organization, 9 Second Avenue, sadly closed down in 1989 after almost fifteen years' activity), the Pedro Albizu Campos Community Center (611 East 13th Street), Solidaridad Humana (107 Suffolk Street), the East 6th Street Community Center (638 East 6th Street), the Grand Street Settlement (80 Pitt Street) [see Mizio and Valiente-Barksdale 1985]. The magazine *The Quality of Life in Loisaida*, founded by Mary McCarthy in 1978, also plays an important rôle in giving voice to the community, keeping it together, and spreading the news. A large portion of the magazine is devoted to such crucial issues as AIDS, recycling, alimentation, teen agers.

25. 'They worked/ They were always on time/ They were never late/ They never spoke back/ when they were insulted/ They worked/ They never took days off/ that were not on the calendar/ They never went on strike/ without permisson/ They worked ten days a week/ and were only paid for five/ They worked/ They worked/ They worked/ and they died/ They died broke/ They died owing/ They died never knowing/ what the front entrance/ of the first national city bank looks like/ Juan/ Miguel/ Milagros/ Olga/ Manuel/ All died yesterday today/ and will die again tomorrow/ passing their bill collectors/ on to the next of kin/ All died/ waiting for the garden of eden/ to open up again/ under a new management/ All died/ dreaming about america/ waking them up in the middle of the night/ screaming: Mira Mira/ your name is on the lottery ticket/ for one hundred thousand dollars/ All died/ hating the grocery stores/ that sold them make-believe steaks/ and bullet-proof rice and beans/ All died waiting dreaming and hating [...]' ["Puerto Rican Obituary", in Pietri 1973, pp.1-2].

26. 'To the united states we came/ To learn how to mispell our name/ To lose the definition of pride/ To have misfortune on our side/ To live where rats and roaches roam/ in a house that is definitely not a home' ["The Broken English Dream", in Pietri 1973, p.13].

27. See Algarín and Piñero, eds., 1975; Barradas and Rodríguez 1980; E. Mohr 1982; Binder 1983; de Laguna, ed., 1987; Algarín, interview, 1987; Mohr 1987; *The Portable Lower East Side* 1988; de la Campa 1988; Maffi and Minganti 1990; Maffi, in Bak, ed., 1993; Flores 1993.

28. "Borinquen" is Puerto Rico's traditional name.

29. Mrs.For is herself a clear example of the Lower East Side cross-cultural, multi-ethnic laboratory. Partly Cherokee and partly Black, she arrived in the neighborhood in the 1940s, and married first a Pakistani and then a Chinese. Also see Rubin 1989.

30. Wong is also the author of "Stanton Near Fourth Street" (1983) and of several other works finely capturing Lower East Side sceneries.

31. I am here using the title of the exhibition organized in 1984 by Arthur Tobier for the Community Documentation Workshop of St.Mark's Church-in-the-Bowery.

32. The Club, on East 10th Street at Fourth Avenue and other locations in the vicinity, provided an informal place for discussions, panels, and lectures on contemporary art. Critics Harold Rosenberg (who lived on East 10th Street, a few yards west of St. Mark's Church) and Clement Greenberg were the most attentive and enthusiastic spokesmen of a scene which took America by storm and was soon discovered by the big art market [Rosenberg 1958-59, 1973; Rosenberg 1959; Greenberg 1961; McDarrah and McDarrah 1961, 1988; Donohue 1980; Tobier, interview, 1987; Ashton, in Wallock, ed., 1988; Barteneff, interview, 1988; Wakefield 1992]. Of great interest are the artists' autobiographical excerpts inserted in the text which accompanied the afore-mentioned exhibition "The Gathering of the Avant-Garde: The Lower East Side, 1948-70" (courtesy of Arthur Tobier). On the spectacular rise of "abstract expressionism" and its obscuring of the realist/figurative tradition, see Jones and Huestis 1986, and Jones, interview, 1987. Such a realist tradition did not however cease to exist on the Lower East Side, good examples being, besides Jack Levine, Philip Evergood and Grace Hartigan.

33. Rauschenberg and Johns had their studios on the Bowery, Oldenburg opened his "Store" on East 2nd Street, Allan Kaprow and Jim Dine staged their early "Happenings" at the Reuben Gallery on Fourth Avenue, and Red Grooms at his Delancey Street Museum. Avant-garde musicians John Cage, LaMonte Young, and Yoko Ono also had their studios on the Lower East Side.

34. Besides these and the already mentioned Five Spot, other places formed an artists' geography — the Brown Bear (an old Russian place, where you could have vodka on tap), the White Whale (a coffehouse where jazz was played), the Stewart Cafeteria, the Sagamore, the old O'Rourke (a veritable relic of 19th-century Lower East Side culture), the famous McSorley's (a traditional avant-garde hang-out), the Old Reliable and, almost opposite, Slug's (where painter Larry Rivers, formerly a professional saxophonist, often used to play).

35. Small presses were born (the Hawk's Well Press, the Trobar Press, the Hesperidian Press) and bookstores opened (the Blue Yak, the Peace Eye). Magazines appeared, such as Dan Saxon's *Poets at Les Deux Megots*, Ed Sanders's *Fuck You/A Magazine for the Arts*, Ted Berrigan's *C*, Allen De Loach's *Intrepid*, Anne Waldman's *The World*. St. Mark's Church held a Lower East Side Neighborhood Arts Festival. At the Charles Theatre on Avenue B, film-maker Jonas Mekas presented the New American Cinema's best authors (Brakhage, Smith, Rice, Jacobs, Frank, VanDerBeek), side by side with such visionary pathfinders as Jean Epstein, Alberto Cavalanti, Maya Deren, Kenneth Anger, and with the more recent school of Morris Engel, Lionel Rogosin, John Cassavetes, and East Sider Rudy Burckhardt. LeRoi Jones, Ishmael Reed, the Umbra poets formed an important nucleus of black artists and militants. Paul Blackburn directed the WBAI-FM poetry programs and Diane Di Prima the varied programs of the American Theatre for Poets at the East End Theatre. Ellen Stewart founded the Café La Mama; Joe Cino, the Café Cino; Charles Ludlum, the Ridiculous Theatrical Company; Ronald Tavel, the Theater of

the Ridiculous; Peter Schumann, the Bread & Puppet Theatre; Ralph Cook, the Theatre Genesis (with a still unknown actor and playwright by the name of Sam Shepard). As for St.Mark's-in-the-Bowery, it has a long history in nonconformity. Originally, it was the church of the gentry who inhabited the neighborhood but was gradually pushed to its borders by the growing immigrant influx. By the early 1910s, it already began to reflect the new socio-cultural composition of the Lower East Side. Its rector William Guthrie started in fact a whole set of new enterprises, from theatre companies to dance performances, from poetry readings to political meetings, that gave the church a progressive configuration. He also turned some of the church's properties into artists' studios, thus fostering the move away from an already fashionable Greenwich Village that would climax in the post-World-War-II years. By the late 1930s, when Guthrie resigned, the church was known by the nickname of "St.Marx's Church". In the following decades, under the new rectors Michael Allen and then David Garcia, its history continued along the same tracks, always in close touch with the social and cultural developments of the surrounding area. The foundation of Theatre Genesis, Poetry Project, Dance Project and Dance Theatre Company, the venues it offered to painters, jazz musicians, and experimental film-makers, the activities it set up with the neighborhood's disaffected kids, its involvement with the civil rights' movement, the Puerto Rican nationalist movement, the Black Panthers, were the church's highlights in the late 1960s and early 1970s — something that even today, in a changing context, remains the Church's main feature. On the scene just sketched, see Bergé 1965; Wirtschafter 1968; De Loach 1972; Waldman 1969; the text of the "Introductory Panel" accompanying the 1984 St.Mark's Church's Community Documentation Workshop exhibition "The Gathering of the Avant-Garde"; Rothenberg 1987 (opening remarks to a panel discussion at the Poetry Project's 20th Year Symposium, May 6-10, 1987. The other panelists were Allen Ginsberg, Anne Waldman, Kenneth Koch and Ed Sanders. Tapes in the Poetry Project archives); Jarolim 1987; Sukenick 1987; Weinstein 1987; Tobier, interview, 1987; Kupferberg, interview, 1987; Schumann, interview, 1990; Tobier, personal conversation, 1991; Ginsberg, in Waldman, ed., 1992.

36. St. Mark's Church, the Peace Eye Bookshop, Café La Mama, the Bread & Puppet Theatre, and several other groups and venues continued their activities through the decade, soon joined by Emmett Grogan's Diggers and by the Up Against the Wall Motherfuckers, which provided all sorts of socio-cultural services; by the Fugs, the caustic and irreverent Lower East Side band composed by Ed Sanders, Tuli Kupferberg, and Ken Weaver; by Crystal Field's and George Barteneff's Theatre for the New City, up to this day one of the liveliest off-off groups; by the Fire-House and the Tompkins Square Community Center. The Fillmore East on Second Avenue hosted the era's big rock concerts, and the Dom on St. Mark's Place (formerly the Arlington Hall, then the Polish National Hall, soon the Electric Circus) was the early home of Andy Warhol's Velvet Underground. Such remains of old-time immigration as Moskowitz & Lupowitz, Rapoport's, Ratner's, the Vazac, McSorley's, O'Rourke's, Veniero's, De Robertis's, Lanza's, the Veselka, the Odessa, the Leshko, were absorbed by an intricate geography made up of eating and drinking places (the Engage Coffeehouse, Stanley's, the Annex, the Paradox Restaurant, the Psychedelicatessen), theatres and cinemas (the Bridge, Orpheum,

Village, Pocket, Far East, Phoenix, the Atelier East, and the Theatre 62, the Gate Cinema, the Charles, the Millenium Film Workshop, the Film-Makers' Cinemathèque), bookstores (the East Side Bookstore, the Peace Eye), collectives (the Mobilization for Youth, the Kerista Free Love Society, the Provos, Jack Scully's Everything for Everybody, the Diggers' Free Store, the Lower East Side Mobilization for Peace-Action), and innumerable other places — a scene that can be best reconstructed through the pages of the *East Village Other* and of the *East Villager* [Weiner, interview, 1987; Scully, interview, 1987; Kupferberg, interview, 1987; Kapralov, interview, 1988; Barteneff, interview, 1988; Stewart, interview, 1988; Schumann, interview, 1990].

37. See Moufarrege 1982; Robinson and McCormick 1984; Kardon 1984; Plous and Looker, eds., 1984; "East Village Performance Issue" 1985; Belsito, ed., 1985; Hager 1986; Musto 1986; Sukenick 1987; Kozak 1988; Howell 1988; Loffreda, ed., 1989. For a stimulating critical analysis of the early 1980s's art scene and its involvement with real estate, see Deutsche and Ryan 1984, 1987.

38. Between 1970 and 1980, the housing stock lost on the Lower East Side through demolition or conversion amounted to 7.5%, as compared to an increase of little less than 1% in the city's total housing supply. In terms of housing conditions, in certain areas more than 50% of the properties resulted below standard, and more than 40% has been substandard over the last 24 years. As far as market value appreciation is concerned, the median sales price increased 254.3% between 1968 and 1984 (New York City's inflation rate in the same period being 186.8%). Between 1979 and 1984, in particular, median unit sales price increased by 146.4% (between 1968 and 1978, the increase had been 43.8%). Data are from DeGiovanni 1987, who also lists, among the displacement pressures resorted to: excessive rent burden, overcrowding, deterioration (possibly the severest one), excessive rent increases, presence of suspicious fires, landlord inducements to relocate, warehousing (i.e., the 'withholding of vacant units from the market — either to improve the chances of "co-oping" a building or as an incremental strategy for clearing a building prior to undertaking substantial renovation', p.38), and tenant harassment (another major pressure). Even when low-income housing was built, such as the blocks on the west and east sides of Avenue C, between East 5th and 6th streets, the materials used were often rather cheap and likely to deteriorate in a few years. Moreover, the architectural conception itself implied a tendency towards community disaggregation. While in fact these new buildings do have a large inner court allowing for the residents' communal life, no space is provided for stores and stoops on the street, thus eliminating a crucial feature in the traditional Lower East Side way of life, and further isolating people. Also see "Three Ethnic Groups" 1980; Goldstein 1980; Gottlieb 1982; Daly 1983; Platt 1984; Xerox 1984; Deutsche and Ryan 1984; Hereijgers and van der Steen 1986; Foderaro 1987; Weinberg 1989; the several articles on the subject regularly appearing during the 1980s on the pages of *The East Villager*; and, above all, Abu-Lughod, ed., 1994. For a more general treatment of the gentrification issue, see Palen and London, eds., 1984; Smith and Williams, eds., 1986; Sharpe and Wallock, in Campbell and Rollins, eds., 1989; and Weitzman 1989. On homelessness in New York City, see Baxter & Hopper 1981, and Hopper, Baxter, Cox, Klein, 1982.

39. By building infrastructures (playgrounds, dog-paths, etc.) mainly catering to a middle-class "gentrified" population, space was gradually subtracted from the tent colony, pushing the homeless more and more to the center of the Park, from where it would be easier to chase them away (personal conversation with Janet Abu-Lughod of the New School for Social Research, New York, January 27th, 1991; as a matter of fact, the tent colony was dismantled by police in early June 1991). The Park has always been a "hot spot" on the Lower East Side, ever since a demonstration by unemployed people was charged by mounted policemen in 1873. The way in which the Park was subsequently redesigned (with its maze-like paths separated by cast-iron fences, which make a mass concentration almost impossible) betrays its character as a critical point in a delicate neighborhood, as is shown by such famous riots as those which occurred in 1967 and in the summer 1988 and by largescale evictions on close-by East 8th Street in May 1989 [see the *East Villager* issues of August and September 1988 and May and June 1989; and Abu-Lughod 1994]. On the human cost of gentrification, among the vast available material, see Osmers 1983; Nachtgeist 1989; and Bernstein 1989.

40. Weiner, interviews, 1987; Unger, interview, 1988; Dolgoff, interview, 1988; Goldin, interview, 1988; Orselli, 1988. Also see the "Poverty and Housing in the Lower East Side" issue of *East Villager* (August 1987); Kaplan 1988 and 1989.

41. The plan would have displaced some 3,000 people and 4,000 homeless living in the Bowery shelters and flop-houses, making room for some 2,900 units that only 7% of the local population could afford. The Committee's Alternate Plan was adopted in 1970, after a ten-year struggle [Goldin, interview, 1988; Orselli, interview, 1988; they are, respectively, a founding member and the present director of the Committee]. For a history of the Committee and its activity, see *Celebrating 25 Years* 1984 and its bulletin *Cooper Square News*.

42. See Pueblo Nuevo's bulletin *The Cornerstone*.

43. Brandstein, interview, 1991. Also see *Sweat Equity* and Brandstein 1984, 1985, 1987, 1990. Also active in the quarter on the issues of gentrification, displacement, and housing, and represented in the Lower East Side Joint Planning Council (61 East 4th Street) together with the afore-mentioned groups, are Action for Progress, the Boys Club of New York, BRC Human Services Corporation, Charas, the Chinese Progressive Association, the Chinese Staff & Workers Association, the Coalition Housing Development, Community Outreach Services, Friends of Tomkins Square Park, 53 Stanton Tenant Association, Grand Street Settlement, Green Guerillas, Hamilton-Madison House, It's Time, Lower East Side Business and Professional Association, Met Council/East Side Branch, New York Hispanic Housing Coalition, Outstanding Renewal Enterprises, Quality of Life Magazine, Roosevelt Park Community Coalition, St.Mark's Church, St.Teresa's Church, Solidaridad Humana, Third Avenue Tenants, Two Bridges Neighborhood Council, University Settlement House. Community Access then provides services for mentally ill homeless (for a panorama of the several groups active in the area, see the July-August 1985 issue of *The Quality of Life in Loisaida*, and Hereijgers and van der Steen). In the past ten years, the neighborhood has also been witnessing the birth of a vigorous squatters' movement, which, from the original stronghold at 537 East 13th Street, spread to several buildings in the area, entertaining often tense

relationships with older and more institutional groups [Xerox 1984; Reinhardt 1988; Nachgeist 1989; Boyle, interview, 1991].

44. By skilfully employing Lower East Side characters, places, and situations, Jerome Charyn's post-Vietnam novel *War Cries on Avenue C* (1985) and the detective novels composing his "Isaac Quartet" (1974-78) offer another demonstration of the neighborhood's metaphorical and mythopoeic force. The view of the Lower East Side as a *different, separate* territory — one in which time, habits, codes are somewhat suspended, even overturned — is at the core of several recent Hollywood movies exploring its realities (and in some cases exploiting them in a rather mystifying way), from Martin Scorsese's *Mean Streets* and *Taxi Driver* and Francis Ford Coppola's *The Godfather* saga, to Joan Micklin Silver's *Crossing Delancey*, James Ivory's *Slaves of New York*, Jonathan Demme's *Married to the Mob*, Robert Wise's *Rooftops*, Matthew Robins's *Batteries Not Included*, Michael Cimino's *Year of the Dragon*, Abel Ferrara's *China Girl*, not to speak of the Hollywood films by such former independent directors as Amos Poe (*Alphabet City*) and Susan Seidelman (*Desperately Seeking Susan*). On this aspect, see Rose 1989. The emergence of a local actor like Puerto Rican Luis Guzman, the success met by such small classic as Jane Morrison's *The Two Worlds of Angelita*, the movie adaptation of Louis Chu's *Eat a Bowl of Tea* by Chinese-American director Wayne Wang, the recent shootings of films dealing with the area's key-problems are encouraging signs that the neighborhood is increasingly speaking its own voice on the cinematic level as well. It is also significant that a writer like Marge Piercy should choose Loisaida for the one of the locales in her *Woman on the Edge of Time* (1976).

45. In 1983, a large exhibition, assembled by Laura Zelasnick under the guidance of the late Penn State University professor Eugenio Battisti and detailing this more political *côté*, reached Milano (Galleria Lo Zibetto), Genova (Circolo Pickwick) and Reggio Calabria University [*Loisaida/New York City* 1983].

46. This was also the case in such more or less contemporary movies as Robert Wise's *Somebody Up There Likes Me*, Jules Dassin's *The Naked City*, Michael Curtiz's *Angels With Dirty Faces*, William Wyler's *Dead End* (although, in this last movie, as in Sidney Kingsley's play on which it was based, the locale isn't really the Lower East Side but the *Upper* East Side in the early times of its own gentrification, themes and issues are exquisitely similar). The old Lower East Side as a circle in Dante's Hell, still ruling the present in a disquieting way, is also at the heart of Jonathan Demme's movie, *The Last Embrace*, based upon a novel by Murray Teigh Bloom.

47. The same kind of careful reconstruction of past realities and atmospheres, throwing an illuminating light upon the present, can also be found in Hy Kraft's 1942 play "Café Crown", recently revived on Broadway, which goes back to the times and places of the Yiddish theatre's great flowering; in *Hester Street*, the 1975 movie Joan Micklin Silver adapted from Abraham Cahan's pivotal 1896 novel *Yekl*; in Isaiah Sheffer's 1983 play "The Rise of David Levinsky", once more based upon Cahan's 1917 novel; in Michael Stewart's 1985 play "Harrigan 'n Hart", which tells the story of the famous Lower East Side theatrical duo; in *The Imported Bridegroom*, the 1989 movie Pamela Berger adapted from Cahan's 1898 short story;

and, among several other examples, in Marlene Booth's 1989 documentary film *The "Forward": From Immigrants to Americans*.

48. Vol. I has already appeared in the U.S. [Roth 1993], preceded in Italy by a slightly different edition of the first one hundred pages [Roth 1989].

49. The series of oral histories is composed by Minnie Fisher, "Born One Year Before the 20th Century" (1976); David Perez, "Long Road from Lares" (1979); Merle Steir, "Making Mud" (1979); Anon., "Between Wars" (1980); Sara Plotkin, "Full-Time Active" (1980); Michael Donohue, "Starting Off from Dead End" (1980); Yuri Kochiyama, "Fishermerchant's Daughter. Vol.I and II" (1981, 1982); Cus D'Amato, "Making Neighborhood Heroes" (1982); Sophie Saroff, "Stealing the State" (1983); Lesia Gaijdycz, "Learning American" (1984) — all of them edited by Arthur Tobier and published by the Community Documentation Workshop at St.Mark's Church-in-the-Bowery. As for the exhibitions, "The Stuyvesant Legacy" detailed the developments in the area immediately around St.Mark's Church between 1795 and 1900. "Portrait of an Emigrant Community" showed the impact of the early German immigrant community. "The Depression, the New Deal and the Lower East Side" dealt with the effects of the economic crisis and of the Roosevelt Administration's programs. "What's Cooking: Restaurant Culture on the Lower East Side" documented one of the ways in which recent immigrant groups maintained an identity of their own. "The Gathering of the Avant-Garde, 1948-70" dwelt on the coming together of the lively artistic community in the post-World War Two years. "Images of a Latino Community: the Lower East Side, 1956-86" recreated the story of the latest immigrant wave in its relationship with the city and the immigrants that preceded it. "Gramercy's Gashouse District: 100 Years of Underdevelopment. 1848-1948" reconstructed the history of the Lower East Side's northern border, New York's first industrial ghetto (Arthur Tobier, letter to the author, October 18th, 1987; interview, 1987; personal conversation, 1991).

50. The 5-days "Chinese American Folk Arts Festival and Exhibition" celebrated the Lunar New Year with lectures on the "Lion Dance" and forums on the activities of the various Chinese American Folk Arts Agencies of New York, workshops on Peking Opera Movement Technique and Cantonese Opera Music, storytelling and table setting, walking tours, performances, and demonstrations. The "Jewish Folk Culture of the Lower East Side: A Celebration of the Visual and Performing Arts" offered events which, in the span of a month and a half, ranged from walking tours of Lower East Side synagogues to lectures on Yiddish theatre and Jewish music, from folk arts fairs to movies and poetry readings, from theatrical and musical performances to oral history workshops.

51. The "Eight Pound Livelihood" (1984) narrated the history of laundry workers in America by using photoes, objects, slides, videos, and a most direct metaphorical image: that of the flat iron's weight. "Chinese Women of America" (1985) told what is still a largely unknown story. "In the Shadow of Liberty" (1986) exhibited rare prints from the Wong Chin Foo Collection, dealing with the times and events around the 1882 Chinese Exclusion Act. "Salvaging New York Chinatown: Preserving a Heritage" (1987) again explored the neighborhood as it was half a century ago through old photoes made available by a member of one of Chinatown's oldest families. "Both Sides of the Clothes" (1989) dealt with the rôle played by Chinese American women in New York's garment industry. "Memories of New

York Chinatown" (1990) and "Remembering New York Chinatown" (1991) reshaped into an installation a ten-year oral history work in the neighborhood, a kind of *summa* of the Project's activities and at the same time an interesting experiment in audience response and work-in-progress.

CHAPTER ONE: AN ALTERNATIVE CITY

She lived in a little wooden house on the corner of the street huddled in the shadow of two towering tenements. There are a few frail buildings of this sort still left in that part of the city, half a mile east of the Bowery and a mile south of Tompkins Square, where the architecture is as irregular, as crowded, and as little cared for as the population.

Brander Matthews, 1894

I.

The old Lower East Side was a tight, self-contained world. In the second half of the 19th century, within a metropolis such as New York that was undergoing a swift, even convulsive expansion, its boundaries remained somewhat stable and precise. The northern edge, East 14th Street, ran from Union Square to the East River. East and south-east, the docks stretched down to the Brooklyn Bridge, following the inward curve of Lower Manhattan. The approach to the bridge from City Hall Park connected them to Lafayette Street and Fourth Avenue, which eventually closed the perimeter to the west. In all, some 1400 acres, with about 450 city blocks [Lagerquist 1910].

Beyond the pale, spread 'a region that lay before us dim and mysterious in the distance on summer nights as we stood on the house-tops' [Ganz 1919, p.98] — the rest of New York being, to most East Siders, a place where one might venture out in solitary, almost dreamlike rambles, or parading in street demonstrations that gathered at Union or Tompkins squares, or searching for work or entertainment, but always as 'a stranger in a strange world' [Ganz 1919, p.21]. Within that pale, there lived — or struggled to live — a world apart, a multi-layered social and cultural microcosm in which '[e]ach group left its deposits, as in geology' [Gold 1930, 1984, p.180]. Side by side on the same street, or just around the corner, different communities had settled decade after decade, with their distinct folkways and traditions, language and religion, till, by the turn of the century, some 500,000 persons lived in the area, with a density, in some streets and blocks, of three hundred and thirty thousand per square mile (the population density of Manhattan being about forty thousand) and a death rate of between 34 and 38 per thousand[1].

The Lower East Side's original core had once formed a residential quarter. The area around Tompkins Square had been part of the large farm owned by Peter Stuyvesant (the first Dutch governor of New Amsterdam), and a legacy in street names was clearly left after those times — the Bowery (from the Dutch *bouwerie*, i.e. farm), Cherry, Orchard, and Mulberry streets bearing witness to a quiet rural past. George Washington had spent some time on Cherry Hill, James Fenimore Cooper on St. Mark's Place, and well into the latter part of the 19th century many "old families" (Fish, Stuyvesant, Rutherford, Livingston, Keteltas, Evarts) still lived on its outskirts [Harlow 1931, p.395] [2]. Already by mid-eighteenth century, however, things had begun to change, when a small group of freed Blacks settled near Werpoes Hill and Collect Pond, in what was to become Chatham Square and the "Five Points". At the same time, the harbor on one side and the Pond on the other had attracted a few industrial establishments (tanning, soap-, tallow-, and candle-making), which could profitably exploit the waters of the pond and the terminus for the Boston Post Road, the most important artery leading north from New York City. In a few years, pollution had ensued and by the early nineteenth century such was the stench from the tanneries that the decision was taken to drain the pond. In 1805, a 20-foot-wide canal connecting it to the Hudson was dug, the drainage effected, and the canal finally covered, soon to become Canal Street. The boom following the War of 1812 and the transformation of Chatham Square into the main entertainment center of the city led to the removal of the Black settlement further West, to Thompson and Sullivan streets, and to the redevelopment of the area into a fashionable quarter. But the buildings erected on the site of former Collect Pond began to sag, and the well-to-do residents moved North.

Thus, for almost half a century, whenever the propertied classes departed northwards, new immigrants moved in, drawn by an area that was rapidly becoming the commercial and manufacturing heart of the big metropolis. As soon as a pocket of immigrants settled, it was inevitable that it be followed by fellow townsmen, and in time the original immigrant enclave attracted new ones, in a process of gradual proletarization. In part, these immigrants had come from Ireland and Germany in the early decades of the 19th century. The Irish were fleeing crop failure, famine, and hunger in their homeland, and settled along (and west of) the Bowery, south of Chatham Square, Division and Grand streets, and on the waterfront, their main workplace. The Germans were escaping political repression at home, and peopled the irregular quadrangle east of the Bowery and Fourth Avenue, south of East 14th Street and north of the Irish neighborhood. The Irish, generally peasants and day laborers, took up the most menial jobs, often living in conditions of abject poverty. The Germans were mainly craftsmen and skilled workers, at times merchants and educated professionals, and as such they soon occupied a higher rung in the social ladder. Then, little by little, the Chinese began to arrive, pressured by the rising tide of racist hysteria in the West. Trickling into Mott, Pell, and Doyers Street, they gave birth to Chinatown with its 'bachelor society', laundries, small restaurants, and grocery shops. Finally, in the last decades of the century, great waves of immigrants poured onto the shores of America: over five millions between 1881 and 1890, more than three and a half in the following decade, more than eight and a half from 1901 to 1910 [United States Department of Commerce 1971, Table 130; Kraut 1982][3]. Italians were the predominant group from the Mediterranean area, followed by Spaniards, Greeks, Turks, and Arabs. But the largest ethnic community was made up of Jews coming from Eastern Europe, from 'every nook and corner of Russia, Poland, Galicia, Hungary, Roumania; Lithuanian Jews, Volhynian Jews, South Russian Jews, Bessarabian Jews; Jews crowded out of the "pale of Jewish settlement"' [Cahan 1896, 1970, p.35]. It was a mass migration, made up of artisans, craftsmen, common laborers, as well as of educated professionals and intellectuals — all of whom would soon be transformed into an underpaid, poorly housed labor-force for the benefit of American business and industry in the throes of unprecedented growth. After staying some time in the city, many proceeded to the interior, or to other cities. But a large number settled in New York, and in the Lower East Side in particular [Gerard 1890; Ernst 1949; Rosenwaike 1972].

Originally the home of middle and upper classes, the neighborhood thus became the immigrant quarter *par excellence*, characterized by a strange, even fanciful urban geography. The Italians settled on Mulberry, Mott and Elizabeth streets, near Chinatown, and between First and Second avenues and East 7th and 13th streets, near to what remained of the German and Irish settlements. The rest of the quarter was inhabited by immigrants from Eastern Europe, who had dislodged earlier communities or had encroached upon them, thus creating additional mini-communities. Then there were less defined settlements: the Greeks, the Arabs, the Syrians, the Gypsies, a cosmopolitan microcosm in which it was enough to cross a street in order to enter a different world. So, Allen Street 'was as exotic as it was erotic with secrecy, darkness, Arabic, Syrian, and Greek music, all of it intermingling with the smell of teas and coffees [...], a Judaic-Arabic Casbah of the senses' [Roskolenko 1971, p.106]. Under the incessant arrival of new immigrants, the neighborhood continued to change. But it kept its boundaries intact — an inner city, always swelling but never reaching the explosion point. If a 'map of [New York], colored to designate nationalities, would show more stripes than on the skin of a zebra, and more colors than any rainbow' [Riis 1890, 1971, p.20], this was even truer of the Lower East Side.

II.

In this 'theater within a theater' [Ravage 1917, 1971, p.87], the streets were 'tenement canyon[s] hung with fire-escapes, bed clothing, and faces' [Gold 1930, 1984, p.13] — mostly long, narrow, and straight. But there were exceptions. Some — the Bowery, Grand Street, East Broadway, Second Avenue, Avenues A, B, C, D — were wide and spacious, thus offering numberless possibilities to passers-by and errand-boys, peddlers and housewives, newsies and boot-blacks, slummers, pickpockets, idlers, theatre-goers, café- and saloon-habitués: the infinite variety of city experience and urban crowds. Others — Mulberry, Mott, Doyers, Clinton streets — were crooked thoroughfares packed with people, and this increased their village-like atmosphere or the aura of mystery they possessed to outsiders or residents of other blocks. The monotony of the New York grid was broken at times by sharp corners opening to sudden, unexpected views: as where Grand — and, farther down, Canal — met East Broadway, or where Third and Fourth avenues separated. Alleys and lanes, backyards and empty lots then added to the maze-like appearance of the neighborhood.

In such a dense and congested quarter, an open area was 'a fairy-tale gift to children' [Gold 1930, 1984, p.45]. Union Square, at the north-west corner of the Lower East Side, was a favorite meeting place for rallies and demonstrations. Close by, Tompkins Square served the same function, and was also a chosen spot for Sunday picnics and evening courtships. Then there were Corlears Hook Park, on the river, and Hamilton Fish Park, halfway up the busy avenue of East Houston Street. And there was Seward Park, 'the center of the universe' [Chotzinoff 1956, p.79], built in 1900 at the intersection of East Broadway, Essex and Canal streets, where people gathered to attend political meetings, to play chess and *bocce*, to talk and to argue, to relax in the sun on the steps of the fountain just across the street, and to read the election results on big billboards hanging from the *Jewish Daily Forward* building.

Tenements dominated the scene. In 1901, in Manhattan alone, some 42,000 of them housed approximately 1,585,000 persons ["The Tenement-House Problem" 1901, p.191, 195][4]. But it was precisely on

68

the Lower East Side that their massive and menacing outline became the sad symbol of what was awaiting immigrants in the *Goldeneh Medina*, the "Golden Land". Here, the 'endless panorama of the tenements, rows upon rows, between stony streets, stretches to the north, to the south, and to the west as far as the eye reaches' [Riis 1890, 1971, p.95]. Surely, tenements were

a brick and stone and tin poem to the architectural conceit of the mushrooming metropolis [...]. Irish, English and Italian masons laid up the intricate patterns of bonds, fretted jambs and stately sills, the curved and flat arches, the showy quoins and stone balconies and stoops. Smiths molded and soldered seamless sculptured shapes of tin for baldachins before entrances and for imposing roof cornices. Iron shops hammered and joined the fanciful wrought-iron of fire-escape landings, railings and ladders. Never again in American construction will be seen the imaginative postures, the flaunt, daunt, myth and craftmanship of the mask of Tenement [Di Donato, in Moquin and Van Doren, eds., 1974, p.414].

But reality behind that mask was often appalling. The Lower East Side had been the site of infamous "Five Points" (the intersection of Baxter, Worth, and Park streets) that had so outraged Charles Dickens when he visited it in 1842, and of the no less nefarious Gotham Court (off Cherry Street), erected in 1851 as a model building and soon turned into one of the area's worst "rookeries". It still was the site of the Big Flat (the block north of Canal, between Mott and Elizabeth streets), of the Mott Street Barracks (between Bleecker and Houston), of the Big Barracks on Forsyth, and of unnumerable other human bee-hives, some of them newly built, most of them nothing else than reconverted old tenant-houses [Dickens 1842, 1972, Chapter 6; Foster 1850, 1990, pp.120-131; Crapsey 1872, 1969, pp.110-114; McCabe, Jr., 1882, 1984, pp.584-590; Riis 1890, 1971, Chapter Four; Bremner 1958].

Generally speaking, there were four types of tenements: the "rear" tenement, built in the yard of another tenement or of a converted single family house; the "barrack" type of the "old law" tenement, with its "railroad flats" made of small, dark rooms strung in a line; the "dumb-bell old law" tenement; and the "new law" tenement. The most common was the "dumb-bell", or "double-decker", first constructed in New York during the 1870s in the hope to better housing conditions in the slums and in the Lower East Side in particular. It was a massive building, 'usually five or six, or even seven, stories high, about twenty-five feet wide, and built upon a lot of land of the same width and

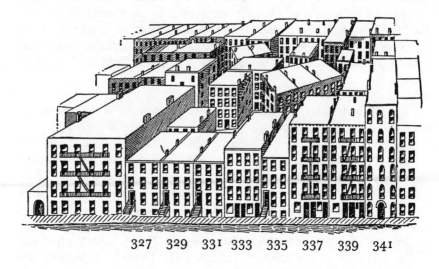

327   329   331 333   335   337   339   341

Ill. 11
A Tenement Block (Drawing by Charles F. Wingate, from Jacob A. Riis's *How the Other Half Lives*, 1890)

about 100 feet deep. The building as a rule extends back ninety feet, leaving the small space of ten feet unoccupied at the rear so that the back rooms might obtain some light and air' ["The Tenement-House Problem" 1901, p.195][5]. The "new law" tenement, a building that extended over several lots, was surely an improvement, but it was still plagued by all the evils deriving from overcrowding and neglect on part of the landlords. Whatever their type, dark halls, small courts, scarce ventilation, common water closets and washing facilities, steep and unsafe fire-escapes (when they existed), narrow air-shafts acting as conveyors of noise, odors, and diseases, or as inflammable flues when fires broke out (a rather common occurrence), were the features that earned for the tenements the sad names of "dens of death" and "perpetual fever nests", breeding alcoholism, tuberculosis, and various epidemics[6]. In 1867 and 1879 (with amendments in 1887 and 1897), a series of laws had attempted to confront the problem of the disorderly outgrowth in an increasingly crowded Manhattan. The 1901 "new law", which contained an accurate documentation of a still little known reality and criteria for future constructions, prescribed that several buildings be demolished and new houses and parks built [Dinwiddie 1908; Lubove 1962]. Still, despite the efforts of law-makers, urban planners, and reformers, tenements continued for decades to hang over the Lower East

70

Side like a dark curse, while the razing of entire blocks for the construction of the Williamsburg Bridge aggravated the situation in terms of congestion.

But huge tenements, fragile wooden buildings, or poor brick houses were not the only elements in the panorama of the Lower East Side. In the decades after the Civil War, as the propertied classes abandoned the neighborhood and the mostly German craftsmen and professionals moved midtown and uptown, a pattern developed that would be repeated again and again in the following decades. The old mansions and the more recent, austere buildings on and around Tompkins Square were subdivided into the greatest possible number of flats, "rear houses" were erected in the former gardens, alleys were cut to connect them to the street, whole buildings were turned into tenements in a very haphazard way — a process of transformation and re-use that originated a peculiar architecture and often gave rise to a sort of 'alternative city, hidden behind a façade of propriety' [Conrad 1984, p.68]. Thus, next to the tenements and the rookeries, there remained Federal and Georgian row-houses and buildings in Classical Revival style, complete with Gothic and Romanesque touches, dormers, cornices, and pediments — a certainly irregular, and rapidly decaying, but often rich and refined architecture.

Other elements enlivened the scene. The iron fire-escapes drew arabesques on the buildings' fronts and, at the same time, offered a disquieting comment on the precariousness of the new urban life. Archways, vaults, piers, and pillars opened out unexpected spaces in the confusion of streets and buildings. More than anything else, the Elevated Railway — the familiar El, or L — added dramatic overtones to an already chaotic scenario. From the junction at Chatham Square, two El lines crossed the Lower East Side: the "Third Avenue line" ran along the Bowery and Third Avenue, the "Second Avenue line" along Division Street and Allen and First Avenue. With its carriages, locomotives, and tracks suspended above a dense and noisy city traffic, the El furnished a conclusive contribution to bustle and din, smoke and speed. Girders, posts, steps to the platform, Swiss-châlet stations drew new lines against the backdrop of a clustered and evolving skyline, while the tracks cut across the façades of buildings at the second floor, enveloping passers-by and street vendors, shops and taverns in their shadows [McCabe, Jr., 1882, 1984, pp.178-194; Howells 1890, I, pp.243-244; J. A. Miller 1941, 1960].

Beyond the crowded streets and the infrequent parks, the tenements everywhere and the El rumbling overhead, there was another component in the geography of the Lower East Side that played a major rôle in the

(From Report New York State Tenement House Commission, 1896,

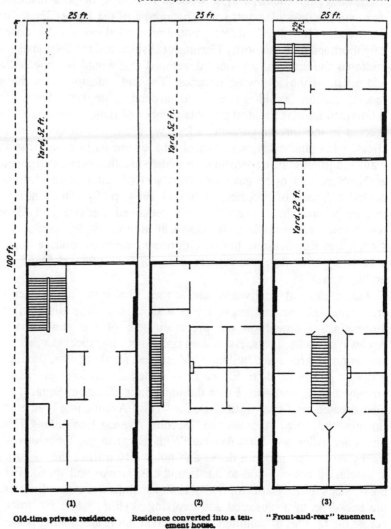

| (1) | (2) | (3) |
| Old-time private residence. | Residence converted into a tenement house. | "Front-and-rear" tenement. |

Ill. 12
The Evolution of the Tenement in New York

and Report New York State Tenement House Commission, 1900.)

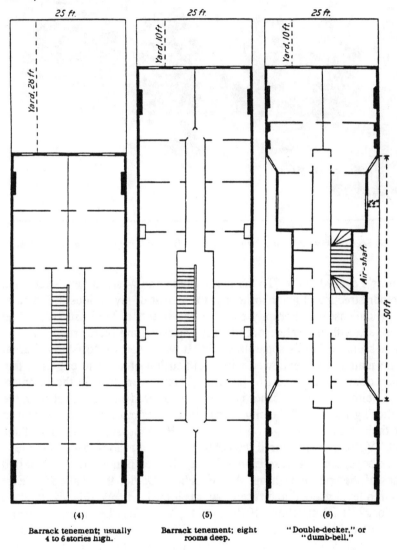

(4)

Barrack tenement; usually
4 to 6 stories high.

(5)

Barrack tenement; eight
rooms deep.

(6)

" Double-decker," or
"dumb-bell."

Ill. 13
A Street Scene (Drawing by Jacob Epstein, from Hutchins Hapgood's *The Spirit of the Ghetto*, 1902)

quarter's everyday life. To the north, south and west, in fact, streets led to other streets and neighborhoods, to the rest of mysterious Manhattan. But to the east they abruptly ended in the waters of the East River. And the river, with its waterfront, docks, wharves, and piers, represented a major scenario in this separate world. It was a sort of "off-limits" area, a "no man's land" endowed with a dimension quite different from that which dominated the rest of the area. People went to it in the summer, when neither the fire-escapes nor the roofs offered enough relief from the sweltering furnace of the city. Kids dived in its murky waters or played out their rites of passage on its banks ('He approached the end of the dock. Voices, as he neared the cobbles, made him look over to the left. Three boys, coming from Eighth Street, climbed nimbly over the snarled chaos of the open junk-heap. At the sight of David, they hallooed, leapt down to level ground and raced towards him. [...] "Wadda yiz doin' on 'at dock?"') [Roth 1934, 1979, pp.245, 246]. By the river, the many gangs of the time (the Short Tail, the Five Pointers, the Baxter Street Dudes, the Swamp Angels, the Whyos, the Crazy Butch Gang, the Dead Rabbits, and the Short Tail Gang immortalized in Jacob A. Riis's 1889 photograph) had their meeting places, their battle grounds, their "fences" of stolen goods. And to the river people went in search of a privacy that was so difficult to attain in the crowded streets and tenement flats.

The river was my refuge when I needed to escape from fatherly rebukes, minor beatings, garbaged streets, dead horses, shrill laments — and the rabbi. Then I would sit on a decaying pier under the Manhattan Bridge or the Brooklyn Bridge and watch freighters slide through the scummy river; or old schooners that still had golden figureheads under the foresail; or the husking ferries going to Brooklyn, passing the fishing boats that put in at Fulton Street with a load of fish caught in the Atlantic. The piers were my second home — before and after the synagogue's spiritual ravishment [Roskolenko 1971, p.14].

III.

But the true heart of the Lower East Side beat in the streets, the inevitable refuge for people forced to live and work in suffocating flats and oppressive sweatshops. From early morning till late at night, 'the throngs going and coming spread off the sidewalk nearby to the middle of the street' [Bunner 1894, p.458], and formed an ever-flowing river, a swarming human tide — people meeting, idling, arguing, playing, courting, going to work and wearily returning home, carrying bundles of clothes, running errands in Chinatown and Little Italy, shouting and gesticulating at the *Khazzer-Mark* (or "Pig Market", the unofficial labor market at the corner of Ludlow and Hester, where each morning a public "shape-up" took place). Streets 'taught [...] the deceits of commerce, introduced [...] to the excitement of sex, schooled [...] in the strategies of survival, and gave [the] first clear idea of what life in America was really going to be like' [Howe 1976, p.256]. In their hurly-burly, things became mixed and entangled, borderlines blurred between old and new, past and present, dreams and reality, hopes and disillusionent, tradition and Americanization, work and leisure, and the myriad acts of survival.

Amid horses and wagons, placards and ash-barrels, stands and shop-awnings, moved hurdy-gurdy men with their dancing train of little children, delivery boys burdened with their heavy loads, ice-cream vendors, flower sellers, newsies. And, above all, peddlers — 'peddlers with pushcarts and peddlers with boxes, peddlers with movable stands and peddlers with baskets, peddlers with bundles, with pails, with satchels and suit-cases and trunks, with an infinite assortment of contrivances designed to display the merchandise and to enthrall the eye' [Ravage 1917, 1971, p.96]. From everywhere came screams and exhortations: 'Fish! Fish! Living, floundering, jumping, dancing fish! Pike, pike, pike! Take pity and buy the living pike! I cash clothes, I cash clothes! *Bubkes*, buy my hot, fresh *bubkes*! Candy, ladies, finest in America! Only a nickel, a half-a-dime, five cents! Potatoes as big as your fist! A bargain in muslin! Buy a calico remnant — calico as good as silk, sweet little housewives!' [Cahan 1899, 1898, in Rischin 1985, pp.63-70, 95-96]. As the pushcart's song went:

Pride of the East Side, Yiska my own,
Hop in my pushcart, I'll drive you home
[quoted in Catapano 1988, p.28].

Along Orchard, Hester, and Grand streets (the shopping district), inside and outside of stores, among pushcarts and stalls, bargaining ruled. Buying and selling was a ceremony, with its rules and rituals [Golden 1944, 1958]. Along Essex Street, the core of the orthodox Jewish community, small shops sold religious articles that were so important for the feast days of Succoth and Purim. Just a few blocks to the west, not far from a synagogue, Allen and Chrystie streets were notorious places of vice and sin ('They call this place "The Klondike". It is worse than the Tenderloin') [Cahan 1898, in Rischin 1985, p.354; also see Foster 1850, 1990; McCabe, Jr., 1882, 1984; Ornitz 1923; Gold 1930, 1984; Gilfoyle 1987]. Chinatown's Mott and Doyers streets were lined with open stores selling fruit and vegetables, Little Italy's Mulberry and Elizabeth streets had tens of small restaurants and grocery shops, East Broadway was busy with *cheders*, congregations, newspaper offices, and cafés. The Bowery was another place of dubious morality and at the same time the heart of popular entertainment, while Second Avenue attracted a cosmopolitan *intelligentsia*.

Odours and smells added to the peculiar geography of the neighborhood:

Each street had its own favorite flavor which it cherished with a certain local and civic pride. If, for instance, the tang of herring was missing from Hester Street, the Hester Streeters thought they were walking in a vacuum. Similarly, the Italian quarter had its air pockets filled with garlic; under Williamsburg Bridge blew strong fish breezes, and no rich supply of ozone was complete without the ingredients of a dozen stables and the thousand and one fumes arising from vegetable push-carts, poultry and meat markets, pickle works, and refuse cans. If one walked down Orchard Street towards Rivington, one knew definitely that the air was literally cheese, sometimes fragrant cream cheese blended with cottage, and sometimes it was stale Roquefort with a dash of Gorgonzola. Subtract the cheese from this region and people would die for lack of air [Cantor 1928, p.27].

In the streets, '[s]omething was constantly happening' [Chotzinoff 1956, p.88], and this made them the reign of kids. Horses collapsed because of heat and exhaustion, soap boxers spoke at election time or in support of strikes, *marionette* shows took place, religious processions paraded, brawls, fires, and *fourjoulahms* (the false alarms no less exciting than the real thing) occurred. In the streets, the rituals of adolescence were staged: games ('We used to play potsie, you know, with the broken tin, you know, and you hop on one foot, and then we used to play we gather hand and ring around the rosie, you know, we'd do that, and then, what else can I tell you, those were the games...') [Begun, interview, 1987], courtings and dates, explorations and raids into other immigrants' *enclaves*, youth gang wars ('what streeter?' being the commonest question, and the gang the most elementary aggregating factor).

We boys lived several kinds of lives...First, there was the queer relationship of American street gamins to our old-world parents...Then there was that strict, rarefied public school world... Again there was the harsh and cruel *cheder* life, with its atmosphere of superstition, dread, and punishment. And then came our street existence, our sweet, lawless, personal, high-colored life, our vent to the disciplines, crampings and confinements of our other worlds [Ornitz 1923, pp.30-31].

Sex was also discovered in the streets, and not only in the "red lights district" or along the Bowery. In their attempt to reproduce native customs and traditions, or to mould them in a new context, immigrants from different places and cultures turned sidewalks, stoops, street corners, fire-escapes, basement stairs into centers of public life, where it was normal not only to talk and gossip, but to court and nurse as well, in a closeness and exposure of bodies that often was an extension of the crowded flats' unavoidable promiscuity.

The women were big-breasted, big-rumped, big everywhere. The black bread or corn bread they habitually ate if they were Jewish created some awesome sexual reveries for us. They would, too, nurse their babies in front of our eyes by merely pulling out the left or the right breast, a nipple to the fore, and into some small mouth it went. If we thought anything, it was very private and most mysterious.

Nursing with complete disregard for privacy was done at home as well as in the streets [...]. But the most engaging of the Orchard Street breast-feeders were the Italian women. [...They] gave off more mystery, though hardly as much as the wandering Gypsy women [Roskolenko 1971, p.98].

The first working experiences also belonged to the streets. Kids of between five and fifteen blacked boots, sold newspapers, flowers, and candies, brought home pants and shirts to be finished, delivered them the day after, did all kinds of errands, not always of the most irreproachable nature. And it was in the streets that behaviors pertaining to both work and play came to be related to each other in very peculiar ways. When future comedian George Burns sold newspapers on Delancey and Clinton streets, he used to holler puffed-up or even utterly invented titles in order to get rid of the last copies left, perfectly grasping the secrets of both show business and advertising. Future vaudeville-star Eddie Cantor 'liked to make funny faces at passers-by. At first they started and then they laughed. This encouraged me and I played such pranks that people would gather about me in the street and wonder when I would pass the hat around' [Burns 1980, p.39; Cantor 1928, p.48]. To them, and to people like Irving Berlin, Ira and George Gershwin, Edward G. Robinson, Paul Muni, Zero Mostel, the streets of the Lower East Side offered a vital source of inspiration and apprenticeship. Whatever their use, it was in the streets, amid yearnings and traumas, discoveries and obsessions, that the difficult process of reinventing one's identity began [F.A.King 1900; Grant 1909; also see C. Goodman 1979 and Nasaw 1985].

IV.

But the world of the Lower East Side was one of congested interiors as well. Tenement flats were usually composed of two or three rooms, rarely ever four, and their standard size seemed to be about ten feet long and eight feet wide.

It was a home of two tiny rooms. The room in the rear was not much larger than a good-sized clothes closet, and not the stuffiest of closets could be more lacking in sunlight and air. The walls were as blank as an undeground dungeon's. There was neither window nor ventilating shaft. The room in front, almost twice as large, though half a dozen steps would have brought anybody with full-grown legs across its entire length, was a kitchen and living-room by day, a bedroom by night. Its two little windows gave a view of a narrow, stone-paved court and, not ten feet away, the rear wall of another tenement. The sunlight never found its way into that little court. By day it was dim and damp, by night a fearsome place, black and sepulchral [Ganz 1919, p.1].

Surely there were larger and more attractive dwellings. But the overwhelming majority of East Siders had to squeeze into stifling, unhealthy, amd miserable quarters, neglected by "czars" (as the landlords were popularly known) who charged between $10 and $20 a month, if not more, for three-, four-room flats ["The Tenement-House Exhibition" 1900; Frankel 1907]. However a flat might look, it was certainly overcrowded with father, mother, at least two children, frequently a relative or two, and almost always a boarder, that universal presence on the Lower East Side — because '[what] squalid home in New York's crowded ghetto is without its boarder? How can that everpresent bogy, the rent, be met without him? He must be wedged in somehow, no matter how little space there may be' [Ganz 1919, pp.1-2].

The real center of the flat was in the kitchen. There, Sabbath prayers were said, card games were held, and homework was done, the family seated around the table overflowing with cuttings, paper flowers, matches, boxes. In the kitchen, contrasts exploded between old and new, traditional mores and gender rôles and the "American way". At times, the kitchen was a quiet harbor protected by the reassuring presence of *mama*; at other times, when the whole family was there and tensions grew as a result of frustrations and lack of privacy, the kitchen became '[one's] own Coney Island' [Zero Mostel, quoted in Howe 1976, p.172] — a deafening and bewildering whirlwind of words, emotions, and strain. All around the kitchen — possibly the one stable place in the house and, within limits, always the same —, the flat's planimetry seemed to undergo continuous changes, as temporary partitions sprang up almost everywhere to accomodate relatives and boarders and separate males from females for the night, in the daily struggle to find a little space where none existed.

During the day my relative kept up the interesting fiction of an apartment with specialized divisions [...]. But between nine and ten o'clock in the evening this imposing structure suddenly crumbled away in the most amazing fashion. The apartment suddenly became a camp. The sofas opened up and revealed their true character. The bureau lengthened out shamelessly, careless of its daylight pretensions. Even the wash-tubs, it turned out, were a miserable sham. The carved dining-room chairs arranged themselves into two

Ill. 14
Back from Work (Drawing by Jacob Epstein, from Hutchins Hapgood's *The Spirit of the Ghetto*, 1902)

rows that faced each other like dancers in a cotillion [sic]. So that I began to ask myself whether there was, after all, anything in that whole surprising apartment but beds [Ravage 1917, 1971, p.72].

The buildings themselves seemed to stretch and swell, and 'quivered and creaked from the weight of humanity stamping about in their bowels' [Crane 1896, 1984, p.11]. As soon as possible, this tightly compressed humanity 'pushed out the wall of their homes to the streets' [Yezierska 1950, 1987, p.101], and poured onto the stoops and the fire-escapes, down the hallways and in the backyards — and, above all, to the house-tops, those flat roofs with low parapets, separated from the mushroom-growth of nearby roofs by narrow urban canyons. On the Lower East Side, 'roofs were social playgrounds and bedrooms' [Gold 1930, 1984, p.127]. There, housewives hung out their wash, children flew their kites or peeked into their neighbors' houses, lovers dated, people raised pigeons and met to talk and sing, to hold political meetings, to recall the past: '[p]eals of laughter and voices in earnest and animated conversations would come from different groups on the roofs, while the melancholic and nostalgic strains of popular Russian folk songs would often resound in the still evening air' [Roskolenko 1971, p.202]. At night, the roofs took on an almost magical aura: 'our housetop had a wonderful fascination to me — the cool breezes, the far vistas over the city's roofs, the mysteries of the night sky, the magic moonlight — a fairyland, a place of romance after the dreary day in the stuffy little rooms below or in the crowded, noisy streets' [Ganz 1919, p.5]. In summer, when the air stagnated in the streets, in the flats, and in the shafts, the roofs became one large dormitory under the stars for men and women of all ages and nationalities.

Like rats scrambling on deck from the hold of a burning ship, that's how we poured on the roof at night to sleep. What a mélange in the starlight! Mothers, greybeards, lively young girls, exhausted sweatshop fathers, young consumptive coughers and spitters, all of us snored and groaned there side by side, on newspapers or mattresses. We slept in pants and undershirt, heaped like corpses. The city reared about us [...]. Sometimes the wind stirred from the Atlantic. Sometimes the hot fantastic moon looked down, and remembered us in the Arabian desert. Some nights it rained. The heavens suddenly split, the thunder rolled down the Brooklyn Bridge. We saw the lightning, like a stroke of insanity, as it created huge nightmare vistas of an unbelievable city of towers, New York...[Gold 1930, 1984, pp.126-127].

At the same time, however, the tenements' forced promiscuity and congestion wove a veritable fabric of communal living. Regardless of geographic, cultural, linguistic differences, people from all parts of the world tended to recreate their East European *shtetln*, their Southern Italian *paesi*, their Sam Yup and Sze Yup villages. But the highly integrated dimension that was at the core of the neighborhood's experience then rearranged ethnic diversities into a whole, into a veritable mosaic, well beyond cultural, linguistic, religious borders[7].

***

The same congestion was to be found at the work-place. The ruling Lower East Side scenario was that of the "sweatshop", a workshop owned by a "sweater" or "cockroach boss" — a small entrepreneur, frequently a former laborer who had arrived not so long ago and had gone into business for himself. The "boss" received the orders directly or through a contractor, and put five to fifteen people to "sweat" in large, bare rooms. Or he distributed orders around, thus adding to child labor and home work. Especially in the clothing industry, the throbbing heart of the downtown area and of the metropolis itself, working conditions were terrible. The "greenhorns" (the recent arrivals who spoke little or no English and were scarcely unionized) fell easy victims of a daily blackmail of exploitation and exhausting work rhythms. The "speed-up" and the "slip" (two systems introduced to enhance productivity), the continuous threats of lockout and dismissal, the menace of the "slack season" (when work slowed down due to a structural contraction of demands), the precariousness of small enterprises, piecework and home work — these were the sad realities of everyday life for thousands and thousands of immigrants. The sweatshop was their most eloquent, dramatic symbol — a 'deathridden loft making a young man middle-aged and the middle-aged ancient, [where the] skin changed daily, the lungs hourly, and the feet every second' [Roskolenko 1971, p.56].

There were three endless tables running almost through the entire length of the loft in parallel lines. Each table was dotted with a row of machines, and in front of these sat the operatives like prisoners chained to their posts. Men and women they were, collarless, disheveled, bent into irregular curves; palpitating, twitching, as if they were so many pistons and levers in some huge, monstruous engine. On the nearer end, around a smaller square table, stood an old, white-bearded man, a young girl, and a boy, marking shirts with a pencil, pulling threads, folding, "finishing". The intermittent whirring of wheels, the gasping and sucking of the power engine (somewhere out of sight), the dull murmur of voices, heightened the oppressive effect [Ravage 1917, 1971, p.141].

In these hellish places — dark, damp and cold in winter, hot and stifling in summer —, people worked for miserable wages from thirteen to eighteen hours a day, six and even seven days a week, amid such a noise that 'if Gabriel had blown his horn on the sidewalk below, the silent women bent over the speeding machines would not have heard — they would have missed the Resurrection' ["Edwards" 1913, p.14]. Accidents were commonplace, slowness was unforgivable, and even the mildest hint of insubordination resulted into being sacked and possibly blacklisted — "If you don't come on Sunday, don't come on Monday" and "Take your Katerinka [the name usually given their sewing machine by the operators] and march" being common experiences for workers. When fires broke out — hardly a rare event, given the scarce or non-existant safety measures —, the sweatshops turned into death traps, as was the case in the most infamous of them, the Triangle Waist Co. tragedy in March 1911. Only with time and the increased unionization did the situation begin to change, though not by much.

82

The sweatshop, like the tenement, thus continued to weigh heavily on the world of the Lower East Side [Schoener, ed., 1967; L. Stein, ed., 1977]. But, oppressive and exploitative as it was, it possessed a communal dimension that was typical of associated labor: 'just as there ain't no bottom to being poor, there ain't no bottom to being lonely. Before, everything I done was alone, by myself. My heart hurt so with hunger for people. But here, in the factory, I feel I'm with everybody together. Just the sight of people lifts me on wings in the air' ["Hunger", in Yezierska 1920, 1987, p.52]. While waiting for the contractor in the early morning hours, or in the brief interruptions for lunch before machines took up their hum and buzz and movements turned frantic again, the sweatshop became a place for talking, reading and studying, for gossip and informations, for politics and trade unionism. Cigarmakers had fought for (and won) the right to have one of them read aloud to the others while they worked, and clothing workers resisted the strict discipline forbidding them to speak or sing during work hours. So, often, the 'spacious, barn-like loft rang and trembled with a chaos of mournful and merry song, vying with the insolent rattle of the machines. There were synagogue airs in the chorus and airs of the Jewish stage; popular American airs, airs from the dancing schools, and time-honored airs

Ill. 15
The Newsie and the Sweatshop Worker (Drawing by Jacob Epstein, from Hutchins Hapgood's *The Spirit of the Ghetto*, 1902)

imported from Russia, Poland, Galicia, Roumania, Hungary' ["Circum-stances", in Cahan 1898, 1970, p.221]. Especially for first-generation immigrants, the sweatshop thus became "a place of memory". In the drudgery of mechanical work, the mind was free to wander across time and space and to re-live Old-World sceneries and experiences [Asch 1918, 1938].

In the closed space of the sweatshop, the New-World culture filtered and mingled with that brought over from Europe or Asia, and a mass culture developed out of the encounter with mass production — the peculiar process by which immigrants became Americans by creating a new America.

V.

A different kind of congestion ruled in other overcrowded places — no longer the inevitable promiscuity of the tenement flat, nor the forced closeness of the sweatshop. The Lower East Side was far from being just the abyss of misery, squalor, and dejection that so many journalists, local colorists, and slumming novelists liked to portray. It was also a quarter that throbbed with yearnings and passions, its inhabitants struggling to maintain and create a sense of personal and collective identity, to weave a fabric that could contain the past *as well as* the present. A lively cultural life thus took forms as varied, and often as unexpected, as were its agents and implements, and expressed itself in specific places [E. S. Martin 1898; Blaustein 1901]. Some of these places were separate ones, the jealous guardians of social and religious traditions. In the Jewish area, there were 'scores, perhaps hundreds, of small congregations [...], each of which had the use of a single room, for the service hours on Saturday and holidays, in a building rented for all sorts of gatherings — weddings, dances, lodges meetings, trade-union meetings, and the like' [Cahan 1917, 1966, p.106]. And there were *shuls* (synagogues), *cheders* (elementary schools), *yeshivas* (Talmud schools), *mikvahs* (ritual baths). Parishes, churches, and chapels dotted the Italian and Irish blocks. Chinatown had its *fongs* (family associations), while Italians and Jews coming from the same town or village attended their respective *società di mutuo soccorso* and *landsmanshaftn*. Other places were veritable channels of Americanization, focal points where different cultures met, clashed, or mingled. At the University Settlement, the Henry Street Settlement, the Educational Alliance, the Cooper Union, the Astor Library, the Seward Park Library, a wide range of activities were made available to immigrants starved for culture, curious about the new world in which they had to live, and impatient to learn, both literally and figuratively, a language different from their own.

In the pockets of that leisure time that was increasingly becoming a necessary base for the birth of a mass culture, still other places had distinctive connotations and played fundamental rôles in the development of collective habits and behaviors. One of the most popular among the younger generations was the candy store, or "Cheap Charlie".

Every street had a "Cheap Charlie". I used to wonder at the singularity of the candy-store business being exclusively in the hands of men of the same name. These candy stores had an extraordinary attraction for children because of the personal attitude of Charlie to his young customers. This was an even more potent lure than the advertised cheapness of Charlie's wares, which we accepted on faith without inquiry or comparison. Charlie was human and understanding, and was not above entering into the problems of his patrons [Chotzinoff 1956, p.75].

With the main room that opened directly onto the street and a smaller one in the back, a 'counter along the length of the store, decked with cheap candies, and perhaps with cigars, some shelving behind filled with cigar and cigarette boxes, and invariably, a soda-water fountain [and] a few cigarette pictures on the wall' [Reich 1899, p.32; also see Cahan, July 1899, 1985; Catapano 1988], the "Cheap Charlie" (or the ice-cream parlor) was a veritable social center and crossroads of cultures, where ordinary codes were put to the test and frequently broken[8].

As the main gathering place in the area, the candy store was not without competition. There were saloons, cafés, beer halls, wine cellars, and other similar resorts. Mainly dating from the times of the early Irish settlement, saloons were by far the most popular. By the turn of the century, again in the Tenth Ward (with a population of 95,000), there were some 150 drinking places, mostly between Allen Street and the Bowery (this last enjoying the record of 29 saloons along seven blocks) [Spaulding 1899, pp.34-35]. Some had very close ties with both the political world and the criminal underworld: it was through them that Tammany Hall was able to influence a large slice of the male electorate and at the same time to control prostitution in the neighborhood. At the two extremes of their wide range could be found the famous McSorley's Old Ale House on East 7th Street, frequented by New York's artistic and political *intelligentsia* and barred to women, and Paddy Martin's on the Bowery, a notorious basement with opium den. But all kinds of gathering places dotted the quarter. Rum-shops, gin-mills, and bucket-shops thrived in the red lights district, right in the heart of the Jewish community; or on the waterfront, where the dives often had no name, just a number painted on a window; and of course on the ever-present Bowery. In most of them, with a drink usually came a free lunch, and customers could help themselves to turnips, corned-beef hash, macaroni, beets, sausages, baked beans, fried liver and bacon, pork, tripe, sardines, pickled-herring hash, chicken, ham, crackers, bread, cheese, and soup. Saloons were above all male resorts, and because of their connection with prostitution, alcoholism, and the criminal underworld, they were a constant target of preachers and reformers (from Anthony Comstock and Carrie Nation to the younger generations of settlement workers), who demanded that they be shut or at least subjected to stricter control. But even here, among smoke, beer, and the "swift, machine-like music" [Crane 1893, 1984, p.71] of little orchestras and honky-tonk pianos, another important chapter in the history of urban culture was being written.

German beer-halls, Roumanian wine cellars, Vienna cafés were of a different kind. Places such as Klein Fritz's *Kneipe* on East 6th Street, Justus Schwab's on East 1st Street, the Atlantic Garden on the Bowery, Moscowitz's celebrated wine cellar on Rivington Street, Levy's café on Grand Street, the Odessa on East Broadway, and many others, were frequented by both men and women *and* by whole families, and, while they generally had strong ethnic connotations, were open to people from all backgrounds. In the 1910s and 1920s, the heart and artery of this world had moved from East Broadway north to Second Avenue, between Houston and East 14th streets. Ordinary passers-by, famous actors of the Yiddish theatre or the music-halls, journalists and writers, politicians, artists, trade unionists, and "new women" made up the miscellaneous clientele of noisy, smoke-filled, lively places. At the Café Royal (on Second Avenue, at the corner of East 12th Street) or at the Café Monopole (on Second Avenue, at the corner of East 10th Street), one could easily run into Meyer London, the popular Socialist lawyer from the neighborhood, or into Yiddish dramatist Jacob Gordin and actress Bertha Kalisch, fresh from their triumphs at the Grand Street Theatre, or into anarchist Emma Goldman, back from a speech at the Victoria Hall, or into Nikolai Bukharin, Alexandra Kollontai, and Leon Trotsky, about to leave for Russia in 1917. Food and beverages were different here from what was offered in saloons. The bill of fare included bean soup, cold fish, *borscht*, chopped herrings with onions, *matzohs*, coffee, tea (sipped from the saucer, a slice of lemon aside, huge lumps of sugar in an open bowl), *schnapps*, and "May wine" (Rhine wine with the addition of champagne and seasonal fruit juices). Here, people came to meet friends and celebrate, to read newspapers and pick up their mail, to play chess and pinochle and to talk, argue, learn, or try to forget; here, union meetings were held, art and literature discussed, gender and social codes assaulted.

And there were Russian and Hungarian eating places (the Budapest Rathskeller and the Pokol at 69 Second Avenue, the Belghov on Second Avenue and East 4th Street), or Spanish and Greek (on the Bowery), or Chinese (on Pell and Mott streets), or Italian *trattorie* with red chequered table-cloths and straw-covered Chianti bottles (along Mulberry Street), and vegetarian restaurants.

VI.

The intense life of the neighborhood manifested itself in other places too. A conspicuous example were the halls. At the beginning of the century, there were some thirty different halls between Houston and Grand streets, east of the Bowery — i.e., one every two and a half blocks [Bovie 1901, pp.31-32]. Again in a delicate balance between ways old and new, between past and present, they hosted weddings and community celebrations, dances organized by *landsmanshaftn* and social clubs, and meetings sponsored by political parties and labor unions.

The halls were long and narrow, poorly heated and lighted, with sawdust on the floor to protect it for the dancing. Usually there was a canopy for Jewish weddings with faded velvet hangings and dusty flowers. On the walls there were charters of "landsmen" clubs and beautiful red banners of Socialist locals and unions, hung carefully under glass, taken out only for special occasions like May Day. [...] At all the meetings there was a constant moving about and a commotion at the back of the hall of people talking together, who did not understand English. These forums were a haven for homesick people. They brought music, art and comradeship before there were any settlement houses or union halls [Flynn 1955, pp.67, 68].

The largest ones in the area could hold between 500 and 1,000 persons, the rental fee for an evening being about $30. But size and prices could vary widely. Among the favourite were the New Irving Hall (214 Broome Street), where the Russian anarchist, Prince Kropotkin, gave a speech in the spring of 1901; the Clinton Hall (151 Clinton Street), one of the largest, often used as a strike headquarters; the Victoria Hall (80 Clinton Street), where Emma Goldman frequently spoke; the Arlington Hall (23 St.Mark's Place), a popular spot for weddings and big celebrations; Eisl's Golden Rule Hall (125 Rivington

87

Street), which housed a renowned dance school and where already in 1882 a meeting was held to organize Jewish greenhorns and keep them from strikebreaking. Other famous ones were Zwieck's Hall (86 Attorney Street), the New Atlantic (26 Delancey Street), the Teutonia (60 Essex Street), the Apollo (160 Clinton Street), the Garden Dancing Hall (10-12 Second Avenue), the Odd Fellows' Hall (67 St.Mark's Place), Liberty Hall (51 East 1st Street), the Clarendon Music Hall on East 13th Street, the Concordia Hall on Avenue A, the Beethoven Hall on East 5th Street, the Pythagoras Hall on East Broadway. Important political venues were Tammany Hall and Mozart Hall, on the outskirts of the neighborhood [Oskison 1899, pp.38-39].

Still other places were noted for specific characteristics, sometimes tied, at least originally, to certain group traditions. It was the case of the *Deutsch-Amerikanische-Schützen-Gesellschaft*, the German-American shooting society at 12 St.Mark's Place, and of the *Turnverein*, the gym society at 66 East 4th Street, which also functioned as a theatre (the Turnhalle, or Turn Hall); or of the Germania Assembly Rooms (291-293 Bowery), the gathering place of rifle clubs, marching societies, music leagues, political organizations, social clubs, and Italian, German, French theatre companies.

Dancing was surely one of the neighborhood's beloved leisure-time activities: 'One day, while walking not more than three blocks on Grand and Clinton Streets, I counted nineteen different posters advertising nineteen different balls and entertainments which were to be given in the near future' [Mead 1904, p.6; also see Betts 1899]. The ball was an important community event, and at the same time an opportunity to forge new relationships and friendships away from the often narrow and stifling boundaries of family and ethnic community. Dancing also offered the occasion to explore emotions and behaviours that skirted the accepted confines of morality and tradition, above all as far as accepted gender rôles were concerned, and in the meantime represented a powerful vehicle for Americanization [Israels 1909; Hapgood 1910; Ewen 1985; Peiss 1986]. Dancing academies thus had an important function akin to that of the halls. Weary from work and hungry for some recreation, people went to them to learn traditional dances (the waltz, the quadrille, the lancers), new steps (the "spieling", the "grizzly bear", the "shaking the shimmy"), and that "tough dancing" which often had overt erotic allusions (the "slow-rag", the "lovers' two-steps", the "turkey trot", and the "bunny hug").

Presently he found himself on the threshold and in the overpowering air of a spacious oblong chamber, alive with a damp-haired, dishevelled, reeking crowd — an uproarious human vortex, whirling to the squeaky notes of a violin and the thumping of a piano. The room was, judging by its untidy, once-whitewashed walls and the uncouth wooden pillars supporting its bare ceiling, more accustomed to the whir of sewing machines than to the noises which filled it at the present moment. It took up the whole of the first floor of a five-story house built for large sweatshops, and until recently it had served its original purpose as faithfully as the four upper floors, which were still the daily scenes of feverish industry. At the further end of the room there was now a marble soda fountain in charge of an unkempt boy. A stocky young man with a black entanglement of coarse curly hair was bustling about among the dancers. Now and then he would pause with his eyes bent upon some two pairs of feet, and fall to clapping time and drawling out in a preoccupied sing-song: "Von, two, tree! Leeft you' feet! Don' so kvick — sloy, sloy! Von, two, tree, von, two, tree!" This was Professor Peltner himself, whose curly hair, by the way, had more to do with the success of his institution than his stumpy legs, which, according to the unanimous dictum of his male pupils, moved about "like a *regely* pair of bears" [Cahan 1896, 1970, p.15].

VII.

But the Lower East Side's true passion was theatre. No sacrifice seemed exorbitant in order to put aside the dime, the quarter, the half dollar necessary for a stage show. All forms of entertainment developing within the modern metropolis, even those less acceptable to religious orthodoxy, attracted a mixed audience of all sexes and ages, curious and informed, who, each night — but above all on Friday and Saturday evenings and on Sunday afternoons — filled the theatres of the neighborhood, and let themselves be swept away by the fortunes of the stage characters.

My appetite for the theater was insatiable, and I stopped at nothing, even theft, to obtain the coveted passes [that allowed free entrance]. Several times I extracted my sister's pass from her pocket-book when she was out of the room, and by the time the loss was discovered I was well on my way to Grand Street or the Bowery. I had no preferences and reveled in every variety of play. I even yearned to attend a performance at Miner's Theater, an English-speaking playhouse on the Bowery, near the Windsor and the Thalia. The posters at Miner's advertised an entertainment called Burlesque, and featured plump ladies in disturbing garments, and funny-looking clowns... [Chotzinoff 1956, p.107].

The number of theatres on the Lower East Side was astonishing. Some were large and refined ones. The Neue Stadt Theatre (43-47 Bowery), built in 1864 at the rear of a big hotel, could seat 3500 persons, the Amberg Theatre (Irving Place at East 15th Street) 2500. The People's Theatre (199-201 Bowery), the Harrigan and Hart's New Theatre Comique (728 Broadway), the Grand Theatre on Grand Street were also very large buildings. Huber's, a dime museum showing freaks and other cheap attractions, occupied a whole block between 106-108 E.14th Street and 103-107 E.13th Street. Other locations were rather singular, churches being frequently transformed into theatres and variety halls: the old Theatre Comique (514 Broadway) was a former synagogue, the New Comique was the former Church of the Messiah. Bunnell's Museum, the first dime museum at cheap prices, showed his "Dante's Inferno" in a basement at 103-105 Bowery, and so did the Chinese Opera House (5 Doyers Street) with its classical dramas[9], while Little Italy's puppet shows were often staged in saloon backrooms[10].

One of the most peculiar theatres was the Grand Duke's, on Baxter Street, opened and managed by a notorious teen-age gang — the Baxter Street Dudes led by Baby-Face Willie. The boys themselves wrote and performed their "blood-and-thunder" plays and "variety acts", admission went from 5 cents for the gallery to 25 for the boxes, and props and scenery were often of very dubious origins.

The house and its appointments are primitive, and the stage and scenery equally so. The orchestra is made up of amateur musicians, and is placed out of sight at the back of the stage. The footlights consist of six kerosene lamps with glass shades. Two red-plush lounges, stuffed with saw-dust, and in a sad state of dilapidation, serve as boxes; while the orchestra stalls are represented by half a dozen two-legged benches, and the balcony and gallery are composed of a bewildering arrangement of step-ladders and dry-good boxes. The manager acts as his own policeman, and enforces order by punching the heads of disorderly spectators, or by summarily ejecting them. The performances are crude, but they satisfy the audience, and never fail to draw forth a storm of applause, mingled with shrill whistles, cat-calls, and other vocal sounds. The boys are satisfied. What more could be desired? [McCabe, Jr., 1882, 1984, pp.579-580][11].

In its heterogeneity, the theatrical scene of the Lower East Side clearly mirrored the complex ethnic and cultural stratification brought on by decades of immigration, each community adding significant contributions to an often rough-edged and garish, but very creative, composite. At the Olympic, the Bowery, the National, the Comique, the Irish immigrants had identified themselves with the popular characters of "Mose the Fireman, and his B'owery B'hoys", passionately followed the events in Dion Boucicault's plays, sung to the tunes and lyrics of Harrigan and Hart. The German community had attended the Neue Stadt, the Turnhalle, the Germania Assembly Rooms; and had taken over the Old Bowery Theatre — a shrine of "blood-and-thunder" melodramas — and rebaptized it the Thalia, starting it off on a glorious history that lasted till its demolition in the 1920s. Little Italy had a sparkling theatre life along Mulberry and Spring streets, with *marionette* shows, farce, *cafés-chantants*, and legitimate theatre, and so had Chinatown, in the thick maze between Mott and Doyers streets. The Jewish community crowded the Thalia (relieved from Germans when they moved uptown), the Windsor (formerly the Neue Stadt and, for a period, also a "blood-and-thunder" melodrama theatre), the People's, the Oriental, and the brand-new Grand Street Theatre. Whatever their appearance and ethnic catering, theatres were invariably crowded. They were something more than pure and simple theatres, but places 'to socialize as well as to be entertained. Houselights were always partially lit during performances to allow for a ready exchange of conversation between members of the audience. There was eating, drinking, and the accompanying din of pop bottles rolling under the seats...' [Sogliuzzo 1973, p.62]. During the week, theatres — or, at least, the most important among them — held benefits for a whole number of different organizations (*landsmanshaftn*, trade unions, congregations, newspapers, individuals), thus playing a vital social and cultural function.

Most of the above-mentioned theatres were on the Bowery and vicinity. Running some 15 blocks from Chatham Square to the intersection of Third and Fourth avenues, this famous thoroughfare had followed the ups and downs of the neighborhood's fortunes. Originally the purposed home to higher-class entertainment, already by the 1830s it had turned into a strange, often equivocal and rough-and-tumble, lower-class Broadway — a sort of updated and Americanized Bartholomew Fair, hosting legitimate theatre (principally Shakespeare, in the interpretation of such local heroes as Edwin Forrest) side by side with minstrel and freak shows, *risqué* burlesque skits, farce and pantomime, sentimental plays and "blood-and-thunder" melodramas, urban *feuilletons* and variety acts, dime museums and opium dens, rowdy saloons and cheap brothels. Other places were also important, in this Bowery world of popular culture slowly evolving into urban mass culture: Steve Brodie's and Mike Lyon's attracted a mixed audience of petty (and even not so petty) politicians and famous actors, celebrated prize-fighters and would-be poets, while the Worth's, the Grand, the Gaiety, the New York, the Globe, the Alexander offered all kind of attractions — from freaks to the Ford brothers fresh from Jesse James's assassination, from fighters and jugglers to singers and talkers (like Brodie himself), who urbanized and modernized the tradition of frontier humorists and antedated a whole string of stand-up comedians. Then there were sleazy dives of rather equivocal atmosphere, such as Paddy Martin's, Barney Flynn's, Billy McKeon's (already a favourite resorts of the B'howery B'hoys Gang), the World Poolroom (theatre of action of the Pretzel Gang), Louie Aressler's Music Hall (a meeting place for crooks and swindlers), Owney Geoghegan's, the Sailor's Snug Harbor, the Mug, Gombossy's Crystal Palace, the eloquent Palace of Illusions and the ill-famed Suicide Hall [Harlow 1931; Sante 1991].

'The Bow'ry, the Bow'ry!/ They say such things, and they do strange things/ On the Bow'ry! The Bow'ry!/ I'll never go there anymore', went Charles Hoyt's popular song. But people *did* go there again and again, and kept going there well into the 1930s, when decline definitely set in and, due to the Depression and other factors, the thoroughfare turned into a sad Skid Row[12].

By the turn of the century, new places then opened up on the Lower East Side that quickly seized public attention and eventually displaced theatre in its various forms as the number-one attraction. Amusement parlors and penny arcades began to feature ever more frequently what were then known as *kinetoscopes* or *penny vaudevilles*. Shortly after, small storefront theatres appeared, called *nickelodeons*, where theatre combined with new and fascinating technological inventions. Cinema was being born, and by 1907, of Manhattan's more than 200 *nickelodeons*, at least a third were located south of 14th Street. Most of these opened up along the Bowery and the streets flowing east from it — like the Automatic One-Cent Vaudeville (48 East 14th Street), the Comet Theatre (100 Third Avenue), or the later, grand Loew's Avenue B and Lowe's Delancey. Again, in these new places, new habits and experiences — both social and cultural — were developing:

Visit a moving picture show on a Saturday night when the house is full, and you will soon be convinced of the real hold this new found amusement has upon the audiences. Certain houses have become genuine social centers where neighborhood groups may be found any

92

evening of the week; where the "regulars" stroll up and down the aisles between acts and visit friends, and where the farsighted proprietor has learned the names of the children and remembers them with a friendly pat on the head [Palmer 1909, p.356].

***

This geography of places was not a cage lowered upon helpless individuals, a grid of unavoidable grooves immigrants could not but passively follow. Germans and Irish, Chinese and Italians, Jews and Slavs, peddlers and rabbis, laundrymen and basters, newsies and small-time thieves, slowly took possession of these places, reshaped and reinvented them in forms that had to do both with the past and with the present, both with Europe and with America — but also, more frequently, in forms that were new to both. From the start, a dialectical process developed. As German novelist Alfred Döblin wrote, '[men] are related to other men as well as to other beings by symbiosis. They touch each other, they approach each other, they grow together. This is already a reality: the symbiosis with other people, and also with the buildings, the houses, the streets, the squares' [Döblin 1924, 1978, p.88]. It was in these places that the laboratory of the Lower East Side soon began to function.

Notes

1. The increase in population was also impressive. For instance, the 31,537 persons that in 1865 inhabited the Tenth Ward — the heart of the neighborhood — had become 70,168 in 1896 [Crapsey 1872, 1969, p.114; Riis 1890, 1971, p.85 and "Appendix"; "City Wilderness" 1900, p.20; Lagerquist 1910; *The WPA Guide* 1939, 1982, p.113; Grebler 1952, p.12 (this last study does not include the Mulberry and Mott streets section)].

2. On the origins of the Lower East Side, also see Urchs in Brown, ed., 1923; Dunshee 1952; Wolfe 1975; Spann 1981; R. Thompson 1988.

3. The shift from the "Old" to the "New Immigration" is clearly revealed by the following data: of the 648,000 Europeans who arrived in America in 1882, 87% came from northern and western Europe and 13% from eastern and southern Europe, while of the 1.2 millions who came in 1907, 19% were from northern and western Europe and 81% from eastern and southern Europe [Kessner 1977, p.7].

4. On tenements and their reality, also see Flagg 1894; "The Tenement House Exhibition" 1900; "City Wilderness" 1900; DeForest and Veiller, eds., 1903; and *First Report* 1904.

5. Also see Riis 1890, 1971, Chapter One; United States Industrial Commission 1901, pp.481-492; Claghorn, in DeForest and Veiller, eds., 1903.

6. 'Every indvidual in normal condition should have at least 35 cubic meters of air [...], and the air we breathe in should not contain more than one per cent of all the expired air [...]. In many tenements, on account of the overcrowding, the quantity of air left for each person is reduced to three or four cubic meters, and the expired air in the sleeping-rooms represents one-half or one-sixth of all the air available' [Stella 1904, p.487]. The terrible heat wave of August 1896, for example, resulted in the death of 420 tenement dwellers in New York City [Seller 1977, p.115]. For a precise description of the various types of tenements, see Gabaccia 1984, pp.66-72.

7. '"Uptown here, where each lives in his own house, nobody cares if the person next door is dying or going crazy from loneliness. It ain't anything like we used to have it in Delancey Street, where we could walk into one another's rooms without knocking, and borrow a pinch of salt or a pot to cook in"' ["The Fat of the Land", in Yezierska 1920, 1987, pp.198-199].

8. By the turn of the century, there were some fifty candy stores in the Tenth Ward alone. Most of them also served as headquarters for the social clubs, which constituted one of the most elementary, and sexually mixed, aggregating factors for the neighborhood's youth. The Cadet's Pleasure Club (176 Broome Street) had some 50 members, the Idlewild Pleasure Club (77 Essex Street) some 30, the Oriental (146 Delancey Street) and the Melrose (414 Grand Street) 25, and so on. The 'object of the club is purely social, and a member of one of them reports that in all "they have kissing all through pleasure time, and use slang language"' [J. W. Martin 1899, p.23]. In some candy stores/social clubs, 'a dozen or more youngsters are entertained [...] by a team of aspiring amateur comedians of the ages of sixteen or seventeen, whose sole ambition is to shine on the stage of some Bowery variety theater. The comedian or comedians will try their new "hits" on their critical audiences (and a more critical one can not be found), dance, jig, and retell the jokes heard by them in the continuous performance or vaudeville theaters' [Reich 1899, pp.32-33]. In others, the breaking of the rules went well beyond kissing and slang, they being often used as bases for the semi-legal activities of street gangs. Candy stores and social clubs retained their fundamental aggregating function in the following decades too. The late Joe Juliano, a Lower East Side prize-fighter of some notoriety in the 1940s, recalled that, in the late 1930s, 'we had a club on 10th Street, right between First and Second Avenue, called [...] "Red Rain", the club was there for almost thirty years. [...] The guys used to get together, from like three, four, five, six blocks, and you had thirty, forty guys, and they would put a dime a week, twenty cents a week, and they would join a club, the rents were like thirty dollars a month, forty dollars a month [...]. Every neighborhood, like 14th Street...I can't remember the name of the clubs...14th Street between A and B had a social club, 14th Street between C and D had a social club, 18th Street between B and C had a social club, 12th Street and Avenue C had a social club, 23rd Street and Second Avenue had a social club...So there were social clubs all over, that was the big thing in that day, that's how the guys used to stay together...social clubs...' [Juliano, interview, 1987].

9. '[The theatre] is fitted up with a stage or platform across the rear end, and [...] is innocent of curtains and scenery. The wall back of it is elaborately painted in high, bright color, representing birds, beasts and reptiles. In the center is a

painted joss [divinity]. On either side of the joss are doors, through one of which the actors enter, and through the other take their exit when they have finished their respective parts. The orchestra is seated on the back part of the stage, immediately in front of the pictured joss. The auditorium is filled with rough wooden benches, enough to accomodate possibly 500 people. At the right of the stage is an enclosure, or private box, which is usually occupied by white people or slumming parties. Two other boxes are located in the corners of the extreme front of the house' [Beck 1898, pp.91-92].

   10. 'Past a more than ordinarily disorderly saloon, along a tortuous passageway, the audience edges through narrow wooden gates into a room about twenty-five feet wide by forty long. There are tiers of raised benches in the rear at ten cents and seats and chairs in front at fifteen cents. The seating capacity is, perhaps, 175; ventilation is through traps in the roof, a method quite inadequate to relieve the marked discomfort of an audience in summertime' [Kimball 1900, pp.5-6].

   11. The theatre was so successful that it soon had to move to a larger location on Water Street, and this aroused other gangs' envy. After several riots, police closed down the place. Also see Alger, Jr., 1904, Chapter 2; Asbury 1928, 1990; Sante 1991.

   12. On the Bowery world, see Bunner 1894; McLean 1899; Connors 1904; Hapgood 1910; Harlow 1931; Shank 1956; Senelick, in Matlaw, ed., 1979; Rinear 1981; Giamo 1989; Sante 1991. An extension of the Bowery in terms of entertainments (and not only because that was also the name of one of its paths), and of the Lower East Side in general, was Coney Island. To recent immigrants, it was 'a wonderful and beautiful place. I took a German friend, a girl who had just come out, down there last week, and when we had been on the razzle-dazzle, the chute and the loop-the-loop, and down in the coal mine and all over the Bowery, and up in the tower and everywhere else, I asked her how she liked it. She said: "Ach, it is just like what I see when I dream of heaven"' [Agnes M., 1903, now in Stein and Taft, eds., 1971, pp.103-104]. Since mid-nineteenth century, eastern Coney Island had been the privileged resort of "nabobs" and "robber barons" (with the luxurious Oriental and Manhattan Beach hotels). Central Brighton Beach had then been discovered by the rising middle classes, while the eastern part, beyond the Cut, had soon become the underworld reign of crooks, swindlers, prostitutes, horse racing and prize-fighting, cheap dives and popular amusements (especially around infamous Norton's Point). By the end of the century, its social and cultural fabric had seemed on the verge of irreparable fraying. But in 1896, thanks to a group of capable entrepreneurs, the *new* Coney Island was born, with the opening of the first amusement park, "Sea Lion Park", followed by "Steeplechase" in 1897, "Luna Park" in 1903, and "Dreamland" in 1904. In part, these parks copied Manhattan's Bowery, with its freak shows and dime museums, its lights and sapid vulgarity, although set within neater borderlines. But, in part, they introduced new elements, of which some directly stemmed from an urban and working-class culture that by then was clearly discernible. So, Coney Island became the favourite destination of many Sunday or summer excursions, a common experience among tenement people. It also became the site for Friday and Saturday evening trips, when hundreds of working girls left the slums to look for amusement and adventure (not always devoid of sexual overtones) in its dance halls. Above all, the world of Coney Island took

on the aspect of a "parallel universe", where the components of modern metropolitan life (which masses of workers and recent immigrants daily felt as alienating) turned for once into a source of pleasure and amusement. In its mechanical rides (such as "Roller Coaster", "Loop-the-Loop", "Shoot-the-Chutes", "Leap Frog Railway", "Helter Skelter") and in its pageants (such as "Fire and Flames" or "Fighting the Flames"), working people experienced technology in terms of entertainment, became familiar to city rhythms and clockwork mechanisms, looked at common city landscapes and events as awe-inspiring spectacles. To them, Coney Island was thus not simply a topsy-turvy world that '[stood] any man on its head' [Anon. 1904, p.3], but also a no man's land where Americanization and socio-cultural transgression, acculturation and remodeling of codes took place, vying with each other to the popular whirling steps of the "spieling". On Coney Island, see Paine 1904; Gillman 1955; Snow and Wright 1976; Kasson 1978; Peiss 1986; Maffi 1989.

CHAPTER TWO: WHO IS MY NEIGHBOR?

It's Ireland and Italy, Jerusalem and Germany,
Oh Chinamen and Nagers, and a paradise for cats
All jumbled up togather in snow or rainy weather,
They represent the tenants in McNally's row of flats.

Edward Harrigan, "McNally's Row of Flats", 1882

I.

Ever since non-WASP settlements started to appear in the area, the Lower East Side took on the aspect of a 'polyglot boarding-house' [Corsi 1925, p.92], a 'miniature federation of semi-independent, allied states' [Ravage 1917, 1971, p.87]. After the early Black community had settled around Chatham Square, the Irish had come, attracted by work on the Erie Canal. Initially, they occupied the buildings abandoned by the propertied classes at the foot of Mulberry Street (what would become the notorious Five Points) and in so doing dislodged the Blacks, who had to move out of the neighborhood — to Baxter, Sullivan, and Thompson streets, where many bars and dives came to be known as "black-and-tan" and catered to a racially mixed clientele. From that initial, small enclave, the Irish then spread almost all over the area, but mainly on the waterfront, along Cherry and Water streets, and on and around the Bowery, where their saloons, theaters, dives, and halls (Paddy Martin's, Billy McKeon's, the Gaiety Musée, the Old Bowery Theater, the World Poolroom, Owney Geoghegan's, Steve Brodie's, Harry Johnson's, MacSorley's, Sailors' Snug Harbor, The Mug, Suicide Hall) offered various types of entertainment and often operated as important links with Tammany Hall and the political underworld.

In the same decades, Germans had also begun to arrive as a consequence of political repression at home. *Kleindeutschland* came to embrace a large area between Avenue B, Clinton Street and the Bowery. It had a *Freie Bibliothek u. Lesehalle* on Second Avenue, a German Dispensary on East 10th Street, a *Deutsch-Amerikanische-Schützen-Gesellschaft* on St.Mark's Place (with the motto *Einickeit-Macht-Stark* inscribed on its front), some Reformed, Lutheran, and Methodist

Ill. 16
Map 2: Main Ethnic Enclaves on the Turn-of-the-Century Lower East Side

98

churches, a few synagogues, a *Turnverein* and a *Konzert Halle* adorned with the heads of Mozart, Beethoven, and Wagner on East 4th Street, a flourishing theatre district on the Bowery and vicinity, Luchow's Restaurant on East 14th Street, Loesling's *Kaffee Haus* and Winkelmeier's on the Bowery, Erhard Richter's *Lokal* on Forsyth Street, Justus Schwab's saloon on East 1st Street, *Kneipen* and *Apfelwein Stuben* serving cider, May wine, and mineral waters (*Klein* Fritz's on East 6th Street, Feser Brothers' on the so-called "Munich Bowery"). The Austro-Hungarian Empire was also well represented: *Klein Wien* was on lower Second Avenue, "Little Hungary" just off East Houston, "Little Ukraine" along and around Avenue A (the "Ukrainian Broadway")[1].

When "new immigrants" came in the 1880s and 1890s, ethnic heterogeneity grew and by the turn of the century complexity and difference ruled the quarter. The coexistence of Old and New World and the interaction of so many communities were a source of unending drama, and the neighborhood soon became a veritable social and cultural laboratory, that possessed rather singular traits and was to play a crucial part in the development of many aspects of twentieth-century American (and, more generally, modern) culture. While Germans slowly abandoned the neighborhood[2] and the Irish moved to the outskirts settling by the "new immigrants" and often acting to them as policemen, saloon keepers, Tammany Hall politicians, bosses of the underworld, Chinese, Italians, East Europeans Jews, Greeks, Syrians, Ukrainians, Turks, Gypsies, Levantines, Arabs and Spaniards started to open their routes of survival in the great metropolis. They conquered its spaces, redrew its map, rewrote its alphabet, remoulded its cultural and social geography. And, while the contribution of the other groups was far from indifferent, it was surely the Chinese, the Italians, and the East European Jews who left the more conspicuous and significant marks [see Map 2].

II.

It is difficult to say with complete certainty if New York's first Chinese really was Quimbo Appo, a tea merchant who came in the 1840s, married an Irish girl, and settled on Doyers Street. Or whether he was really followed by Lee Ah-Bow, Ah-Kent and Wah Kee, and then by Lou Hoy Sing, a sailor who jumped ship, also married an Irish girl, and settled on Cherry Street. At any rate, by 1859 there was a clearly definite Asian enclave on and around James Street, south of Chatham Square, where a small group of Chinese men lived with Irish women as common-law wives ["How New York Lives" 1859]. The 1860 census reported 51 Chinese in New York City, a figure due to grow to 120 in

1870, to 853 in 1880, to 2559 in 1890, to 6321 in 1900 [Fessler and China Institute 1983, p.244][3].

For the most part, Chinese immigrants came from the districts around Canton, in the province of Kwangtung, and fled famine, political unrest, and economic distress. To reach *Gum Shan* (Cantonese for "Golden Mountain", i.e. San Francisco), they risked — and many lost — their lives: not only because the Pacific crossing was an ordeal as hazardous as the Atlantic crossing, but also because it was the imperial policy to punish with death by decapitation anyone caught in the act of emigrating. By 1860, the number of Chinese in the United States — most of them in the Western states — was 35,000 [Chen 1981, p.16]: something very different from the "swarming hordes" of the racist propaganda that would break out in a few years. They generally were "male sojourners", men who had left China in the hope of making a small fortune and then going back home (custom and traditional codes conspiring to discourage women from setting out on such a perilous voyage).

In San Francisco and thereabouts, Chinese were considered "outlandish", and racist episodes were not infrequent. But they were hard workers and earned for themselves a certain amount of respect. Between 1848 and 1869 — what with the Gold Rush and the building of the first transcontinental railway (a turning point in the development of the United States) —, jobs were not lacking in California and, while they had come as peasants, skilled laborers, artisans, merchants, these "male sojourners" were ready to pick up whatever job was at hand — a first adaptation strategy common to all immigrants. Chinese contract labour thus provided mines and companies with a very cheap workforce, and a very good one: accustomed to team-work discipline and equipped with millenarian building skills, the Chinese made a fundamental contribution to the economic development of the West [Chen 1981; Fessler and China Institute 1983]. But mining and railroad construction were not the only sectors to employ Chinese labour. Frontier society was essentially a male society, and important chores such as washing and cooking were considered "women's work". Racism, sexism, and adaptation strategies thus allied in entrusting those jobs to the Chinese, who soon developed very specific skills in both fields, and more generally in services. Besides, San Francisco and other Western towns and villages were in a state of transition. Their urban structure was still rather fluid, and this allowed the cultivation of vegetables or the breeding of animals indispensable to Chinese cooking, which soon became an attractive alternative to the Frontier's rough and monotonous diet.

Things started to change drastically in the 1870s, when the first serious economic depression after the Civil War hit the country with

100

unparalleled violence. Unemployment soared in California, where mines were by now worked out and the transcontinental railway completed. Such a situation was immediately blamed upon the most recent (and visible) immigrants. Racist leaders, such as Denis Kearney, drew out the usual, rabid repertoire, and they were soon backed up by national figures like AFL president Samuel Gompers, who wrote that the 'superior whites [had] to exclude the inferior Asiatics, by law, or if necessary by force of arms' [quoted in Chen 1981, p.132]. Episodes of overt racism became more frequent, and mob violence blood-stained the Western states. Meanwhile, local and state anti-Chinese laws multiplied, climaxing in the 1882 Chinese Exclusion Act, and its subsequent amendments.

A new phase of adaptation strategies then opened. Chinese immigrants (numbering at the time 107,488, i.e. 0,2 % of the total American population) [Chen 1981, pp.3, 148-155] abandoned all those jobs entailing some kind of competition with whites on the labor market, and turned to those in which contact with the outside society was reduced to a minimum — they increasingly became laundrymen and cooks. At the same time, a real exodus began. Whole groups moved to the Eastern cities, and "Exclusion Chinatowns" were thus born. They were isolated communities, folded in upon themselves and, within limits, self-sufficient. Soon, the so-called "bachelor society" developed, made up of "single" men and "paper sons", inevitably breeding deep isolation, cultural and social traumas, and personal frustrations[4]. Indeed, not only the Act was the root of the evils which racist propaganda blamed upon Chinese as if they were specific ethnic traits (opium smoking, gambling, involvement in prostitution or assumed white slave traffic), but it also nourished the nightmare of miscegenation that had tormented America's dreams since the end of the Civil War[5].

Soon, New York (a city of immigrants from all parts of the world, where a certain degree of anonymity could be attained) hosted the largest Chinatown after San Francisco. Upon arriving there, the Chinese immigrant found a thick net of community relationships, because 'every trade, profession or calling, however exalted or lowly, is governed by a union of its own members' [Beck 1898, p.2]. In the tiny maze of Mott, Doyers, and Pell streets, soon to expand to Park, Bayard, Baxter streets and to part of Chatham Square (see Map 2), feudal China's traditional hierarchies and associations were soon reproduced, side by side and often in osmotic relationship with new organisations made necessary by the realities of American life. At the basis of this social structure was the *fong*, a social and mutual-assistance group of persons from the same clan and village. Different *fongs* of the same village formed the *tung hung woy*, which had functions similar to the *fong*'s, but a larger scope (for instance, it kept in touch with the village of origin). It was by these structures that the newcomer was welcomed and offered a substitute for that family life of which he had been deprived first by immigration, and then by the Exclusion Act. They organized traditional festivals, sent back home the deceased's bones after six years' burial as tradition required, and provided temporary accomodation to the elderly, unemployed, and homeless — the real connective tissue in a community that was developing under strain and menace. Then there was a top tier, more complex and articulate, which took care of the community's economical and political interests, also with respect to American society. This was the rôle of the *kung saw* and of the *hui kuan*. The first grouped individuals with the same surname, even if they came from different villages (the powerful "The Four Brotherhood", for instance, with headquarters at 22 Pell Street), the second brought together persons from the same district or speaking the same dialect (the Ning Young, the Hakka) [Kwong 1979, pp.34-44; Wong 1982, pp.15-23].

The running of such a mechanism rooted in medieval China was far from smooth in modern America's Exclusion Chinatowns, where the community was placed under pressure and agitated by often contrasting internal tensions. Precisely to remedy this, the *Jung Wa Kung Saw* or "Chinese Public Assembly Hall" (better known as the "Chinese Consolidated Benevolent Association", CCBA) was born in San Francisco in 1868. In New York, where it was incorporated in 1884, the CCBA was Chinatown's unofficial city-hall. Its headquarters at 16 Mott Street were a focal point in the quarter, the very same building also housing the *Fan Tan Hong* (or "Fan Tan Syndicate"), the *Quong Ying Lung Company* (a merchantile establishment), the *Sing Me Hong* (a laundrymen's union), the meeting room of the *Mee Shing Kung Saw*, and the "Joss House" (or temple) dedicated to Quang Kong[6]. The CCBA was to arbitrate internal disputes, to centralize a whole series of community services, to offer educational and leisure-time activities, and to represent Chinatown outside its borders. As such, it should have been an element of balance. In fact, it was a tool of the richest and most powerful regional associations and business organizations, to the exclusion of the great mass of the labouring poor (the "mayor", an office not recognized outside Chinatown, was elected yearly in March by the *kiu lings*, the leaders of the traditional associations, and by the principal merchants of Mott, Doyers, and Pell streets). Internecine rivalries and the peculiar rôle played by the CCBA inevitably gave ground and strength to the *tongs*, secret societies dating back to the seventeenth-century China and reborn in the United States, where they came to control the community's illegal activities and in turn were often controlled by the merchants' top tier.

Other organizations also existed. There were gamblers' and peddlers' unions, and the *Fan Tan Hong*, which regulated *fan tan*, the most popular game in Chinatown. There were two laundrymen's unions (more guilds than modern unions) that fixed prices and tarifs — the *Sing Me Hong* and the *Chop Sing Hong* (at 28 Mott Street). And, at 7 Mott Street, were the headquarters of the *Kuomintang*, where Dr.Sun Yat Sen used to meet his followers before the overthrow of the Manchu government in 1911.

Chinatown thus seemed to be the most structured community of the entire Lower East Side. But this complex social fabric could not mask the reality of a clear class stratification. Merchants were at the top, labourers at the bottom, and a host of different social figures in the middle. Partly, this was the heritage of the Chinese feudal system, but in the United States it had acquired very recognizable capitalist traits. Sheltered as they were from the Exclusion Act, and notwithstanding anti-Chinese hysteria, merchants were in fact able to live rather normal lives, to increase their economic exchange with American society, to enrich themselves. But, against the lower classes, the "bachelor society" functioned as a double instrument of oppression: from without (from American society at large), and from within (from Chinatown's growing bourgeoisie).

At the same time, Chinatown suffered from a withdrawal on itself both in terms of culture and social adaptation and in terms of gender. It was a "male society" for different sets of reasons. Traditional Chinese thought placed women in a very subordinate position. Man was the family's supreme authority, and women acquired a limited amount of prestige *if* they bore a male child. They rarely appeared in public, and when they did it was invariably in the company of their husbands walking a few steps ahead. Such customs did not change in America, at least for a long time. The few women living in Chinatown — either merchants' wives or the rare labourers' wives who had been able to reach their husbands before 1882 — led very secluded lives, and not only in the turn-of-the-century years. In the 1910s, a Chinese woman recalled, when 'my mother needed to go from one block to another in Chinatown, even from Mott to Pell Street, she would call for a coach. Women were ashamed to be seen on the street in those days'. And in the 1920s, 'I was very lonely. I sewed, read newspapers. [...] Women were not allowed to help out in the store. They said that if women went down to the store, business would be driven away and men would stop shopping there. For a few tens of years I didn't go down to the store' [quoted in Luk 1985].

***

In a certain way, the temptation of exotica and local color was inevitable for the chance visitor. The narrow, crowded streets, the buildings painted red, green, and yellow, the open stores with unusual kinds of fish and vegetables, the almost total absence of women, the colorful wall signs, the sound of the quick speech, the banners, effigies, and paper lanterns, the *bu gao ban* (community bulletin board) in front of the "Joss House" or outside the sailor's rooming house at the corner of Doyers and Pell: many things conjured up to make Chinatown a world apart to the outsider[7].

But, to thousands of Chinese, that tiny maze of streets was the place of work and identity, where, together with the memory of the past, it was possible to keep alive the dream, or the illusion, of the "Golden Mountain" [Siu 1985]. Chinese "sojourners" mainly worked in laundries and restaurants, job sectors that required only a rudimentary knowledge of the American language. At the turn of the century, there were some 8,000 laundries in New York City, but their real headquarters was Chinatown. The same was true of Chinese restaurants: there were some ten first-class ones, among which the renowned Port Arthur (7 Mott Street), the Hong Heong Lau (11 Mott Street), the Kum Sun (16 Pell Street); and as many second-class ones, like the Chay Heong Hen (13 Doyers Street); while Wing Sing's Chinese American Restaurant (3 Pell Street) offered American food only. Cheap eating-places, catering to the great mass of the community and to people from other immigrant groups, were also rather numerous. The bill of fare, the quality, and the prices varied accordingly (the restaurants' daily receipts could be estimated at about $500, of which some $200 came from white customers, $250 from Chinese, and $25 from Blacks), but in all places the *chop suey* could be tasted — a dish of rather uncertain origins which soon became a favourite in turn-of-the-century America. New York's Chinatown also had a large number of bar-restaurants, where white entertainers often sang and acted for a free lunch and tips.

Then there were the myriad other occupations — barbers with traditional tools to shave heads leaving the queue, herb doctors (some fifty of them, plus a Chinese Hospital on Pell Street), peddlers able to carry up to 300 pounds in their wicker baskets balanced on a long pole, grocers and jewellers, lithographers and sign painters, artisans and small shop-keepers. A certain amount of Chinatown's activities was also taken up by illegal occupations. If prostitution, opium, and gambling were among the inevitable consequences of the Exclusion Act, another was their control by the *tongs* and, in certain cases, by some family associations as well. The scarcity of Chinese women led to a community of mainly white *lo ki* (prostitutes), who rarely showed themselves around and thus had to rely upon the services of a network of *low gui gow* ("the common woman's dogs"): there were some fifty of these "dogs" in turn-of-the-century Chinatown, mostly Whites with a few Blacks, led by one George Pappe and centered at the corner of Doyers and Pell and around 11, 17, and 18 Mott Street [Beck 1898, pp.118-120]. As to opium, a person assailed by "the *yen-yen* terrible" could "hit the pipe" or buy brands like the Fook Yen ("Fountain of Happiness") or the Li Yen ("Fountain of Beauty") in 25-cent and 50-cent portions in some twenty opium dens, one of the most popular being at 10 Pell Street (for the sake of "slummers", there was also a fake one, with actors pretending to smoke).

*＊＊＊

Only a part of New York's Chinese lived and worked *on* Mott, Pell, or Doyers: still, Chinatown was the heart of the community, the place of collective identity. On Sundays, its short and narrow streets filled with "sojourners" who came to visit friends and relatives, to attend *fong* and *kung saw* activities and ceremonies, to read advertisements written on the *bu gao ban* or to buy *The Chinese American*, the bi-lingual edited by Wong Ching Foo, whose first issue appeared on February 3, 1883. Grocery stores, like Wah Kee's at 8 Mott Street, provided the main meeting place. Here, the family association's reunions were held and friends gathered after a week's gruelling work in the laundries of Manhattan, Brooklyn, Hoboken, and Jersey City, to collect the mail from China and to dictate letters to those who could write [Tseng 1985; Lui 1991][8]. Then there were several places where one could play *fan tan* and *mah jong*, the nine lotteries were always busy, and so was the *tsz fa*, or riddle game, with its colored boards.

Apart from Sundays, the community's main moments of cohesiveness were during the traditional festivals. The Chinese New Year (between mid-January and the second half of February) was celebrated with street parades, dragon and lion dances, and fireworks, while houses were decorated with paintings and augural inscriptions. The first six days of the *t'son* (the first month) were named for an equal number of animals, whose meat it was forbidden to eat on the respective day, and were spent in visits, feasts, and gift exchanges. In China, the holiday lasted more than two weeks, but in the United States it had to be drastically reduced. During the Dragon Boat Festival — also known as Double Fifth Festival, because it falls on the fifth day of the fifth month of the Chinese calendar (end of June), and honoring the death of the patriot and poet Chu Yuan —, *jung* was usually eaten, a glutinous rice filled with beans, pork, lotus seeds, and eggs. The Moon Festival — or Mid-Autumn Festival, falling on the fifteenth day of the eighth month (mid-September) — celebrated the new harvest and the full moon, and "moon cakes", filled with lotus or bean paste, ham and nuts, were eaten along with melons, pomegranates, grapes, apples, and peaches — symbols of fertility and longevity. Ching Ming (around April 5) and Chung Yung (around October 4) were also called "Sweeping of the Grave Festivals", and were dedicated to remembering the dead [Beck 1898, pp.193-196; Wong 1982, pp.88-89].

Then there were other rituals, like the one accompanying the birth of the first son: on the third day, he received his first bath in water scented with herbs and aromatic leaves and was given an onion and some cash, while after a month a big dinner was served to relatives and association members, during which the baby was named and his head was shaved but for a small tuft at the top, which in time would grow to be the traditional queue. In a community so far from its homeland and for the most part forcefully deprived of family life, these were rituals and holidays that gained special distinguishing features, even if they often had to be modified and adapted to a radically different situation.

***

In the evenings, on Sundays, and on holidays, one of Chinatown's most important rendezvous was with theatre. The Chinese Music Hall Theatre (opened in 1890 at 12 Pell Street) was one of the favourite places, before becoming The Pelham in 1905. Then there were the Chinese Opera House (5 Doyers Street, inaugurated in 1895 and managed by the Chay Ding Quay Company — twenty persons led by Chin You, with Lee Sang as leading actor), and the Opera House (75 East Broadway, built in 1897). By the turn of the century, the theatre on Doyers Street was perhaps the most celebrated, showing a classic Chinese repertoire with an admission charge of between 20 cents and $1. It also had a rather dramatic history because, in the early 1900s, it became involved in the *tong* wars. The building was in front of the Arcade that from the bend of Doyers Street — the notorious "Bloody Angle" — led to Mott Street, thus allowing an easy retreat during gun fights. Actor Ah Hoon, a gifted comedian, was a member of the On Leong Tong and during his performances often interpolated gibes and remarks against the rival Hip Sing Tong. Riots repeatedly occurred, till Ah Hoon was killed in 1909. After his death, the situation became so tense that the theatre had to close down. The building was turned into a movie house and, after a few

106

Ill. 17
A Wedding in the Chinese Quarter, Mott Street, New York (A Drawing by W.A. Rogers for the *Harper's Weekly Magazine*, Nov. 22, 1890) (Archives of the New-York Historical Society)

months, in 1910, it was taken over by the New York Rescue Society and turned into a mission [Asbury 1928, 1990, pp.308-313].

Meanwhile, secluded though it was, Chinatown was being discovered by white artists as well. In its bar-restaurants, catering to a mixed and often far from refined audience, people like Eddie Cantor and Jimmy Durante made their debuts, as did 'the Russian Jew who holds the foremost place among American song-writers and whose soulful compositions are sung in almost every English-speaking house in the world' [Cahan 1917, 1960, p.529] — that Isadore Baline, who, while working as a waiter at "Nigger" Mike Salter's resort (The Pelham), used to entertain the members of the Chatham Club at 6 Doyers Street, before changing his name to Irving Berlin [*The WPA Guide* 1939, 1982, p.107; Asbury 1928, 1990, p.315; Ornitz 1923, passim].

III.

From Chinatown's Mott Street, one had only to turn into Bayard Street and walk one block westward to be on "Boulevard des Italiens" — Mulberry Street, 'swing[ing] in a dirty curve northwest from Park Row, chang[ing] its direction at every foot, and finally run[ning] north parallel with Broadway. [All around, the houses were] chiefly tumble-down old rookeries not originally built for tenements, and [...] therefore worse than the worst of those constructed for the purpose[, or ancient] one-story stables [...] converted into cheap shops and drinking places' [Roseboro 1888, p.397].

Italians first settled in New York in the early nineteenth century. By 1850, the colony had some 700 persons, who grew to 1,500 by 1860, and to 2,700 by 1870 [Rosenwaike 1972, p.68; also see Moncada 1937 and Marraro 1945]. Patriot Piero Maroncelli and Mozart's *librettista* Lorenzo da Ponte were among the most famous Italians in New York in that period, the bulk of the colony being made up of political exiles and professionals from Northern Italy, as well of artists, musicians, ragpickers, organ grinders, fruit sellers, boot-blacks, and the like. The *real* immigration, however, took place in the 1880s and 1890s, as part of the massive flood-tide from Southern and Eastern Europe. Italians started to spill over from "Boulevard des Italiens" to Baxter, Mott, Elizabeth, Bleecker, and Hester streets, and in the process other Little Italies were also born — on the Lower East Side, in the area bordered by East 10th-East 14th streets and First and Second avenues, and, outside the Lower East Side, in Greenwich Village, in East Harlem, in Yorkville, in Brooklyn[9]. The Mulberry Street area was portrayed as 'probably one of the most filthy localities in the city' [*Real Estate* 1893, p.905], where congestion, lack of air, light, and water, and precariousness of the buildings shocked newcomers. In many cases, the arrival of the "new immigrants" even meant some kind of betterment in the general conditions of the neighborhood, contrary to the common opinion, voiced by so many reformers and journalists, that the "the scum of Europe" was the cause of such evils [Gabaccia 1984]. The 20,000 Italians who lived in New York in 1880 became 114,877 in 1890, 225,026 in 1900, 382,775 in 1904, and 544,449 in 1910 ["The Italian Population" 1904, p.445; Rosenwaike 1972, p.67-68; Pozzetta 1971, p.76-78]. The great majority now came from Southern regions (Campania, Abruzzi, Puglie, Calabria, and above all Sicily), that had lived through centuries of ill government and political instability and were presently affected by a chronic misery, a rigid social structure, a difficult post-unification political period, and an economy based upon *latifondo* (vast, privately owned estates). All this resulted in agricultural backwardness, ruthless exploitation, low wages, and widespread unemployment[10].

It was a "chain migration". Lured by the letters of previous emigrants, working-age males from the same village left one after the other. They were peasants, *giornalieri* (day laborers), unskilled workers, small artisans, frequently illiterate and often used to conditions of extreme misery. At least in the beginning, they were mostly "birds of passage", i.e. sojourners who planned to spend a few years in the country of *dolci dollari* (sweet money), put aside a nest-egg, and then return to the homeland — maybe to leave again after some time. The flow was continuous throughout the turn of the century, and began slowly to decrease only around 1914. By then, women and whole families had also begun to arrive, giving the colony a more stable aspect[11]. Like the rest of the "new immigrants", Italians had no choice but to settle in certain quarters of New York, where rents were cheaper and jobs at walking distance. The very character of the "chain migration", the force of centuries-old traditions and prejudices and above all of *campanilismo* (to stick to one's village, distrusting the other villages' inhabitants), and the need to live in the vicinity of people speaking the same dialect, dictated the peculiar distribution of Italians in the city, and especially in Little Italy.

The Mulberry district showed an extraordinary uniformity in terms of ethnic settlement and thus came to be known as the Italian quarter *par excellence*. In the Sixth Ward (with lower Mulberry as its core), several blocks were 80-95 percent Italian; in the Fourteenth (upper Mulberry, and Hester and Bleecker), 29 blocks out of 41 had more than 50 percent Italian occupancy; on "Elisabetta Stretta" — as Elizabeth Street was known in "Italglish" — only one family out of 193 was not Italian in 1904 [Pozzetta 1971, p.98]. Neapolitans lived on Mulberry and Mott streets between East Houston and Prince streets (with a colony of people from Basilicata on the opposite sidewalk), Western Sicilians on Elizabeth, Eastern Sicilians on Catherine and Monroe, Calabrians on Mott between Broome and Grand, Pugliesi on Hester, Genoese on Baxter and Bleecker, and so on [Pozzetta, in Harney and Scarpaci, eds., 1981, p.18]...

***

Back home, Southern Italian society was not so tightly structured as was the Chinese one. But it too had a top tier of *prominenti* (land owners, lawyers, and rich merchants), a middle tier made up of clergymen, doctors, teachers, and of the ubiquitous *padroni* (middlemen), and, at the bottom, the great mass of *cafoni* (peasants and day laborers). This three-tier structure was quickly reproduced in the United States. In New York, the *prominenti* were bankers, merchants, and lawyers, the *padroni* operated as contractors for the American job market, and the large mass of peasants were soon reborn as unskilled workers or as "pick-and-shovel" labourers for the building trades of an expanding metropolis and a thriving interior (tunnels, reservoirs, railroads, tenements, etc.).

Italian banks (the Banca Termini, the Banca Caponigri, the Banca Legniti, the Banca Barsotti, and many others on Mulberry Street) were a focal point in the community. In metropolitan New York alone, there were some 400 of them by 1900, all chartered, and perhaps as many without charter [LaSorte 1985, p.127]. The rule for opening a bank was, 'the more crowded the street on which the bank is, the better for the banker; better yet, the more crowded is the block where the bank has its habitat; best of all, the more crowded with *paesani* [townsmen] the tenement in which operates the banker' [Speranza 1908, pp.55-56]. Often 'attached to a saloon, grocery store, or cigar store — sometimes to a cobbler shop' [Mangano 1904, pp.481-482], or simply a corner in 'the general merchandise store, where spaghetti and Italian cheese were on display' [Tresca, n.d., p.100], the bank provided important services to the neighborhood. It kept deposits, sent money home, functioned as an informal post office and travel agency, was a meeting place for friends and unemployed. The business transaction was a friendly affair between fellow countrymen and receipts were rarely used. But unscrupulous "bankers" were many, and not infrequently such "friendly affairs" ended tragically for the immigrant[12]. In 1896, following the failure of several such institutions, a panic spread, out of which emerged the one substantial Italian bank of the time. By 1904, the Italian Savings Bank at the corner of Mulberry and Spring had deposits of $1,059,369.19, with average sums on deposit of about $170 [Mangano 1904, p.482].

The banker belonged to the top tier of the immigrant hierarchy, and thus exercised a considerable power within the colony. No less central, at least in the early decades of Italian immigration, was the *padrone*'s rôle. In nineteenth-century Southern Italy, his figure was already familiar. A veritable *padre padrone*, he had strong personal ties both with the *prominenti* and with the *cafoni*, recruited *giornalieri* for field work, and often was entrusted with young boys (in some cases he was even sold them) that were to become apprentices in agriculture or in artisan work. In the United States, this figure became the essential contractor or middleman for the American entrepreneurs who needed the cheap labor offered by this new immigrant flood-tide, but neither could hire it personally, nor spoke or understood the various dialects, nor knew Italian customs, traditions, and prejudices. The *padrone* filled this gap. He personally knew the available workforce and so promised and distributed jobs (first of all to his own *paesani*), careful not to hire Neapolitans in a work gang made up of Sicilians. In exchange, he got a job fee (the *bossatura* or *senseria*) that could be as much as two thirds of the worker's pay. Often ruthless as a slave-master, he was a "boss" of the streets and of the work camps, of the bars and of the gambling dens. By 1900, there were some 2,000 small *padroni* in New York, and in time some of them became powerful and rich enough to enter business on their own, above all in the construction field, or to become ward heelers in the city's political scene, while others soon established connections with a budding criminal underworld [Merlino 1893; Koren 1897; Speranza 1903; Nelli 1964 and 1983; La Sorte 1985].

Unskilled workers, who formed the great majority of Italian immigrants in New York[13], initially turned to selling fruit, candy, artificial flowers, religious figurines in plaster, and to rag- and bone-picking, organ-grinding, boot-blacking, or came to control the barber trade and the macaroni market. By the turn of the century, Italian labor was mainly employed in the construction camps scattered around the country, with a high rate of geographical and seasonal mobility. Transiency was thus very high, and Little Italy was a sort of 'great sojourning base camp' [Pozzetta, in Harney and Scarpaci, eds., 1981, p.17]. Still, it had all the features of a real sub-society: 'All sorts of stores, pensions, groceries, fruit emporiums, tailors, shoe-makers, wine merchants, importers, musical stores, toy and clay molders, are found and abound here. There are notaries, lawyers, doctors, apothecaries, undertakers — followers of every profession and business, in fact, found in a great city'[14]. The *colonia*'s transient character started to change by the turn of the century, when Italians steadily entered the city labor market (construction and docks), thus gaining a more stable foot-hold in New York. At that stage, women began to arrive in greater numbers. As immigration increasingly took on a family aspect, homework became another important source of income. Finally, by the early decade of the new century, Italian women turned to factory work as well.

***

The Lower East Side's two Little Italies did not rest upon the same closely-knit social texture that was peculiar to Chinatown. Too many factors worked against this, the most important being *campanilismo* and the initial high rate of transiency. Nonetheless, the *colonia* had a certain structure that allowed for social and cultural identity, survival, and interaction with the external society. The most elemental and important organization was perhaps the *società di mutuo soccorso* (mutual aid society), such as the Società Italiana di Unione, Fratellanza e Beneficenza

Ill. 18
In the Italian Quarter: Mulberry Street on a Winter Evening (A Drawing by W.A. Rogers for the *Harper's Weekly Magazine*, Nov. 22, 1890) (Archives of the New-York Historical Society)

founded by Piero Maroncelli in 1839, or the Fratellanza Italiana, the Società Stella d'Italia, the Società Protezionista e di Mutuo Soccorso dei Barbieri Italiani di New York, the Società dei Reduci delle Patrie Battaglie, or, most famous of all, the Sons of Italy, founded in 1904. These societies provided medical assistance, organized a ball in winter and a picnic in summer, took part in the preparation of various religious festivals, and in the case of death of a member donated $100 to the widow ($50, if it was the *woman* who died). Most of Little Italy's social and cultural life expressed itself through these societies, which represented a vital cementing factor within the community [C. Adams 1881; Mangano 1904], even though the control of the *prominenti* made itself heavily felt.

The religious festivals were an important moment in Little Italy. There were some 20 or more calendar *feste*, to which the local or village patron saints' days were to be added, and all of them were occasions for crowded, colourful, and noisy parades along the streets.

Mulberry Street was on holiday: from the windows of the Italian houses hang tapestries, flags, and three-coloured lanterns, and everywhere were garlands of light-bulbs. It felt like being in one of those characteristic quarters in Naples, where religious feasts still cherish the old customs. In the street, the crowd was happy and noisy: women — and among them several were very young and handsome — wore their holiday dresses and brought the gay note of gaudy colours amid the dark suits of the men and the uniforms of the military societies. San Rocco was being celebrated, and the Italians of Mulberry wanted to do things properly. Towards 11 A.M., the call of the trumpets was heard and in the distance flags and banners appeared. The crowd thronged the sidewalks to enjoy the parade in honor of San Rocco. A squad of policemen headed the procession, followed by the Conterno Band, and right after by a banner on which San Rocco was painted in oil, with all his wounds and his dog. Two flags, one Italian, the other American, flapped at the banner's sides, thus placing the saint under a double protection. Then came the members of the Società San Rocco, stern and proud in their blue dresses with golden buttons and stripes, as if the whole world belonged to them. In the buttonhole of their parade dresses, they had flowers, ribbons, and cockades. After another musical band, a military society paraded, in the uniform of the military engineer corps, with the three colours flapping in the wind; and then came a colossal banner of San Rocco, wounded more than ever, and after it the congregations of the Carmine, of the Madonna Addolorata, and of other saints like San Cono, Sant'Antonio, etc. It was a gorgeous parade, something that really made a hit in a country such as this where parades of every race and form are the order of the day. The bands played, the crowds watched in awe and cheered, the windows, the street, the sidewalks were thronged with people [Ciambelli 1893, p.234, my translation].

The Festa di San Rocco was on August 16. On February 5, the Baxter Street's Catanesi celebrated the Festa di Sant'Agata, and on September 19 the great Festa di San Gennaro began, a Neapolitan feast at the core, but one that, lasting several days and paralyzing Mulberry Street, often merged together the whole Italian community. Then there were the *feste* of Santa Rosalia and San Donato, and of many other saints and patrons. And there were secular holidays — the Festa di Garibaldi (on September 20th) and Columbus Day (on October 12th) being the two most important.

To the homesick peasant who hangs about the Mott-street café for hours, hungrily devouring with his eyes the candy counterfeit of Mount Vesuvius in the windows, with lurid lava-streams descending and saffron smoke ascending, predicting untold stomach-quakes in the block, the saint means home and kindred, neighborly friendship in a strange land, and the old communal ties, which, if anything, are tightened by distance and homesickness. In fact, those ties are as real as they were at home. Just as the [villagers of Auletta] flock in Elizabeth street, so in Mulberry, Mott, and Thompson streets downtown, and in the numbered streets of Little Italy uptown, almost every block has its own village of mountain or lowland, and with the village its patron saint, in whose worship or celebration — call it what you will — the particular camp makes reply to the question, "Who is my neighbor?" [Riis 1899, p.494].

***

The question could find its reply in other places and occasions as well — at the benefit societies' balls and picnics; or during the wedding and christening parties held in the tenements, in the backyards, or in the hired halls; or in the Sunday amusements at home, when the whole extended family was present along with neighbors. And in the numerous cafés along Mulberry Street — that ever-present meeting place, where men gathered to chat and discuss work opportunities, to talk politics, and to play *morra* and such card games as *briscola* and *tresette* (because

'Italian men are noticeably less domestic than Jews and Germans, and they avail themselves of the alternatives to tenements — street corners, clubs, and cafés. The cafés differ from American saloons in that very often they do not have doors to hide those inside from the street [...]') [Kimball 1900, p.5]. Among the most renowned were the Caffé Moretti — a dingy, smoke-blackened place famous for its Lachryma Christi wine, 'for years [...] the *foyer* of operatic artists' [C. Adams 1881, p.683] —, and the Caffé Ronca, numbering actor Eduardo Migliaccio among its most regular customers. Other popular meeting places were, in the Mulberry Street area, Francesco Ruocco's Caffé e Ristorante Cilentano, Moneta's Restaurant, the Caffè Santa Lucia, and, on First Avenue and East 10th-East 13th streets, Veniero's, De Robertis's Pastry Shoppe, Lanza Restaurant.

In the evenings, Italians could go to the various small places which specialized in legitimate theatre (Goldoni, Shakespeare, Schiller), Italian-American melodrama (Bernardino Ciambelli and Rocco Metelli), puppet shows, and Pulcinella skits. Antonio Maiori's company played at 24 Spring Street, in a 'building [...] so small that the constant vociferation of the prompter is heard throughout the audience' [Hapgood 1900, p.546]. The Eldorado on Spring Street, the Villa Giulia on Grand Street, the Villa Vittorio Emanuele on Mulberry Street were *caffè concerto* (or *cafés chantants*), staging *macchiette coloniali*, farces and *sceneggiate*, while Little Italy's great family entertainment was the *teatro dei pupi e delle marionette* — the puppet show.

Theatre companies also played an important social rôle within the community. Among its members and actors, for instance, the Circolo Filodrammatico Italo-Americano had such noted personages as bankers Fausto Malzone and Angelo Legniti, who linked the company to many of the business enterprises and social agencies of the neighborhood. It also contributed money to the victims of cholera and earthquakes in Italy, to the construction of the Italian hospital, of the Italian school, and of the monument of Columbus, and to the Knights of Labor, one of its member being a prominent Knight [Aleandri and Seller, in Seller, ed., 1983, pp.241-243].

***

Theatre was not the *colonia*'s only passion. Illiteracy rates were surely high among Italian immigrants, but the number of bookstalls and small libraries on Mulberry and the adjacent streets and the substantial list of titles of the Balletto & Frugone publishing house on Park Row suggested a widespread love of reading, with — it seems — a very small divide

115

between "highbrow culture" and "mass culture". People read classics and such Italian popular authors as Carolina Invernizio. They also read the works of a group of young poets living in New York (Arturo Giovannitti, Luigi Carnovali, Salvatore di Leo, and Emanuel Carnevale) and Bernardino Ciambelli's novels and stories about life in the Great Metropolis. And they read Italian-American newspapers. *L'Eco d'Italia*, a weekly founded in 1849 by G. F. Secchi de Casali, and *Il Progresso Italo-Americano*, a daily founded in 1880 by former *padrone* Carlo Barsotti, were the most widely read. They tried to react to the stereotyped descriptions of Little Italy that were the daily fare of much of the American press, but they themselves often fell prey to the same fascination for sensationalism and local color in order to attract a wider audience. In a way, they expressed the official position of the community — the *prominenti*'s point of view —, but not infrequently also voiced the tensions arising within it.

Little Italy in fact was not a homogeneous whole. The immigrant in New York often met with the same exploitation and class divisions to which s/he had been accustomed back home. S/he also might be a Socialist or an Anarchist, with a certain political and trade-union experience. And so consumers' cooperatives and *circoli operai* (workers' circles, one of the most important being the Circolo di New York — Bassa Città, with Camillo Cianfarra as delegate to the Socialist Labor Party Central Committee in 1901) were born, which operated in opposition to greedy merchants, shop-keepers, *strozzini* (loan sharks), and travel-agents, or as alternatives to the mutual aid societies often in the hands of *prominenti* and bankers. Unions slowly became rooted in the neighborhood, and figures like socialist Cianfarra and Giusto Calvi, *Wobbly* Arturo Giovannitti and Joseph Ettor, anarchist Giuseppe Ciancabilla, Saverio Merlino, and Carlo Tresca, were rather popular. The Knights of Labor, the Industrial Workers of the World, the Socialist Labor Party, the Socialist Party of America, and various anarchist groups, attempted (and to an extent managed) to gain a foothold in the area, and, from 1902, an Italian Socialist Federation of the United States endeavoured to provide an organizational structure for these *émigrés* and a necessary link with the larger American socialist movement. The Italian radical press — such famous papers like *Il Proletario*, a weekly started in Pittsburgh in 1896 and soon moved to New York, where it remained several years, or the anarchist *L'Adunata dei Refrattari*, *Il Martello*, and *Il Grido del Popolo*, and the various journals and bulletins published by union locals, such as ILGWU Local 89's *Giustizia* — was thus an important element within the community. It spread precious informations about life and survival in America, criticized the *colonia*'s social

116

structure and the conservative rôle of *padroni, prominenti,* and of the Church, and by facing the delicate issues of Americanization and assimilation proved a very special instrument in the definition of a new identity [*The Italians* 1938; Pozzetta 1973; Cartosio, in Harzig and Hoerder, eds., 1985].

IV.

Crowded and busy as they were, Chinatown and Little Italy seemed but tiny enclaves on the Lower East Side's outskirts, if compared to the broad expanse that lay just beyond the Bowery and south of East 14th Street — the throbbing Jewish Quarter. German Jews had arrived as part of the German immigration, and early clusters of Polish Jews had formed in the 1840s at the corner of Mott and Bayard streets. Mostly tailors, they had soon moved nearer to the shops Germans were establishing beyond the Bowery, around the intersection of East Broadway, Canal and Essex streets [R. Sanders 1969, p.48; Howe 1976, pp.81-83; Rischin 1962, 1977, p.79]. The big flood of East European Jews of the 1880s and 1890s thus found a neighborhood already settled by coreligionists. The enclave at the foot of Canal Street swelled and spilled over onto the adjoining streets, moving east, west, and north, beyond Delancey and East Houston streets and directly into *Kleindeutschland.* Disturbed by their social and cultural diversity, German Jews started to abandon the quarter and, in their drive towards Americanization and respectability, moved uptown, from where they looked down upon the newly arrived with a condescension not devoid of hostility [Rischin 1962, 1977, Chapter 6].

East European Jews had come from their communities in the Pale of Settlement (Lithuania, Byelorussia, Ukraine, Volhynia, and Poland) and in nearby Galicia, Bukovina, and Rumania, in the wake of tragic circumstances: the 1868 cholera epidemic, the 1869 Polish famine, the 1871 Odessa pogrom. In the 1880s, the May Laws had prohibited Jews from owning land outside cities and new pogroms had followed Tsar Alexander II's assassination. Finally, in the new century, there followed the 1903 Kishinev massacre and the repression after the 1905 revolution. Chronic misery and economic paralysis, fear and desperation, religious and political oppression and the lure of America skilfully kindled by the German trans-Atlantic shipping companies facing a decline of emigration from Central Europe — many reasons combined to send to America 40,000 East European Jews in the 1870s, over 200,000 in the 1880s, 300,000 in the 1890s, and another 1,500,000 between 1900 and the outbreak of World War I[15]. The great majority remained in New York, and by 1900 more than 250,000 lived in the 7th, 10th, 11th, and 13th Wards — the core of the Lower East Side, of whose population they represented the 79% [Dwork 1981, p.5].

Theirs was essentially a "family migration". Single immigrants arriving in the 1880s toiled hard with the aim soon to send for wives, children, and relatives, even if families sometimes did not survive the transplantation, and wives were often deserted. Between 1886 and 1896, an average of 41.6% of the Jews arriving in New York were women, and 33.8% children under 16; between 1899 and 1910, the figures were respectively 43.4 and 24.9 %. "Birds of passage" were comparatively rare (from 1908 to 1924, 94.8 % of Jewish immigrants remained in the United States) [Dwork 1981, pp.2-3]. Most immigrant Jews actually *fled* the Old World, and had very little chance of going back. Nostalgia for a homeland that often did not exist or that was linked with memories of pogroms and social and economic distress thus took on very peculiar traits. It was one of the main differences with other immigrant groups, probably also accounting for the Jews' higher social and economic mobility as compared, for instance, to the Italians', among whom the repatriation quota was undoubtedly higher.

By and large, Jews arriving in New York before 1900 were skilled workers. In the Old World, they already had a trade, but in the New World they had to adapt to the opportunities at hand, because it was soon clear that, there, 'the *Goldeneh Medina* was a pushcart or a store on Orchard Street' [Roskolenko 1971, p.93]. Between 1900 and 1925, Jews (10.3% of the total immigrant population) made up one-quarter of the skilled workers entering the United States: one-half of the clothing workers, jewellers, and watchmakers; one-third of the printers; 41.4 % of the leather workers; one-fifth of the merchants and shopkeepers [Lestschinsky, in Finkelstein, ed., 1960, p.1569]. In those very years, the clothing industry of New York was undergoing an extraordinary process of expansion, and it immediately attracted immigrant Jews. Many of them had been tailors in the Old World or had had some experience in the sector (the textile industry was rapidly developing in Lodz and other cities of the Pale). Besides, it was not uncommon for East European immigrants to stop in London on their way to America, and there to find employment in a growing clothing industry. Very often, women too came to the United States with a certain experience in factory work [Rischin 1962, 1977, pp.26-30; Ewen 1985, Chapter 14; Kessner 1977, Chapters 3 and 4].

But the great reality of the Jewish Quarter in its early period was a continuous process of proletarization. Talmud scholars, *melameds* (teachers) and students, *chazans* (synagogue cantors) and rabbis,

118

merchants of all sorts and artisans in various trades — almost all had to start anew and were reborn as peddlers or sweatshop workers, rich Jews generally belonging to the German community which was by now moving out of the Lower East Side. The area thus took on a rather homogeneous aspect, and it was only by the turn of the century that a social stratification became apparent. A few among yesterday's *maki* or *griner tukes* (the "greenhorns", the newly arrived) became contractors for uptown firms, and then small entrepreneurs ("cockroach bosses", or "moths" as they were called as compared to the uptown "giants"). In time, they might even buy some flats in the Ghetto, perhaps not far from their shop, and thus exercise a double pressure upon their neighbors and fellow people — as bosses and as landlords: the source of new, dramatic tensions. A local bourgeoisie emerged, whose best symbol probably was the Jarmulowsky Bank (its building was called "the Lower East Side's skyscraper") and whose sons went to City College, became lawyers and dentists, and then moved to new, more respectable neighborhoods.

***

The Jewish Quarter undoubtedly was the most congested area of the Lower East Side. In 1896, its core — the 10th Ward — had a density of more than 750 persons per acre (that of Paris being, in those same years, of 125), and several blocks were inhabited by from 1000 to 1800 persons each. It counted 989 tenements, 8 public schools, 3 large theatres (with a total seating capacity of 9,500), 16 stables, 13 pawnshops, 72 restaurants, 31 synagogues (and 10 Protestant or Catholic churches), 65 factories, 172 garment shops, 60 cigar shops, 34 laundries, 236 saloons (half of which could more appropriately be called brothels), and 18 "disorderly places" [*Report* 1897, p.3; Walling 1905; Lagerquist 1910]. By 1907, among the most crowded blocks was the one on Orchard, Rivington, Allen, and Stanton streets, with 2,943 inhabitants and a resulting density of 1,281 persons per acre:

A street-full of push carts, a pushing to and fro of Jewish men and women — the former predominating among the sellers, the latter among the buyers — the bargaining not confined to the pavement, but spreading far into the street, — this is the first view of Orchard Street to the passer-by. Looking up from the shouting crowds, huge tenements rise — five-story tenements housing families and "boarders" living with the families. The basement fronts and the first floor fronts are often shops and stores; sometimes the basements are used as stock rooms by the keepers of the stands. Meat, poultry, fish, bread, groceries, crockery, white goods, knit goods are the predominating wares sold from Orchard Street between Rivington and Stanton. Butcher shops recur throughout the block, and so do other shops for the sale of the necessaries of life. This apart from the forty-odd street stands which sell fruits, nuts, newspapers, shoe laces, articles of apparel, and the like. Going on Stanton Street to Allen Street we find a saloon and a dancing academy to vary the monotony of food, fuel and clothing shops, and proceeding up Allen Street — this narrow street made dreary by the Second Avenue Elevated — we come to restaurants, barber shops, tobacco shops, soda-water stands, pants' pressing places and other varieties. Turning the corner at Rivington Street toward Orchard again, the predominance of such signs as "Entrance to the Lawyer on the First Floor" and signs indicating the presence of real estate men and dentists attract attention, apart from the usual shops and stands [Bernheimer 1908, pp.26-27].

Russian Jews, possibly the most articulate group (and also, at the same time, the most radical and America-oriented), settled in the area between Grand and Monroe streets, with East Broadway — New York's *Nevsky Prospekt* — as its main artery. Rumanian Jews made up the most congested inner community, south of Houston, north of Grand, between the Bowery and Allen Street (with, after 1907, an enclave of Levantine Jews, often strangers even to the rest of the community, in the few blocks on Chrystie, Forsyth, Eldridge, and Allen streets). Galician Jews lived between Houston and Broome, Clinton and Willett streets. And Hungarian Jews in what had once been *Kleindeutschland*, between East 10th and Houston streets, Avenue B and the river [Rischin 1962, 1977, pp.76-78][16].

A few thoroughfares cut across such a crowded scene. East Broadway was the main one — the street of physicians and dentists, of the Jews who had "made it" but had not yet left the Lower East Side. It was also the street of the Ghetto's "storefront synagogues", of the *kosher* food shops, of the small stores where religious objects were sold, of the famous Garden Cafeteria and of the popular Katz's music store. And it was the street of the public institutions — the Educational Alliance, the Home for the Aged, the Hebrew Sheltering House, the *Machzike Talmud Torah*, the offices of the *Jewish Daily Forward* and other newspapers. Grand Street was second in importance, at least until the opening of the Williamsburg Bridge, with its approach on Delancey Street, brought about the decline of the Grand Street Ferry and consequently of the street itself. It was the Lower East Side's major retail shopping center, the place where one could have a glimpse of midtown and uptown fashion — buying a "Grand Street hat" at Ridley's often being a decisive step in the process of a Jewish girl's Americanization. Orchard and Hester streets were the domain of stalls, shops, and peddlers, a wild confusion of bodies and languages, of offers and refusals, where one bargained, bribed, and bought. Allen Street offered the peak of congestion, contradiction and racial mixture: here, vice and orthodoxy lived side by side, a long line of brothels opening just a few steps from the Congregation of Tifereth Israel.

[Allen Street] was as much Romanian as it was Greek and Arabic. There were Jewish restaurants for the Hungarian-Romanian Jewish cuisine — heavier, spicier — and you ended up as a fat man. The Greeks and Arabs sold leaner dishes. The Gypsies there sold your future, very thin. There were halvah, sesame seeds, dates, figs, pictures of Muhammad, pictures of Christ, pictures of fat women with their breasts in view — and the entire mixture went along with candies from Egypt, the carpets from Persia — and the whores that walked on Allen Street...for everything was tolerated there. Vice was normal on Allen Street...Over the stores, one flight up, were the coffeehouses of the Greeks, Syrians, and Arabs. They offered up coffee, cognac, and belly dancers — and the bigger the belly the greater the applause. [...] More than several types of sin were up one flight, we knew...[Roskolenko 1971, pp.106-107].

Finally, the Bowery, with its theatres and amusement resorts, was 'the western edge of the world [...], the jumping-off place into the unknown' [Ganz 1919, p.21], an International Rialto that was a border line and a no man's land.

***

Coming to the Lower East Side of New York from the closed universe of the European *shtetl* (the small village), Jews had to face a bewildering new world. They reacted as other immigrants did — by reinforcing a group solidarity that was already part of their experience, even more so than it was for Italians or Chinese, and by trying to recreate a neighborhood of their own, to rebuild the past in the present. A deep-rooted sense of community and social responsibility and the concept of *tsedaka* (charity conceived as justice), stemming both from religious tenets and from a history of past and present persecution, received new strength and meaning on the American soil, and originated a host of

121

hevras, voluntary organizations built around the *shul* (the ever-present synagogue).

The most immediate and central among these was the *landsmanshaft*, a fraternal lodge composed of fellow townspeople and devoted to the daily assistance of the immigrant. Originally connected to a synagogue, in time it evolved into a purely secular body, similar to the Italian *società di mutuo soccorso* or to the Chinese *tung hung woy*: the Bialystoker Sick and Death Benefit Society on East Houston Street, the Kletzker Brotherly Aid Association on Ludlow Street, and several others [Soyer 1988; Weisser 1989]. There were also a Russian-American Hebrew Association, a *Roumanisch-Amerikanischer Bruderbund*, a *Magyar Tarsulat* (a society of Hungarian Jews), a Federation of Galician and Bukovinian Jews, and several other organizations of Galician Jews that, in their very names — the Crown Prince Rudolph *Verein*, the *Franz Joseph Kranken Unterstutzung Verein*, the Franz Ferdinand Benevolent Society —, reflected the different relationship this group entertained with the country of origin, the Austro-Hungarian Empire (they were the ones who most frequently returned to Europe). More directly traditional and religious were the *heder*, an elementary school where a *melamed* taught the *Khumesh* or Pentateuch (there were some 300 of them in 1903); the *yeshiva* or *talmud torah*, a school of Talmudic studies (the *Machzike Talmud Torah*, the *Jacob Joseph Yeshiva* on Montgomery Street, the East Side Hebrew Institute on East 8th Street at the corner of Avenue B, and many others); and the *beth-hamedrash*, a place of study and prayer (like the *Beth Hamedrash Hagadol* on Norfolk Street).

Other organizations were the direct result of the American experience: the United Hebrew Charities (formed in 1874), the Hebrew Free School Association and the Hebrew Technical School for Girls (1878), the Hebrew Emigrant Aid Society (1881, soon to find its headquarters in the building on Lafayette Street formerly housing the famous Astor Library), the Hebrew Technical School for Boys (1890), the *Hevra Hachnosas Orchim* or Hebrew Sheltering Society (1890), the *Gemillat Hasodim* or Hebrew Free Loan Society (1892), the famous Workman's Circle, and a host of other organizations, often funded by uptown German Jews in their effort to Americanize the *kikes*, as they called their East European coreligionists (from the "ki" with which so many of their surnames ended).

In 1889, some of these organizations came together to promote the Hebrew Institute which in 1891 found its permanent headquarters on East Broadway, and in 1893 changed its name to Educational Alliance, popularly known as "Edgies". Especially under the direction of David Blaustein, the Alliance became the settlement house *par excellence* of the

Jewish community, organizing classes in English, history, and music, which met from 9 a.m. to 10 p.m., special courses in personal hygiene and physical training, art exhibits, dramatic clubs, and working closely with other settlement houses active in the quarter even if not strictly Jewish in their origins, such as the University, the College and the Henry Street settlements. Some 37,000 persons attended the Alliance weekly, with an admission charge of 10¢: a good measure of an Americanizing effort that did not go without criticism (Yiddish, for instance, was forbidden) [Roskolenko 1971; Shustko n.d.; Rischin 1962, 1977; Howe 1976; C. Goodman 1979][17].

Of course, for the Orthodox Jew, religion regulated everyday life. The observance of *kosher* food norms and of the *bar-mitzvah* (religious confirmation), of the Sabbath and of the various *yoim tojv* (festivities like the eight days of Chanukah, Passover, the festival of Purim, the New Year celebration of Rosh Ha-Shanah, the feast-day of Succoth, the days of fast of Tish'a Be-av and of Yom Kippur)[18] was a powerful element of identity and at the same time, inevitably and from the very beginning, a source of tensions between Ghetto and America. Sabbath, for instance, began at sundown on Friday, and from then to Saturday evening it was forbidden to do any kind of work, to travel, to touch money or to light a fire (orthodox families usually depended upon a *shabes goy*, a Gentile "firelighter" who received a 2-3 cent tip to light the stove or turn on and off the gas mantle). The big Friday night dinner, anxiously anticipated the whole week, consisted of *gefüllte fish* (stuffed fish), sweet and sour roast meat with potatoes and carrots, soup, sweets, and was a treat often made possible only by daily sacrifice. On Saturday, there was the *cholent*, a meat and vegetable soup accompanied by *chala* (brown, unleavened, braided bread).

***

But there was more than religion and survival in the Ghetto. Jewish migration occurred at a time in which, in Europe, the *Haskalah* (the Jewish enlightenment) had gathered sufficient strength to influence a large sector of the community. Also, the revolutionary experience of many immigrants, especially young students, and the curiosity about the new American reality made the abandonment of strict orthodoxy easier[19]. The whole neighborhood was thus animated by an extraordinary cultural activity — 'a veritable intellectual fermentation' [Hapgood 1902, 1967, p.39] that fascinated outsiders (and sometimes disconcerted them, as was the case with Henry James) and was brightly captured by Hapgood, William Dean Howells, Lincoln Steffens. People met in Russian tea-houses and Rumanian *kazín* (coffee-houses), at Sussman and Goldstein's on Ludlow Street, at Herrick's on Division Street, or in the literary cafés on Canal Street, East Broadway, and Second Avenue, 'the living centers of a liquid culture flowing from some earnest immigrant's soul' [Roskolenko 1971, p.186; Fisher 1976]. Or they went to 'the little café on Grand Street where the Socialists and Anarchists of the Russian quarter were wont to meet late at night and stay until the small hours' [Hapgood 1902, 1967, p.297], or to Justus Schwab's on East 1st Street and to Sachs's on Suffolk Street — 'the [two] headquarters of the East Side radicals, socialists, and anarchists, as well as of the young Yiddish writers and poets' [Goldman 1934, p.5]. Other favourite meeting-places were the *delicatessen*-stores on Rivington and Allen streets, famous for their salted vine-leaves, goose-*pastrami*, moon-shaped *caciocavallo*

Ill. 19
A Café Scene (Drawing by Jacob Epstein, from Hutchins Hapgood's *The Spirit of the Ghetto*, 1902)

cheese made of sheep's milk, and for their 10-cent dishes of chopped eggplant with olive oil and pot-roast with mashed potato and gravy; or the pastry-shops and dairy lunch-rooms where only milk products were served (most of them Rumanian, the Rumanians being well-known *bon vivants*, as compared to the more somber Russians) [E. G. Robinson 1973, p.8; Ravage 1917, 1971].

Above all, '[l]earning...that really was the driving force at that time...education and learning, and learning to speak English, it was very important, very important' [Begun, interview, 1987]. And learning meant libraries, like the one on Seward Park or the Astor Library on Lafayette Street, and lectures and speeches of all kinds. At the Cooper Union, at the Educational Alliance, at Justus Schwab's, at the Ferrer Center and School on St.Mark's Place, one could listen to Felix Adler speak on "Ethical Culture", Johann Most and Emma Goldman on "Anarchism", Abraham Cahan, Joseph Barondess, Meyer London on "Socialism and Trade Unionism". Rallies and meetings then took place at the Clinton, New Irving, Golden Rule, Clarendon halls, at the Workmen's Circle, at the United Hebrew Trades' locals, at the Socialist Labor Party's or the Industrial Workers of the World's headquarters on East 4th Street, at the Anarchists' headquarters on East 6th Street, at Union Square and Tompkins Square Park. This was the daily and nightly fare of the Lower East Side's Jewish Quarter, a ferment that invariably attracted members of other immigrant groups and many an American intellectual desirous to break away from the stiffness of mainstream culture.

This scene, as well as the scene of everyday life and survival, was dominated by Yiddish, the Judeo-German *zhargon* that in Europe, in those same decades, was being rescued from obscurity and given literary dignity by such writers as Mendel Moicher Sforim, Sholem Aleichem, and Sholem Asch. Newspapers were the main vehicle of its revival and diffusion in New York, and at the same time an eloquent testimony to the quarter's energy and vitality. The Yiddish press was without doubt the most thriving among the immigrant presses on the Lower East Side. Even before the "new immigration", the small Jewish community of New York could rely upon such newspapers as the *Yiddishe Zeitung*, the *Yiddishe Post*, the *Yiddishe Volks-Zeitung*, the *Tageblatt*, to name just a few, of different cultural and political orientation. When East European Jews arrived, this small handful of newspapers increased tenfold: between 1885 and 1914, the great age of the Jewish Quarter, some 150 dailies, weeklies, monthlies, and quarterlies appeared, some of them nothing more than short-lived attempts, others destined to enjoy a long and important history. In particular, the social and political unrest that steadily characterized the Jewish Lower East Side was chronicled by a lively and aggressive radical press: the socialist *Naye Tsayt, New Yorker Yiddishe Volks-Zeitung, Naye Welt, Zukunft,* and *Arbeiter Zeitung,* the Anarchist *Freiheit, Wahrheit, Freie Arbeiter Shtimme,* and *Freie Gesellshaft,* and many others (some of them in Russian, the expression of Marxist organizations, such as the *Novy Mir* with offices on St.Mark's Place and Leon Trotzky, Nikolai Bukharin, and Aleksandra Kollontay as contributing writers). They had a troubled but fascinating life, and were also a veritable arena for such Ghetto intellectuals as journalist-novelist-trade-unionist-socialist Abraham Cahan (a major figure on the Jewish Quarter, in the Yiddish world, and more generally on the Lower East Side, a friend to Howells, Hapgood, Steffens), poets Morris Rosenfeld, David Edelstadt, and Abraham Wald, playwright Jacob Gordin. The most famous of all was the socialist *Vorwärts,* or *Jewish Daily Forward.* Founded by Cahan in 1897, it really became the cultural backbone of the community. With its "Bintel Brief" ("Bundles of Letters") section, to which common men and women unburdened their souls asking for advice on any issue, with its articles on life in the Ghetto

Ill. 20
The Poet Abraham Wald (Drawing by Jacob Epstein, from Hutchins Hapgood's *The Spirit of the Ghetto,* 1902)

126

and life in America written in an often notably Americanized language, with its attention to the large social and political issues as well as to the daily drama and comedy of its common readers, with its acute literary and theatrical criticism, the *Forward* — even if it grew more and more conservative in time, as was the case with Cahan — provided a precious daily nourishment to thousands of immigrants [R. Sanders 1969; Howe 1976; Metzker 1971].

The other great reality of the Jewish Quarter was theatre. Even more than for other immigrant groups, it was the cementing element that gave an identity to the community and at the same time fruitfully interacted with America. To the Jewish masses, theatre was more than simple entertainment. It was 'educator, dream-maker, chief agent of charity, social center, and recreation hub for the family' [Rischin 1962, 1977, p.133]. Coming a long way from Rumania and Russia via London, Yiddish theatre received new life in New York and became a veritable obsession in the Ghetto, something like a "national" accomplishment which had a social as well as a cultural relevance. Yiddish companies

Ill. 21
The Editorial Office of a Ghetto Newspaper (Drawing by Jacob Epstein, from Hutchins Hapgood's *The Spirit of the Ghetto*, 1902)

took over many German theatres on the Bowery, and by 1910 the area was a Yiddish Rialto, the centre of an intense and creative experience. Actors and actresses, playwrights and directors were public figures on the Lower East Side. Their plays, acting, and private life were openly discussed in the sweatshops, in the cafés, and in the theatres, between acts, and often even on stage.

The mobbing audiences came from the Jewish trade unions, from *vereins*, from sick-and-death-benefit societies and benevolent organizations. [...] They did not come with popcorn. They brought Turkish halva, Jewish bagels, farmer cheese — sandwiched into a newspaper; American fruit, Russian candy, something to drink, and they carried on, equal in ego, as if they were the actors. Too often one could not hear the real actors, who were drowned out by the the frightening comments, the extraterritorial noise, the public and private deep critiques, and then the overdone applause. The Yiddish theater of those days resembled the early English theater with its hurrahs, gusto, and lampooning. The only element lacking was Anglo-Saxon accents [Roskolenko 1971, pp.149-150].

When, in the late 1910s and early 1920s, Yiddish theatre slowly began to move north, first to Second Avenue and then to Irving Place and East 16th Street, that was the first sign that changes were occurring within the Jewish community as well. Another diaspora had begun, from the Lower East Side out, towards the rest of America — and Yiddish theatre would be one of the first casualties.

V.

That such a 'smorgasbord of [...] nationalities' [Catapano 1988, p.2] should provide a fertile soil for powerful tensions among the various communities was inevitable. Partly, this was the result of received stereotypes already active back home or already affecting American culture. Partly, it was the outcome of the Lower East Side's specific economic and social conditions. When, for instance, Italians settled in the Mulberry Street area and steadily moved into the city's labor market, they did so by displacing the Irish from houses and jobs, and this — more than the two groups' different shades of Catholicism — often provoked brawls and fisticuffs, especially in the occasion of Italian patron saints' parades. When Chinese arrived from the West, their forced separateness from white society initially saved them from open hostility. But their world was always viewed as a mysterious and menacing one,

128

thus giving rise to lurid tales about strange Oriental rituals and encircling Chinatown with a *cordon sanitaire* of suspect and morbid sensationalism.

For their part, the Jews — fresh with memories of *pogroms* — often had to face hostility and distrust ('I remember, where we lived, in Henry Street, nearby there was a tremendously large Catholic church, and [...] attached to it there was a parochial school, and I remember when the Jewish boys would go to school, we'd go to school, we'd fight with the other boys, you know, "Oh, you Christ-killer!". You know, that sort of things...') [Begun, interview, 1987]. It was a "poor people's war", most likely to be exacerbated by periods of economic depression or by transformations in the city's labor market. By and large, however, no real battle was ever fought in this war. Prejudice undoubtedly existed, but it rarely took the form of overt racism. Mainly, it expressed itself in the "protection of the neighborhood" and in street gangs' activity — something that was already inscribed in the Lower East Side's past history (the B'howery B'hoys, the Plug Uglies, the Dead Rabbits had been famous gangs in the mid-nineteenth century) and now became common to all immigrant groups, further complicating the already complex urban geography of the area with innumerable territories and border lines[20].

Of course, the step that could lead from the "protection of the neighborhood" to some kind of illegal activity was not a long one. Petty criminality had always existed on the immigrant Lower East Side as part of the everyday struggle for survival. It often was nothing less than the attempt to follow shorter routes to economic security, by conforming to a concept of social mobility that was part of the American work ethic. From this point of view, youth above all were amenable to petty criminality. Street gangs (the most immediate and elemental unit outside the family) became involved in picking pockets, rolling drunkards, stealing wares from pushcarts — a fertile ground for the development of more serious criminal behaviors. Crime patterns were essentially similar for the various ethnic groups. In the early years of settlement, loose organizations were born out of the need to preserve identity, to protect the small clusters of immigrants, and to channel desires and frustrations the official organizations often did not meet. Social isolation, ignorance of language and mores, competition in the labor market made them an unavoidable reality. In time, a stable structure evolved, often moulded upon similar societies back home, and these organizations became real gangs in the Lower East Side's variegated underworld, still very much neighborhood-centered and generally linked — in a subterranean way — to the community's economic potentates. Such were, for instance, in Chinatown, the *tongs*, and, in Little Italy, the "Black Hand".

129

Tongs dated back to seventeenth-century China, when they were secret societies fighting the Ch'ing dynasty. The most famous (the *Hung* League, or Triad) was reborn in California in the 1860s, and soon gave rise to other dissident *tongs* all over the country. In New York, the *Ong Leong Tong* (Chamber of Tranquil Conscientiousness, at 41 Mott Street) and the *Hip Sing Tong* (Hall of Victorious Union, at 34 Bayard Street) fought for the control of prostitution, of the 250 gambling houses, and of the opium joints. They had close links with certain family associations and with the CCBA itself, and in the first two decades of the new century waged a real war in the heart of Chinatown. In 1906, 1910, and 1912, the Chinese government itself was called upon to make peace — which it did by threatening reprisals on the *tong* leaders' relatives in China. Only after 1925 — in connection both with Chinatown's internal changes and with China's social and political events — did the *tongs* reduce their activity, although they did not disappear from the scene [Beck 1898; Asbury 1928, 1990; Longstreet 1975; Sante 1991].

The first public appearance of crime in Little Italy was the August 1904 Black Hand panic. The gang probably stemmed from some illegal organization already active in Italy, and specialized in blackmail, bombings, and kidnappings (to avoid having their activity severely damaged or destroyed, shop- and stall-keepers had to pay a fee to the racketeers) [Denison 1908; Watchorn 1909][21]. The *prominenti* blamed the Black Hand on Southerners, adding new divisions to an already divided community. In 1906, the Italian Squad of the Central Detective Bureau (30 men headed by Joe Petrosino) was formed, followed, in 1908, by the Italian Vigilance Protective Association of New York, which was staunchly opposed by *Il Proletario* as a further repressive tool in the hands of the community's power structure, likely to be used against labor. In March 1909, Petrosino was killed in Palermo, possibly by Ignazio "Lupo the Wolf" Saietta and Giuseppe Morelli — a murder that immediately fed anti-immigrant, anti-Italian fears and prejudices —, but the peak of the Black Hand's activity was reached in 1911, notwithstanding the arrest and sentencing of "Lupo", Morelli, and their lieutenants the year before ["Black Hand" 1910; Pozzetta 1971; Sante 1991].

A Jewish "Black Hand" existed as well, a fact that scarred the community more than it did the Italian or Chinese ones, already familiar with some kind of illegal organizations in the countries of origin. Jewish crime, on the contrary, was a completely American phenomenon, the result of many factors: the scarce possibilities of economic and social advancement on the Lower East Side, the impact of the American credo of quick success with its "self-made-man" and "rags-to-riches" myths, the feeling of being insufficiently represented and defended by existing legal institutions, the loosening of family ties, the breakdown of orthodoxy, and the peculiar aspect of Ghetto economy in which stalls, stores, warehouse, and sweatshops represented as many opportunities for petty crimes. As a reaction to the sensational use the press and the political world made of the issue[22], the community always tended to deny the existence of criminals among its members. But figures such as pickpockets Stiff Rivka and Ikie, Sam, and Max Schorr, fences Annie Kahn and Frederika Mandelbaum, store and warehouse burglars Joseph Marks, Max Belsky, Harry Goldstein and David Kalisky were well known in the area. The Yiddish Black Hand was headed by Joseph "Yushke Nigger" Toblinsky, had its headquarters in a Suffolk Street saloon, and was involved in extortions through horse poisoning and "Jewish lightning" (arson).

Even more shameful, prostitution came to be a distinctive Jewish illegal activity: Jenny Silver, Rosie Solomon, Rosie Hertz were popular names in the "red lights district", Abe "the Rabbi" Ratelles headed some kind of white slave traffic, and the Max Hochstim Association (based in Charles R. Solomon's Essex Street saloon and also known as the Essex Market Court Gang) organized some 200 "ladies managers" and 85 "employment offices" supplying prostitutes to dance halls and brothels. Finally, figures like "Big Jack" Zelig (a gunman who led a small private army to defend the quarter from other groups' incursions) and "Dopey" Benny Fein (who worked as strong-arm in several labor disputes, carrying on a practice inaugurated by Monk Eastman in the 1880s and 1890s and due to have tragic consequences in the future) occupied a rather peculiar position in the Ghetto, one that not infrequently was a source of awe and admiration [Harlow 1931; Joselit 1983; Sante 1991].

At that point, a new phase opened. Firmly rooted in the community, these gangs represented an enormous potential as power brokers to the outside society. Besides their illegal economic activities, they could function as vital links between the two main parties and the great mass of immigrants-as-voters. Such was the rôle, for example, of Paul Kelly and his Five Pointers. Heirs to older gangs, they had their headquarters at the New Brighton Dance Hall on Great Jones Street, and their territory extended between Broadway and the Bowery, East 14th Street and City Hall Park. Born Paolo Vaccarelli, Kelly could count upon an army of 1500, mainly Italians, but Jews, Irish, and others as well. The Five Pointers had important political connections, Kelly being the Lower East Side strong-arm of Tammany Hall boss "Tim" O'Sullivan. Between 1901 and 1903, a war raged between Kelly and Monk Eastman, who ruled the area just beyond the Bowery, in the heart of the Jewish quarter. The climax came in August 1903, when some 100 armed men from the two gangs engaged a gun-fight under the Second Avenue El at Rivington and Allen streets, 'the heaviest concentration of firearms in gang history' [Asbury 1928, 1990, p.281][23]. Several peace meetings followed, and even a prize-fight between Kelly and Eastman, and some sort of arrangement was reached. Kelly opened a new bar on Great Jones Street in 1906, the Little Naples, and turned respectable, starting a career as consultant to various labor unions and becoming vice-president of the International Longshoremen's Association, while Monk Eastman was killed a few years later, on East 14th Street.

A similar rôle was initially played by two young Jewish immigrants, Arthur "The Brain" Rothstein and Louis "Lepke" Buchalter. But their activity within and without the neighborhood signalled the beginning of still another, completely new, phase, ushered in by Prohibition. Skilfully using his political connections, Rothstein built up a powerful economic empire based on gambling as well as liquor and narcotics, and was immortalized as Meyer Wolfsheim in Scott Fitzgerald's *The Great Gatsby*. "Lepke" — a veritable son of the Lower East Side — was involved in all major illegal enterprises, and was responsible for the decisive transformation of the neighborhood's diverse and incoordinated criminal activities into a tight, centralized structure. By the early 1930s, crime on the Lower East Side had become simply a part of a larger scene [Rockaway 1980]: that of the Syndicate, or Murder, Inc., with its strong political connections and control of gambling, prostitution, lotteries, narcotics, and liquor. Among Kelly's followers were "Little Johnnie" Torrio and Al Capone — both soon active in Chicago —, and Charles "Lucky" Luciano, who arrived in the United States in 1907 at the age of 9 and lived on First Avenue and 13th Street. Luciano was soon involved in the activities of the Unione Siciliana (headquarters at 222 Chrystie Street), founded by Black Hander "Lupo" Saietta and headed by Joe Masseria in the 1920s. During the Prohibition years, the Unione established a "curb market" for bootleg liquor along Kenmare, Broome, Grand, and Elizabeth streets, and controlled Italian lotteries and the narcotic trade. Luciano also worked with two other East Side "combinations": the one headed by Buchalter and Jacob "Gurrah" Shapiro, and the one headed by Benjamin "Bugsie" Siegel and Meyer Lansky [Thompson and Raymond, 1940, pp.9-26; Nelli 1983, pp.93-99].

By then, the pyramid of crime born of ethnic enclaves had moved out of its original field of action and its Americanization was complete.

VI.

A terrain of ethnic diversity and dispute, the Lower East Side was also the place where, in a complex interplay, different cultures came together, influencing each other *and* America. Similarities and oppositions, affinities and anomies kept surfacing, at the same time that a process of *contaminatio* occurred, which gave the neighborhood its aspect of ever-working laboratory. To it, the various immigrant communities brought the materials of their history, experience, and everyday life in America, and out of it came new products, often incomplete, often rough-hewn, often uncouth, but endowed with an extraordinary social and cultural vitality. This osmotical and dialectical coming together and blending of differences took place on several levels, one of the most elemental and emblematic being the linguistic one.

While immigrants, often slowly and laboriously, appropriated the American language, they also more or less imperceptibly remoulded it, carrying on a century-old process. And, while each community tended to settle in a separate territory, the degree of physical contiguity and cultural exchange was high, both through common daily experiences and through not infrequent intermarriages. The outcome was that sort of *lingua franca* or "pidgin English" spoken on the Lower East Side, which contained, in a very fluid relationship, the elements of various original dialects and languages and the modifications the American language had meanwhile undergone.

The tenants in our building were from Palermo, Naples, Minsk, Bucharest, and Warsaw, with a number of unidentifiables thrown in. How did we communicate? In Yiddish, partly. [...] My father, [an Italian] tailor, mastered conversational Yiddish in the needle trades; conversed in Italian with his compatriots; and spoke English at home. My [American] mother spoke enough Italian and Yiddish to shop and communicate with in-laws and neighbors [Catapano 1988, p.7].

It was, first of all, a matter of loan words. Yiddish in particular — with its capacity to incorporate outside elements that came to it via an experience of survival across time, space, and cultures — easily absorbed the fundamentals of the American language, even though several interesting phenomena occurred which had rather telling socio-cultural implications[24].

In "Yinglish", suffixes were usually added to American words. So, the feminine and diminutive *-ké* gave rise to *hatké, dresské, watchké*; *-chick* and *-ige* to the affectionate *boychick* and *next-doorige*; *-nick*

133

(agency) produced, among the many variations, the well-known and culturally symbolic *allrightnick*, to indicate the wholly (and fastidiously) Americanized immigrant. At the same time, American words underwent changes, "lounge" becoming *lunch*, "tenant" *tenner*, "fellow" *fella*. Apart from everyday life experience, it was Yiddish theatre that functioned as a veritable two-way channel contributing to a wide linguistic dispersion, by presenting characters that struggled to appropriate English words in their common Yiddish speech[25]. Syntactical structures also developed that were a mixture of Yiddish and American ones, as was made increasingly clear by such authors as Abraham Cahan and Anzia Yezierska, who wrote in English but with their eye and ear still geared to the words and sounds of the Ghetto.

Although the Italian-American linguistic exchange was not so intense as the Yiddish-American one, "Italglish" followed similar patterns. American words, slightly modified, entered Little Italy's common speech, like *barra* for "bar", *visco* for "whiskey", *blacco enze* for "black hands", *sciabola* for "shovel", *sanemagogn* for "sun of a gun", *tocco* for "talk", and so on. At the same time, mainly for purist preoccupations on part of the *colonia*'s intellectuals, many of the most commonly used American words were translated into Italian, often by coining new words or meanings: thus, "subway" became *sotterraneo*, "downtown" *basso città*, "pressers" *pressatori*, "operators" *operatori*. This often gave rise to unintentional puns — *Il Forte Gelato* (=the frozen fort, the great freeze) was "The Fourth of July", *sciocchezza* (=trifle, stupid joke) the "showcase". And often these had noteworthy socio-cultural significance: *Re Erode* (=King Herod, with a doubly negative implication, linked both to the Biblical personage and to the use of the word "king", which so evoked the American "robber barons") meant "railroad"; *temeniollo* meant "a large glass of beer" and possibly came from the well-known custom, on part of Tammany Hall's local bosses, to pay for drinks at election times; *flabussce* was a deeply pessimistic interjection that came from Flatbush, the site of a great Italian cemetery in New York. Again, as for "Yinglish", it was theatre which provided the most vital instrument of linguistic dispersion in the *colonia*, above all with Farfariello's *macchiette coloniali* [Mencken 1923; Turano 1932; La Sorte 1985]. Finally, as we have seen, linguistic exchange between Chinatown and America was very limited, due to the specific condition of Chinese and Chinatowns. But at least one word immediately entered American culture, and that was *chow mein*.

134

***

There was, however, a subtler way of reciprocal exchange, a field in which more than simply words encountered and "contaminated" each other, in the literal sense of the word — i.e., went from the (relative) original "purity" to something that "pure" was no more, although it still contained some parts of the original "purity". In the streets of the Lower East Side, different cultural products came together, often with a clash, often with a blending, and, no matter how that coming together took place, it gave birth to new forms. One's own Old-World traits and expressions (*descent*, to use Sollors's terminology) [Sollors 1986] met with other enclaves' mores and traditions and with the imperatifs of life and survival in the New World, and together they entered into a relationship with the pressures and lures of mainstream America (*consent*).

In the streets, this happened daily. Fascinated by American entertainment as they came to know it along the Bowery, immigrant boys experimented new songs and steps:

"[...] first an Irish reel, very zippy, see, and when I am good and warmed up in the middle of the Irish jig, giving the regular Irish steps, I wants the music to slip into a Jewish wedding *Kazzatzka* with a barrel of snap, and that's when I'm gonna show them a combination step that's gonna knock them for a good... Get this right, Al, I'm gonna give you the two airs and I'm gonna show you how to join them up. But the hard part is the windup — when you gotta get a medley of the Irish reel and the Russian *kazzatzka*"...Sam hums, beats his hands and feet in time and Al follows, lamely, with the harmonica, but they keep it up, patiently, for over an hour until the desired Irish-Russian-Jewish potpourri is accomplished. The tremolo and whining strains of the harmonica have attracted a mixed audience. Mothers with babies in carriages, a mob of kids pushing and shoving, [...] a few pushcart peddlers have moved their vehicles nearer the excitement and the Canal Street horse cars wait while the conductors investigate and report back to the drivers, and the passengers stick their heads out of the windows, asking one another what is the matter...[...] Sam signals, "Let her go — gimme a few bars — to open up, and then start again and go right through"...Sam's dance begins...and the audience is noisily appreciative...and then came the knock-them-dead climax...it almost made us dizzy. Sam's feet don't seem to touch the ground. The windup is acrobatic. He does marvelous bodily contortions on his heels with original, difficult variations of the *kazzatzka* whirligig, and suddenly he leaps into an Irish jig in time with the music and then as suddenly twists himself into wild Russian back-breaking steps that seem impossible to do [Ornitz 1923, pp.116-118][26].

***

This was "Americanization" — not the linear, passive adaptation to a ruling ideology, nor the patronizing influence from above (that "trickling down" on which so many settlement workers were at work), but a basic modification of the ethnic cultures *and* of America itself, in the very process by which immigrants became Americans. It contained a fresh class and gender antagonism that in time helped to disrupt, and sometimes break down, Victorian and genteel rules and assumptions, thus introducing into mainstream America new dimensions of speech, thought, and experience, and gradually but deeply influencing contemporary mass culture and future modernism.

Notes

1. On Black, Irish, and German settlements, see Manson 1888; Gerard 1890; Riis 1890, 1971; Janvier 1893; Merwin 1896; "Foreign Population in New York" 1898; Lagerquist 1910; Harlow 1931; *New York Panorama* 1938, 1984; *The WPA Guide* 1939, 1982; Ernst 1949; Morris 1951; Kouwenhoven 1953, 1972; Wittke 1956; Rosenwaike 1972; Nadel 1981; Smindak 1987; *Chinatown* 1988.
2. A decisive turning point in the presence of the Germans on the Lower East Side was the tragic sinking of the excursion steamer "General Slocum" in the East River, in July 1904. 1,020 persons — mostly working-class families from the Lower East Side — died in the disaster, the result of criminal indifference on part of owners and managers. The German community — those German laborers who had not yet moved midtown and uptown — was the most affected by the tragedy and soon left the area in large numbers [Casson 1904].
3. The question of *how many* Chinese lived in New York Chinatown and *how many* in the metropolitan area is as debatable as that of *who* came first. According to Beck [1898, p.12], by 1898 in Chinatown lived '*4,000* traders, artisans, gamblers, amusement caterers and prostitutes who minister[ed] to the wants and entertainment of the *13,000* of their more industrious countrymen [...] scattered throughout the metropolitan area' (italics added). Rosenwaike [1972, p.78] has 12 Chinese in 1870 and 1,970 in 1890. On the problems to be encountered in writing about New York Chinatown's early history, see Fessler and China Institute 1983, pp.238-245.
4. In 1890, the male/female ratio among Chinese in the United States was 27:1, declining to 14:1 by 1910 — a still rather high figure [Yung 1985]. In 1898, in New York Chinatown, with a population of about 6,000, there were 84 married couples:

36 wives were Chinese, 48 were white [Beck 1898, p.38]. During the 1890s, "paper sons" in the United States amounted to some 110,000 [JWG 1985].

5. The fact, for instance, that so many early Chinese residents in New York married or lived with Irish women is not without meaning, if one remembers that by mid-century Irish immigrants were considered to be at the lower rung of the ladder. As for the "white-slave trade", a later witness recalls: '[t]here were at least 100 to 200 white women in Chinatown during the 1920s, most of them happily married to Chinese merchants, or working as missionaries. This was probably the basis for the white slave myth. Women could and did fall in love with Chinese men, which was intolerable to those who called the Chinese "chinks"' [Catapano 1988, p.42].

6. The term *Joss*, with which outsiders called traditional Chinese divinities, came from the Spanish *Dios*, God.

7. Perhaps more than other immigrant communities, the Chinese were the victims of persistent racial stereotypes, also fueled by miscegenation theories. Chinatown was regarded as a separate world, impossible to come to terms with both culturally and socially. Two clear examples of the way in which these racial stereotypes were quickly appropriated by other immigrants as well are the chapter "Chinatown" in Jacob A. Riis's *How the Other Half Lives* and the following passage from Bernardino Ciambelli's novel *I misteri di Mulberry Street* (1893): 'Not far from Eugenia's house was a Chinese laundry. The owner, like all the sons of the celestial empire, was disgustingly ugly: with his flat face, his bullet-like eyes, and the sparse hair — or better bristles — on his lips, he looked like one of those masks built to scare kids' [Ciambelli 1893, p.278, my translation; also see Meloney 1909].

8. Luis Chu's novel, *Eat a Bowl of Tea*, carries several telling descriptions of these places.

9. For an interesting account of an Italian-American family living on the Lower East Side but outside the borders of Little Italy, see Catapano 1988.

10. On the background of Italian immigration, see Pozzetta 1971; Nelli 1983; Ewen 1985.

11. 76,055 Italians entered the United States in 1891, 100,135 in 1900, 285,731 in 1907. Between 95 and 98 percent landed in New York City and of these 54.5 percent gave New York City as their final destination. Between 1892 and 1896, the rate of repatriation was of 43 going back to Italy for every 100 leaving for the United States; between 1907 and 1911, it was of 73 out of 100 [Pozzetta 1971, pp.72-73; Kessner 1977, p.28; Speranza 1888-1889; Beede 1901-1902; Aronovici 1906].

12. See the colorful portrait of Don Arcangelo, with his Banca Centrale, in Bernardino Ciambelli's *I misteri di Mulberry Street*.

13. Between 1899 and 1910, out of a total of 2,284,601 Italian immigrants arriving in the United States, only 275,906 were skilled workers (mainly shoemakers, masons, tailors, miners, clerks and accountants). 563,200 were classified as "farm labor", 767,811 as "labor", and 516,320 gave no occupation; engineers were 543, teachers 599, physicians 617, musicians 2,803 [Kessner 1977, pp.33-34].

14. *New York Times* (May 31, 1896), quoted by Pozzetta, in Harney and Scarpaci, eds. 1981, p.24.

15. For the background of the Jewish immigration, see Blaustein 1905; Rischin 1962, 1977, pp.19-20; R. Sanders 1969, Chapter 1; Howe 1976, Part 1, Chapter 1; Ewen 1985, Chapter 2.

16. Of course, these geographical divisions cannot be taken too rigidly: according to Ravage [1917, 1971, p.88], for instance, 'Little Rumania [...] was bounded on the east by Clinton Street, with Little Galicia extending on the other side to the East River; by Grand Street on the south, with the Russians and Lithuanians beyond; and on the north lay the untracked wilds surrounding Tompkins Square Park, which to me was the vast dark continent of the "real Americans"'. It must also be remembered that, although predominantly Jewish, the East European immigration was not exclusively Jewish: by and large, the area in the Ghetto bounded by East 14th Street, the East River, East Houston Street, and Third Avenue was of Slavic origins [Smindak 1987].

17. The Educational Alliance's art classes were of particular importance, especially for future developments. The fact itself that a Jewish institution got involved in the field was, at the time, quite significant, given the Orthodox sanction against "graven images". The Alliance functioned as a crucial venue for ghetto artists, who otherwise would not have either the material means or the channel to express themselves and exhibit their work. In the early years of the new century, an embryonic realist movement developed in the Jewish quarter, that clearly paralleled what was happening in the field of fiction and art (see below, Chapters Four and Six), but also had very specific features. Jacob Epstein was its first, great name. Born on Hester Street in 1880, Epstein was 'an East Side boy who [...] met with sensational success in Paris and London' [Cahan 1917, p.530]. In the years he lived in the Jewish quarter, he was essentially a Lower East Side artist. The neighborhood provided him with his first inspiration and subject matter — the pushcarts and the markets, the Bowery, the alleys and the people of Chinatown and of Little Italy [Epstein 1965]. Unfortunately, all of his early work went lost after his departure for Europe, where he took on sculpture and gained world-wide celebrity. But we still have the beautiful illustrations he drew for Hutchins Hapgood's *The Spirit of the Ghetto* (1902), so important because they were the first artistic expression to come *from the inside*, and thus helped to break down that negative sanction and contributed to the battle for a non-stereotyped, non-sentimentalized image of the quarter. Not merely a gallery of famous people (Jacob Gordin, Jacob Adler, Morris Rosenfeld, Abraham Wald), Epstein's drawings are also a series of portraits of common people caught in the common places of everyday life and portrayed in a mood of serious and melancholy dignity that mirrors the pathos of the ghetto experience — a sequence of situations, faces, and figures, which already foretell the future sculptor in their robust outline and ability to capture a personality in a gesture, a pose, an expression. In a chapter of his book, dealing with an artistic production which seemed to promise a future that was not achieved — or was differently achieved —, Hapgood described Epstein as a serious and dedicated young artist who 'will devote himself to his art', to 'the plastic picturing of the life of his people in the Ghetto'. And reported him as saying: 'It is only in the Ghetto, where there is human nature, that I have ideas for sketches' [Hapgood 1902, 1967, p.257, 258; Howe 1976, pp.573-585; Rischin 1967, p.xxxii-xxxiii]. In later years, Epstein would add, not without a bit of nostalgia: 'I sometimes think I should have remained

in New York, the material was so abundant. Wherever one looked there was something interesting, a novel composition, wonderful effects of lighting at night, and picturesque and handsome people. Rembrandt would have delighted in the East Side, and I am surprised that nothing has come out of it, for there is material in New York far beyond anything that American painters hunt for abroad. I took this East Side drawing work very seriously, and my drawings were not just sketches. With Gussow, my Russian artist friend, I drew the life in the East Side, and one or two other artists joined us, so that we might have developed a School had we kept on' [quoted in Hindus, ed., 1971, p.12]. The "school" longed for by Epstein and Gussow never came to be. For some time, between the early 1880s and 1905, and again after 1917, the Alliance was at the forefront in this enterprise. It had Jerome Myers and Abraham Walkowitz, Raphael and Moses Soyer, as instructors at its art classes, and organized periodic exhibitions (a big one, in 1895, was put together with the help of a 15-year-old Epstein). In the early years of the new century, unions like the International Ladies' Garment Workers Union and the Amalgamated Clothing Workers Union then sponsored a Workers' Art Traveling Scholarship to enable talented pupils to go and study in Europe. In 1915, a People Art Guild was organized, and in the mid-twenties the Jewish Art Club (Second Avenue at East 12th Street) and the Leonardo Da Vinci Art School (East 10th Street at Avenue A) were active on the Lower East Side. But nothing more permanent or organic emerged from the ghetto. What did emerge were individuals: some of them — Nathaniel Loewenberg, Samuel Kalisch — would soon fall back into obscurity, while others — Moses and Raphael Soyer, Ben Shahn, Louise Nevelson, Louis Lozowick, Barnett Newman, Mark Rothko, all of them students at the Educational Alliance art classes — would soon embark on different roads, after giving their own contribution to a Lower East Side's iconography (see for example, Abraham Walkowitz's "Rutgers Square", Ben Shahn's "Sound in the Mulbery Street", Raphael Soyer's "In the Park" and "Dancing Class", Louis Lozowick's "Allen Street — Under the El"). William Gropper, a famous cartoonist for radical magazines *The Masses* and *The Liberator*, was another son of the Lower East Side, and later on social realist Philip Evergood was also a student at the Alliance.

18. See the description of some of these festivities as they adapted to the new reality, in the articles written by Abraham Cahan for the *Commercial Advertiser*, and in particular "Rejoicing of the Law" (Oct.19, 1897), "Feast of Chanukah" (Dec.20, 1897), "Dead After Purim" (March 9, 1898), "Passover on Clinton Street" (April 6, 1898), "We Mourn the Loss of Our Temple" (July 27, 1898), "When Angels Shudder" (September 26, 1898), "The New Year" (September 5, 1899), and "Ghetto Full of Sighs" (September 14, 1899), now in Rischin, ed., 1985, pp.76-92, 97-98, 103-107.

19. A clear example of the loosening of orthodoxy was the decline of the figure of the *rabbi* within the community, something that had deep consequences as regards the observance of food norms, of the Sabbath, and of such prescripts as the wearing of a wig for married women. The attempt in 1899 to set up a Chief Rabbi in New York in the person of Jacob Joseph (specifically summoned from Vilna) was met with failure.

20. '[The] whole river front was in Mick [Irish] territory, and during the days when the Jew was a newcomer in this wild section of Manhattan the Irish hoodlums

regarded him as legitimate prey. [...] The Irish lads shouted, "Kill the Christ killers", and the Jewish boys cried, "*Mopolize* the Micks" (A strange word, probably coming from the root of *mopel*, to abort. In any event it implied the direst punishment). [...Later] when they became acquainted they were amiable neighbors and the most powerful local gangs were made up of an admixture of Irish, Jews, and Italians' [Ornitz 1923, pp.48-49]. Inter-ethnic frictions were also vividly recalled by Joe Juliano in an episode from the late 1930s, in which the pugilist's pride tends to overshadow the racial implications: 'The gangs were only there to protect the neighborhood, they were not there to start trouble...See, like if the Jews that were down on Delancey Street, Grand Street, would come to this neighborhood [East 10th Street-First and Second avenues] and start trouble, then the Italians would get a gang together and beat th' hell outa 'em and chase 'em back...As a matter of fact, we had a big fight one time, we knocked out ten of 'em. You know what happened? We had a club on 10th Street, right between First and Second Avenue, called the "Red Rain" [...]. We were having a dance one night...You see, every Friday, every Friday, we used to have a dance, we used to charge a dime to come in [...]. So, there's a couple of girls...This was a club that was...you go downstairs, you walk ten feet, and then there's a wall, there's two windows, and the club was behind that...So, we had a couple of beautiful girls that's hangin' outside, so there's six, ten, fifteen Jewish kids from Delancey Street who never came to the neighborhood...So they're hanging around in front of the club, they watch the guys dancing, and so on...And one guy gooses a girl in the ass. So, finally she turns around and smacks him in the face. So, my friend, I'm standing outside with two guys, one Joe [...], and this guy Joe [...] he says to the girl, "Whadda matter?", and she says, "That guy goosed me in the ass". "That's why you slapped?". So this guy Joe — there's three of us, there's fifteen o' them — says to the guy: "What are you, a wise guy?". So that guy says: "Mind ya fuckin' business!". Bam!, this guy Joe hits him [...] ! Now, the fight starts, they got sixteen guys, we got three! A guy called for help...Who do you think they were up against? Joe Juliano, [...], Lou Lou Concertino, Rocky Graziano... They didn't have a chance!...Harry Di Pizzo...These all professional fighters!... There was seven professional fighters from the club, in the club, and they all come up...*Minchia*, bim, bam, bam, bim...[...]. The cars were coming down the street, we guys halted 'em, we had the cars back up to Third Avenue, they couldn't come through 10th Street so many guys were laid down the street...Now, it's all over...And a guy comes over and he says, "Ehi, you guys are in trouble, now... Those guys, they are tough Jews, those guys...". "Where they come from? Ya know those guys?". "Ya, I know 'em". "Where they come from?". "Well, they hang out on Grand Street". So what do you think we did? We had two or three crazy guys in the club, they went home and got pistols, they come down, start givin' out pistols, say "Let's go down!"...So we went down to Grand Street...So now there's a couple of guys there, there wasn't many guys in the club, in their club... "See, you don't want any more trouble, don't you...I mean, you guys beat us up, and see, that's it, we forgot about it, and now you are comin' back lookin' for more trouble...And you're comin' back with guns...Weeell...[...]". When they seen the guns, they copped out: "Look, we don't wanna any more trouble, we'll never come to 10th Street as long as we live"...And they never came back...' [Juliano, interview, 1987].

21. For an early and interesting attempt at dealing with Italian immigration and

crime in a non-sensational and non-stereotyped way, see Howerth 1894, that mostly takes in account the situation in Chicago.

22. See especially Moss 1897 and the reports of the "Lexow Committee" (1894) and of the "Mazet Committee" (1896). On this aspect, see Joselit 1983.

23. It must be remembered that Asbury was writing in 1928.

24. For instance, while *ingle* (Yiddish for "boy") was 'wholly obliterated by the English word', the same was not true of *meidel* (Yiddish for "girl"), which was still preferred to the English word, so that '"Die *boys* mit die *meidlach* haben a good time" was excellent American Yiddish' [Mencken 1923, p.417]. It is also possible to read this in terms of gender — "boys" being somewhat projected *outside*, towards America, and *meidlach* being instead jealously kept *inside*, in the traditional place and culture. At the same time, however, it is true that, after the first impact with America, it was often women who more directly came to terms with outside society and entertained the thickest linguistic exchange with it, given their rôle as housekeepers, shoppers, and soon wage-earners [on this, see Abraham Cahan's articles now in Rischin, ed., 1985; Anzia Yezierska's short-stories; Henry Roth's *Call It Sleep*; and Ewen 1985]. A similar speculation, although not in terms of gender but in terms of inside/outside, could be advanced on the different use of "window" and "door": the first completely displaced *fenster* (on this, see in particular Cahan's novel *Yekl*), while *tür* continued for a long time to be preferred to the second. Was it because the window is something opening towards the exterior, while the door (essentially the door of the apartment) is rather something that protects familiar and cultural intimacy? Once more, immigrant novels (and Roth's *Call It Sleep* in particular) are extremely telling on the subject. Another socio-cultural implication was at the heart of the difficult relationship between original language (or dialect) and American language as an expression of the widening gap between first- and second-generation immigrants (and this was common to other ethnic communities as well). This relationship was often further complicated by a third element — that street language that was so distant from Yiddish but also, culturally and socially, from genteel America: '[Uncle Philip] intimidates: not he, but his way of speaking Yiddish. It is not just Yiddish — guttural, jargonish, haphazard; but an arresting, rhythmical, logical language...Yiddish, the lingo of greenhorns, was held in contempt by the Ludlow Streeters who felt mightily their Americanism. [...] "Meyer [...], remember that learning without breeding is like a *kugel* (pudding) without *gribbenes* (rendered chicken fat). It is food without flavor [...]. [...] Speak to me *momme loschen* (mother tongue), not that nasty gibberish of the streets". [...] Again he humiliates me — he — the greenhorn. He knows I am not speaking genteel American' [Ornitz 1923, p.14, 15, 16]. It must also be remembered that not all Jewish families on the Lower East Side spoke Yiddish. For instance, 'Avrum is a new kind of Jewish boy in the Ghetto. He came with his folks from the Balkans. At first the neighbors thought they were not Jews because they did not speak Yiddish. Their everyday speech was *Ladino*, melodious Old Castilian garnished with Hebrew and bits of the universal patois of Mediterranean ports' [Samuel Ornitz 1923, p.44]. Neither can it be forgot that, beside Yiddish, East European Jews generally spoke their respective languages. And, lastly, that not all East European immigrants were Jewish.

25. In the melodrama "The Aristocracy of a Province", the villain's vanity is

that he can 'speken Engleesch', his speech being interspersed with 'Tankaiou', 'meine lufly goil', 'Was ist de matter mit you?', 'Kom on, let's have a little lunch-room' [Corbin 1898, p.40].

26. The *Kazzatzka* is a lively, Russian-Jewish wedding dance. For other vivid and rather interesting descriptions of musical "contaminations", see the two short-stories by Robert Howard Russell ("The Bells of Aberdovey") and Edward W. Townsend ("A Tenement-Court Festival"), in the series called "True Picture Among the Poor" 1894. Also see Cantor 1928 and Burns 1980.

CHAPTER THREE: A CRY FOR BREAD

Ot azoy neyt a shnayder,
Ot azoy neyt er doch!
[...]
A shnayder neyt un neyt un neyt,
Un hot kadoches, nit kayn brot!
[...]
Farayorn, nit haynt-gedacht!
Hob mir gehorevet fun acht bis acht!
[...]
Ober die struksie hot ongemacht,
Mir arbetn shoyn mer nit fun acht biz acht!

Anon., "Ot Azoy Neyt A Shnayder" (ca. 1890)[1].

I.

Ethnic diversity could perhaps conceal, but not cancel, the basic homogeneity underlying the Lower East Side's experience — the fact that the neighborhood was essentially a *proletarian community*. In a way, its social history can be better understood in terms of urban geography. On its eastern border, the quarter had a busy harbor, for decades the country's most important. On its western boundary was Broadway, the route along which the city shifted northward, the main commercial and shopping artery, and the principal link between downtown and uptown, New York and the interior. This very location dictated some four score years of continuous change, out of which, by the time of the "new immigration", the Lower East Side emerged with its distinctive features and character.

In terms of labor market, the harbor meant not only the loading, unloading, and refitting of ships, and the various associated jobs, along with saloons and boarding-houses. It also meant sailors' outfitting, which had to be quick and cheap. By the end of the eighteenth century, a certain number of "slop-shops" had already appeared on the waterfront — garrets and basements where pants, shirts, and jackets were roughly cut and sewn out of coarse material. Following the war of 1812, this new business had received a great impulse from a series of related factors. A tariff imposing a 30 percent duty on ready-made clothing (risen to 50 percent in 1828) had fostered a rapid development of domestic industries. In New York City, the clothing industry was among the first to benefit from the unprecedented economic boom and could easily diversify its production. To the demands from sailors and soldiers were thus added those coming from a new urban consumer class and from various sections of a rapidly expanding nation [Stansell, in Frisch and Walkowitz, eds., 983, pp.82-85; Wilentz 1984; Stansell 1986; Harzig 1989]. Then, between 1846 and 1850, the sewing machine was invented and perfected, and, a decade later, the Civil War did the rest — it augmented the demand for ready-made clothes, gave further impulse to domestic production, and ushered in decisive social transformations, two of the most important ones being the definitive rise of an urban middle class and the birth of an urban proletariat increasingly immigrant in background. By the 1870s, the small core of workshops had become a central industry in the economic set-up of the country, and of New York in particular[2].

Three different working processes had developed within the industry, ready to employ the great mass of immigrants soon to pour into the country. The "home" shop had the family as a production unit, and a somewhat hierarchical organization often reproducing socio-cultural mores. The "inside" shop (or "Boston system", which was to reach New York only a few years later) consisted of a real factory operated by a manufacturer who directly hired and paid 50-100 workers. The "outside" shop was a loft where between five and twenty laborers, hired by a contractor, "sweated" to the rhythm of the "task system" (a way to increase productivity by paying a team of workers according to the work done during the day), at very low wages and in very unsanitary conditions[3].

II.

New York City quickly became the center of the garment trade. In 1890, it produced 75 percent of the total output of women's clothing and 38.6 percent of the total output of men's clothing (45.7 percent a decade later), employing some 90,000 persons by 1900. By 1910, the city's cloak and suit branch could boast an invested capital of $40,000,000, an annual output of about $250,000,000, and some 37,000 workers in 1,200 shops, swelling to over 47,000 at the peak of the season [Price 1911, p.221].

To the needs of such a booming industry the Lower East Side offered a wide range of answers. Its physical conformation (the narrow streets, the huge tenements, the congestion arising from the waterfront activities) and the high rents throughout downtown Manhattan worked against the building of large factories [Sakolski 1906, p.21]. At the same time, these negative factors proved decisive because they favored an unprecedented growth of the "sweating system". An unlimited supply of cheap labor, largely composed of women and children and continually swelled by successive immigrant waves, was at hand in the neighborhood. Small shops could be set up everywhere thanks to the quarter's disorderly architectural growth, and work could be done in all tenements, thus easily avoiding inspections and overtime regulations. Even the hindrances caused by differences in language, religion, traditions, and culture could be turned into powerful instruments of division and exploitation, because '[these] greenhorns, Italian people, Jewish people, all nationalities, they cannot speak English and they don't know where to go and they just come from the old country, and I let them work hard, like the devil, and these I get for less wages' [quoted in Hardy 1935, p.18].

Once more, ethnicity and gender were crucial in the development of the clothing industry. Its New York history can indeed be read in terms of ethnic displacement. Between 1850 and 1880, the Irish dominated the New York market, with some layers of skilled Germans. After the Civil War, a few Swedes came and, in the 1880s, another great number of Germans (many of them Jews), who carried with them a precious wealth of skills. This frequently enabled them to turn from workers to bosses (initially employing Irish), and in the 1890s made it easier for the newly arrived Russian and Polish Jews to find work in the trade, thus displacing earlier ethnic communities [Supple 1957; Rischin 1962, 1977, pp.95-111]. This new (unskilled) immigration supplied the first cheap, mass labor indispensable to the clothing industry's initial stage of capitalist accumulation[4]. By the end of the nineteenth century, Italians too had started to arrive in greater numbers, slowly entering the labor market from the bottom, as unskilled labor. Their presence in the clothing industry steadily increased in the early years of the new century, and by 1910 they were already beginning to displace the Jews.

These developments, as well as the distinctive features the industry was acquiring, also had to do with the rôle women played in it. From the start, this was by and large a woman's trade. As an embryonic industry rooted itself in the city in the early decades of the nineteenth century, it attracted an increasing number of women and young girls, part of a widespread movement from the country to the city. Side by side with the lamplighter, the newsboy, and the fireman, the seamstress thus became a common figure in the rising urban literature and folklore[5]. With the post-Civil War boom, other factors combined to define more strictly the women's place in the industry.

At the beginning, before considerable improvements were introduced, work at the sewing machine meant a heavy physical strain. Men were thus often preferred, and women were hired as basters and finishers — tasks that could be easily performed at home; put-out work soon became the norm, and gave birth to the "outside" or "sweating" system, to home work and child labor. Here, gender divisions were quite apparent, not only because, generally speaking, women were paid less than men, but also because a gender hierarchy ruled. In the family production unit, for example, the man usually functioned as a sub-contractor and skilled laborer, while the woman, often aided by the children, did most of the unskilled and underpaid finishing work. This was especially true for Italian women, for whom the "outside system" reinforced the patriarchal mores of the *colonia* to confine women to a domestic rôle. It was they who slowly displaced Jews in the trade, both in home work and, later, in factories. By 1902, they monopolized the felling and finishing of garments, and by 1910 — at a time when the shift from the "sweating system" to the "factory system" was well under way — they accounted for over 75 percent of the women in the men's clothing industry and for over 36 percent in the ladies' [Odencrantz 1919, p.60; Kessner and Caroli, 1978; Cetti 1984-85; Vezzosi 1984-85].

***

The Lower East Side thus became the kingdom of the "Katerinka", the sewing machine:

> Take the Second Avenue Elevated Railroad at Chatham Square and ride up half a mile through the sweater's district. Every open window of the big tenements, that stand like a continuous brick wall on both sides of the way, gives you a glimpse of one of these shops as the train speeds by. Men and women bending on their machines, or ironing clothes at the window, half-naked. [...] The road is like a big gangway through an endless work-room where vast multitudes are forever laboring. Morning, noon, or night, it makes no difference; the scene is always the same [Riis 1890, 1971, p.100].

In the shops, the "task system" ruled. Mass production was increased by accelerating working times and prolonging the workday. Profits soared as costs were cut and wages reduced. The same coat that once was ready-made by a journeyman tailor receiving $2.50 to $3 could now be done at a cost of $1.50 to $2 by a team of five persons who often worked up to 20 hours per day in order to finish their assignments

[United States Census Ofice 1900, p.296][6]. Conditions in general worsened, and the work-day became a long, exhausting nightmare, which led to such professional diseases as pneumonia and consumption, eye- and back-strain, malfunctions in the genital apparatus[7]. The "sweating system" also meant a savage competition at all levels, among manufacturers, contractors, and laborers. Its inevitable consequences were home work and child labor, two aspects which, perhaps more than other features of the "system", came sadly to characterize domestic life on the Lower East Side. A vicious circle linked the family to sweatshops and factories. In order to supplement a meagre family income, a large portion of the immigrant population was forced to accept this kind of work. This in turn had several important effects on the labor market. On one hand, the fact that the woman worked at home with the help of the children put the man in the position of accepting whatever job was available, even the worst paid, thus depressing wages in that sector. On the other, home workers and children could be paid considerably less than shop and factory workers, and the wages in the trade concerned were thus once more depressed, compelling many shop and factory workers to carry work home, there to be finished by wives and children. At that point, the circle started again.

By 1901, there were 16,068 family workrooms in New York (most of them in the Lower East Side), licensed by the Bureau of Factory Inspection of the State Department of Labor, for a total of 27,019 persons authorized — seven ninths of them women, and of these, six sevenths working on clothing. Among the predominating home industries were finishing clothing, making artificial flowers and willowing ostrich feathers. A finisher could get from 6 cents to 10 cents for a coat or a pair of pants, with a weekly income of between $2.40 and $4.20, while an artificial flower-maker could get from 3 cents to 18 cents a gross, according to the size and number of petals, with a weekly income of between $2.75 and $4.00.

By 1910, Italians controlled 98 percent of these home industries, while Jews made all kinds of women's neck-wear and fancy bows and plaited hat straw [Van Kleeck 1908, p.1412; Watson 1911, p.778; Van Kleeck 1913]. By 1907, some 60,000 children — a "conservative estimate" [Markham 1907, 1967, p.163] — worked in the Lower East Side's "home shops", lending their own specific skills to adult work and adding between 50 cents and $1.50 a week to the family income. They pulled out bastings, sorted and sewed buttons on cards and tapes in kid gloves, helped in millinery, made garters, shelled nuts, put cords on pencils for souvenir cards, worked on passementerie, finished corset covers, separated petals, and even willowed pluming, a rather more

Ill. 22
Cheap Clothing — The Slaves of the "Sweaters" (A Drawing by W.A. Rogers for the *Harper's Weekly Magazine*, April 26, 1890) (Archives of the New-York Historical Society)

complicated task for small fingers. In a day, working till 9 p.m., a mother helped by her three children could finish between 1400 and 1700 flowers, thus earning from 35 to 40 cents ["Table", in Van Kleeck 1908, p.1413; J. B. Adams 1908; Van Kleeck and Barrows 1910]. As the modified child rhyme went, side by side with the mother

This little child made laces,
This little child made flowers,
This little child made willow plumes,
This one held baby for hours,
And all of them worked in a close, warm room,
Through the good, bright summer hours
[quoted in Watson 1911, p.776][8].

III.

Given these conditions, it was inevitable that tensions should arise and conflicts erupt. What took place in the clothing industry at the labor level and on the Lower East Side went however beyond a simple list of class-struggle episodes. The perennial social unrest and the ways it expressed itself in the neighborhood were in fact part of a series of important developments within the American labor movement, which had to do with the presence of a new mass and unskilled workforce, with the rôle played within it by women, with the emergence of an immigrant leadership, and with its relationships with the labor bureaucracy [Dubofsky 1968; Hoerder, ed., 1986; Cartosio 1989].

Seamstress turnouts had taken place in New York in 1831, 1836 and 1845, the real problem always being that of organizing the "outside" workers — those women who performed their work at home. In January 1865, a meeting of sewing women was called by the Working Women's Union at the Early Closing Hall (267 Bowery) [Andrews 1911]; but the first, real "immigrant" strike in the industry took place in July 1883, when 700 men and women turned out demanding $2.50 a day and hours from 8 A.M. to 6 P.M., formed the Cloak and Dress Makers' Union, affiliated to the Knights of Labor, and won most of their demands [Leiserson, quoted in L. Stein, ed., 1977, p.33].

The 1885 general strike, which mobilized between 3,000 and 5,000 cloakmakers in New York City and soon spread to Chicago, then ushered in a period of endemic, although isolated, shop struggles; and it was only in October 1889 that the first attempt was made to unite workers engaged in separate strikes. With the help of the United Hebrew Trades (an organism born the year before from the fusion of three small Jewish unions and originally under the tutelage of Daniel De Leon's Socialist Labor Party), 3,000 workers on strike formed the Operators' and Cloakmakers' Union No.1 of New York and Vicinity (headquarters at 92 Hester Street) [Barondess 1903, 1977, p.38; Hardy 1935, p.23; Rischin 1962, 1977; Howe 1976]. In May 1890, it was the turn of 4,000 cutters, trimmers, and operators, who engaged a bitter 15-week struggle in answer to another lock-out. Led by the Amalgamated Board of Delegates (headquarters at 92 Hester Street) which took care of all the aspects of the strike, a "triple alliance" was formed against the manufacturers. The situation was dramatic, of utmost misery and even starvation. A huge hunger demonstration marched through the streets of the Lower East Side, anticipating scenes that would become rather familiar within two years, and a reporter wrote that '[upon] the Jewish proletariat of New York is forced the problem of freedom from a servitude worse than that of Egypt' [quoted in Rischin 1962, 1977, p.178].

Another attempt to form a stable, national structure was made in May 1892, when the International Cloak Makers' Union of America was organized by representatives of the New York, Chicago, Boston, Baltimore, and Philadelphia workers. But these were already hard times, further complicated by factional struggles between the AFL and the Knights of Labor, the Socialists and the Anarchists, and by 1895 the union had disappeared. Meanwhile, the tragic 1893 depression had hit the country. Armies of unemployed roamed the streets, and 32,000 out of New York's 100,000 unemployed were clothing workers. Suffering was particularly acute in the Lower East Side, where the "sweating system" showed its ruthless face and devastating effects. The Labor Lyceum on East 4th Street was busy in dispensing aid, the University Settlement (then in Delancey Street) sponsored a huge unemployment conference, a trade union relief committee was organized, meetings and demonstrations took place almost daily. By October 1894, the cloakmakers were again on strike, led by such an increasingly popular figure as Joseph Barondess. The situation grew tenser (it was the year of the bitter Pullman strike in Chicago), and police repeatedly clubbed and dispersed parading strikers. But support was strong in the city and on the Lower East Side in particular, where even peddlers and unemployed contributed to the strike funds ["Police" 1894; Rischin 1962, 1977, pp.178-180].

In July 1895, the Brotherhood of Tailors, led by Meyer Schoenfeld and representing workers from some 630 shops, called its members to action. Some 13,000 operators, basters, finishers, and pressers (men, women, young girls) stopped working and, to cries of "No task work! Down with the sweating system!", crowded the streets around the strike headquarters at the Walhalla Hall (54 Orchard Street). Their demands were a 59-hour week, a 10-hour day (nine hours on the sixth day), no overtime, minimum wages of $13 a week for basters and $9 for finishers, the abolition of the tenement sweating system, and the employment of union members only. Most of them were rejected, but the strike was one of the first to attack the "system" and to propose the closed shop — two passwords that would become more and more important ["13,000 Tailors" 1895]. Three years later, it was the turn of the children's jackets' makers, a remarkable episode because most of the striking "basting pullers" (with weekly wages of $2-3 a week) were teen-age boys and girls, who organized into the Machine Tenders' Union (75 members, and headquarters at 78 Essex Street) led by 15-year-old Harry Gladstone[9].

The end of the century was then stirred by another wave of unrest. The Cloakmakers' Union (headquarters at 158 Rivington Street) and the Pantsmakers' Union (headquarters at 62 Pitt Street) repeatedly struck, enthusiastically supported by young members who often had very little of the traditional "greenhorn" types, and by walking delegates who toured the neighborhood organizing the shops and making familiar a figure that would have a great importance in labor's future history. Once more, the "task" and the "sweating" systems were the targets of battles that, victorious or defeated, made the Lower East Side alive with such a continuous turmoil that it was by now possible to speak of 'the big annual tailor strike, *the* strike on the East Side, where hundreds of sweatshops were deserted, the streets of the ghetto were swarming with gesticulating, chattering, groaning men and women, and the newspapers were full of pictures of long-bearded patriarchs' [Cahan Aug.25, 1900, 1985, p.381]. But the extraordinary militancy of a rank-and-file mostly composed of newcomers barely speaking English clashed with a complex situation. The moment was a rather delicate one in the American labor movement. On one hand, the disappearance of the Knights of Labor and the conservatism of the AFL bureaucracy — its stubborn craft unionism, elitism and resistance to unionization of unskilled workers, Blacks, immigrants, and women — weakened and split labor in a phase of great struggles. On the other hand, dual-unionism of the SLP kind threatened to foster yet other divisions within the working class, aggravated by factionalism and internecine struggles in the ranks of Socialists and Anarchists. Ethnic affiliations had their weight too, since they could easily be employed to pit immigrants against immigrants, or to thwart more classist tendencies in the name of ethnic solidarity and communal responsibility. Turn-of-the-century unions were thus often 'anything but a deep-rooted growth. They toppled over the moment they reached their

151

highest point; they began to pall as soon as they ceased to be a novelty. Few of the numerous labor organizations were strong enough to survive their own triumphant strikes' [Cahan Febr. 13, 1899, 1985, p.373].

The new century opened instead with a decisive step forward for the clothing workers. On June 3, 1900, a meeting was called at the Labor Lyceum by the United Brotherhood of Cloakmakers No.1 of New York and Vicinity (organized in 1896, and soon grown from 28 members to 10,000 in 1899), out of which came the decision to form the International Ladies' Garment Workers Union (ILGWU) [L. Stein, ed., 1977, pp.46-49]. A month later, a two-week strike led by the Shirtwaistmakers' Union (headquarters at 77 Essex Street) made it clear that a new militant subject had appeared in the industry and within the trade unions' ranks, 'the majority of the strikers [being] well-educated immigrant girls come to seek higher education in the American colleges' [Cahan Aug.24, 1900, 1985, p.398][10].

IV.

By the end of the new century's first decade, rank-and-file militancy had grown in the needle trades, and with it the workers' capacity to organize autonomously *vis à vis* the new unions' precariousness and the old ones' wait-and-see policies. With the entrance of disadvantaged categories, such as women, children, and recent immigrants, the battle front had also widened. Conditions in the industry had surely changed in those years. The shift from pure and simple "sweating" to factory work had been accomplished, and traditional contracting had been somewhat reduced. At the same time, however, home work and child labor had all but disappeared, and a new form of contracting had been developing *within* factories, known as "inside contracting" — i.e., learners, finishers, operators (mostly girls in their teens) were employed by a skilled worker who negotiated wages and output with the manufacturer. "Section" work, or piece work, was flourishing, and as a consequence speed and productivity had greatly increased, with a general aggravation of working conditions [R. Cohen 1918; Ganz 1919]. Times were now ripe for a major confrontation, and this took place in the latter part of 1909.

By then, over 600 shirtwaist factories operated in New York City. The larger shops were on the outskirts of the Lower East Side, and employed up to 300 power machines in long rooms or lofts. The smaller ones were mostly in the Lower East Side, or generally downtown, and usually had from 20 to 30 foot machines. The total workforce was more than 30,000, three quarters of it made up of 16- to 25-year-old girls, with many helpers and learners between 11 and 13. A good 55 percent were Jewish girls, 35 percent Italian, and 7 percent native American [Ippolito 1979, p.3, 6, 9; also see Gutman 1987, p.386]. Wages were between $3-4 per week (the finishers) and $8-13 (the operators), reaching a top of $16-18 for custom-making, a skilled job. But learners and helpers received lower wages, and women were generally paid less than men, who usually held the skilled jobs. The workday was from 8pm to 6pm, with a 56-hour week that became a 70-hour one in high season. The trade was in fact a typically seasonal one: shirtwaist makers could count upon a full 6-day week only for four months, while for three months the week was reduced to five days, for four months it dropped to three or four days, and for one month inactivity was complete. Working conditions were made even more intolerable by a strict factory discipline, by a severe system of fines, by the fact that workers had to pay for appliances, and by the continuous harassment and abuse to which helpers and learners, and more generally women and girls, were subjected on part of the overseers [Clark and Wyatt 1910, p.72; Goodman and Ueland 1910; Ewen 1985, Chapter 14]. So it was that

In the black winter of 1909
When we froze and bled on the picket line
We showed the world that women could fight
And we rose and we won with women's might
[quoted by Ewen 1985, p.242].

Unrest had been simmering all through the summer. Repeated stoppages had taken place at such large factories as Solomon & Leffler, Leiserson's, Triangle Waist Co., and once more manufacturers had resorted to thugs and prostitutes to intimidate pickets. Trouble finally erupted at Triangle, when 100 employees held a meeting to discuss grievances and possible actions, and were immediately laid off. They applied to ILGWU Local 25, which at the time had no more than 100 members and but $4 in its treasury. Picketing began on September 25, and workers at Leiserson's soon joined in. The demands were abolition of "inside contracting", a 10 percent wage increase, a 52-hour week with limitation of overwork to three evenings per week for less than two hours, appliances to be paid by the firm, suppression of the fine system, equal distribution of work during the slack season, and recognition of the union. From the very start, picketing girls were attacked by policemen and hired thugs and prostitutes, were arrested and sentenced, and could count upon little more than moral support on part of the weak ILGWU and small sums from the United Hebrew Trades. Still, they stubbornly held out.

Ill. 23
The Foreman and the Worker, in an Anonymous Late 19th Century Cartoon

On October 21, a meeting was called to discuss the possibility of a general strike, and the manufacturers immediately answered by forming an Employers' Mutual Protective Association. By then, however, the struggle had enlisted more supporters. Besides ILGWU Local 25 and the UHT, the Women's Trade Union League — a middle-class organization founded in 1903 to help women workers to organize for better wages and working conditions, with a mixed membership of college girls, settlement workers, and laboring women — had started to support the strike, and cap-maker Rose Schneiderman was appointed its organizer for the Lower East Side [Schneiderman 1967; Dye 1974 and 1977; Basch 1980]. Suffragist associations then mobilized, as did the Socialists and the Anarchists. Little by little, workers at other firms also struck, and the union's membership swelled to nearly 2,000. The Lower East Side was in a great ferment, speeches and meetings were held in its halls, leaflets in Jewish, Italian, and English were distributed daily. On the night of November 22, a great meeting was called at the Cooper Union, and a general strike finally proclaimed[11].

The day after, a mass walk-out took place in Manhattan, the Bronx, and Brownsville. In a few days, more than 20,000 shirtwaist makers had abandoned work, 80 percent women no older than 20. Started as a spontaneous action, the conflict now grew into a well organized affair and soon, almost out of nothing, a strike machine was born. At Clinton Hall — the central headquarters and, like the Cooper Union, a pivotal site for the whole Lower East Side —, a committee sat till late in the night to plan the day after's activities, to receive reports and delegates from the factories, to prepare and distribute leaflets and placards, to teach picket rules, and to collect funds. Other halls — most of them in the neighborhood — functioned as meeting places for the striking workers of the various factories. The WTUL women took care of all the office work, collected bail money, and set up a legal council and a bureau of information. Walking delegates went from shop to shop to organize pickets and help convince scabs. Everywhere speakers exhorted the girls in Yiddish, Italian, and English. Working girls, whom to that day patriarchal values and socio-cultural mores had often relegated to a subordinate position, discovered a new dimension and a new rôle, and became organizers and agitators, speakers and walking delegates. And, out of the activity of such popular figures as Clara Lemlich, Fanny Zinsher, Rose Schneiderman, Rena Borky, Yeta Roff and Mary Effers, a sort of unofficial leadership developed, often in contrast to the union leaders[12].

Money was the most urgent problem. $2,500 were needed daily to free the 10-15 pickets arrested, and — although strike benefits were kept as low as possible ($2.50-3.00 a week for workers with family, $1.50 for single workers) — by the end of the 13 weeks' fight they amounted to some $60,000. Aid came from the UHT, the WTUL, the New York Central Federated Unions, the Teachers' Association, *The Jewish Daily Forward*, *The New York Call*, *The New York Evening Journal*, the Socialists and the Anarchists, and from the Lower East Side community as a whole. It was a severe winter, but not a day passed without pickets, marches, demonstrations, meetings, and fund-raising, and the shirtwaist makers were able to hold out through it[13]. Meanwhile, negotiations, which had been interrupted due to the big manufacturers' refusal to consider recognition of the union, had resumed again, and, by late December, after a general strike had started in Philadelphia to block scab work being done there, some 236 small shops had signed up, for a total of 17,000 employees. Attempts to break the strike increased. Scab use caused more scuffles at the picket-lines and new arrests, but soon the strikebreakers (mainly Italian women, often accompanied by their husbands or brothers, and some hundred Blacks) started to join the strikers' ranks, thanks also to the efforts of Socialist organizers such as Arturo Caroti and Salvatore Ninfo and of the Italian Women's Mutual

Fellow Workers!

Join in rendering a last sad tribute of sympathy and affection for the victims of the Triangle Fire. THE FUNERAL PROCESSION will take place Wednesday, April 5th, at 1 P. M. Watch the newspapers for the line of march.

צו דער לויה שוועסטער און ברידער!

די לויה פון די הייליגע קרבנות פון דעם טרייענגעל פייער וועט זיין סימוואך, דעם 5טען אפריל, 1 אזהר נאכטטטאג.

קינדער פון אייך מער נים פערבלייבען אין די שעפער! שליסט זיך אן אין די רייהען און די טרויריערענדע! דרוקט אויס אייער סימפאטיע און מיטגעפיל בעדויערען אויף דעם נרויסען פערלוסט וואס די ארבייטערוועלט האט געהאט.

געבלייגען די קעפ — סים ציטעטתע הערצער זעלען מיר פיהרען אונזערע פאהיייע שפעסערם צו זייער לעצטער רוה.

וועטם די ציימוגנען דוך וועלכע מיר וועלען לאזען וויסען וואו איהר קענט זיך צוזאמענקומען.

צו דער לויה פון די הייליגע קרבנות, קומט שוועסטער און ברידער!

Operai Italiani!

Unitevi compatti a rendere l'ultimo tributo d'affetto alle vittime dell'imane sciagura della Triangle Waist Co. IL CORTEO FUNEBRE avra luogo mercoledi, 5 Aprile, alle ore 1 P. M. Traverete nei giornali l'ordine della marcia.

Ill. 24
A Poster Announcing the Funeral Procession for the Triangle Fire Victims (from *The Survey*, April 15, 1911)

Benefit Association [Seller 1975; Kessner and Caroli 1978; Furio 1980; Ewen 1985].

On December 27, a compromise was presented to the workers assembled in five different halls. It offered a 52-hour week, but said no to the union shop, and was thus overwhelmingly rejected. From mid-January on, more and more manufacturers settled, and on February 15 the strike was finally called off, even if some 1,000 workers were still out [Leupp 1909; Mailly 1909; Comstock 1909; "A Souvenir" 1910; Clark and Wyatt 1910; Schneiderman 1967; Kessler-Harris 1976]. Manufacturers had agreed to a 52-hour week and to raises of between 12 and 15 percent, to reduce night work to 2 hours per day and not more than twice a week, to divide work among all workers in the slack season, and to curb "inside contracting". On the issue of union recognition, the agreement was somewhat vaguer, some of the manufacturers remaining adamant in their refusal. A year later, the deadly fire at the Triangle Waist Co. (the factory where the 1909 strike had originated) was a tragic commentary on the precariousness of the shirtwaist makers' gains, above all for what concerns working conditions in the shops[14]. Still, the 1909 strike, with its spontaneous class solidarity, remained as a milestone both in labor and in women's history [Luhan 1936; Flexner 1968; Sochen 1972].

Another great episode soon followed, when the cloakmakers completely paralyzed their trade from early July to early September 1910. This new general strike differed from that of the shirtwaist makers' in many respects. On one hand, it was *mainly* a male workforce to leave the shops this time — labor veterans who had lived through several years of unrest, especially during the 1890s. On the other hand, these veterans could now count upon a stronger ILGWU than a few months before. It was now a union galvanized by the working girls' superb struggle and thus ready to plan and organize, to lead and control the strike with care and determination. At the same time, however, its leadership remained cautious and unwilling to stay out any longer than was absolutely ecessary. When the strike was finally called off, the agreement signed by the ILGWU alarmed shopfloor activists. In their eyes, it appeared (and in the following years proved to be) bad and ambiguous. The mobilization *around* the strike — the active support from various community organizations, the attention from public opinion — was also less widespread than with the shirtwaist makers' struggle, which had taken the city by storm and stimulated more emotional responses.

Hostilities in the branch began towards the end of June 1910, as a revolt against sweating and inside contracting. Working hours went from 14 to 16 a day (plus home work), only in the busy season did wages average $14-18, and there were long periods of total unemployment[15]. On June 28, after a few weeks' insistence on the part of the rank and file, a huge meeting was finally held at the Madison Square Garden. In its June 30, 1910 issue, the *Jewish Daily Forward* called it 'the greatest Jewish labor meeting the world has ever seen', but the workforce also comprised a substantial number of Italians and other recent immigrants, as well as some American-born workers. A decision was taken to hold a referendum on July 2, 3, and 4. The results were overwhelmingly in favor of a general strike, and the union, although rather hesitatingly, called for it, to start at 2pm sharp, July 7. At that hour, some 70,000 cloakmakers left their shops and from various parts of the city converged on the Lower East Side, a veritable river swelled by hundreds of streamlets. The huge, impressive procession headed for East 4th Street, where it packed the Labor Lyceum and blocked the surrounding streets, and listened to Abraham Cahan, editor of the *Forward*, who gave a speech from a fire escape. The largest strike in the city's history up to that time had begun, and would last two months.

Notwithstanding the critical situation of those years, the Lower East Side once again responded with great enthusiasm and mobilized to support the workers in all possible ways. Several committees were organized to collect funds and offer relief, saloons and cafés provided free meals to the strikers, bakers gave out free bread, and — as a Speakers' Committee, a Law Committee, and a Pickets' Committee were set up to take care of the various aspects of the struggle — some 50 halls were hired, mostly in the neighborhood, to serve as meeting points for workers from the various shops. The union's journal *New Post* (in Yiddish, Italian, and English) put out special issues to detail the strike's developments, the *Evening Journal* published a strike edition as it had done for the shirtwaist makers, and Morris Rosenfeld — the sweatshop poet — wrote a song that became the battle hymn. Everywhere, the call for a "closed shop" took on the aspect of an almost ritualistic password.

Negotiations started with Morris Hillquit and Meyer London to represent the union, and a first attempt at a settlement was made at the end of July. But manufacturers were totally opposed to the closed shop, the rank and file was ready to reject any compromise on the issue on the part of the union's Joint Board, and a stalemate ensued. By August, the strike was declared illegal on the issue of the closed shop, and it was clear that a test of strength was building. Then, on September 2, after a hurried meeting of only a part of the shop's representatives, the strike was called off on the basis of a "Protocol of Peace" proposed by the union leadership, which laid down a definite wage scale and a fixed number of hours per week, established a Board of Sanitary Control, and introduced the concept of "preferential union shop" in the place of the "closed shop" — i.e., the manufacturers had to give preference in order of hiring to union members, but were not compelled to employ union members exclusively.

Huge crowds headed towards Seward Park and gathered in front of the *Forward* building, to get the latest news about the strike's conclusion. Italian cloakmakers met at nearby Orchard Hall, and then marched to the park, with an Italian speech printed in phonetics to be read by union officials to the crowd. Some 1,000,000 people, by police estimate, thronged the city streets that night, in the great enthusiasm for the end of the struggle. The day after, wagons with flags and bands drove through the Lower East Side, to publicize the settlement. But in several shops the strike went stubbornly on till September 17, a sign of the rank-and-file opposition to a compliant leadership [Hardy 1935; L. Stein, ed., 1977; Perry 1982].

Although it severely forfeited the right to strike by setting up a complex apparatus of arbitration and conciliation, the "Protocol of Peace" did not put an end to unrest in the trade. 10,000 fur makers and 50,000 men's tailors struck in 1912, shirtwaist makers walked out again in 1913, 20,000 white goods workers (mostly young girls) soon followed them, and so did the 15,000 kimono workers, who were even visited by former president Theodore Roosevelt at their strike headquarters at the Odd Fellows' Hall at 67 St.Mark's Place. By then, a new period of unemployment and near starvation was beginning. A veritable hail of unofficial stoppages fell on the industry, while a rank-and-file opposition formed within the ILGWU. By 1914, the success story was largely complete: the whole industry was unionized by the ILGWU (which became the third largest union), the UHT, and the new-born Amalgamated Clothing Workers' Union.

V.

While the clothing industry undoubtedly was the Lower East Side's pulsating heart, by no means was it the only sector in which tensions accumulated and exploded. Cigar making was the second most important industry in the city, closely resembling clothes making in terms both of dimensions and of working processes. Originally, it had clear craft features, with employers and skilled employees working side by side in the same shop. Then, the introduction of a certain amount of machinery (principally the "mold", to shape the filler or "bunch" of the cigar for the wrapper, and the "suction table", to roll cigars) opened it up to semiskilled and unskilled workers. By the mid-1870s, there were some

10,000 cigar makers, mostly skilled Germans and unskilled Bohemians, with already a few Puerto Ricans establishing decisive footholds for future immigration trends [Riis 1890, 1971, Chapter 12; Gompers 1925; Kaufman et al., eds., 1963; Iglesias, ed., 1984; Schneider 1985]. A handful of large factories (Kerbs & Spies, De Bary's, Stachelberg's) had up to 500 workers or more, the great majority employing from 10 to 50 and the small shops up to 10, with weekly wages of $5-$7. The "tenement house factories" characterized this industry as well, with buildings rented by manufacturers and licenced as factories, and rented again to whole families who lived and worked there, with wages that were one quarter less than the average and daily 15-18 working hours. In 1890, a row of houses on East 10th Street

> contained thirty-five families of cigarmakers, with probably not half a dozen persons in the whole lot of them, outside of the children, who could speak a word of English, though many had been in the country half a lifetime. This room with two windows giving on the street, and a rear attachment without windows, called a bedroom by courtesy, is rented at $12.25 a month. In the front room man and wife work at the bench from six in the morning till nine at night. They make a team, stripping the tobacco leaves together; then he makes the filler, and she rolls the wrapper on and finishes the cigar. For a thousand they receive $3.75, and can turn out together three thousand cigars a week [Riis 1890, 1971, p.111].

The small cigar shops were particularly common on the Lower East Side. They employed from eight to ten workers — men, women, children, often the employer himself —, used little or no machinery outside the "mold", and produced low-quality cigars to be sold in the neighborhood. It took an average of two years to become a skilled "hand" cigar maker, but many workers in the trade left the small shops after a few months to find employment in the larger factories outside the neighborhood. The small shops, however, continued to thrive in the area. In fact, while it was not a manufacturing district, from the beginning of its history as an immigrant quarter the Lower East Side had always hosted several small industries employing that portion of its population who did not go to work outside its borders. The small shops that flourished in the neighborhood thus served as important stepping stones for hundreds of newcomers faced with the immediate problem of surviving in a foreign country and of looking for an industrial foothold. Such shops were generally 'characterized by the entire absence of machinery and mechanical appliances or by the use of very small

Table 1
View of the Bowery, North from Canal Street (Anon., 1884)
Table 2
Mullen's Alley (Jacob A. Riis, ca. 1888-89)
Jacob A. Riss Collection, Museum of the City of New York

Table 3
Bandits' Roost, 39 1/2 Mulberry Street (Jacob A. Riis. ca. 1888)
Jacob A. Riis Collection, Museum of the City of New York
Table 4
A Sweatshop in a Ludlow Street Tenement (Jacob A. Riis. ca. 1899)
Jacob A. Riis Collection, Museum of the City of New York

Table 5
Mulberry Bend (Jacob A. Riis. ca. 1888-89)
Jacob A. Riis Collection, Museum of the City of New York
Table 6
Northwest Corner of Hester Street, Looking East Side of Norfolk Street, NYC (anon., 1898)
The New-York Historical Society, New York City

Table 7
Pell Street, Chinatown (anon., 1898)
New York Chinatown History Museum Archives
Table 8
A View of Mulberry Street (anon., ca. 1906)
Library of Congress, Washington

Table 9
A Tenement Flat (anon., ca. 1905)
Brown Brothers Archives, Sterling, Pennsylvania
Table 10
View of Mulberry Bend, The Italian Section of New York (anon., ca. 1907)
The New-York Historical Society, New York City

Table 11
Samuel Gompers Addressing Shirtwaist Strikers at the Cooper Union, Before the
Proclamation of the General Strike (anon., 1909)
Brown Brothers Archives, Sterling, Pennsylvania
Table 12
Clothing Workers' Strike (anon., possibly 1910)
Brown Brothers Archives, Sterling, Pennsylvania

Table 13
Chinatown and the Bowery (anon., 1930s)
New York Chinatown History Museum Archives

Table 14
Louis Sontag, "Bowery at Night" (1892)
Museum of the City of New York
Table 15
John Sloan, "McSorley's Ale House" (1912)
Founders Society Purchase, The Detroit Institute of Arts

Table 16
George W. Bellows, "Cliff Dwellers" (1913)
Los Angeles County Museum of Art, Los Angeles County Funds
Table 17
George B. Luks, "Hester Street" (1905)
Dick S. Ramsay Fund, The Brooklyn Museum, New York

Table 18
Jerome Myers, "Life on the East Side"
Museum Purchase, Collection of the Corcoran Gallery of Art, Washington
Table 19
Louis Lozowick, "Allen Street (Under the El)" (1929)
Collection of the Whitney Museum of American Art, New York

Table 20
Reginald Marsh, "The Bowery — Strokey's Bar" (1953)
Collection of the Whitney Museum of American Art, New York

Tables 21-22
Lower East Side Scenes (Marlis Momber, 1980-85)
Marlis Momber, New York City

Tables 23-24
Lower East Side Scenes (Marlis Momber, 1980-85)
Marlis Momber, New York City

Table 25
A Garden Among the Tenements (Marlis Momber, ca. 1984)
Marlis Momber, New York City
Table 26
Poet Jorge Brandon in Front of the Loisaida Avenue Mural "From One Generation to
Another", Designed and Directed by John Weber (Marlis Momber, 1985)
Marlis Momber, New York City

Table 27
Roofs of the Lower East Side (Marlis Momber, 1983)
Marlis Momber, New York City
Table 28
"Baile Bomba", in Front of the Clinton Street Mural, Designed and Directed by Maria
Dominguez (Marlis Momber, 1983)
Marlis Momber, New York City

Table 29
Martin Wong, "Attorney Street Handball Court With Autobiographical Poem by
Piñero" (1982-84)
The Edith C.Blum Fund, The Metropolitan Museum of Art, New York

machines readily operated by inexperienced hands' [Sakolski 1906, pp.21-22], and thus did not require skilled workmanship. At the same time, they answered the needs of the quarter and offered its inhabitants a good chance to get accustomed to "working American-style" (sweating, contracting, speed, task-system, home work), enabling newcomers either to move to larger industries which required more skills, or to become a contractor and, if the case be, a "cockroach pharaoh".

Important small industries thus were brush-making (a trade where little capital was needed and products could be easily distributed to local retailers, wages were low, but no slack season affected the workers as in the clothing industry); trunk-making (which took advantage of the fact that many immigrants had been joiners or carpenters at home, although it made very little use of their skills); wig-making (an occupation that offered reasonable wages but, directly linked as it was to the ethnic character of the neighborhood — Jewish religious tenets required married women to wear wigs — was rather limited); the manufacture of brass and copper implements (a more skilled trade, whose workers earned an average $10 per week but labored in basements and cellars under very unhealthy conditions) [16].

***

Each immigrant community then had its own specific activities. While at least by the turn of the century Jews monopolized the garment industry, street-peddling, and most local shops[17], Chinese worked mainly in laundries and restaurants, within and without Chinatown, within and without Manhattan. The "Eight Pound Livelihood" was a telling image to characterize a laundryman's life. It was a tough job, which required physical strength, quickness, and endurance. It easily took up between 12 and 14 hours a day — often more, since the workday ended only once the orders for the following day had been cleared. For that reason, and due to the high rents to be paid for shops, many owners and labourers practically lived in the laundry during the week, to the scandal of a public opinion who could not understand the reasons why. Tarifs were set by the two laundrymen's unions, and a labourer could put together between $8 and $12 a week plus board and lodging, while two owners, working together without outside help, could make $1000 a year [Beck 1898, p.57-62]. For their part, restaurants multiplied in Chinatown by the turn of the century, when it became somewhat fashionable to go slumming in the area and a local-color tourism developed. But there was also a large number of smaller eating places catering to the community's working population, both Chinese and not, who found Chinese food healthier and more economical. A first-class restaurant, like the Port Arthur or the Hong Leong Lau, could pay its cook some $80 a month plus board, while a cook in a second-class restaurant received some $60, and in other places between $33 and $40 [Beck 1898, pp.49-54].

Italian workers were mainly unskilled and semi-skilled men, common laborers who principally used *picca e sciabola* (= "pick and shovel", the tools of construction workers). As masons, carvers and carpenters, they helped to build tenements and houses on the Lower East Side, and elevated railways, reservoirs, stations, tunnels, and subways in the rest of the city (the Lexington Avenue subway in 1900, the Bronx aqueduct and Manhattan's Grand Central Terminal in 1904). In 1890, 90 percent of the public work laborers in New York were Italian; in 1900, one out of every four common laborers was Italian. Seasonally, they left Little Italy to work in construction camps scattered across nearby states (Maine's railways, for instance). It was the toughest job, most likely to scar deeply the community by continuously breaking up family units just reunited after long periods of separation. The work-day in construction camps was generally ten hours, and Italians received wages of between $1.46-3.00 per hour, as compared to $2.00-5.00 normally paid the Irish. They also worked as longshoremen, an occupation where another ethnic take-over occurred in the last decades of the nineteenth century. By 1880, 95 percent of the waterfront workforce was in fact Irish. To break the 1887 strike led by the Knights of Labor, employers turned to Italian workers, thus undermining the Irish presence on the job, and by 1896 the process of displacement was well under way. Italians then worked as teamsters, hackmen, peddlers, street-musicians, cooks, bartenders and, above all, as barbers (in a trade once dominated by Germans and Blacks, they came to account for at least half of New York's haircutters) and as boot-blacks (of the 2,648 boot-blacks listed for New York State in 1900 2,561 were Italian) [Kessner 1977, p.58; La Sorte 1985, p.65].

Italian women worked as fellers and finishers in the garment industry, making between $50 and $125 a year, and in the artificial flower industry (72 percent of the entire workforce), where four persons working together on the kitchen table could put together some $7.00 a week [Kessner 1977, pp.73-74]. When home work declined, Italian women found employment in factories, and another ethnic displacement began — from a principally Jewish trade to an increasingly Italian one. In 1910, 36.2 percent of the female workforce in the garment industry in New York City (i.e., the largest proportion) was in the hands of Italian women [Nelli 1983, pp.87-88].

VI.

From these and from many other sectors, a 'cry for bread [was] rising ever so louder' [Malkiel 1910, p.32]. On January 13, 1874, at the peak of a terrible depression that had left some 180,000 people without work in the State of New York alone, a meeting of mainly German unemployed in Tompkins Square Park was attacked by mounted policemen, and demonstrators were chased down Avenue B and the intersecting streets, beaten, and arrested, in what came to be known as the "Tompkins Square massacre" [Hillquit 1903, 1971, pp.182-183]. In the fall of 1877, 10,000 cigarmakers formed a combative union (the *Vereinigte Cigarren Macher von Nord-Amerika*), held meetings at the Germania Assembly Rooms and demonstrations at Tompkins Square Park, and struck for several weeks, demanding higher wages and better living and working conditions. They met with a severe defeat, but they struck again in 1890 and, for sixteen weeks, in 1900 [Riis 1890, 1971; Cahan Sept.8, 1900, 1985; Gompers 1925; Schneider 1985].

Unionization was not an easy process in a neighborhood which annually experienced the arrival of thousands of immigrants from all parts of the world, mostly unskilled and ready to pick up whatever job was at hand. Newcomers fell prey to unscrupulous middlemen, accepted starvation wages, often ended up as strikebreakers, and all this tended to divide the laboring classes of the Lower East Side and to reinforce racial hatred and stereotypes[18]. Ethnic specificities and gender rôles also had their say in making the unionization process even more complex. Due to Chinatown's self-defensive seclusiveness, very little is known about trade-union activities on Mott and Doyers streets, or about relationships with the larger labor movement in the city and on the Lower East Side in particular. Yet, two unions existed, although — as we have seen — they probably resembled traditional guilds rather than modern labor organizations. And for some time, the Industrial Workers of the World had a branch in the area. On the West Coast, Chinese workers monopolized cigar making — a fact that surely had its weight on Gompers's reactionary attitude towards these immigrants —, and it is thus to be supposed that a certain number of Chinese cigar makers worked in New York too and was possibly involved in some episode of unrest in the trade. But the particular social organization of Chinatown, the daily realities of the "bachelor society", and the open hostility expressed by many craft unions to Chinese immigrants undoubtedly militated against their joining ranks with the American labor movement. The birth of the Chinese Unemployed Council in 1932 and of the Chinese Hand Laundry Alliance in 1933 thus signalled important changes in Chinatown's social and cultural identity [Kwong 1979].

At least initially, attempts to organize Italian immigrants were also rather unsuccessful. The peasant background, the *campanilismo*, the age-old traditions, and, in the new country, the rôle of the *padrone* and the high rate of transiency, all worked against an easy process of unionization. Italians soon occupied the lower rungs of the social ladder, depressing wages and acting as strikebreakers. Nonetheless, after a few years, unions began to appear within the community — the United Brotherhood of Carpenters and Joiners, the Amalgamated Society of Carpenters and Joiners, the Progressive Carpenters, the Bricklayers' and Masons' International Union, the Italian Mosaic Marble Workers, and many others in the same fields, as well as among barbers, street-sweepers, longshoremen, bakers, and so on [Fenton 1957, 1975, pp.141-142]. Strikes soon followed, and in 1900 socialist organizer Salvatore Ninfo led the subway workers in the first successful effort at union activity in the *colonia*. Barbers then repeatedly struck and so did longshoremen, and large demonstrations took place in occasion of great class conflicts such as the 1912 Lawrence Strike and the 1913 Paterson Strike, in which Italian workers were in the forefront. The increasing presence of Italian women in the clothing and artificial flowers industries and, consequently, their more independent economic position also had important effects, both on the community and on union activity. As a growing number of Italian girls got accustomed to factory work and socialized with their German or Russian-Jewish fellow workers, they were slowly drawn to union activity, or at least to less backward gender conceptions. Especially with younger girls, factory work meant a physical and economic independence from family and the house, that was almost inconceivable in Southern Italy. Italian women organized in the WTUL, and then, increasingly, in the ILGWU, and often gained leading positions in the unions, as was the case of Angela Bombace, or, in the 1920s, in Communist activities, as was the case of Angela Delfino. Little by little, traditional patriarchal values were being eroded on Mulberry Street and along First Avenue.

In a way, Jewish women were in a different situation. The very subordination in which they were placed by religious Orthodoxy was socially so explicit and outspoken that it made rebellion somewhat easier than for the Italian woman, whose subordination was exerted in a subtler way, more as a set of habits than as a corpus of tenets[19]. To this, other important facts must be added. First of all, the economic developments that were taking place in Russia and other areas of the Jewish Pale of Settlement had already opened up the factory gates to an increasing number of women, and a certain amount of independence both economically and psychologically had thus ensued. Secondly, the influence of the *Haskala* (the Jewish enlightenment) had made itself felt among women as well, pushing them to challenge and break orthodox rules, especially for what concerns gender. Thirdly, Jewish women had experienced pogroms which had dramatically called for more militant attitudes in order to survive, or had been involved in revolutionary activities, especially in Russia, where women were numerous among Anarchists and Social-revolutionaries. The result of all this was that, on the Lower East Side, Jewish women were not only readier to fight than Italian women, but often more so than Jewish men as well, having also to take care of all the difficult household problems of day-to-day survival. Admiration for them is clear in such texts as Hutchins Hapgood's *The Spirit of the Ghetto* or Theresa Malkiel's *The Diary of a Shirtwaist Striker*, and it was from within their ranks, more than from those of the middle-class liberated women, that the model of the "new woman" would develop [Ewen 1985].

VII.

Spontaneous militancy and communal solidarity were also at the basis of a series of collective actions that went beyond the purely labor level, involving the neighborhood as such and using streets, rather than factories or shops, as their theatre of action. In turn-of-the-century New York, streets provided the main setting for a host of jobs employing children, who preferred their fascinating possibilities to home work in stifling tenement flats. At the same time, streets were the places where most of the neighborhood's life was lived, often in a close interaction between private and public [C. Goodman 1979; Nasaw 1985]. And precisely in the streets a significant episode occurred in the summer of 1899, when newsboys struck against William Randolph Hearst's *New York Journal* and Joseph Pulitzer's *New York World*.

"Newsies" were a familiar figure in city lore. Many novels and plays had romanticized them, while reformers Charles L. Brace and Jacob A. Riis had expressed worry at these potentially dangerous "wild angels", used to all kinds of street-life tricks and hardships. When new technical developments were introduced into the newspaper industry (photoes and banner headlines, afternoon and evening editions), their use in the streets became crucial.

The strike broke out in response to the decision of the two papers to increase the wholesale price from 5 to 6 cents per ten journals, as part of a bitter competition. A meeting was called in New York on July 19, and on the following day the strike began [Nasaw 1985, Chapter 12;

Maffi, in Filippelli 1990]. The kids (10-to-15-year-old boys and girls, mainly Jewish and Italian, but Black and Irish as well) formed a union, appointed a "strike committee" and a "committee on discipline", and sent walking delegates to adjoining cities. Day after day, they intercepted delivery wagons and pelted them with stones and rotten fruit, scattered bundles of papers to the ground and fought scabs. For two weeks, they gave proof of great organizational skills and a real knack at dealing with public opinion — something that probably came to them through shared family experiences and contemporary struggles — and support was widespread. Huge meetings were held in the Lower East Side. After a few days' strike, some 5,000 "newsies" gathered at the New Irving Hall and listened to speeches by Kid Blink and Bob the Indian, Newspaper Annie and Warhorse Brennan, and to a song by newsboy mascot Hungry Joe Kernan. Demonstrators paraded through the streets, and a mass march on Manhattan of Brooklyn kids had to be stopped by the police on the Brooklyn Bridge.

Initially, the two newspapers did not take the children seriously. But, as the strike spread to other cities and states and merged with bootblacks' and messenger boys' strikes (almost a "children's general strike"), sales began to plummet and advertisers to desert, while the press run dropped from 360,000 to 125,000 and returns rose from 15-16% to 35%. In a memo to Pulitzer, the *World*'s managing editor wrote that "the loss in circulation [...] has been colossal" [quoted in Nasaw 1985, p.176][20]. At that point, the papers gave in. They did not abolish the increase, but agreed to take back unsold copies at a 100 percent refund. On August 2, the newsboys accepted the deal. They called off the strike, disbanded the union, and made no attempt at a more permanent organization — too volatile was their workforce, and too precarious was the labor situation in the city, to allow for more stable results. When strikes occurred again in 1918 and 1919, the newspapers could thus easily defeat the "newsies", who, besides, were already being rendered obsolete by a whole set of changes in city life.

Another important episode took place a few years later, and showed the spontaneous but organized way in which the neighborhood could respond to attacks on its living conditions — the "*kosher* meat boycott". By early May 1902, the retail price of *kosher* meat was raised from 12 cents to 18 cents a pound by what went under the name of "Meat Trust", mainly composed of German Jews. Sharply affecting day-to-day survival, the increase immediately caused a stir in the Jewish component of the Lower East Side. For a week, the small retailers tried to exert some pression on the Trust, hoping to have the previous prices restored. But their action proved unsuccessful, and women took the matter into their own hands to the cry of 'If *we women* make a strike, then it will be a strike' [quoted in Hyman 1980, p.93; Rischin 1962, 1977; Howe 1976]. A boycott began which lasted three weeks, mobilized (and even split) the community, and led to several bitter confrontations with the police.

It originated in a few blocks on Monroe and Pike streets, where women (mostly housewives in their thirties, several years in the United States, and thus rather different from the young girls that would soon be protagonists of many labor struggles) set up a committee of 19 and started to canvas the neighborhood for active support. On May 15, thousands of women were in the streets, to talk, argue, and — if the case be — forcibly convince other housewives or their husbands to boycott *kosher* meat shops. Pickets were placed in front of shops, and often, when tension rose, meat was thrown out or used as a missile against "scabs" and police[21]. When a meeting was called at the New Irving Hall, and 20,000 persons gathered in front of it, a riot soon broke out, and 70 women and 15 men were arrested for disorderly conduct. The day after, another 100 followed them when police intervened to protect shops from pickets and assaults. Brushing up expressions reminiscent of past attitudes as regards city proletariat, *The New York Times* labelled the more resolute women a 'dangerous class', 'a swarm of ignorant and infuriated women'.

A grass-roots leadership developed. The Ladies' Anti-Beef Trust Association, led by Sarah Edelson and Caroline Schatzburg, started to agitate among non-Jewish women as well. And on Saturday, May 17, in order to discuss the boycott with men, the strike committee went from synagogue to synagogue, resorting to the traditional practice of interrupting Torah reading whenever an important matter was concerned. By May 18, the boycott had spread to Brooklyn and Harlem, and most of the shops had finally closed down. Preoccupation was now apparent even within the community, and contrasts began to surface in the Association itself. The chance was taken by the more moderate spokesmen (former radical Joseph Barondess, among others) to set up another mostly male leadership, the Allied Conference for Cheap *Kosher* Meat, which tried to regain control of the situation by convincing women to step aside. Meanwhile, the Retail Butchers Association had joined the boycott, and on May 27 even the initially hesitant Orthodox leaders declared themselves in favor. On June 5, retail prices were reduced to 14 cents a pound, and the boycott was over.

This early "folk" struggle (as *The Jewish Daily Forward* termed it) set the pattern for other episodes which stirred up the community even more in the following years — the "rent strikes". The first one, in spring 1904, was a reaction against rapidly escalating rents (+20-30 percent) which severely affected the home budget of most families. Two figures in the neighborhood's social panorama were in fact deeply and widely hated: the "czar" (in most cases an absentee landlord) and the "lister" or "cockroach landlord" (a lessee, or a sort of contractor in the housing field). The innumerable cases of meanness and stinginess on their part had become part and parcel of the community lore [Cahan 1902, 1985; Blaustein 1904; Hill 1904; Ganz 1919, pp.83-85; Joselit, in Lawson, ed., 1986)[22], but for most households it was not simply a matter of local color. The situation on the Lower East Side *was* dramatic. Housing was limited, and recent constructions (such as Seward Park and the Williamsburg Bridge) had caused the razing of whole blocks at a time when population grew 14 percent [Kessner 1977, p.133]. The reaction was spontaneous, but, at the same time, the expression of the quarter's growing politicization and unionization. Women were again at the vanguard and turned the neighborhood into their favorite battle ground. By resorting to the established net of personal relationships and familiar meeting places (streets, stoops, markets, stores), they canvassed and mobilized it. They held meetings and planned outdoor demonstrations, picketed buildings and opposed evictions, formed "unions" and proclaimed "rent strikes", fought "scabs" and gave the movement an embryonic organization. Again, after this early stage, a male leadership was set up — the short-lived New York Rent Protective Association, which functioned more or less as a mutual aid society.

The 1904 strikes thus ended with a tenants' victory for what concerns rents, but with no stable organization to carry on the battle. A more widespread and bitter strike wave followed in 1907-1908. Rents had soared again, and a three-room apartment that could be rented for $11-12 in 1904 now rented for $16-17 [Dinwiddie 1908; Bernheimer 1908]. Scenes of evicted families huddling on the sidewalk, with their household equipment piled nearby, had become sadly common. Besides, the country was now in the grip of another economic depression. Unemployed on the Lower East Side amounted to some 75,000-100,000, tension was high (in 1908, the Unemployment Conference in Union Square was charged by mounted policemen), and some sort of test of strength was inevitable. Tenants barricaded themselves in their houses and raised red flags; in the streets kids hanged landlords in effigy and women fought "scabs"; delegations from other neighborhoods and towns paraded in protest. The strike soon spread to Brooklyn, Harlem, and New Jersey, and a Tenants' Union and Anti-High Rent League was formed. Support came from several labor unions (teamsters refused to remove household equipment from flats of evicted tenants), and, much to the scandal and worry of public opinion, the Socialist Party was actively involved. The police and

168

the courts dealt quite severely with the movement, and newspapers and magazines expressed much less support than they had in 1904.

In the following years, tenant mobilization on the Lower East Side was continuous, often intertwining with other expressions of unrest on the labor as well as the community level. In 1913-14, several banks went bankrupt and conditions became tragic in the quarter. Hundreds of evicted and unemployed roamed the streets in search of work, food, and shelter, major protests were led by IWW Frank Tannenbaum, and not a day passed without spontaneous demonstrations born of improvised street-corner speeches.

As I turned into Rivington Street the way was blocked by a long line of men standing outside a tall old shop building waiting for a chance to earn fifty cents a day from the Mayor's Committee for the Unemployed by rolling bandages and sorting cast-off clothing, which had been sent for the relief of the destitute. Many of these men had already come into possession of some of the cast-off clothes, and there were all sorts of fantastic costumes in the line. Here was a man wearing a high silk hat, striped evening trousers and a sweater. Another was in rags except for an immaculate pair of white kid gloves. So the rich people were trying to help at last. Surely it was time. But what a farce it was. Here was a problem involving two hundred thousand unemployed people, and these wealthy philanthropists were trying to solve it through a system that could reach out only a few hundred persons a day at most. And among those few hundreds were many who deserved help the least. What of all the homeless women and children I had seen? Where were they? Most of them too proud to beg, too ignorant or bewildered to know which way to turn [...]. Everywhere wretchedness and suffering. How long, I asked myself, would the ghetto bear its burden of woe so meekly. [...] I took my stand on the curb and began to speak aloud, raising my voice high. [...] A little group of people gathered round me, and quickly from streets and alleyways and tenements streams of eager men and women poured in to join them. Soon there were thousands of them, standing in silence, blocking the whole street. Suddenly there came a stirring in the tightly massed crowd. Men were pushing their way to the outer edges. In a few seconds fully two hundred of them had worked their way free of the rest, and, forming in a body, were marching away for uptown. "We're going to get a square meal, Marie", they called back. [...] Followed by several hundred men and women, I led the way to Rivington Street [Ganz 1919, pp.122-123, 124-125, 126, 127][23].

In mid-February 1917, violent food riots broke out in Brooklyn, soon spreading to other working-class neighborhoods, with women again on the front line. In years of celebrated prosperity, and just before the United States's entry into World War I, food prices had gone up 82 percent. To East Siders, it meant that butter and poultry had become a luxury, cheese and potatoes had increased by more than 100 percent, flour was more expensive than at any time since the Civil War, onions sold for 15-18 cents per pound as compared with the 10-12 of a few months before [Lasker 1917, p.639; Kirkland 1969, p.475][24]...The situation was further aggravated by the conversion of many industries into war industries with the ensuing imbalances in the labor market, by the constant flow of country people attracted to the city by illusory war prosperity and job opportunity, and by President Wilson's Preparedness Campaign with its 'massive appropriations for armaments' [Freiburger 1984, p.231]. What followed was a dramatic worsening of living conditions and a rise in infant mortality in working-class neighborhoods, due to lack of food, clothing, and heating[25].

On February 19, pushcarts were attacked and overturned in Brooklyn, and soon the whole Lower East Side was in turmoil. Some 400 women assembled in Rutgers Square and marched to City Hall, where Marie Ganz and a few members of the Mothers' Vigilance Committee met officials and called for city intervention. When "Sweet Marie" tried to speak to the crowd after the meeting, she was immediately arrested. A riot then broke loose, bare-handed women charging policemen, tearing buttons and scratching faces [*The New York Evening Journal* (February 21, 1917)]. In the evening, some 10,000 persons met at the Forward Hall on East Broadway, where bases for organization and plans for future actions were laid. As food riots occurred elsewhere on the East Coast, other major disturbances took place in New York. On February 20, a boycott of onions, potatoes, and poultry was started. Pickets were formed to enforce them, and whenever 'a woman, basket or bag on arm, approached a poultry market there were dozens to tell her that she must not buy fowl of any kind. If she ignored the warning and emerged with a chicken she was seized, as was the chicken, which was torn limb from limb' [*The New York Times* (February 23, 1917)]. A few days later, for several hours in the afternoon, 5000 persons literally sieged the Waldorf-Astoria Hotel, a symbol of prosperity, and fought policemen and hotel detectives, overturned motor cars, and beat their occupants, trying to break through the revolving doors. Mounted policemen charged, and women and children were trampled over.

The whole Lower East Side was ebullient with revolt — Anti-High Price League pickets boycotted groceries and butcher shops and, on

170

The Shoe & Sandel Trade Union!

Monster Massmeeting

WILL TAKE PLACE

ON THURSDAY SEPT. 11th, 1913, 8 p. m.

At CLINTON HALL, 151 CLINTON STREET

The best Speakers of the United Hebrew Trades will Address the Meeting.

New members will be adjusted at this meeting. The Union meets every Thursday at its Cuate St

Come all. **The Boot and Shoe Workers Ur.ion.**

שוו־דיא שזה אזן סזענדזעל ארבזייסזער זיניאזן

ניידזער שזה אזן סזעדזל ארדזיסזור ! נידם, סבארין אך סבבזד אך דזר ארדזיסזור. הזן זד אד
ארזאבזיידם, מאבזקזן אך זזד ארדזיסזור, הזן זד אד נזם ארסאבזחים, אך אדח דזם אלזב א בזיסזאל.
בזינב אך דזא אבזג אזן דזי שזה אזן סזעדזל ארדזיסזור, הזאבזם אדזים בד רזידזב די אבזג זב זי זזה אזן סזעדזל.
ארדזיסזור, האב די זניאב בן דזזן סזרזי אבזאמזסזדם א

א גרזייסזען מאסזסמזיטזינג

דזאנזערסזאבז, דזן 11זען סזעפזסזעמבבער, 1913.
— אזב א אהר אבזנדם —

אזן קלזינסאן האלל, 151 קלזינסאן סזרזם

הזג די סבזעסזע זזהזם זזה זן די נזדזירזצאבזן, דזם דזם לזהאן ארזקזהזין. נזג סבאבאזן־ זזהם.
ארזענזסזע זזהזקם. די זדזא אך סזע זזדם אגזערזסאם, אך לזהאן זאל, 151 האבאן יאל.

Tutti i Lavoranti Shoe & Sandel Makers

Sono invitati venire ad un

GRANDE RIUNIONE

CHE AVRA LUOGO

Giovedi 11 Settembre, alle ore 8 p. m.

Al Nr. 151 CLINTON ST. Clinton Hall

Questo riunione e di grande importanza precio si pregano tutti di compagni nessuno non mancare,

Dave parleranno valenti oratori in Italian.

The Boot and Shoe Workers Union.

March 1, 100 persons were arrested for attacking food shops. Unless a remedy was found — declared Senator George Norris —, 'ultimately there will be a revolution' [quoted in *The New York Sun* (February 21, 1917)], and while Lower East Side representative to Congress Meyer London repeatedly spoke on behalf of the hungry masses, and various, mostly useless, attempts were made to set up committees to take care of the crisis, patriotic propaganda seized the opportunity to blame the riots on "German agents", as part of a generalized anti-radical strategy that would climax in the 1919 "Red Scare" hysteria. Then, entry into the war pushed to the background the dramatic problem of hunger in the city. But — together with the housing and unemployed problems — it remained an open issue all through the 1920s, and above all in the 1930s, when, under the pressure of the Depression, the tenant movement was revived. This time, it was mainly led by the Communist Party through its Unemployed Councils, whose squads of militants were ready to go from block to block to resist evictions or to move back evicted families' furniture — an often victorious action made possible by the militant solidarity of entire blocks[26].

VIII.

Mobilization on the Lower East Side, however, was far from limited to local level. As an immigrant quarter, the neighborhood always showed a keen attention for the issues that affected the American as well as the international working class. Solidarity with the striking railwaymen and coalminers had been expressed in the 1870s, and with the Chicago stockyard workers in the 1880s. Then, in 1886, the Haymarket riots in Chicago, with the subsequent indictment of seven radical leaders and the hanging of four of them, represented a dramatic turning point for the Lower East Side as well. On November 11, a huge commemoration was held at the Cooper Union, and the date remained a fixed one on the calendar of a neighborhood thriving with radical politics. Also in 1886, the New York mayoral campaign was another relevant event, which drew many immigrants (like Gompers and Cahan) into American politics for the first time. And, from their very beginning in 1890, May Day parades, during which '[bands] played the *Marseillaise* and other workers' songs[, the] people were dressed in their best, [...] red flags fluttered from hundreds of windows[, and the] streets of the East Side took on a new, more cheerful air' [M. Epstein 1950-53, I, p.178], were more than simply ritual occasions. In those same years, the arrival of East European immigrants (most of them engaged in revolutionary activity back home) added new strength and nourishment to an already combative community, and forcibly enlarged its horizon.

All Russians seemed to be revolutionists. Girls as well as men told me of dangerous plots in which they had taken part against the czar's government. Many of them were students in the preparatory schools of the neighborhood. All seemed to be hungry for knowledge. [...] In the evening I would go to Jackson Park, where groups of them were always to be found. They discussed their favourite authors, Nietzsche, Schopenhauer, Ibsen, Tolstoy [...]. When they were not carrying on animated discussions they sang their folksongs or danced. There was nothing apathetic about them. Their minds and emotions were always wide awake [Ganz 1919, p.108].

In the 1890s, the unemployed armies crossing the country and the bitter strikes at the Carnegie Steel Works (Homestead, Pennsylvania) and at the Pullman Company (Chicago) deeply stirred the neighborhood. Anarchist Alexander Berkman, who tried to kill Carnegie's manager Henry Frick, was a popular figure on the Lower East Side, as was his comrade and companion Emma Goldman. Several large meetings were held on his behalf, with James Barondess, Saverio Merlino, and other well-known radicals as speakers. Eugene V. Debs, imprisoned as a labor leader during the Pullman strike, was to become another beloved figure in the quarter, as was shown by the huge rallies welcoming him there during his presidential election tour in 1912 [Ginger 1949, 1962].

When news of the 1903 Kishinev massacre and subsequent pogroms in Russia reached New York, 100,000 paraded the streets, and emotion was deep well beyond the boundaries of the Jewish ghetto. The Friends of Russian Freedom, a section of the Narodnaya Volya (the Socialist-Revolutionary Party), was already active in the area, and when its most famous militant, Catherine "Babushka" Breshkoskaya, arrived in New York, a meeting was called at the Cooper Union to welcome her. Shortly after, news of the 1905 Russian Revolution arrived, and again the Lower East Side 'lived in a delirium, spending almost all of its time at monster meetings and discussing these matters in cafés, forgetting political differences and brought into close comradeship by the glorious events happening in the fatherland' [Goldman 1935, p.372]. And when Bloody Sunday followed, and revolution was crushed in terror and repression, such a virulent anti-Russian sentiment developed in the neighborhood that the Orleneff Theatre on East 3rd Street, performing mainly Russian plays, had to close down [Goldman 1935, p.373]. The first anniversary of the 1905 Revolution was celebrated in Union Square, with "Mother" Jones and Jack London among the speakers.

Meanwhile, the veritable semi-civil war raging in the Western coal-mining regions was being followed with great passion, and the attempt to frame Western Federation of Miners's officials William "Big Bill" Haywood, Charles Moyer, and George A. Pettibone again stirred the neighborhood into action. "Mother" Jones, the miners' beloved activist, was asked to speak on several occasions, while, after the formation of the Industrial Workers of the World in 1905 and above all during the 1913 Paterson strike, "Big Bill" often spent time on the Lower East Side, staying at Emma Goldman's place at 210 East 13th Street (the 'home of lost dogs', as it was termed by writer and bohemian Hutchins Hapgood) [Goldman 1935, p.489, 517]. And Elizabeth Gurley Flynn, a young IWW militant who played a major rôle in the 1912 Lawrence strike, came to be well-known for her eloquent and passionate street-corner speeches [Flynn 1973; M. Green 1988]. Anger once again exploded, this time in 1914, when miners and their families were shot and burned to death in Ludlow (Colorado) by the Rockefeller Company's private police. Stormy meetings were held at the Cooper Union, and several demonstrations at Union Square broke into violent rioting. Militants from nearby IWW headquarters on East 4th Street called for action and left for the West by bumming rides on freight-trains. "Sweet" Marie Ganz even tried to reach and shoot John D.Rockefeller in his office. The whole Lower East Side was literally seething with revolt [Homberger 1986]. The prospects of a war with Mexico, the news of the February and October revolutions in Russia (with the emotion they provoked among such exiled revolutionaries as Leon Trotzky, who was in New York at the time), and the United States's entry into World War I — all were occasions of great turmoil.

***

Out of this intense radical activity, a sort of international leadership soon developed in the quarter. Its early history was dominated by German immigrants, most of whom had been deeply involved in socialist movements at home and were now ready to carry on revolutionary activity in America. In 1852, the Proletarian League was organized in New York by Joseph Weydemeyer, a close friend and comrade to Karl Marx and Friedrich Engels, who tried to overcome the German-Americans' sectarian attitudes and started to agitate for the unionization of skilled *and* unskilled workers. Five years later, Weydemeyer moved to Chicago, and his place in New York was taken by another friend and comrade of Marx and Engels's, Friedrich Sorge, who reorganized the Proletarian League into the Communist Club of New York, joined the anti-slavery battle, and carried on the task of Marxist agitation and propaganda [Aveling and Marx Aveling 1891, 1969; Sorge 1891, 1977][27]. Even in this early period of American radicalism, the Lower East Side was a crucial area — not by chance, when the General Council of the International Workingmen's Association was moved to New York in 1872, it set up its headquarters in the Tenth Ward Hotel, at the corner of Broome and Forsyth streets.

With the arrival of East European immigrants, political activity increased in the neighborhood, and managed to overcome many of the limitations of the earliest period. The need to reach out to the American workers and the American situation, so often stressed by Engels, was now deeply felt, and a veritable radical community was born, whose activities occupied much of the quarter's daily life. Militants met in halls, parks, newspaper offices, and cafés, and engaged in heated discussions which often stirred the neighborhood for days. The most famous radical centre was Liberty Hall, Justus Schwab's saloon at 51 East 1st Street, whose rear room was

a Mecca for French Communards, Spanish and Italian refugees, Russian politicals, and German socialists and anarchists who had escaped the iron heel of Bismarck. Everyone gathered at Justus's. [...] The circle was interspersed with many Americans, among them writers and artists. John Swinton, Ambrose Bierce, James Huneker, Sadakichi Hartmann, and other literati loved to listen to Justus's golden voice, drink his delicious beer and wine, and argue world problems far into the night [Goldman 1935, p.119].

Each ethnic community contributed in its own way to this atmosphere. The Russian immigrants and the East European Jews surely were the ones who expressed the higher potential for politics on the Lower East Side. As an oppressed people they had known persecution in the Old World and out of their ranks had come many militants of revolutionary organizations — the Narodnaya Volya, the Bund, the socialist and the anarchist groups —, all of which were revived in the New World under one aspect or another [Leviatin, ed., 1989]. In particular, Jews were able to clothe their politics in a language that could be easily grasped by the large masses. They recurred, for instance, to familiar religious concepts and bended them to the needs of the class struggle, as when strikers were invited to take the "old Jewish oath"; or Cahan wrote his socialist commentaries in the *Arbeiter Tseitung* in the form of the *sedra* (the

175

traditional weekly reading of the Bible) and signed them *"Der Proletarishker Maggid"* (a *maggid* being a traveling preacher); or *kosher*-meat boycotters interrupted the reading of the Torah[28].

For its part, the Italian Socialist Federation of the United States (born in 1902) endeavoured to overcome the difficult obstacle represented by the transient nature of Italian immigration, especially in the first two decades, and to provide a viable organizational structure and a necessary link with the larger American socialist movement. The problems it met before its disbanding in 1921 were many, and most of them also derived from the rather delicate situation in which the American labor and socialist movement found itself, on the theoretical and on the organizational level. But Little Italy continued to be a hotbed of radical politics. Antonio Giovannitti and Carlo Tresca were popular figures, *Il Proletario* was one of *the* Lower East Side newspapers together with the New York *Call* and the *Jewish Daily Forward*, the Paterson strike was a stirring event for the New York's community, and all this continued well into the 1920s and 1930s, when the neighborhood had to face the rise of Fascism [Cianfarra 1900; De Ciampis 1959; Seller 1975; Vezzosi 1984-85].

Isolated Chinatown also gave its contribution to the radical panorama, but this happened later on. In the late 1920s, the nationalist Kuomintang had a strong branch in New York, which was instrumental in bringing about some kind of politicization in the community, and it was out of this that a leftist group developed which was expelled from the KMT in 1927 and joined the U.S. Communist movement. In 1930, the Chinese Anti-Imperialist Alliance, with headquarters on Union Square, was formed and started organizing in Chinatown. During the Depression, which dramatically hit the community's small businesses with an official unemployment rate of 30%, the Unemployed Council and the Chinese Hand Laundry Alliance, soon claiming several hundred members, for the first time challenged Chinatown's traditional social structure. But the two levels, the labor and the political, always remained somewhat distant [Kwong 1979].

In a way, this was the problem for the Lower East Side at large. Such a high level of radicalization, in fact, was not matched by a corresponding level of political organization. The Socialists could probably boast the largest following. When it was born from the Workingmen's Party of America in 1877, the Socialist Labor Party of North America had a mostly German membership. In the 1890s, under the leadership of Daniel DeLeon, it made an effort to reach out to the larger ranks of recent immigrants and American workers hit by the decade's economic crisis. To the old *New Yorker Volks-Zeitung* and

Arbeiter Zeitung were now added new papers such as *The People* and then *The Jewish Daily Forward*, able to speak more incisively and convincingly to the working masses. After playing an important rôle in the ranks of the Knights of Labor, the Party failed to exert a decisive influence on the American Federation of Labor and thus founded its own Socialist Trade and Labor Alliance. While it entered the sterile road of dual unionism, nonetheless the Alliance was instrumental in the birth of such important unions as the United Hebrew Trades. DeLeon was the party's most magnetic personality and repeatedly ran for Congress from the Lower East Side (with votes growing from a meagre 10 percent to a stable 30). Out of the SLP, also came many of the future leaders of the socialist and labor movement of years to come, from Morris Hillquit to Abraham Cahan.

But by the turn of the century, on the Lower East Side as elsewhere, the SLP's influence was beginning to die off (a decisive factor probably being some kind of resistance to relate to struggles that went beyond the purely factory level). In those same years, the Socialist Party of America was born, which was soon able to gain a larger membership thanks to a rather eclectic and "progressive" platform. In the neighborhood, the SP could claim deeper class and ethnic roots, notwithstanding a moderate and even conservative leadership, especially on the issue of immigration. Towards the end of the new century's first decade, the party on the Lower East Side made a greater effort to reach out to the recent immigrants, and soon the garment workers made up its backbone. The breadth of its programme also appealed to a radical *intelligentsia* that often sought and found a source of inspiration in the Lower East Side. On the other hand, this very breadth was the party's main weakness. Its members joined and often led numerous labor and social struggles in the quarter and showed a great capacity for mass work and street mobilization, and from all this the party gathered strength and thrust (running from the neighborhood in 1914, Meyer London was the first Socialist to be elected to Congress). But at the same time the party was unable to offer the masses of the Lower East Side a credible outlet other than that of the ballot box [Leinenweber 1977 and 1981; Perrier 1981].

The anarchist scene was possibly the most complex one, various groups and newspapers contending a dwindling but constant membership. The Pioneers of Liberty had began their activity in the Lower East Side by desecrating Yom Kippur and other Jewish festivities. The group Autonomie was among the most active ones. So were the groups formed around Johann Most's *Freiheit* and David Edelstadt's *Freie Arbeiter Shtimme*. In the 1910s, Emma Goldman and Alexander Berkman — long-time activists and residents in the area — founded *Mother Earth*, another important organ of political as well as cultural anarchism. On the whole, the movement often presented itself in a rather fragmented way, internecine rivalries creating splits and dissident groups, while strong personalities like Most, Goldman, Berkman did their best to gain following among the masses [Ganz 1919; Goldman 1935; R. Sanders 1969]. When the Industrial Workers of the World were born in 1905, they added to the anarchist and syndicalist scene, even if their presence on the East Coast (apart from the big episodes of Lawrence and Paterson) always was rather weak.

***

The creativity with which, at all levels, the Lower East Side reacted to an adverse reality in order to survive (and in so doing at least partially managed to reverse it) thus expressed itself in the field of class struggles as well. A widespread militancy, coupled with a high degree of spontaneity and fed by immigrants from all backgrounds and experience (and often from sectors which age and gender traditionally kept away from such a field), came to characterize the neighborhood from the very beginnings of its history, and remained one of its distinctive features also in years to come. At the same time, however, such an almost instinctive radicalism rarely succeeded in translating itself on a political level, and the outcome was a tragic dispersal of creative energies. Wrote Trotzky: "Without a guiding organization the energy of the masses would dissipate like steam not enclosed in a piston-box. But nevertheless what moves things is not the piston or the box, but the steam" [Trotzky 1930, 1980, p.xix]. And in a way, the Lower East Side's social and political experience (this never-ceasing production of steam, lacking a piston-box) made crystal clear the substance of a crucial problem, which was not limited to the Lower East Side.

Notes

1. "Here's how a tailor sews/ He sews like this!/ A tailor sews and sews and sews/ And he owns nothing, not even his bread!/ Once upon a time I could not believe/ that we should work from eight to eight!/ But now with the strikes/ we have no more to work from eight to eight!" (from *Yiddish Folk Song Sung by Ruth Rubin* [Folkways Records, 1978]).

2. On the national level, clothing establishments almost doubled between 1860 and 1870, invested capital increasing by 83.9 percent [Seidman 1942, p.20-21; Greenfield 1947-48, p.182; Wilentz 1984]. Men's clothing was the first branch to develop. In its early phase (1830-1880), skilled Germans introduced important

technical innovations and a veritable division of labor, leading to those strictly interrelated features which were to become characteristic of the industry — sweatshops, contracting, home work, child labor. The "sweating system", analyzed in those same years by Karl Marx in England, meant put-out work done in small, poorly equipped shops, with few overhead expenses and a high rate of exploitation (low wages, long hours, great productivity), and a complex chain joining the main entrepreneur to the mass of workers through the links of the contractors. The introduction of the sewing machine and the growing division of labor made it possible to distribute work *outside* the main factory, to a large number of unskilled operators. At least initially, contractors were often laborers who could afford to buy a sewing machine and to whom other workers applied to have their stitches done, or former workers displaced by the sewing machine's competition, who found it easy to turn middlemen since a capital of only $50 was needed to set up a loft with a few foot-power machines. In time, their rôle became essential. They picked up orders and were responsible for final results. Often resorting to sub-contracting, they hired "hands" where they liked, placed them in lofts and garrets, paid them out of their own pockets, and dismissed them whenever the period was "slack". In immigrant neighborhoods, they became central figures: 'The man best fitted to be a contractor is the man who is well acquainted with his neighbors, who is able to speak the language of several classes of immigrants, who can easily persuade his neighbors or their wives and children to work for him, and who in this way can obtain the cheapest help. [...] The contractor is an important factor in the clannishness of the immigrant nationalities. It is to him due in part that we have in large cities the Jewish districts, Polish districts, Swedish districts, etc., with very little assimilation. The contractors establish their shops in the heart of the district where the people live, and since they can practically earn their living at home, they have no opportunity of mingling with others or of learning from the civilization of other people' [Commons, in United States Industrial Commission 1901, pp.320-321]. Contractors were also responsible for the spreading of home work and child labor, the last links in the chain and the worst ones — a veritable plague, not limited to the garment trade alone. At this stage of development — dominated by intense competition and by the demands of ruthless accumulation —, women and children were an ideal unskilled workforce. They could work longer hours at home for lower wages, escape inspections more easily, be withheld work at any time, and were not dangerously concentrated in a factory or a shop. Home work and child labor also answered other needs. Gender rôles, cultural prejudices, religious tenets had their say in the matter. If, generally speaking, Victorian America considered home the "woman's place", home work could become a "woman's work" *par excellence*. If, to speak more specifically, many immigrant cultures placed the woman in an even more subordinate position, home work could solve the problem of contributing to the family income without violating socio-cultural norms. And, if it was imperative to orthodox Jews to observe the Sabbath, home work allowed them to work on Sundays, when most factories closed.

3. Though largely defective due to the great dispersion and the amount of work done in tenements, figures clearly show the industry's growth in the turn-of-the-century years. For what concerns men's clothing, on the national level and between 1890 and 1900, the number of the larger shops increased from 20,113

to 29,470, and invested capital from $209,125,560 to $213,510,177. The smaller shops went from 13,591 to 22,134, with a slight fall in invested capital (from $54,109,273 to $52,167,653), probably due to the peculiar character of these enterprises, very precarious in their set-up and able to reduce to a minimum their overhead expenses. In the same period, as a consequence of the introduction of new machinery and the widespread use of the "outside" system, the number of workers in both the larger and the smaller shops decreased (from 269,255 and 71,179 to 259,751 and 69,149, respectively) and so did wages (from $102,985,835 and $36,245,655 to $100,540,110 and $33,596,967, respectively), while the value of production went from $441,532,354 and $126,219,151 to $508,181,398 and $137,714,282, respectively — i.e., productivity increased, working conditions worsened, living conditions became dramatic, and endemic the plagues of sweating, contracting, home work and child labor [Greenfield 1947-48, p.185, 186; Wilentz 1984]. Almost nonexistent before 1880, women's clothing had become the most important sector by 1900, under the pressure of such social changes as the birth of a mass market, the development of a consumer culture, the rise of the middle class, and the new rôle of the "woman as buyer" in the post-Civil War decades [Barth 1980; Trachtenberg 1982]. As a consequence, all figures in this trade, for the same 1890-1900 decade, show an increase — in number of shops (+120.7 percent), in capital (+127.8), in value of production (+133.8), and also (although at a reduced rate as compared to the other figures) in number of workers (+113.9) and wages (+111.2) [Greenfield 1947-48, p.188].

4. In the years that followed, the proportion of skilled Jews rose, because the industry had been developing in East Europe and news of the American situation had led many young men and women to pick up the trade before leaving for the *Goldeneh Medina* — a fact that in turn put many of them in the position of rising quickly to a higher status and soon becoming contractors or small entrepreneurs (the notorious "cockroach pharaohs"): 'The old cloak-manufacturers, the German Jews, were merely merchants. Our people, on the other hand, were mostly tailors or cloak operators who had learned the mechanical part of the industry, and they were introducing a thousand innovations into it, perfecting, revolutionizing it. We brought to our work a knowledge, a taste, and an ardor which the men of the old firms did not possess...' [Cahan 1917, p.374; also see Cahan July 1901].

5. A good example is Francis S. Smith's novel, "Bertha, the Sewing Machine Girl, or Death at the Wheel", serialized by the *New-York Weekly* in 1871, and dramatized by Charles Foster the year after [A. Siegel 1981].

6. In 1891, the weekly wage of a cutter was $3.33 (four years later, it was still the same), that of a coat-maker $2.33 ($2.50), that of a presser $2.16 ($2.50), that of a baster $2.16 ($2.33), that of a bushelman $1.33 ($1.50), that of an operator $1.33 ($1.33) [New York Bureau 1896, p.738 ff]. In terms of economics, it must be considered that, by the turn of the century, six rolls of bread cost 5 cents, fish about 8 cents a pound, 15 potatoes 10 cents, three and a half pounds of oatmeal 10 cents, half a dozen eggs about 13 cents, half a pound of tea 18 cents, two pounds of chops or a steak about 20 cents; that, in 1900, the average annual income of a man was $591, of a woman $254; that, in 1902, a three-room apartment in an old-law tenement rented between $10 and $12 per month; and that, in 1907, the monthly disbursements for food were $20-22, for clothing $90, for fuel and light

180

$35 [Frowne 1902, 1971, pp.116-117; Greenfield 1947-48, p.187; Bernheimer Jan. 18, 1908, p.1403; Frankel 1907, p.1050; other family budgets, for the turn-of-the-century years, can be read in Cahan 1902, in Rischin, ed., 1985, pp.402-409, and in Ganz 1919, p.41].

7. 'I get up at half-past five o'clock every morning and make myself a cup of coffee on the oil stove. I eat a bit of bread and perhaps some fruit and then go to work. Often I get there soon after six o'clock so as to be in good time, tho the factory does not open till seven. I have heard that there is a sort of clock that calls you at the very time you want to get up, but I can't believe that because I don't see how the clock would know. At seven o'clock we all sit down to our machines and the boss brings to each one the pile of work that he or she is to finish during the day, what they call in English their "stint". This pile is put down beside the machine and as soon as a skirt is done it is laid on the other side of the machine. Sometimes the work is not all finished by six o'clock and then the one who is behind must work overtime. Sometimes one is finished ahead of time and gets away at four or five o'clock, but generally we are not done till six o'clock. The machines go like mad all day, because the faster you work the more money you get. Sometimes in my haste I get my finger caught and the needle goes right through it. It goes so quick, tho, that it does not hurt much. I bind the finger up with a piece of cotton and go on working. We all have accidents like that. Where the needle goes through the nail it makes a sore finger, or where it splinters a bone it does much harm. Sometimes a finger has to come off. Generally, tho, one can be cured by a salve. All the time we are working the boss walks about examining the finished garments and making us do them over again if they are not just right. So we have to be careful as well as swift. But I am getting so good at the work that within a year I will be making $7 a week, and then I can save $3.50 a week. I have over $200 saved now. The machines are all run by foot power, and at the end of the day one feels so weak that there is a great temptation to lie right down and sleep. But you must go out and get air, and have some pleasure...' [Frowne 1902, 1971, pp.117-118. At the time of writing, Miss Frowne was sixteen. For other evidences of working conditions, see Lemlich 1909, 1977, p.66].

8. The possibilities of control on home work and child labor were even scarcer than with sweating and contracting. Preoccupations for the public health, however, led to inquiries and surveys, and this allowed for a better knowledge of the ways and conditions in which work was done in the tenements. After the 1892 Tenement House Commission made public its appalling reports, the demand for a safeguard of both workers and consumers became very strong, and a series of laws were passed by the New York State legislature in 1892, 1899, 1908. They made it mandatory that a permit or license be granted in order for work to be done in private houses, and listed a certain number of products whose manufacturing was forbidden in tenement apartments. Section 100 of the labor laws thus prohibited, except when licensed, the use of a room or apartment for "manufacturing, altering, repairing or finishing" some thirty different articles, from coats to vests, from caps to blouses, from underwear to skirts and furs, from umbrellas to artificial flowers, from paper boxes to cigars and cigarettes, and "for the purpose of manufacturing, preparing or packing macaroni, spaghetti, ice cream, ices, candy, confectionery, nuts and preserves". But it left out a much longer list of activities commonly done in

181

tenement rooms and apartments, such as finishing gloves, making baby bonnets, pasting labels on cigars and boxes, embroidering pillow tops, sorting and sewing buttons on cards, making kimonos, setting stones in celluloid combs, making passementerie — all activities thus to be considered perfectly legal. Besides, given the small number of city inspectors and the strategies used by homeworkers in order to avoid inspections, the factual possibilities of enforcing such legislation were really limited. If it was difficult to control home work, it was even more difficult to control child labor. The child labor law in fact prevented employment of any child under 14 in factories, restaurants, mercantile establishments, places of business. But no provision dealt with homeworking children. The only law that could in some way safeguard them was the compulsory education law, which however had jurisdiction over the children's school day only. If a child, after his/her school day, worked at home till late in the evening, nothing could be done. Progressive legislation thus did not eradicate home work and child labor. Its provisions were too vague and ineffectual, and too difficult to enforce. Above all, home work and child labor were too important for the development of the turn-of-the-century city economy, and getting rid of them would have meant for entrepreneurs and manufacturers serious losses in a stage of desperate accumulation. Laws thus simply tried to regulate these sectors, and in so doing they helped to bring about the shift from the "outside system" to the "factory system". The change did not however significantly better working conditions. As a 1911 survey made clear, factories kept resembling the old sweatshops. Most of them were ill-lighted and ill-ventilated death-traps, with appalling sanitary conditions and mostly lacking safety provisions [Poole 1903; Stella 1904; Van Kleeck 1908; Watson 1911; Price 1911; Schereschewsky 1915].

9. '"What we wanted was $1 per machine", said Harry. "While the operators are workin' on them jackets we must keep turnin' the sleeves and the flaps and the collars, and sometimes three or four operators commence to holler at us, so that we get mixed up and nearly go crazy tryin' to attend to them all. But the boss, he don' care; he pays us the same. That won't go. We want a dollar for each machine and no more 'n nine hours a day. It's enough, ain't it? [...] The only way to get the bosses to pay us good wages is to stick together, so let us be true to our union"' [quoted in Cahan Aug. 13, 1898, 1985].

10. The years between 1905 and 1909 witnessed other important episodes, among which a 13-week capmakers' strike for union recognition and closed shop led by Rose Schneiderman, a 20-year-old girl soon to become one of the most popular organizers on the Lower East Side; a strike against waist contractor Izzi Lock of 150 girls between 14 and 17, who demanded a 10-hour workday and recognition of the Ladies Waistmakers' Union; and the "battle of 1907", a bitter and victorious 11-week strike for a union shop by the reefermakers, who had to defend their pickets from thugs hired by the manufacturers [Schneiderman 1905, 1971, pp.24-27; L. Stein, ed., 1977, p.51-54; Hourwich 1912, 1969].

11. The Cooper Union meeting was the strike's turning point. The hall was so packed that many hundred workers had to be accomodated in other four nearby halls. Speech after speech, WTUL, AFL, SPA, ILGWU leaders and officials voiced the shirtwaist makers' grievances, but still no decision was being taken. Then, shortly after Samuel Gompers's speech, a young girl of 16, Clara Lemlich, one of the most active strikers at Leiserson's, climbed up the platform, and very simply

182

said: "I have listened to all the speakers and have no more patience for talk, as I am one of those who feel and suffer from the things described. What we are here for is to decide whether we shall or shall not strike. I offer a motion that a general strike be declared — now!". The hall was immediately on its feet, cheering and waving hats and handkerchiefs. Amid the general tumult, the motion was seconded, thousands of hands were raised, and the old Jewish oath was taken — "If I turn traitor to the cause I now pledge, may this hand wither from the arm I now raise". A committee of 15 girls and one boy was sent to the other four halls, and everywhere the motion was endorsed [Lorwin 1924, p.154; see also *The New York Call*, Nov. 23, 1909; *The New York World*, Nov. 23, 1909; Stein, ed., 1977].

12. "[It's] a good thing, this strike is; it makes you feel like a real grown-up person [...]. Upon my word, we ought to be glad that we went out on strike — it teaches us self-respect. [...] Growth — whatever else we'll gain from this strike it certainly was an eye-opener to some of us..." [Malkiel 1910, pp.5, 9, 5. The book is a vivid and reliable fictionalization of the 1909 events, written by an active participant and detailing an American working girl's development into a class and gender conscious militant. Another fictionalization of the strike is in "Albert Edwards" (pseud. Arthur Bullard)'s *Comrade Yetta* (1913)].

13. On December 3, led by Rena Borky, Yeta Roff, and Mary Effers, 10,000 marched to City Hall to present the Mayor a written protest against police brutality and the courts' severe sentences. Public opinion was often roused at the judges' behavior. Asked by the WTUL to comment on the remarks made by Judge Olmstead while sentencing a young picket ("You are on strike against God and Nature, whose firm law is that man shall earn his bread in the sweat of his brow. You are on strike against God"), British playwright George Bernard Shaw telegraphed: "Delightful. Medieval America always in the intimate personal confidence of the Almighty". Notwithstanding public opinion, courts kept sending young strikers to Blackwell Island. On the same December 3 night, Socialist organizers Rose Pastor Stokes and Theresa Malkiel and WTUL members Leonora O'Reilly, Pauline Newman, Rose Schneiderman, and Meta Stern spoke at a packed Liptzin Theatre. On December 5, a mass meeting sponsored by the Political Equality Association was held at the Hippodrome Hall, while a solidarity meeting took place at Newark, N.J., with ILGWU speakers S. A. Stodel, Max Danish, and Publio Mazella. On December 9, beloved "Mother" Mary Jones appeared at the Thalia Theatre, to incite to action and express the Western miners' solidarity [*New York Call*, December 10, 1909; P. Foner, ed., 1983]. On December 13, thousands packed the Grand Central Palace to hear reports from the arbitration conference which had met for the first time three days before. Rose Schneiderman for the WTUL, Morris Hillquit for the Socialists and the ILGWU, John Mitchell for the AFL were among the speakers. On December 16, Rose Schneiderman and other girls met the rich women of the exclusive Colony Club, who donated $1,300 — what would increasingly become a key strategy in Lower East Side labor disputes. On December 19, the Socialists appointed a special committee of 12 women to support the strike. On December 21, an automobile parade with placards drove from picket-line to picket-line to encourage strikers and inform public opinion. On December 22, a party and reception, with music, dances, speeches, and medals for the girls who had been arrested and sent to the workhouse, was given at the Arlington Hall on St.Mark's

Place. On December 29 and 30, the Socialist *New York Call* donated a special edition detailing the shirtwaisters' struggle, to be sold in the streets by the girl strikers themselves as a way to raise funds. On January 2, 1910, a new demonstration was held at Carnegie Hall to protest arrests and imprisonments, and Morris Hillquit, Leonora O'Reilly of the WTUL, and teen-ager striker Rose Perr spoke to a packed audience. Between January 12 and January 15, solidarity meetings took place in Buffalo, Boston, and even at Vassar College in Poughkeepsie.

14. The tragedy was only the most shocking of a long list. On March 25, 1911, a fire broke out on the eighth floor of the building at the corner of Washington Place and Greene Street, and soon spread to the two top stories. Not only the one fire-escape was utterly inadequate, but the doors had been locked in order to prevent workers from leaving and walking delegates from entering. It was a real carnage. 146 workers, mostly Jewish and Italian girls from the Lower East Side, burned to death, were smothered by smoke, or died jumping from the windows and smashing on the streets below. On April 5, in a long funeral procession attended by some 50,000 people, the Lower East Side mourned its dead. On December 27, 1911, the two owners of the Triangle Waist Co. were acquitted after trial by jury ["The Triangle Fire" 1911, 1967, pp.171-172; Shepherd 1911, 1977, pp.188-193; the two addresses by Rabbi Stephen S. Wise and Rose Schneiderman at the memorial meeting held at the Metropolitan Opera House on April 2, 1911, in L. Stein, ed., pp.195-197; "Silent Parade" 1911; L. Stein 1962].

15. For a fictional treatment of working conditions in the trade, see Abraham Cahan's "A Sweatshop Romance" [Cahan 1898, 1970].

16. Food shops were also of primary importance in the community. In 1899, the Tenth Ward alone counted 140 groceries and 3 grocery stands, 131 butcher shops, 10 sausage stores, 2 meat markets, 36 bakeries, 9 bread stands, 2 *matzo* (unleavened bread) stores, 14 butter and egg stores, 62 candy stores, 24 candy stands, 1 cheese store, 7 coffee shops, 5 tea shops, 10 delicatessen, 9 fish stores, 7 herring stands, 7 fruit stores, 21 fruit stands, 16 milk stores, 20 soda water stands, 11 vegetable stores, 13 wine shops, 15 grape wine shops, and 10 confectioners [Rischin 1962, 1977, p.56]. While most of these were family businesses, bakeries were not infrequently large enterprises with numerous workers (Goodman and Son had 114 employees, Gottfried and Steckler 102, the medium-size bakeries between 20 and 30). The rate of exploitation was high, and hygienic conditions were often awful, especially in the smaller bakeries. Not surprisingly, bakers were among the most militant food workers. They often struck demanding shorter hours, higher wages, better and cleaner working conditions, easily supported by the whole community [Cahan Jan. 12, 1901, 1985; Sumner 1910; Rischin 1962, 1977, p.57].

17. By 1890, in the Jewish Quarter, there were some 900 painters and carpenters, 400 tinkers and plumbers, 150 printers, and some 100 coppersmiths working in basement shops along Allen Street. By 1900, peddlers were some 25,000, the majority of them Jewish, with Italians, Greeks, and Chinese as well. Most of the food shops quoted above were also Jewish.

18. Many were however the instances in which, as soon as they realized what they were being used for, scabbing immigrants spontaneously left work. This was the case of the 1882 longshoremen's strike, when attempts were made to replace German and Irish strikers with newly-arrived Jewish immigrants. As soon as the real

situation was explained to them, these "greenhorns" immediately refused to scab and, with the help of German Socialists active in the strike, formed a Propaganda Society for the Dissemination of Socialist Ideas among Immigrant Jews [Chametzky 1977, p.7].

19. 'God didn't listen to women. Heaven and the next world were only for men. Women could get into Heaven because they were wives and daughters of men. Women had no brains for the study of God's Torah, but they could be the servants of men who studied the Torah. Only if they cooked for the men, and washed for the men, and didn't nag or curse the men out of their homes; only if they let the men study the Torah in peace, then, maybe, they could push themselves into Heaven with the men, to wait on them there' [Yezierska 1925, 1975, p.9-10; Kessler Harris 1975].

20. When, in order to break the strike, attempts were made to enlist Bowery bums as scabs by offering them $2 a day plus commission, the proposal was turned down: "I'm a Bowery bum [...] and one of about a hundred that's signed to take out *Worlds* and *Journals* to-morrow. But say, we ain't a-going to do it. It's all a bluff. We told them scouts that we'd do it when they offered $2 a day, but everyone of us has decided to stick by the boys and we won't sell no papers" [*New York Sun*, July 23, 1899, quoted in Nasaw 1985, p.174].

21. From the very beginning, women involved in the boycott resorted to the terms of "strikers" and "scabs", a clear sign of a widespread use of labour terminology.

22. An interesting fictional treatment is in Anzia Yezierska's short-story "The Lost 'Beautifulness'" [Yezierska 1920, 1987].

23. These direct action episodes also made apparent the cleavage that was opening between the rank and file and the Socialist Party. The *New York Call*, a Socialist daily, was very critical of them, and went so far as to approve of Tannembaum's arrest during a jobless' demonstration [Goldman 1935, pp.523-525].

24. Remarked a Broome Street mother: 'I have estimated that I have $4 a week upon which to feed and clothe myself and my children. It is hard work, but the greatest fear I have is that my children will not have sufficient nourishment [...]. Fish is a luxury with us, and I have not had meat for so long that I have forgotten when. I can recall, however, that the Sisters gave us a chicken for Christmas. If you have ever been very poor you will know what it meant to us. We even hated to see the bones go after they had furnished substance to the soup. For breakfast we have bread and coffee. For the coffee I pay 19 cents a pound. We cannot save for clothing. This dress I have worn for five years, and the shoes were made for a man, but I picked them up at a bargain' [quoted in *The New York Times* (February 25, 1917), p.5]. An Irish neighbor echoed her with the following written statement: 'Meat we cannot buy. Cheakean [sic] we cannot buy. Eggs we cannot buy. Poteos [sic] we cannot buy. Onions we cannot buy. Butter we cannot buy. Vagitables [sic] we cannot buy. [...My] husband and my children are eating mainly oatmeal and rice; and I know that if I don't feed the children, I won't get anything off of 'em when I'm old, because they will be all skin and bones' [quoted by Lasker 1917, p.640].

25. 'Where milk is being given to babies it is being diluted until it is little better than water. The people are buying "loose" milk — the cheapest that can be bought — usually one or two cents worth at a time. Tea they have found to be cheaper

because a small quantity will last a week. Water is added to the same tea leaves day by day, until the elements of tea have been entirely blotted out' [Deputy Charities Commissioner, quoted in *The New York Call* (February 23, 1917), p.1]. Also see Lasker 1917 and Freiburger 1984, on which I largely depended for the details of the events.

26. On January 27, 1933, a veritable battle took place on "Paradise Alley", an artist colony at Avenue A and East 11th Street, where a rent strike was going on. Police reserves had to be called to fight some 500 jobless men and women, resisting the eviction of seven members of the colony. In the following years, the Lower East Side Public Housing Conference and the Knickerbocker Village Tenants Association led several important actions and strikes, and in 1935 formed the City-Wide Housing Conference, a short-lived umbrella organization. The year after, the experiment was repeated with greater success, and gave birth to the City-Wide Tenants League, in which the neighborhood was represented by the Lower East Side Tenants Union [Lawson, in Lawson 1986, p.16; Naison, in Lawson 1986, pp.94-133; Boyer and Morais 1955, Chapter 9]. Meanwhile, the neighborhood's face was changing, what with the exodus of several thousand inhabitants moving uptown, the Bronx and Brooklyn (the so-called "exit option"), and with the first public houses built as part of the New Deal reform program, such as the First Houses, the Vladek Houses, etc.

27. In several occasions, Engels lamented the German-American Socialists' obstinacy in using their language only, both in speeches and in print. See especially the Preface to the American edition of *Condition of the Working Class in England in 1844* (1887).

28. An interesting fictional example of the use of religious texts and concepts for unionization purposes is in Asch 1918, 1938.

CHAPTER FOUR: ACCENTS OF THE FUTURE

You know, dear Mr.Howells, that our readers want to have a novel about richly-dressed cavaliers and women, about women, about love which begins in the fields while they're playing golf. How can a novel about a Jewish immigrant, a blacksmith who became a tailor here, and whose wife is ignorant, interest them?

Anonymous editor (1896)

I.

By the turn of the century, many factors contributed to make the Lower East Side an articulate neighborhood. Its closely-knit social texture, the variety of cultural influences, the daily struggle for survival, the many-fold stories of success and failure, the lingering, vivid memories of the Old World, the complex experience of coming to terms with America — all this required, stimulated, and molded specific verbal and literary expressions that were due to have consequences of the utmost importance. The quarter's cultural density thus expressed itself in words written and printed, uttered and sung — words which, borrowed or lent, invented or distorted, could easily criss-cross ethnic and geographic boundaries. Street gossiping and shop talk, strike meetings and church, temple, synagogue ceremonies, newspaper reading and theatre attending, Old World traditional songs and new American popular songs helped to weave a thick linguistic net, from which more complete and consistent literary forms would, in time, inevitably evolve.

It was primarily on this level that the laboratory-like character of the Lower East Side stood out. Such a character was founded upon a fervid internal dynamics and a continuous dialectics between inside and outside, and was the most effective denial of a *purely* assimilationist view of the relationship between immigrant and American (mainstream or mass) culture. As W. D. Howells and Henry James noted (the former with warm curiosity, the latter with bitter annoyance), 'a New York jargon [was being born in its streets, theatres, and meeting places,] which shall be to English what the native Yiddish of [Cahan's] characters is to Hebrew, and it will be interlarded with Russian, Polish and German words, as their present jargon is with English vocables and with American slang' [Howells, quoted in Chametzky 1977, p.71]: a language resulting from a continuous tension between past and present, and already evolving into an 'accent of the very ultimate future' [James 1907, 1987, p.99].

In this regard, the rôle of newspapers was decisive. Such Yiddish ones as the *Arbeiter Zeitung* and the *Forward* literally bred a generation of writers and poets and were thus instrumental in the process of cross-cultural, multi-ethnic circulation and dissemination. Not only did they familiarize their readers to the American language by frequently recurring to it and thus creating a kind of ever-evolving *lingua franca*. They often took side in favour of certain aspects of the American way of life, which tended to be dismissed or attacked by conservative or orthodox leaders worried about the possible loss of socio-cultural roots. By so doing, they expanded the tension between those two contending fields of forces ("descent" and "consent") from the purely linguistic terrain to a wider, socio-cultural one. This taking side never was, in fact, a supine acceptance of ruling, mainstream values. It was always a deeply dialectical process, tending, in due course, to reshape both sides. Such columns as, in the *Arbeiter Zeitung*, the "*Proletarisker Magid*" or "*Fun a Vort a Kvort*" ("From a Word a Quart", signed "The Hester Street Reporter" and recounting everyday accidents of common people's lives), or, in the *Forward*, the *Bintel Brief*, thus encouraged people to read and to write, by resorting to (and updating and transforming) familiar patterns and traditional schemata. Without doubt, this was especially true of the Jewish press (Yiddish historically being a kind of cultural sponge, used to attract and recycle elements from the languages with which it was forcedly brought into contact). But something similar took place in the press of other communities as well, in the pages of *Il Proletario* or of *The Chinese American*. Language (both the written one of the newspapers and the spoken one of the streets and daily occupations) also came to mark the emergence of a widening "generation gap" between the older generations (or the very recent "greenhorns") and the American-born "hyphenated". The former used to speak the mother tongue, while the latter spoke, if not the neat "school American", at least some kind of modified "American street jargon". And this contributed to the formation of a thick, cultural texture, so favorable to the development of literary forms.

II.

The degree of articulateness clearly varied according to each ethnic group. In Chinatown, the sense of being socially under siege and the daily imperatives of survival led the "bachelor society" to an almost

188

complete withdrawal within itself. As a consequence, the cultural exchange between the community and the external world was rather limited, and this severely hindered the development of an indigenous intelligentsia capable of speaking beyond its pale. The only places in Chinatown where a certain degree of osmosis occurred were those dives, theatres, and restaurants in which new forms of popular entertainment were being born. But the fact that for a long time to come those places met with sharp cultural and social disapproval had the effect of reinforcing isolation and defensiveness[1].

The situation in Little Italy was slightly different. Here, too, some kind of cultural withdrawal manifested itself, but rather as the result of different factors. As we have seen, the great bulk of Italian immigration came from rural, backward regions with high illiteracy rates and a tradition of oral communication. Once in America, the "bird-of-passage" character of this immigration and the great geographical mobility kept most of these immigrants, at least initially, from rooting themselves in America and there establishing a cultural tradition of their own. A gap also developed between them and the earlier, more advanced, Italian settlements, which looked down upon these new arrivals with a fastidiousness similar to that manifested by the German Jews towards their East European coreligionists. In the turn-of-the-century years, while oral tradition was kept alive by such figures as Farfariello or more generally by the various forms of popular theatre which employed a high level of linguistic and cultural *contaminatio*, most of Little Italy's reading and writing was done in the mother tongue, which led to the same problem of withdrawal that so conditioned, within the Jewish community, those writers who resorted to Yiddish. But, whereas in the case of Yiddish authors the use of an ethnic language was part of a larger, international movement of cultural reaffirmation (and also helped to give birth to an "indigenous" intelligentsia, capable of responding to the hostility shown by the German Jews), in the case of the Italian *colonia* it was rather the expression of a still imperfect and defensive relationship with America.

That is not to say that promising Italian authors, writing in English, did not exist along "Boulevard des Italiens". One of them was Arturo Giovannitti, the passionate IWW member imprisoned at the time of the 1912 Lawrence strike. A leading spirit both of the lively socialist journal *Il Proletario* and of the political and literary magazine *Il Fuoco*, and a contributor to *The Masses* and *The Liberator*, Giovannitti wrote often turgid poetry with clear Whitmanesque echoes ('I will sing of your slums where you bleed,/ Your machines, iron claws of your greed,/ And your jails, viscid coils of your mind...') ["New York and

I", in N. Thomas, ed., 1975, p.8], and was a popular figure on the Lower East Side. But the urgencies of militancy always led him well beyond its borders and his literary relationship with it was tenuous. The same can be said, although for different reasons, for the even more promising poet, Emanuel Carnevali, whose literary interests gravitated towards the modernist circles of Ezra Pound, William Carlos Williams, Harriet Monroe, Kay Boyle and Robert McAlmon. Carnevali's promises were dramatically undercut in 1922, when he was struck down by sleeping sickness and had to return to Italy, where he died in 1942. Both culturally and geographically, his links with the Lower East Side were marginal, but his autobiography contains several vivid references to the teeming atmospheres of Little Italy, the Jewish quarter and the Bowery[2].

Giovannitti and Carnevali remained *rarae aves*, and in turn-of-the-century Little Italy no author emerged, sufficiently endowed with the capacity to address himself to a public larger than the one who lived along and around Mulberry Bend, and thus to start a "hyphenated" tradition upon which to build an osmotic relationship with and a specific contribution to American literature[3]. For this, the *colonia* would have to wait till the 1930s, when such writers appeared as Pietro Di Donato, John Fante and Garibaldi Lapolla. By then, however, the community's axis had moved to Brooklyn and Harlem, and in such new realities would those writers be rooted. Still, the name of journalist and novelist Bernardino Ciambelli cannot be quickly dismissed, notwithstanding his many limitations and the fact that he too wrote in Italian. His novels (*I misteri di Mulberry Street*, 1893; *I misteri della polizia*, 1895; *I misteri di Bleecker Street*, 1899; *I sotterranei di New York*, 1915; and many others) made use of all the typical tricks of *Trivialliteratur*, *feuilletons* in particular: serialization, length, formulaic characters and situations (the innocent young woman kidnapped by the villain, the sincere lover unjustly jailed, the "dark woman" as the quintessence of sensuality and wickedness, the avenging detective as the final "equalizer", the chorus of good and bad characters, the twins ignorant of each other, the pursuit in the city's bowels, the final agnition, the escape of the criminal leaving the door open for a sequel) [Bernabei 1986; R. B. Green 1974; Tamburri, Giordano, Gardaphé, eds., 1991].

Ciambelli clearly worked in the tradition of Eugene Sue and, perhaps even more, of his American counterparts George Lippard (*The Quaker City; or, the Monks of Monk Hall*, 1844) and E.Z.C. Judson (*The Mysteries and Miseries of New York*, 1848). He insisted on that multiplication of melodramatic elements that was so characteristic of much *fin-de-siècle* culture: diffuse patheticism, standardization of characters, ethnic stereotyping, open eroticism[4]. From this point of view, Ciambelli's realism betrays many weaknesses. Nonetheless, it existed, and his *feuilletons* can even be read as chronicles of Little Italy that resorted to the formulae of popular literature, not only because they were the more directly recognizable and widely known among his readers (as is shown by the fact that the Italian masters of the genre, from Francesco Mastriani to Carolina Invernizio, were on the list of all the Italian publishers in New York), but also because they contained that element of reassurance that, at the time, was both culturally and socially necessary to the *colonia*. In order to achieve and convey that reassurance, Ciambelli used familiar situations and settings (the inauguration of the Colombo monument in *Mulberry*, the building of the first subterranean railways in *Mulberry* and *Sotterranei*, the war against Spain and the news of the 1898 Milan uprising in *Bleecker*). He had real-life characters (Theodore Roosevelt, Joe Petrosino, Mayor Grant) freely mix and interact with fictional ones. He gave detailed portraits of cafés, restaurants, banks, and dives, and lengthy descriptions of feasts, funerals, and religious processions. He repeatedly made use of "Italglish" expressions and often referred to different regional dialects and dishes. In this way, not only did he confer credibility to his melodramatic stories, but also offered his readers powerful instruments to find themselves in them.

To the same strategy pertained the recurring (and often fastidious, in a writer who elsewhere shows unusual open-mindedness in attacking death-penalty and defending divorce) use of racial stereotypes to delimit the *colonia*'s "ethnic space" (Franca Bernabei). Drawing from the *feuilleton* repertory (the Apaches of the Paris bowels) but adding clear American overtones, he painted negative pictures of Irish, Chinese and Jewish immigrants, the variegated world encircling Little Italy. At the same time, he placed the adventures of his criminals and innocents in a slightly past time, taking pains to remind his readers that many of the infamous dens in which his wicked ones lived and acted had been by then razed. Lastly, he almost invariably concluded his *feuilletons* with rituals during which the Italian heroes are finally "welcomed" by mainstream America — marriages and parties, to which city authorities are present to show their admiration for (and physical contiguity to) Little Italy. Not yet in terms of economic success, perhaps, but surely in terms of socio-cultural acceptance — so Ciambelli seems to say —, the "American dream" is possible for Italian immigrants. And in a way, from the point of view of their strategies of reassurance and search for identity, Ciambelli's works, although in Italian, although naive and

191

often badly written, can really be taken as the first step *towards* Italian-American fiction.

III.

By far the most articulate group was the one that came from Eastern Europe and, within it, the Jewish one. There were many reasons for this. The Word and the Book were familiar elements in Jewish everyday life, more than they were for other immigrants — the traditions of *midrash* (the rabbinical notes and commentaries to the Scriptures) and of *pilpul* (the quick, cutting argumentation on the sacred texts) involving, at least among males, a high degree of articulateness[5]. In addition to this, revolutionary activity under the Tsarist regime had brought about the diffusion of a knowledge that went beyond the pale of the Biblical one. Besides, at that time, the *Haskala* had broadened the Jewish cultural horizon, *Yiddishkeit* already being a reality in the Old World soon to be revived in the New as well.

The Lower East Side's most important literary experience was thus the birth of Jewish-American fiction. In 1896, on W. D. Howells's advice, D. Appleton and Co. published *Yekl. A Tale of the New York Ghetto*, a short novel by Abraham Cahan, a Lithuanian Jew born in 1860 and emigrated to the United States in 1882. Previously rejected by several publishing houses, it was *precisely* a novel about 'a Jewish immigrant, a blacksmith who became a tailor here, and whose wife is ignorant' — but it *did* interest the American audience. Two years later, Cahan followed it up with *The Imported Bridegroom, and Other Stories of the New York Ghetto*, which contained the unpublished title novella and four pieces already appeared in *Short Stories, Cosmopolitan, Atlantic*. Finally, in 1917, Cahan published his last and most accomplished work, the novel *The Rise of David Levinsky*. In the meantime, he contributed novels, stories and articles, both in English and in Yiddish, to several newspapers and magazine, and was the editor of the *Arbeiter Zeitung*, of the *Tsukunft*, and of the *Jewish Daily Forward* (which he helped to found in 1897). A major figure in the Lower East Side scene, deeply involved in union work and socialist agitation, Cahan wrote and argued about American society and Yiddish culture, was a "guide" to Howells and Hapgood in their literary explorations of the neighborhood, spent four years on the staff of the *Commercial Advertiser* edited by Lincoln Steffens, and from 1903 to the day of his death was the real soul of the *Jewish Daily Forward*. An outspoken advocate of Yiddish as a literary, theatrical, and political language, at the same time he fully understood the inevitable necessity, for *all* immigrants, to come to terms with the American reality, with its language, culture, and way of life, and to do this *without* losing touch with one's own identity. And his writing, structured upon a recurring pattern of growing disillusionment, revolves precisely around this basic and dramatic dilemma[6].

In *Yekl*, the title character, better known to his mates as Jake and well on his way to Americanization, sends for his wife and child. But their coming to New York brings about a radical change in his habits of fake 'tzingle man' and results in bitterness and divorce. The last chapter portrays Jake, bound for City Hall to marry his *Amerikanerin* Mamie, as 'a defeated victor' [Cahan 1896, 1970, p.87]. In *The Imported Bridegroom*, old Asriel Stroon, during a visit to his native village, buys a husband for his daughter Flora in the person of Shaya, an *illui* or 'prodigy of Talmudic learning' [Cahan 1898, 1970, p.112]. But, once in New York, Shaya disappoints both father and daughter: the first, by turning into an *appikoros* (atheist), the second, by not becoming the refined doctor she used to fancy as a husband. Present in most short stories as well, the pattern climaxes in *The Rise of David Levinsky*. A story of material success and emotional failure, it follows David's rise from a frightened orphan boy in an Old-World *shtetl* to the top of the New-York garment industry. But the price David pays for this extraordinary career is one of devastating solitude and inner aridity: 'I am lonely. Amid the pandemonium of my six hundred sewing-machines and the jingle of gold which they pour into my lap I feel the deadly silence of solitude. [...] No, I am not happy' [Cahan 1917, 1960, p.526]. Over and over, when they are not crushed by the hoaxes of destiny, Cahan's characters experience a cultural as well as physical displacement. As 'defeated victors', they are, in Isaac B. Singer's words, 'lost in America' — a theme that will recur again and again in the Jewish-American fiction, and is perhaps best summarized by Levinsky himself: 'I cannot escape from my old self. My past and my present do not comport well' [Cahan 1917, 1960, p.530].

Were this the only register in Cahan's fiction, his writing would be desperately gloomy. On the contrary, a clearly discernible vein of humour runs through it, often turning into bitter irony and self-irony — the Yiddish capacity to laugh at tragedy itself. The eye with which Cahan looks at his "greenhorns" and "allrightniks" is a sympathetic one, and an affectionate warmth fills his portraits of the Lower East Side people, both Jewish and non-Jewish. The picture he thus conveys of the neighborhood is that of a teeming ant-heap where tiny individuals, for all their dejection, ignorance, meanness or narrowmindedness, heroically strive in the anguished effort to keep alive memories and traditions of old under the awesome spell of a new reality. By creating plausible characters and at the same time by painting a large, collective backdrop to their daily life, by detailing their path to disillusionment and at the same time by viewing their experiences with humour and irony, Cahan clearly followed in the wake of the Russian realists he loved so much (Chekhov, Gogol, Turgenev) and of such contemporary Yiddish authors as Mendele M. Sforim and Isaac L. Peretz. He also caught up with American letters' most recent tendencies: a local color attentive to the geographical, cultural, historical, linguistic, psychological regions; a realism that was drawing a new literary map; a naturalism that was giving voice to the country's forgotten people; and a city fiction that was exploring the new urban reality's literary possibilities. Placed as he was at the cross-roads of three different cultural traditions, to them Cahan added the immigrant experience's specific voice and thus authoritatively prepared a niche to be enlarged by subsequent Jewish-American writers.

More than that, he also began to disassemble the common Horatio-Alger mechanism (that "rags-to-riches" pattern which seemed to rule contemporary American culture and imaginary), and, by creating a peculiar, *negative*, form of American *Bildungsroman*, he helped to open the path that would lead to Theodore Dreiser's *Sister Carrie, The Titan, An American Tragedy*, to Sherwood Anderson's *Poor White*, to Francis S. Fitzgerald's *The Great Gatsby* and *The Last Tycoon*, to Nathanael West's *A Cool Million* — all bitter, disillusioned explorations of the success theme [Lhamon 1976; Maffi 1982-83][7]. And he started an important critical reflection on the real meaning of "Americanization". In *Yekl*, Jake concludes a heated discussion on the American way of boxing, by saying: '"Do you mean to tell me that a moujik understands how to *fight*? A disease he does! He only knows how to strike like a bear [...], *an' dot' sh ull*! What does he *care* where his paw will land, so he strikes. *But* here one must observe *rulesh*"' [Cahan 1896, 1970, pp.3-4][8]. In the same novel, the couples at Professor Peltner's dancing academy are shown while patiently and laboriously learning the new American dances; and, further on, Mrs. Kavarsky states: '"It can not be helped; when one lives in an *edzecate* country, one must live like *edzecate peoples*. As they play, so one dances, as the saying is"' [Cahan 1896, 1970, p.57]. It would thus seem that, to the author, "Americanization" is simply a matter of "observing *rulesh*". But Cahan is skillful in showing that there is more in it than the newcomers' simple obedience to codes and plain assimilation of a different way of life. The point is made even clearer in the articles he wrote for the *New York Commercial Advertiser*, in which the issue of Americanization is

194

transformed from a simple matter of *acculturation* and *adjustment to* another culture, to a more complex one of *confrontation, interaction,* and *dialectics between* host and guest culture [Chametzky 1977; Rischin, ed., 1985; Kramer 1985].

In order to do so, Cahan resorts to a kind of "didactic realism". With great precision, he recreates Lower East Side realities and atmospheres, describes traditional mores and orthodox ceremonies, gives graphic accounts of the developments in the garment industry and of the birth of immigrants' unions in New York. By speaking of things familiar, he clearly sets himself the task of reinforcing the immigrants' sense of identity in the loneliness of the urban wilderness, but also (and perhaps, even more) that of familiarizing the American audience with aspects of the immigrants' life that would otherwise remain unknown and, as such, possible sources of anxiety. This "didactic realism" (so different from Ciambelli's "melodramatic realism") is rendered even more effective by a distinctive use of language. In *Yekl*, the first novel written in English by a Jewish immigrant and the one where the linguistic texture is thicker, the characters are supposed to speak a Yiddish amply interspersed with mispronounced American words and sentences and, here and there, hints are given as to the varieties of Americanized Yiddish, or the different Polish or Lithuanian inflexions. From the very beginning, the Jewish-American novel inevitably deals with what initially appears to be the Babelish quality of the immigrant life. Writers following in Cahan's wake will, in one way or another, tackle the issue over and over again[9].

At the same time, however (and this was to have important consequences), Cahan's "didactic realism" is endowed with a peculiar element that enlivens and even transforms it — an oneiric dimension that often gives objects and situations an almost surreal meaning:

And as she thus sat brooding and listlessly surveying her new surroundings — the iron stove, the stationary washtubs, the window opening vertically, the fire escape, the yellowish broom with its painted handle — things which she had never dreamed of at her birthplace — these objects seemed to stare at her haughtily and inspired her with fright. Even the burnished cup of the electric bell knob looked contemptuously and seemed to call her "Greenhorn! greenhorn!" [Cahan 1896, 1970, pp.73-74].

In the same novel, Gitl's wig is charged with a sort of symbolic meaning, and so are, on the housetop where Jake's and Mamie's idyll is consumed, the sheets that menacingly and reproachfully resemble shrouds. In *The Imported Bridegroom*, Flora's hat literally hypnotizes Shasha, while the objects dangling from the headstones in the Pravly cemetery 'had an effect of mysterious muteness, as of erstwhile animated beings' [Cahan 1898, 1970, p.115]. Things become magical, and their magic enters the story, conditions the characters, opens up a Chagallesque world of dream and unconscious. Moreover, such a magic also contains the dimension of memory — the memory we saw thriving in the interstices of working time and leisure, in the new rituals of city life as well as in the old ceremonies of orthodoxy. Either as a sweet remembrance of days gone or as a bitter nightmare of oppression suffered, the past is ever hovering over the Lower East Side's Ghetto, and in its fiction receives a mythical, often unreal and ambiguous, quality. It is the sense of a far-away identity, the tortured nostalgia for an Old World which meant *pogroms* and for a home which was no home, the sudden realization of the difficulty/impossibility to come to terms with America...And, in all these versions, it will remain a specifically Jewish-American experience.

Abraham Cahan's career as a novelist climaxed and ended in 1917 with *The Rise of David Levinsky* — a year and a novel that can be taken as a turning point in the development of a distinctive Jewish-American fiction. In those twenty years, not only had Cahan been instrumental in inspiring a host of minor Ghetto authors writing in English. But he also served as an inspiration to those immigrant artists who were trying to rekindle the flame of the *tzargon* in New York. On the whole, the literary production of Ghetto authors writing in English was rather naive. They frequently leaned towards the melodramatic and sentimental, especially when dealing with the central theme of the relationship between parents and children, as in Herman Bernstein's *Contrite Hearts* (1905). Or they spoiled their novels by recurring to racial stereotypes one would not expect in immigrant fiction, as in A. H. Frankel's *In Gold We Trust* (1898) — a sign of that self-hatred and introjection of ruling images that would often plague ethnic writing. When their locale was the underworld, they were easily tempted by the grotesque, sensational, and bizarre, as in David Warfield's and Margherita Hamm's *Ghetto Silhouettes* (1902) or in Nathan Kussy's *The Abyss* (1916). More balanced works, often striking an intimate chord, were Herman Bernstein's *In the Gates of Israel. Stories of the Jews* (1902), or Ezra Brudno's *The Fugitive: Being Memoirs of a Wanderer in Search of a Home* (1904) and Edward Steiner's *The Mediator* (1907), both following Russian-Jewish characters who grow up in misery and persecution in the Old World and eventually escape to New York, where they face yet another form of misery and oppression at the hands

196

of their German coreligionists. Thematical ambiguity, structural confusion, stylistic weakness seemed to be the price to be paid for the development of a literary identity. At the same time, however, by so vividly portraying the Ghetto experience, and especially by turning their attention to the critical issues of parents vs. children, New-World mores vs. Old-World traditions, and of Americanization via intermarriage and cultural fusion, these minor authors helped to enlarge the path opened by Cahan [Howe 1976; Fine 1977].

As to the turn-of-the-century authors writing in Yiddish, they were scarcely known outside the Lower East Side. But, within its borders, they were cherished by masses hungry for a poetry and prose that be a vehicle and expression of their condition. The neighborhood thus became a real crucible of Yiddish writing. There were the so-called "sweatshop poets" — people like Joseph Bovshover, the *Freie Arbeiter Shtime*'s editor David Edelstadt, or the greatest and most celebrated of them all, Morris Rosenfeld, who left a large *corpus* of poetry full of the pathos and tragedy of life in the Ghetto. There were such poets of *Yiddishkeit* as Abraham "Liessen" Wald, 'an imaginative critic, a violent socialist, and an excitable lover of nature' [Hapgood 1902, 1967, p.107], and Abraham Reisin, who composed simple stories about everyday's occurrences in the streets and tenements. Other well-known authors were Zalman Libin, whose sketches full of bitter humor appeared on the *Arbeiter Zeitung*, the *Zukunft*, the *Jewish Daily Forward*, and captured 'the poignant moment in the flow of daily events' [Hapgood 1902, 1967, p.210] along Hester and Suffolk streets; playwrights Leon Kobrin, who also wrote warmly satirical sketches of Ghetto types for the *Arbeiter Zeitung*, and Jacob Gordin, whose short stories were full of the same love for the emotionally extreme that so often characterized his plays; and David Pinsky, B. Gorin, Moshe Nadir, Zalman Schneur...[M. Rosenfeld, ed., 1967].

More interested in the aesthetic side of literary creation than the "sweatshop poets" or the sketch writers, who rather viewed themselves as Ghetto bards and prophets, were the components of the *Di Yunge* group — Moshe Leib Halpern, Mani Leib, David Ignatow, and Joseph Opatoshu (who also chose the Jewish underworld as his main subject matter, but avoided morbid sensationalism by infusing it with a vivid warmth)[10]. Finally, there were such internationally acclaimed Yiddish masters as Sholem Asch, Sholom Aleichem, and I. J. Singer, who came to New York in the early years of the new century and there spent much of their careers. A feature that was common to most of these authors was that they were really and intimately people of the Ghetto, living and working side by side with their audience, in a close

197

relationship that had its appointed places in the cafés. Their writing touched a wide range of themes, and dealt both with past life in the East European *shtetln* and with a present in which the Jewish community struggled to defend a separate identity and at the same time inevitably opened up to a larger world[11].

Probably the best example of this early Yiddish production, although only marginally dealing with the Lower East Side, is Sholem Asch's novel *Onkl Moses*, which the *Jewish Daily Forward* started to serialize in 1918 [Asch 1918, 1938]. A sort of continuation of *David Levinsky*, it told the story of Moses Minsky, a widower in his mid-fifties and a boss in the New York garment trade, who literally imports his native village and puts it to work for him, in a mixture of paternalistic and autocratic attitudes. Struck by the independent, rebellious nature of Masha, the teen-age daughter of one of his relative-laborers, Moses falls in love with her. After many vicissitudes, the two marry and a baby is born. But these events mark the beginning of Masha's growing estrangement from her husband and of Moses's progressive expulsion from his shop's management. The climax is reached when a strike breaks out in the shop, a real rebellion against "Uncle Moses". Masha sides with the strikers and leaves her husband, who will soon turn into a pathetic old man, almost a *shnorrer* in perennial search of his lost wife and past. We find here the same reflection on the costs of Americanization, the same dimension of memory and nostalgia for the past, the same outspokenness in describing the characters' sexual arousings and urges, the same attention to the new urban culture as opposed to Old-World traditions, that were a constant of this early phase of Jewish-American writing. The problem with these Yiddish authors was more or less the same as with Italian Ciambelli. Although they surely contributed to the dissemination of several literary and cultural elements through the publication in the most widely read newspapers of the New-York Jewish community, still the fact that they wrote in an ethnic language placed them in a somewhat separate position as regards the development, from within the Lower East Side's laboratory, of a Jewish-American literature[12].

V.

David Levinsky and the year 1917 were a turning point in other respects as well. By and large, the above-mentioned works (Cahan's early production included) dealt with the present, with life as it was in the same years in which they were being written. The past was the Old-World past, a region of the mind and of the soul to be reëxplored and regained through one's memory. After *David Levinsky*, and already implicit in it, a significant change took place. Not only the rôle of memory became more and more decisive, but, side by side with the Old-World past, a *new* past developed as an intermediate layer (no more Old-World past, not yet American present) and began to exert its fascination upon the Jewish-American authors. It was the *recent* past of the Lower East Side experience, which already took on the shades and hues of a nostalgic myth. There were several reasons for this development. With the end of World War I, the immigrant flow turned to a small trickle and then, by 1924, stopped altogether. The epoch of the first traumatic impact with America was over, and the Jewish community in New York and in the Lower East Side in particular was reaching a relative social and economic stability. Besides, a new generation of American-born Jews was coming of age, and the first hints were already apparent of that veritable diaspora that would take place during the mid-1920s and 1930s. The Lower East Side was increasingly becoming *the past* — a past to revert to in memory and to be infused with all the magic qualities of remembrance, but also with the deeply felt realization that, however hard and often desperate life there had been, still those streets and tenements, sweatshops and pushcarts had meant a close-knit neighborhood[13].

And so, after 1917 and *David Levinsky*, Jewish-American fiction increasingly took on the character of the semi-autobiographical large canvas covering the span of several years in the author's experience. That was the case, for instance, of Rose Cohen's *Out of the Shadow* (1918). Beside marking the emergence of a woman writer within the New-York Jewish community (at the time, a rather unusual occurrence), the book was an important first attempt at looking back, in anger and hope, in fiction and memory, and from a female point of view, to one's past in the quarter. Written in a plain, almost understated and murmured style, which perfectly rendered the drudging monotony of survival in the Ghetto[14], the book did not win the fame and success it deserved, and Cohen's foray in literature almost ended in tragedy when, four years later, she attempted suicide, before completely dropping from sight.

Much more successful was another woman writer, who started to write in the same years as Rose Cohen did and, in the 1927 short-story "Wild Winter Love", implicitly acknowledged the debt she had with that early, unappreciated pathfinder. Anzia Yezierska certainly had none of the renouncer or of the sedate personality, all her life being a fiery affirmation of individuality. Born in 1881 (or 1885) near Warsaw, she emigrated to America in the 1890s and settled on Hester Street. Her large family was a typically orthodox one, dominated by a Talmud-scholar father; and by leaving home at the age of 17 Anzia epitomized the new immigrant generation's (and woman's) will to fight for one's independence. After working in laundries and sweatshops, Yezierska won a tuition scholarship to Columbia University, taught for a few years, for some time got involved in settlement work, and by 1910, when she married, she had already left behind the quarter [Kessler-Harris 1975; Krut 1987; Henriksen 1988; Dearborn 1988; Burstein 1989].

In 1915, *Forum* printed one of her short-stories, "The Free Vacation House" and, two years later, "The Fat of the Land" received the Edward J. O'Brien Award for the Best Short Story of the Year. Together with eight more, the two stories were collected in *Hungry Hearts and Other Stories* (1920). The book had an incredible success and was immediately bought, for the dazzling sum of $10,000, by the movie mogul (and former East Sider) Samuel Goldwin, and Anzia was called to Hollywood to work on the film script [Yezierska 1950, 1987]. Her second book, a novel called *Salome of the Tenements* (1922), was freely based on the love story between immigrant activist Rose Pastor and WASP millionaire and settlement worker James Graham Phelps Stokes (a story that had deeply moved the Lower East Side and in a way paralleled, but with a happy end, Anzia's own secret relationship with John Dewey). It too was bought by Hollywood and, in the newspapers, Yezierska's tale of success was quickly exploited to show that the "rags-to-riches" myth could easily apply to the Lower East Side as well. Other books followed: *Children of Loneliness* (1923), a collection of short stories and essays, and *Bread Givers* (1925), a largely autobiographical narrative of an immigrant girl's efforts to free herself from the domination of her autocratic father ('a tyrant more terrible than the Tsar from Russia') [Yezierska 1925, 1975, p.65], which, along with *Hungry Hearts*, remains her most convincing work. Then, decline set in: she kept writing — *Arrogant Beggar* (1927), *All I Could Never Be* (1932) —, but somehow either her talent had exhausted itself or her formerly enthusiastic audience had abandoned her. More probably, the terrible strain suffered in the struggle to emerge from the Ghetto had in a way limited her creative scope to Ghetto themes solely — a material to which she felt the urge to go back again and again, almost as a liberation and at the same time as a curse, and which now, after being largely exploited by Hollywood, was becoming bothersome. In a way, Yezierska's story was similar to that of other contemporary Ghetto writers who, after laboriously opening a path, suffered a creative paralysis that made them unable to go beyond one book.

Even more than in Rose Cohen's book — in which the first-person (autobiographical and/or fictional) narrative somehow conditions the range of possible points of view —, in Anzia Yezierska's work the universe of the Lower East Side is portrayed through the eyes and collective experiences of immigrant women. The real core of her fiction, however, lies not so much in the realistic description of life in the neighborhood as in the expression of an enormous, almost obsessive, yearning — a hunger for love, beauty, knowledge, identity, that swells and grows and yet so often remains unfulfilled, because '"[a]lways something comes between the immigrant and the American"' ["How I Found America", in Yezierska 1920, 1987, p.294]. Her heroines, however, are more than simply individual immigrant women struggling to survive, looking for 'dream America' in the streets, tenements, and sweatshops, and 'praying, ceaselessly praying, the dumb, inarticulate prayer of the lost immigrant: "America! Ach, America! Where is America?"' ["Soap and Water", in Yezierska 1920, 1987, p.174]. Rather, they are the embodiment of all the yearnings of an oppressed people, and primarily of women choked and silenced by autocracy and tradition, *shtetl* life and religion ('"And woe to us women who got to live in a Torah-made world that's only for men"') [Yezierska 1925, 1975, p.95; also see Burstein 1989], who now, in America, suddenly wake up to new possibilities: '"I am a Russian Jewess, a flame — a longing. I am the ache of unvoiced dreams, the clamor of suppressed desires. I am the unlived lives of generations stifled in Siberian prisons"' [Yezierska 1923, p.65]. The fire in them is '"not just the hunger of a woman for a man — it's the hunger of all [their] people back of [them], from all ages, for light, for the life higher!"' ["Hunger", in Yezierska 1920, 1987, p.63].

Yezierska's fiction thus develops around the by-now familiar themes of the "promised land" (Mary Antin's narrative often echoes throughout *Hungry Hearts*), of the immigrants' dreams and realities, of the generational conflicts, and of the contrast between immigrant and American psyche and culture. But it remoulds them by using a female point of view and endowing them with an element of passion almost unknown before. This last aspect in particular is extremely interesting, because it elaborates upon a common image in the literature of the time — that of the passionate immigrant woman who rescues the Anglo-Saxon male from coldness and self-denial[15]. What could (and did, in much sensational fiction, even by immigrant writers) so easily turn into a trite, almost racist, stereotype is here transformed into the positive assessment of a fire that threatens to consume these heroines, *unless* it reaches and envelops another human being. To Yezierska, intermarriage and cultural fusion thus seem to be the only ways out of an otherwise self-devastating hunger. At times, the insistence upon this obsession tends to become excessive, and a certain degree of sentimentalism results, perhaps even of *schmaltz*, which often risks to transform these fiery and searching heroines in women wholly dependent upon *him*, as in "Wings", "Hunger", "The Miracle", "Where Lovers Dream" (in *Hungry Hearts*). But in several other stories, and in the novel *Bread Givers*, Yezierska is at her best when she retains that bitter humour (that was Cahan's as well) in depicting the gulf between desires and reality.

In "The Lost 'Beautifulness'" — the story Yezierska used as a pivot for her Hollywood script from *Hungry Hearts* —, Hanneh Hayyeh is waiting for the return of her soldier son Aby from the battlefields of Europe, and plans to have her tenement kitchen white-washed 'exactly like that in the old Stuyvesant Square mansion [where she washes silks and linens for one Mrs.Preston]. Now her own kitchen was a dream come true' [Yezierska 1920, 1987, p.66]. To her husband who reproaches her for spending so much, she answers: '"What do I got from living if I can't have a little beautifulness in my life? [...] Shining up the house for Aby is my only pleasure"' (p.67). But the landlord seizes the opportunity of the unexpected renovation to raise the rent and, when they cannot cope with it, they are evicted. In a fit of fury, Hanneh destroys her grand work, and the night Aby comes home he finds 'on the sidewalk before their house [...] a heap of household things that seemed familiar and there on the curbstone a woman huddled, cowering, broken. — Good God — his mother! His own mother — and all their worldly belongings dumped there in the rain' (p.98). In "The Free Vacation House" [Yezierska 1920, 1987], the narrator tells of how she has finally resolved to apply to charities in order to have some days off with her children in a vacation house. To do so, she has to endure never-ending humiliations ('suppose somebody from my friends should see me walking into the charity office with my children', pp.101-102) that, together with the vacation house's strictly enforced rules ('"Gott im Himmel!" thinks I to myself; "ain't there going to be no end to the things we dassen't do in this place?"', p.109), transform the long-awaited holiday into a veritable ordeal.

To the hypocrisy of charities and the arrogance of settlement workers, Yezierska would return again and again, with a bitter sarcasm that is telling in itself. For instance, in "My Own People" [Yezierska 1920, 1987], a group of hungry tenement neighbors are invited by old Shmendrik to help themselves to some cake and wine sent by a friend. In the middle of the merry little party, they are caught by the charity's "friendly visitor" who charges Shmendrik '"with intent to deceive and obtain assistance by dishonest means"' (p.246), since — by having a friend who can send him a box of cake and a bottle of grape-juice — he is not wholly destitute. The theme of solitude and nostalgia for the Lower East Side is instead developed in "The Fat of the Land" [Yezierska 1920, 1987]. Hanneh Breineh, after years and years of hard work in the neighborhood (when she even wished some of her children would die, so as to relieve her of a life of unending toil), sees her sons and daughters grow up and become successful. They move uptown to wealthier neighborhoods, but she misses her old blocks, habits and friends. In order to get a taste of life as it was, something her children do not understand and even despise in their Americanized way of life, she goes back to Delancey Street and in the pushcart market rejoices in 'the rare sport of bargaining, which had been her chief joy in the good old days of poverty' (p.213). But she soon discovers how terribly uprooted she is now, having lost her Old-World past and severed what linked her to the neighborhood, and not belonging either to her children's present.

A great accomplishment of this woman writer was also her capturing the rhythm and melody of a language — that of the Jewish immigrant already settled in America —, at a time in which it had already evolved from the uncertain stammering of Cahan's characters to the more melodious fusion of Yiddish and American, still another rough result of the ever-working laboratory. In their "Yinglish" syntactical and grammatical quaintness, such formulas as "What say you to a bite of eating with me?", "It only dreams itself in you how to make yourself for an American", "For why is it necessary all this to know?", "Why don't it will itself in you to give your daughter the moon?", seem to approach Henry James's fastidious prediction.

***

Another variation upon the *David Levinsky* theme had also appeared in 1923. With its vivid and well-written first half and rather disappointing second half and ending, *Haunch, Paunch, and Jowl. An Anonymous Autobiography* (in reality, by Samuel Ornitz) is too often relegated to the standing of pure Ghetto curiosity. The story of young Meyer Hirsch, who turns from street urchin and gang leader to crooked lawyer, however, is an interesting one, although structured upon a by-now predictable pattern of success-*cum*-solitude. Gang activity is the main theme of the novel's first part[16], but the author also manages to weave several different aspects of Ghetto life into his narrative: the variety of small trades thriving in garrets and basements, the peculiar sentimental education with its violent sexual drives, the complex net of relationships among the various immigrant groups, the birth of a local criminal world deviously acting between unions and bosses...In the background, but as a majestic protagonist, stands the city with its scenery, colors and sounds, with its pulse and rhythms, with the peculiar quality of experiences and feelings it nurtures:

> [...] the quiet that we call quiet in the city — only an occasional rattle of an empty wagon and the clatter of hoofs, a moment's hush like a fevered sleeper's sigh, the rattle and jangle of car horses' bells to the slipping and grating of their iron shoes on the cobblestones of their bumpy treadmill; a cry, a greeting, now there is a laughter, the saloon's ribald guffaw, doors shutting like the sounds of a slazey drum; cats sputtering and spitting over the garbage heaps in the gutter...the city's bedtime quiet [Ornitz 1923, p.39].

Even more than the success-*cum*-solitude story of a Jewish boy turned lawyer for both the bosses and the unions and thus loosing touch with his own past and world, *Haunch, Paunch, and Jowl* is a fascinating document on the development of a street culture on the Lower East Side and on the birth, out of it and out of its interactions with older or different cultural expressions, of show-business, and, if only as such, it deserves to be rescued from obscurity.

***

By 1930, the stage was set for a final summing up of the neighborhood's early experience in fictional terms, and two authors in particular seemed to be able to carry such a responsibility. Itzok Isaac ("Irwin") Granich was born on the Lower East Side in 1893, and adopted the pseudonym by which he became famous, "Michael Gold", during the 1919-1920 anti-Left Palmer Raids. Henry Roth was born in Galicia (then part of the Austro-Hungarian Empire) in 1906 and a year after emigrated with his parents to New York, living first in Brooklyn and then in the Lower East Side.

Jews Without Money (1930), Gold's only book-length literary work, had a strange fate. Initially praised as one of the best examples of "proletarian literature", it was later dismissed for the very same reason — both short-sighted or at least imperfect judgements. Ever since his famous 1921 essay "Towards Proletarian Art", Gold surely was a most passionate proponent and devotee of a politically committed literature and the protagonist of several heated literary controversies steeped in the particular atmosphere of the Depression and of the American brand of Stalinism [Folsom, ed., 1972][17]. Still, with the exception of its very last page's (almost mystical, to be sure) invocation of the revolution, very little in *Jews Without Money* can be considered as falling within the category of "proletarian literature", let alone of some kind of Americanized "socialist realism". What immediately strikes the reader of this semi-fictional autobiography is rather its impressionistic quality. Especially in the first two thirds (in the last part, the book's pace slows down, almost unable to move beyond the established groove), bright, almost violent, images light up one after the other, in a veritable triumph of the senses — true epiphanies charged with memory's high emotional voltage and woven together by narration's continuos thread:

> [My street] was an immense excitement. It never slept. It roared like a sea. It exploded like fireworks. [...] Excitement, dirt, fighting, chaos! The sound of my street lifted like the blast of a great carnival or catastrophe. The noise was always in my ears. Even in sleep I could hear it; I can hear it now. [...] Spring excited us. The sky was blue over our ghetto. The sidewalks sparkled, the air was fresh. Everything seemed hopeful. In winter the streets were vacant, now people sprang up by magic. Parades of Jews had appeared in these first soft days, to walk, to talk. To curse, to bargain, to smoke pipes, to sniff like hibernating bears at the spring. Pushcart appeared. Pale bearded peddlers crawled from their winter cellars, again shouted in the street. Orange blazed on the carts; calico was for sale, clocks, sweet potatoes, herrings, potted geraniums and goloshes. Spring ushered in a huge, ragged fair. [...] [C]rowds always sprang up on the East Side like dynamite explosions [Gold 1930, 1984, pp.13-14, 16, 139][18].

This is not to say that neither a realistic, nor polemical, intention is present. 'I will write a truthful book of Poverty; I will mention bedbugs' [Gold 1930, 1984, p.71], Gold proclaims, and painstakingly depicts the dirt, the squalor, the violence ('Now we knew the [East Side] as a jungle, where wild beasts prowled, and toadstools grew in a poisoned soil — perverts, cokefiends, kidnapers, firebugs, Jack the Rippers...', p.59-60), the brutality and physical contiguity so often menacing and perverting one's own sentimental education ('It took me years to learn that sex can be good as well as evil; more than the thing truck drivers bought for fifty cents on my street', p.26)...If Gold's portrait does not gloss over the widespread suffering, the heavy physical and emotional toll exacted by life in the neighborhood, at the same time, however, it acknowledges the particular experience implicit in it — the fact that the Lower East Side was an *integrated community* sharing a daily struggle for survival[19]. When Gold's little sister is killed by a truck in the street — his mother '[sinking] in [a] stupor' and his father '[crawling] off his sickbed to hunt for work' (p.288) without result —, '[t]he neighbors helped us. They brought in portions of their suppers, and paper bags containing sugar, coffee, beans, flour. Jake Wolf the saloonkeeper quietly paid our rent for months. Other people were kind. Once Rosie the prostitute placed a crumpled five-dollar bill in my hand. "Give this to your mother", she said. "Tell her you found it in the street"' (p.290). This was possible because

[joy] and grief were social in a tenement. [...] How often have I seen my mother help families who were evicted because they could not pay rent. She wrapped herself in her old shawl, and went begging through the tenements for pennies. Puffing with bronchitis, she dragged herself up and down the steep landings of a hundred tenements, telling the sad tale with new emotion each time and begging for pennies. But this is an old custom on the East Side; whenever a family is to be evicted, the neighboring mothers put on their shawls and beg from door to door (p.283, 161-162).

There is no romanticizing the good and evil that were part and parcel of everyday experience. There is no temptation to give rosy portraits or bleak treatments of poverty and the underdog, so common instead in the "tenement tale" or "urban local color" traditions. The neighborhood contained the *connected extremes* of dejection and rebellion, of misery and solidarity. Above all, good or evil, '[a]ll these things happened. They were part of our daily lives, not lurid articles in a Sunday newspaper' (p.35).

What *Jews Without Money* admirably expresses, through the vehicle of a memory that reshapes the past, is the sense of a vital street (tenement, sweatshop) culture. People craved for knowledge and expression, and conceived the word and one's capacity to use it as powerful weapons in the daily fight to regain identity and organize experience, to face America and reinvent it ('My father was an unusual story-teller. [...] Very often, my father told stories. Some of his stories took weeks to tell, five or six hours each night', p.81, 83). It was this hunger for a collective identity, for culture as a social experience and not as a private matter, that made life endurable and above all remained

206

'burned into [the] mind' (p.24) as a source of perennial fascination for those writers who turned to *that* past in search of inspiration. What is more, in Gold's book, the reality and experience of the Lower East Side take on an almost metaphorical dimension. They become *the place* and *the occasion* for one's initiation to life: 'in my mind you still blaze in a halo of childish romance. No place will ever seem as wonderful again' (p.46).

Of such a metaphorical dimension (the neighborhood as the physical, mental and emotional *locus* of initiation), Henry Roth's *Call It Sleep* (1934) is the most telling epitome, although no single definition is apt to convey the complexity of a novel that rightly climaxed the Lower East Side literary experience. In a way, Roth's book met with a fate almost opposite to that of Gold's. It was initially criticized and even dismissed on the grounds that it was not sufficiently rooted in the "proletarian literature"'s soil, to be later rediscovered and praised as one of the neglected great works of American fiction[20].

The book is really a novel of many languages. On one level, it stretches into a somewhat Balzachian/Dickensian dimension, along the Cahan-Yezierska-Gold line. Life in the streets and tenements, kids' games and rituals, *cheder*'s experiences, the multitude of characters, cultures, tongues and episodes — all the traditional materials are there, to weave a large tapestry that is exquisitely held together by a masterful literary style, a sensitive ear and eye, a clearly symphonic intent, and a vividness that often betrays the partially autobiographical nature of the work. But on another, more complex and significant level, the book speaks the language of Freud and Joyce, by following a search which is as much inward as outward. In this way, the city (and in particular the Lower East Side, which occupies three of the four parts of the book) becomes very much what Dublin is in Joyce's *Ulysses*, or Berlin in Döblin's *Berlin Alexanderplatz* — not a backdrop but a protagonist, a *real* city described with a *non-naturalistic* purpose, whose outer maze of streets and places corresponds to one's inner maze of thoughts and emotions, so that the slow and difficult conquest of the one coincides with the dramatic and precarious conquest of the other.

Young David Schearl is a frightened kid who, less than two years old, arrives in America with his loving and protective mother, to find there a paranoiac and violent father and an alien world, made even more alarming by ethnic heterogeneity, by obscure death images and sexual hints, by uncertainties as to his own parentage, and by the lack of a substantial Old-World past. His search for an identity thus develops both within his family — in the soothing and all-encompassing relationship with his mother and in the turbulent and regularly shocking clash with his father — and within the strange world outside, where the streets form a confusing network, the other kids offer friendship and at the same time reveal cruelty, and ethnic and cultural differences (however predominant the Jewish community might have been in the area described) are a constant source of anxiety and peril. From this point of view, *Call It Sleep* is a true *Bildungsroman* ('"When am I going to be big enough?"') [Roth 1934, 1979, p.18], structured not so much upon a progression of experiences as upon a (potentially infinite?) series of concentric circles. David moves along the inner circle of his own self, with his self-created images and language, ever brooding over things seen or heard till they become either interiorized experiences or menacing entities:

> "You! You! Watchuh lookin'! Yoop! Don' step on de black line! Bing! Don' step on de black line. Ain't I ain't! Ain't I! Pooh fuh you too 'lilulibuh! Don' step on de black line! I'm sommbody else. I'm sombody else - *else* - ELSE! Dot's who I am. Hoo! Hoo! Johnny Cake! Blt! Dat's fuh you! Blyoh! Stinker! Look out fuh de fox. Fox; fix fux, look out! Don' step on de black line. Yoop! Take a skip! In de box! Yoop! Yoop! Two yoops! Yoop! Hi! Hop, skip an' a yoop! Hi! Funny! Ow! Owoo!" (p.368).

He then moves along the still inner circle of the kitchen and of his own privileged relationship with his mother (one of the unforgettable female characters of American literature, as Irving Howe once wrote) [Howe 1964], till something or someone disruptively breaks into it. He anxiously tries the outer circle of the stairs, the cellar, the street, the block, the school, the *cheder*, of friends, relatives, and neighbors, till some other frightening experience pushes him back to his most inner self or to his mother's protective arms. At last, on the verge of a mystical experience almost coincident with death, he dramatically attains the most external circle — the city chorus of different voices, languages, and fragments of life that gathers around him, after he is shocked and burnt in the attempt to find "angel coal" and divine light by the sexually metaphorical act of slipping a dipper '[between] the livid jaws of the rail' (p.418) of the Tenth Street Crosstown tram. The climax of initiation is now reached, and the 'pain of consciousness' (p.430) is coupled with a 'sense of triumph' (p.436) at hearing his father's voice falter as he answers the questions of the policeman who has saved David. But, when the novel ends — with David slowly abandoning himself to something that is 'not pain, not terror, but strangest triumph, strangest acquiescence. One might as well call it sleep' (p.440) —, the reader almost feels that this is just a provisional suspension, that the (potentially infinite?) series of concentric circes is still awaiting David[21].

Call It Sleep is a novel of many languages also because the complexity of the topographical grid along which David's search develops is paralleled by the complexity of the linguistic universe that surrounds him and conditions it [Mortara Di Veroli 1984 and 1985]. Indeed, David's search is clearly embedded in language. It is the progressive quest and conquest of identity and expression not only at the conceptual and existential level, but at the linguistic level as well, and perhaps above all. The book's many languages are, first of all, the author's one, and this language is intimately linked, in a veritable stream of consciousness, to David's one, so as to form a fluid, ever-changing, private language, which follows the boy's progress from darkness to light, his difficult and painful coming of age:

> Eagerly, he scanned the streets ahead of him. Which one was it. Which? Which one was - Long street. Long street, lot of wooden houses. On this side. Yes. Go through the other side. The other corner...Right away, right away. Be home right away...This one?...Didn't look like...Next one bet...Giddyap, giddyap, giddyap...One little house...two little house...three little house...Corner coming, corner coming, corner - Here? (p.94).

All around, and deeply entwined, echo the Yiddish spoken at home and rendered by Roth in correct English (the melodious speech of the kid's relationship with his mother, the fractured stammering of the few words exchanged with his father); the Hebrew David studies at the *cheder* (the language of mystery and revelation, of mystical search and emotional initiation); the street jargon spoken with the other kids (a language of sonorities assimilated from different cultural sources, a *patois* that often corresponds to the most transgressive experiences: '"Foist yuh put sompin ove' hea, and on 'iz little hook. An' nen nuh rat gizzin. Dey uz zuh big fat rat inna house, yuh could hear him at night, so my fodder bought dis, an' my mudder put in schmaltz f'om de meat, and nuh rat comes in, an' inna, mawingk, I look unner by de woshtob, an'ooh — he wuz dere, runnin' dis way like dot"', p.48); the Polish his mother and aunt lapse into when talking about an Old-World past which holds a "secret" (his mother's early love for a *goy*, a Christian), 'the realm of another speech' from which he (and the reader) are drastically excluded; and finally that chorus of different, ethnically connotated languages that symphonically emerges in the last chapters, stressing and enveloping the book's end.

In David's fragmented reality, words and languages form the brightest and more emotionally charged fragments, and it is clearly in this net that young David is struggling to give order to confusion and meaning to words: '"Boddeh Stritt [...]. Maybe it was Poddeh Stritt, like he said. Didn't sound the same, but maybe it was. Everybody said it different anyhow. His mother said Boddeh Stritt, like that. But she couldn't talk English. So his father told her Boddeh Stritt, like that. And now the man said Poddeh Stritt. Puh. Puh. Poddeh. Buh. Buh. Boddeh"' (p.96). Never before — with the one possible (and partial) exception of John Dos Passos's *Manhattan Transfer* (1925) — had the complex, kaleidoscopic quality of city experience been rendered with such dramatic intensity and immediacy. And to this literary accomplishment, the Lower East Side lent its vivid materials, its metaphorical potentialities, its evocative atmospheres. On these two levels — of a search for one's place in the world and of a search for one's words in it, on the level of Balzac and Dickens and on the level of Freud and Joyce —, Henry Roth's *Call It Sleep* rightly climaxed and summed up a forty-year-long quest for identity and expression, begun by Cahan and continued by Yezierska and Gold[22].

***

In this early phase of Lower East Side experience, ethnic writers thus seemed to fulfill Hamlin Garland's prescription [1894, 1960, pp.59-65] that the "local color" writer, and even more so the "slum novelist", be a part of the scene he describes. Although their being insiders never resulted in a compulsive homogeneity of purpose, style and solutions, still it exercised a powerful unifying influence. But sharing a common locale meant more than simply sharing a common *physical* place. It also meant belonging to a *socio-cultural* area which — however fragmented within — was as clearly and sharply, if not more, defined and separated from the rest of the city. At the same time, this separation was not absolute. It implied the dialectical relationship between inside and outside, between descent and consent, which we saw at work in all Lower East Side expressions and which would result in deep, significant changes within American culture itself. That this separation existed, what this separation implied, and how this *contaminatio* functioned, were made especially clear by the theatrical production directly stemming from the neighborhood and by those writers and artists who, although not from the Lower East Side, still chose it as a valuable source of inspiration.

Notes

1. As we have seen, a Chinese Writers' Society did exist in New York in the 1920s. But, notwithstanding the researches done both by such institutions as the New York Chinatown History Project (Museum) and by such cultural activists as Fay Chiang, informations about Chinatown's turn-of-the-century literary scene are quite scarce. It is thus difficult to say if very little actually *existed* or, rather, very little *remained*.

2. Compiled by Kay Boyle, Carnevali's *Autobiography* [1967] shows heavy traces of her hand in the form of various materials extrapolated from Carnevali's other works. Thanks to David E. Stivender's pioneering work, the Italian edition, by Maria Pia Carnevali and Luigi Ballerini [Carnevali 1978], restores the book to its original version, with the addition of several poems, stories and critical materials.

3. Rather significant too is the fact that so many autobiographies (Gaetano Conte's *Dieci anni in America*, 1903; Adolfo Rossi's *Un italiano in America*, 1907; Franco Ciarlantini's *Al paese delle stelle*, 1931) were published in Italy — probably as a result of "bird-of-passage" experiences —, and that the one and most significant among them to be published in America, Camillo Cianfarra's *Diario di un emigrante* (1900), was written in Italian — which clearly had didactic reasons, but surely reinforces the impression of a withdrawn community.

4. Prostitution, rape, homosexuality, venereal diseases are widely dealt with, even if usually in a very sensational manner. In the case of *I misteri di Mulberry Street*, the morbid temptation is heightened by Giacomo Nasi's illustrations.

5. See Halper 1932; Fiedler 1958; Guttman 1971; Fine 1977; Hartman and Budick, eds., 1986; Fink and Morisco, eds., 1988; Materassi, ed., 1989.

6. For a thorough assessment of Cahan's work, see R. Sanders 1969; Marowitz and Fried 1970; Howe 1976; Chametzky 1977; Fine 1977; Maffi 1985 and 1987; Orsini, in Fink and Morisco, eds., 1988; Buelens 1990. Also see Cahan's autobiography [1926-1931].

7. He also contributed a sense of physical concreteness generally lacking (or amply veiled) in contemporary American writers, even of the naturalist school. In his writing, the body's pangs and desires are presented with an intensity almost unknown even to Norris and Dreiser, and sexuality is a reality neither hidden nor overlooked. It is revealing that exactly this aspect disturbed Howells, who had discovered and warmly supported Cahan at the beginning of his literary career, but felt that, in *David Levinsky*, he had been too 'sensual in facts' [quoted in Chametzky 1977, p.151; also see Sollors, in Bak, ed., 1993].

8. Here and below, italics are Cahan's, and mark the words that the characters, who are supposedly speaking Yiddish, mispronounce in English.

9. Such terms as "Babel" and "Babelish" are in a way improper. It seems to me that the creative tension expressed (yesterday as well as today) by immigrant

artists in New York and in the Lower East Side in particular is rather towards an *overcoming* of such a chaotic separateness and incommunicability, in favor of an organic recomposition (or, at least, of a search of it). See below, Afterword.

10. It is noteworthy that, already in the early '900, the *Die Yunge* group (and, later on, the "Introspectivists": Jacob Glatshteyn, A. Leyeles) stood on a strongly proto-modernist ground, in terms both technical and conceptual. If it is true that the use of Yiddish sharply limited the group's influence, it is also true that the contribution offered to modernism by such authors as Ignatow himself, Charles Reznikoff, Louis Zukofsky (and, more generally, by the Lower East Side artists) was rooted precisely in *that* experience [Howe and Greenberg, eds.; Harshav, eds., 1986; Kramer, ed., 1989; Boelhower, ed., 1990].

11. Under the pseudonym of Yehoash, Solomon Bloomgarden composed several poems with Chinese subjects: "The Empress Yang-Ze-Fu/ Has palaces fourscore/ A hundred rooms each palace has/ Each room, a golden door" [quoted in Howe 1976, p.426]. One is tempted to think that such a peculiar choice was fed not so much by the typical turn-of-the-century American fascination for Eastern culture, as by the physical contiguity of Ghetto and Chinatown on the Lower East Side and by their growing social integration on the job level.

12. On the New York Yiddish literary scene, see Cahan's articles for the *New York Commercial Advertiser*: "'They Have Got So Used to Daily Papers'" (February 12, 1898), "'Rosy's Eyes Were Full of Tears'" (April 9, 1898), "An East Side Extra" (April 6, 1899), "'When I Write Yiddish, It Is Pure Yiddish'" (July 23, 1898), and "'I Saw Paradise Open Before Me'" (November 10, 1900) [all reprinted in Rischin, ed., 1985]; Hapgood 1902, 1967 (especially chaps.IV and VII); Zunser 1952. Also see Howe and Greenberg, eds., 1953; Rischin 1962, 1977; Howe 1976; Howe and Greenberg, eds., 1976; Slobin 1982.

13. The same shift can be detected in autobiographies. In such early ones as Marcus Eli Ravage's *An American in the Making* (1917) and Marie Ganz's *Rebels* (1919), in the foreground are the sordidness of slum life and the hardships of survival, even though, like veritable "pilgrim's progresses", both of them end with an extollment of American values and way of life. In such later ones as Samuel Chotzinoff's *A Lost Paradise* (1956) and Harry Roskolenko's *The Time That Was Then* (1971), although misery and dejection are far from overlooked, the filter of memory creates a sort of magical aura that envelops and colours the past [Boelhower 1987; Boelhower, ed., 1990; Buelens 1990; Singh and Skerrett, eds., forthcoming].

14. 'It was three months now since father and I had earned anything. We owed the landlord five dollars for this third month. We gave him just what the lodgers had paid us. What there was left of our own money we kept just for bread and a little milk for the two smaller children. Father used to bring the big round loaf of bread from the bread stand on Hester Street when he came home at night. We were always in bed then and the light in the lamp was turned low but I was often awake. Mother would sit up to wait for him and open the door and he would come in on tip toe, lay the bread on the table and sit down heavily beside it. Then mother would cut some of the bread, sweeten some hot water in a glass and give it to him. Then she would sit down on another chair near the table and sit staring on the floor in front of her while he ate his supper. He used to chew every mouthful a

212

long time and drink the hot water slowly. Sometimes in the stillness I could hear a deep half-stifled sigh' [Cohen 1918, p.159].

15. '"We Americans are too much on earth; we need more of your power to fly. If you would only know how much you can teach us Americans. You are the promise of the centuries to come. You are the heart, the creative pulse of America to be.[...] You can save me," he said. "You can free me from the bondage of age-long repressions. You can lift me out of the dead grooves of sterile intellectuality. Without you I am the dry dust of hopes unrealized. You are the fire and sunshine and desire. You make life changeable and beautiful and full of daily wonder"' ["The Miracle" in Yezierska 1920, 1987, p.137, 141]. On the theme of inter-ethnic fusion, and on the implicit and complex one of the "melting pot", see both Fine 1977 and Sollors 1986.

16. 'Civil war has begun [...] between the two principal Jewish gangs, the Ludlow Streeters and the Essex Street Guerrillas. The first battle is expected tonight. [...] A great bonfire burns in the cobbled square at Ludlow and Canal Streets. [...] Barrels, boxes, plundered wooden signs, canvas signs, cellar doors, chicken coops, a broken pushcart, lumber, abandoned mattresses and couches, paint cans, beer kegs and the countless clutter of city streets form a huge blazing pyramid — a fiery challenge and defiance' [Ornitz 1923, p.35].

17. The standard reader on "proletarian literature" is Hicks, Gold, et al., eds., 1935. Also see Rideout 1956; Aaron 1961; Madden, ed., 1968; De Biasio 1982.

18. That this kind of coloristic impressionism, sometimes reminiscent of Stephen Crane, was a cipher of Gold's writing is shown in such earlier works as "Birth. A Prologue to a Tentative East Side Novel" [Gold 1917], as well as in such later ones as "A Jewish Childhood in the New York Slums" [Gold 1959]. This physical quality — the resort to such a dense texture of sensory perceptions — will remain a favorite register in those semi-fictional autobiographies written with a few years' interval between writing and actual experience.

19. On this theme, but from the point of view of the Afro-American community, see Morrison 1981.

20. On the rediscovery of Roth, see Kazin 1956; Fiedler 1960; Lyons 1976; Materassi, ed., 1985.

21. In a way, this will be the fate of Henry Roth as a writer, too — that of writing, not in progression, but in concentric circles. To *those* experiences, to that scaring and scarring initiation to an alien world, he would in fact go back again and again, both in the few short stories he wrote while vainly trying to overcome what appeared to be a writer's block, and in the long flow of pages that, under the title of *Mercy of a Rude Stream*, seems to signal that block's definitive overcoming [Materassi 1990, Roth 1994].

22. Among the other authors who also carried on this quest by dealing at least marginally with the Lower East Side, one must remember Charles Reznikoff and Albert Halper, whose respective novels *By the Waters of Manhattan* (1930) and *Union Square* (1933), although thematically and stylistically rather different, are also too-long forgotten masterpieces.

CHAPTER FIVE: AS LONG AS IT IS THEATRE

I go to a heart-rending drama because my boss has deducted a cent-and-a-half a dozen sleeves and my heart is heavy — and I am ashamed to cry. Therefore when I see [...] how Hamlet holds in his hands the skull of his friend Yorick and speaks of life and death, I suddenly recall that they have deducted a cent-and-a-half a dozen sleeves and I cry real tears.

Moishe Nadir, 1918

I.

There was a field in which words — even the separate ones of Yiddish, Chinese, Italian, Russian — joined with images to speak both to the heterogeneous peoples of the Lower East Side and, beyond the pale of the ethnic enclaves, to an outside audience. If, as the saying went, in the Jewish Ghetto one ate *broyt mit teater* (bread smeared with theatre), that was also true of the whole quarter. From classics (Euripydes, Shakespeare, Goldoni, Goethe, Schiller, Molière) to contemporaries (Sardou, Hauptmann, Chekhov, Ibsen, Shaw), from popular American plays to the various forms stimulated by the new urban experience (farce, musical comedy, dime museums, vaudeville, etc.), theatre literally *saturated* the neighborhood. Ethnically, socially, and culturally, the dozens of large and small theatres that studded the area had a very mixed audience. All classes and communities of the Lower East Side sat side by side with slummers, theatre-goers, journalists in search of copy, artists in search of local color, outsiders interested in the neighborhood's cultural life, and a large repertory was needed to satisfy them all[1].

Labor-weary masses turned to theatre for knowledge, entertainment, emotion, and comfort — for the opportunity it offered to enter a world that, physically and metaphorically, lay beyond often unbridgeable confines. No matter how romanticized, Buffalo Bill's "border melodramas" spoke of experiences miles away from everyday drudgery, while Shakespeare led greenhorns and sweatshop workers into a dimension of drama and comedy, passion and desire, that they perceived as their own as well[2]. Other plays, though drawing directly upon Lower East Side material, were of a particular, often mystifying, character. Charles B. Hoyt's "A Trip to Chinatown" (1892, originally set in San Francisco, but amply modified for its New York run), Robert N. Stephens's "On the Bowery" (1894), Theodore Kenner's "The Bowery After Dark" (1898), Horace B. Fry's "Little Italy" (1902) were structured on the well-established formulae of city exposés and sentimental urban novels, with their stereotyped characters and situations. To outsiders, they offered a doubly thrilling experience — that of actually *going downtown* and that of *being shown* the dangers of such a descent. To insiders, they could result doubly ambiguous, because they functioned according to the same ideological operation implicit in the sensational or sentimental "tenement tales" — the superimposition of mainstream values upon the Lower East Side reality[3]. As Crane put it,

> this was transcendental realism. Joy always within, and they [...] inevitably without. Viewing it, they hugged themselves in ecstatic pity of their imagined or real condition [Crane 1893, 1984, p.36].

Still, superficial and mystifying as they were, such farces and melodramas also worked from within a lively and fruitful tradition of mid-century successes — Benjamin Baker's "A Glance to New York" (1848), Dion Boucicault's "The Poor of New York" (1857), John Brougham's "A Day in New York" (1857), Augustin Daly's "Under Gaslight" (1867) —, and as such they were stepping stones to more elaborated and convincing formulae, to which they passed on potentialities too often stifled by purely melodramatic intentions. Besides, the presence in the cast of such popular figures as Steve Brodie or James J. Corbett had a realistic (and at the same time "distancing") effect on insiders, which probably went lost to an outside audience. By sparking a kind of emotional identification, their presence stimulated a momentary meditation upon the audience's life, not without importance in the development of self-identity. And in the continuous dialectics between inside and outside that was becoming so typical of the Lower East Side culture, all this was to have crucial consequences [Hapgood 1910; Harlow 1931; Grimstead 1968; Gerould 1983; Giamo 1989; Sante 1991]. As to the songs these melodramas made famous ("The Bowery", "My Pearl, the Bowery Girl", "The Belle of Avenoo B", "The Sunshine of Paradise Alley"), they further contributed to that process of mythopoeia which in time would turn the neighborhood into a place of reality *and* imaginary charged with an impressive metaphorical dimension [Fremont, ed., 1973; Appelbaum, ed., 1974; Charosh and Fremont, eds., 1975; Slobin 1982].

216

II.

Ethnic theatre was surely one of the most interesting elements in the scene [Wittke 1952; Seller, ed., 1983]. From the 1840s, a great effort had been made for instance to establish a German theatre in New York, and by mid-century it had begun to bear fruit. For their Kotzebue and Goethe (as well as for Shakespeare in German), for their *Volkstück* (folk drama), *Schwank* (farce), *Schicksaldrama* (fate tragedy) and *Posse mit Gesang* (musical folk comedy), Germans went to the Turnhalle, the Germania Assembly Rooms, the Teutonia Hall, the Thalia, the Alte Stadt, Hoym's, the Neue Stadt, which had first-rate productions and companies, with important actors like Hoym, Elise Hoym-Hehl, Karoline Lindemann, Alexander Pfeiffer and Daniel Bandmann.

Although impressive, the repertoire was however almost exclusively made up of classics, and this — coupled with the fact that the language spoken was German — had the consequence of severely limiting the impact of this theatre on the developing Lower East Side culture. Beside, after the Civil War, the German community began to move midtown and uptown in a strong integration drive, and the shift was graphically mirrored by the departure of German theatres from the original Bowery-and-vicinity location. And so, when a German stable professional theatre finally opened in New York, the chosen site was on the outskirts of the Lower East Side. In 1888, after hosting such different events as Fallon's stereopticon, Artemus Ward's lectures, "The Beggar's Opera", Kinney's diorama on Lincoln's funerals, George Christy's Minstrels, the Irving Hall (at the corner of East 15th Street and Irving Place) became in fact the 2500-seat Amberg Theatre, and in 1893 the Irving Place Theatre, a "permanent German theatre" managed by Heinrich Conried and soon considered one of the best professional theatres in the United States[4].

Among these early immigrant enclaves, it was the Irish — whose Americanization pattern was somewhat different from the Germans', allowing for a more protracted and significant permanence in the neighborhood, also *via* the political and criminal underworld — who left a deeper mark on the Lower East Side theatrical scene. They could count on a lively tradition that dated back to the early nineteenth century, when the "stage Irishman" was born — a colorful ethnic caricature that would soon give way to the "stage Irish immigrant" and, in a few years, to such a key creation as "Mose, the B'howery B'hoy". First appearing in Benjamin Baker's "A Glance to New York" (and in its various sequels), Mose, especially in the interpretation of F. S.

Chanfrau, was one of the great "urban folk heroes" — half Macheath and half Paul Bunyan — directly drawn from a street culture made up of gangs, fire companies, brawls, and brogue. Most important, he became a veritable cultural catalyst, and as such reappeared again and again in farces and melodramas, bringing to them its own typical slang and gestures, ideological meanings and social situations [Dorson 1943-44; Senelick, in Matlaw, ed., 1979; Rinear 1981]. A variation on the Mose figure (Dan the Fireman) would also appear in Dion Boucicault's "The Poor of New York", with which the Irish playwright started an American career that would be marked by such great successes as "The Octoroon" (1859), "The Colleen Bawn" (1860), "Arrah-na-Pogue" (1864); while John Brougham gave the character a frankly farcical twist in "Life in New York; or, Tom and Jerry on a Visit" (1856) and "A Day in New York" (1857).

Although not devoid of great stage effects (with its final fire in the Five-Points tenement), Boucicault's play still employed a typical mid-century contrast between rich and poor, uptown and downtown, light and shadow. And so it was up to the Harrigan-and-Hart duo to give perhaps the best Irish contribution to the Lower East Side ethnic theatre — something that, at the same time, went well beyond the purely Irish enclave and amounted to a fresh meditation on the quarter's culture and society, and on ethnicity and its stereotypes. Edward Harrigan as author, actor, manager and director, Tony Hart (Anthony Cannon) as his partner and main actor, Harrigan's father-in-law David Braham as composer, and Ann Yeamans as *prima donna*, were the creative core of an incredible theatrical adventure — one which William D. Howells went so far as to consider the true beginning of American comedy [Howells 1886].

It all started in the early 1870s, at Tony Pastor's Opera House and at Miner's, where Harrigan acted in other authors' plays and in his own sketches and skits, before moving to longer and more complex works ("Old Lavender", 1877, can be taken as a turning point, with its logorroic main character who seems to have inspired the later W. C. Fields) [Wittke 1952; Kahn 1955; Moody 1980, p.79; Murphy, in Seller, ed., 1983]. And it ended up first at the Comique Theatre (514 Broadway) and then at Harrigan and Hart's own theatre, the New Comique (728 Broadway). Here, the company — some 90-person strong and a very well disciplined one — developed its own poetics and became a veritable attraction for turn-of-the-century theatre-goers. The shift to the Lower East Side's outskirts greatly enlarged the audience, but Harrigan-and-Hart kept their prices down (from 15 cents the gallery to 75 the orchestra chair), and the great bulk of their audience, its real heart, continued to be made up of East Siders who had learned to view a Harrigan play as something directly stemming from their self-same experience. In the words of a contemporary reviewer, it was 'a thoroughly American audience in our first thoroughly American theatre' [quoted in Moody 1980, p.123].

The characters, situations, and language in Harrigan's fifty sketches and forty plays (and innumerable songs) were the well-oiled cogs of splendid machines to make people laugh intelligently. More than that, drawn as they were from a world their author (a true-blood East Sider) intimately knew, they portrayed the Lower East Side's multiethnic population "warts and all", with an immediacy of language and themes and a sympathetic understanding that made the use of stereotypes totally acceptable and even necessary. Side by side in the audience, immigrants from different ethnic enclaves were thus offered a warmly humourous exhibition of their own, and their neighbours', defects and idyosincrasies. Around the central place of the "Alley" — finally given over to theatrical dignity, with important consequences —, Harrigan created a colorful but not cheap panorama of the neighborhood, an "America" with which spectators could easily identify. His best production, the one that had the greatest relevancy to the quarter's culture, was the "Mulligan series". From "The Mulligan Guard Picnic" (1878) to "The Mulligans' Silver Wedding" (1881), these nine plays dealt with the adventures and misadventures of Dan Mulligan, his wife Cordelia, their son Tommy, and their neighbors, the German Gustavus and Bridget Lochmuller (other characters, such as the Blacks Sam Primrose and Palestine Puter and the Italian-Chinese couple, the Hop Sings, introduced ever new, exhilarating contrasts), and were followed by such variations as "Mordecai Lyons" (1882) and "McSorley's Inflation" (1882) — a veritable pageant in which stock characters kept reappearing under new names, in a sort of never-ending work-in-progress.

A certain degree of realism was extremely important in such a theatre. The main action usually developed around one or more key issues of the day: the accidents and rituals of metropolitan experience as viewed from (and experienced in) the tenements, the complexities of multi-ethnic coexistence, the incidence of outside values upon a self-contained community (the drive to respectability, the alluring power of city politics, the dream of moving uptown, the various degrees of Americanization)[5]. At the same time, however, what took place in such a neatly presented microcosm acquired a sort of absurdist aura. Not only Harrigan's was a theatre in which even the most dramatic situations contained a powerful comic nucleus. It was also (perhaps, mainly) a theatre of physical effects and verbal acrobatics, a cross-fire of wisecracks and nonsense, of skits and accidents, of surreal punchlines and aggressive monologues: a theatre that was rooted both in the suggestive world of vaudeville and in the more secluded one of ethnic comedy[6]. For the whole length of the plays (up to three hours and a quarter), actors argued, wrestled or jumped through the windows, pigs and rats scrambled on stage, cigars exploded, fires broke out and smoke filled the theatre, floors sagged in and crashed down, and in most endings everything went "slambang, melée and general melée" — a sort of climaxing and liberating destruction that resorted to the most astounding stage effects. In the words of a contemporary critic, 'Harrigan and Hart have created a new order of entertainment. It is an American order. Nothing like it exists anywhere in the world' [Crinkle, quoted in Moody 1980, p.139]. An important part of this social commentary was occupied by Harrigan's and Braham's songs. "Maggie Murphy's Home", "Paddy Duffy's Cart", "The Babies on Our Block", "McNally's Row of Flats", "Mulberry Springs", and so on [Moody 1980], were real favourites, sung along in the theatre and in the streets — another contribution to the Lower East Side mythopoeia, and to that kind of self-scrutiny and self-revelation that to immigrants of all sort was so important in their discovery of America and of themselves in America.

III.

Theatre was an even more vital source of entertainment, education, and aggregation to the "new immigrants" of the 1880s and 1890s. Chinese, Italians and East European Jews turned to it not only to relieve the hardships of their new life, but to maintain links with their homeland *and* to come to a better understanding of their new reality. This social and educational character was particularly apparent in New York's Chinatown. Theatre had reached it via San Francisco, where the Hong Took Tong Cantonese Opera Troupe had landed in 1852 with a company of 123 and a repertoire of classical Chinese operas (a synthesis of music, song, dance, acrobatics, and costumed drama). During the anti-Chinese riots and the following diaspora, and after the birth of the "bachelor society", theatre had played a key rôle in keeping the community together. The Chinese Music Hall Theatre and the Chinese Opera House staged adaptations of historical novels — "Cao Cao at the Pass", "Fight at the Crossroads", "Romances of Three Kingdoms", "Heroes of the Marshes" —, that were 'long, highly stylized productions consisting of hundreds of acts, often taking many weeks for

220

a completed performance' [Seller 1977, p.182]. With its diverse styles (Kunqu, Peking, Cantonese, Sichuan, Pingju, Fujan), its conventions, rôles and subrôles (*sheng*, the male character; *dan*, the female; *jing*, the painted faces; *chou*, the clowns), its props reduced to the essential and intended to stimulate the audience's imagination, its contrast between elaborate costumes and scant scenery, its pantomime and symbolic gestures to suggest action and the passing of time, Chinese theatre was an important collective ritual and a stabilizing cultural force[7].

It was also an entirely new experience in New York and on the Lower East Side, and some of its features (the use of placards to indicate time and place, the distancing effect produced by stagehands giving actors the needed objects in full view of the audience) were not without effect on the future developments of the American theatrical scene. In fact, although the Chinese community understandably maintained a rather more separate position than the other Lower East Side ethnic groups, its theatre managed to reach a certain degree of interaction with America. Nearby Bowery theatres were often rented and special bills offered to more mixed audiences (in 1889 and 1890, Chinese opera troupes repeatedly appeared at the Windsor with different plays, the most successful being what 'purported to be a "sacred concert", but was really a heavy tragedy entitled "Li Khi Han Kan"') [Brown 1903, 1964, p.372]. Variety acts were also presented, with juggling, knife-throwing, and other attractions, similar to the ones that, in those very same years, were being performed in concert saloons and vaudeville houses elsewhere on the Lower East Side. Also, amateur comedians from other ethnic groups started to work as singing waiters in the Chinatown restaurants and clubs. Little by little, some kind of *contaminatio* occurred and gave rise to a mixed form of theatre, above all in its lightest forms. By the turn of the century, stylization had become less extreme and realism more pronounced, and greater attention was being given to new themes and stage effects — what soon came to be known as American Cantonese Opera, a cross-fertilization that made use of Chinese materials and American music-hall techniques. The presence of a still unknown Harpo Marx in the cast of the 1911 adaptation of the "persecution drama" "The Yellow Jacket" tellingly signalled the change. But, due to Chinatown's peculiar situation, it was hard to go beyond that[8].

IV.

After their 'spaghetti, chianti, and *fernetbranca*' [Hapgood 1900, p.545], Italian immigrants could go to 6 Spring Street, where a puppet

221

show awaited them, or to 24 Spring Street, headquarters both of the *caffè concerto* Eldorado and of the noted Maiori and Rapone company. Or they could go to the Germania Assembly Rooms (291-293 Bowery), the Teutonia Assembly Rooms (144 East 16th Street), the Teatro Garibaldi (31-35 East 4th Street), the Turnhalle (66-68 East 4th Street), the Dramatic Hall (44-46 East Houston Street), the National Theatre (104-106 Bowery, also known as Teatro Italiano by the late 1890s, before turning Jewish), the Concordia Hall (on Avenue A) — all places where Italian-American theatre clubs frequently performed, alternating with German, American, Yiddish, Chinese ones. Or they could go to the many saloon backrooms along Elizabeth, Baxter, and Mulberry streets, where farce and skits were put up. Prices were always between 10 and 50 cents, ladies were generally admitted free, and in the saloons you only paid the drinks [Aleandri, in Caroli, Harney, Tomasi, eds., 1978; Aleandri and Seller, in Seller, ed., 1983].

The *colonia*'s great attraction surely was legitimate theatre, and several companies offered well-staged and well-acted productions. Antonio Maiori specialized in Shakespeare ("Othello" and "The Merchant of Venice" being his celebrated *tours de force*) and between 1898 and 1913 was recognized as Little Italy's foremost exponent of classic drama, capable of attracting to his theatre uptown audiences as well, while his wife Concetta, herself a good actress, played Ophelia and Desdemona in a 'graceful, touching and poetical' way [Hapgood 1900, p.552; also see Corbin 1898; Cautela 1927]. They also staged melodrama and generally ended every bill with a farce. Other noted companies were the Circolo Filodrammatico Italo-Americano (Goldoni, Schiller, Verga, Giacosa, not to mention Ciambelli's and Rocco Metelli's Italian-American melodramas, farce, and Pulcinella's skits), the Compagnia Galileo Galilei, the Compagnia Drammatica Napoletana [Aleandri and Seller, in Seller, ed., 1983].

Steeped in the Italian tradition of *feuilleton* (the *romanzo d'appendice*), melodrama was one of the legitimate theatre's great competitors. Generally speaking, Guglielmo Ricciardi's, Armando Cennerazzo's, and Rocco Metelli's works, turgid with passions and betrayals, illegitimate sons and unfaithful lovers, were set in Italy, and mainly in Naples. In "La Jena del Cimitero", for instance, a little girl is kidnapped by sailors in Naples. For twelve years, sure of her death and mad with pain, her mother searches the graveyards of Italy, virtually reducing herself to the level of a beast. Meanwhile, the little girl grows up to be a beautiful woman, and one of her sailor kidnappers (now a rich man) falls in love with her. But she is promised to another man, and the marriage is arranged. Her former kidnapper then drugs her in

TEATRO ITALIANO

24 SPRING STREET N. Y.

Compagnia Comico Drammatica Italiana
A. MAJORI & P. RAPONE
No. 1

GIOVEDI' 26 Aprile 1900, ore 8 pom.
SI RAPPRESENTERA'

AMLETO

PRINCIPE
DI
DANIMARCA

Tragedia in 5 atti di WILLIAM SHAKESPEARE

PERSONAGGI	ATTORI
AMLETO	ANTONIO MAJORI
Claudio, Re di Danimarca	L. Colombo
Polonio, Ciambellano	Lucio C. Zumbo
Laerte, suo figlio	B. De Vincenzis
Orrigo, Cortigiano	A. Alessandri
Orazio	Francesco Minciotti
Marcello / Ufficiali	Eduardo Migliaccio
Bernardo	C. Eduardo
L'ombra del padre di Amleto	G. Zacconi
Un Sacerdote	B. Cappello
Un Beccamorto	Pasquale Rapone
Primo Commediante	S. Lampiase
Secondo Commediante	Giuseppe Majori
Gertrude, Regina di Danimarca	Renata Brunorini
Ofelia figlia di Polonio	Concetta Arcamone
Una Commediante	A. Maurelli

Signori, Dame, Ufficiali, Grandi di Corte.

La Scena è ad Elsinoro.   Vestiario e Scenario Analogo.

L'orchestra sara' diretta dall'Egregio Professor PASQUALE PENZA.

PREZZI D'ENTRATA
Platea 10c., Posti distinti 15c., Poltroncine 20c., Loggione 25c.

Domenica di giorno dale ore 3 1|2 alle 6 1|2 si dara'

IL VECCHIO CAPORAL SIMON alla BATTAGLIA D'ULMA

Tipografia Telesca & Orienta, 223 Grand Street, New York.

Ill. 26
Theatre in Little Italy (from *The Bookman*, August 1900)

223

order to simulate her death and steals her from the graveyard. Of course, in her desperate and brutish wanderings, the mother has come precisely to that graveyard, and when the body is left there, she recognizes her lost daughter and carries her off. Each night, Antonio Maiori as the "jena" received a storm of cheering.

A few melodramas then dealt with American materials, in the attempt (often naive, seldom successful) to set the typical *feuilleton*-like ingredients in the new *milieu*: "Maria Barbieri" told the well-known case of an Italian woman sentenced to death in New York for killing her brutish husband; "Jack lo Squartatore" staged a New York story of unsolved murders which echoed the almost contemporary ones in London; "I misteri di Mulberry" was an adaptation of Ciambelli's novel; "La catastrofe del Maine" was set against the Spanish-American War of 1898; and "Il condannato a morte" turned around the theme of the immigrants' assimilation[9]. This "Americanization" was however relative, and on the whole Little Italy's melodramas tended to lack that kind of realistic structure that made contemporary Yiddish-American theatre — often performed just a few blocks away — such a compelling commentary on "life in America".

Both in legitimate theatre and in melodrama, an interesting aspect, due to have important even if overlooked effects on the American theatre's subsequent history, was the rôle of the prompter. Since often as many as five or six different dramas were given during the week, mainly non-professional actors couldn't be expected to know by heart such an incredible amount of lines. Thus, the prompter 'simply reads aloud the entire play [...]. But the audience, simple and at the same time sensitive to what is fundamentally dramatic, do not mind in the least. [...] That they ignore what are really trivial incongruities points to feeling and imagination, and in aesthetic competency puts them far ahead of those blasé rounders on Broadway who watch closely the mechanics of the scene...' [Hapgood 1900, pp.546-547]. The physical presence of the prompter — his voice clearly audible but separated from his body — thus came to be accepted as an integral part of the performance, and as such it helped to break down many realistic or illusionistic conventions, creating a veritable distancing effect.

Melodrama and legitimate theatre apart, two other theatrical forms gave a peculiar nourishment to Little Italy's entertainment and Lower East Side's culture. The *teatro dei pupi e delle marionette* (puppet theatre) staged the humorous misfortunes of *commedia dell'arte* stock-characters, Arlecchino and Colombina, Pulcinella and Pantalone, and, above all, the never-ending adventures of Roland against the Saracens. In small, crowded rooms on Spring, Mulberry, and Elizabeth

TEATRO ITALIANO
24 SPRING STREET, N. Y.

Compagnia Comico Drammatica Italiana
A. MAJORI & P. RAPONE
No. 1

Lunedi' 30 Aprile 1900, alle ore 8 pom.
Si dara' per l'ultima volta

LA

JENA

del

CIMITERO

DRAMMA SPETTACOLOSO IN 5 ATTI.

PERSONAGGI	ATTORI
Matteo La Rocca	Giuseppe Majori
Giorgio	Eduardo Clairella
Marchese Tractta	Giuseppe Zaccoal
Milord Eraesto	B. De Vincenzis
Carlo	Francesco Minciotti
Michele	Pasquale Rapone
Biagio	C. Ruggi
Brigadiere	Luigi Colombo
Custode	Eduardo Migliaccio
Marchesa Giulia Tracta	Renata Brunorini
Gemma	C. Arcamone
Giaccolna	I Scarlati
Caterina	A. Maurelli
Teresa	E. Clairella
Filomena	B. Savarese
Maria detta la Jena	ANTONIO MAJORI

Soldati, Marinai. Popolo.
La Scena e' in Napoli e dintorni. Dal Prologo al Dramma passano 12 anni.

L'orchestra sara' diretta dall'Egregio Professor PASQUALE PENZA.

PREZZI D'ENTRATA
Platea 10c., Posti distinti 15c., Poltroncine 20c., Loggione 25c.

Tipografia Talocca & Oriente, 225 Grand Street, New York.

Ill. 27
Theatre in Little Italy (from *The Bookman*, August 1900)

225

streets, the seven-nights-a-week performances could last a year or more, in order to go through the forty-six cantos of Ariosto's *Orlando furioso* or the twenty of Tasso's *Gerusalemme liberata* — a fascinating tradition that was carried on by Remo Bufano in the 1920s and by the Manteo family in the early 1930s, before slowly dying out and being revived under new forms in the 1960s, for instance by the Bread and Puppet Theatre.

The players are gaily-tinselled wooden puppets, dressed as Saracens, Turks, crusaders, knights, nuns, maidens, warriors, and, as an apparent survival of the early miracle plays, the devil is ushered in by flame. The stage is but six feet high, so that the puppets seem also heroic in size as they jerkily respond to the impassioned words of the dramatic readers behind the scenes, who, in very truth, declaim the pure classics of Italy [Kimball 1900, pp.5-6; Cautela 1927; Greene 1933].

Farce and Pulcinella skits were also the fare of well-known companies. But soon specific places began to stage this kind of light theatre, based on both the Italian tradition of *commedia dell'arte* and Neapolitan farce and on the more recent developments from France and United States as well. The *caffè concerto* were very popular places, and in time some of them emerged as important entertainment resorts in the *colonia*, no matter how dubious their character could appear in the eyes of *prominenti* and conformists. At the Eldorado on Spring Street, at the Villa Vittorio Emanuele on Mulberry Street, at the Villa Giulia on Grand Street, at the Ferranda Music Hall on Sullivan Street, at the Olympic Theatre on Fourteenth Street, a new form of theatrical art was developing, in osmotic relationship with what was happening on near-by Bowery.

It is buffoonery, farce, or simply burlesque pantomime. Often the fun is exquisite in its spontaneity and native drollness. The excellence of the acting here also rests in the naturalness with which the unsophisticated characteristics of the race are rendered. They never play the hard, metallic farce so popular at the uptown theater — the same play may be given, but by the Italians it is softened, made more natural, and more simply enjoyable. The construction of the farce is generally loose, which leaves room for the actors to infuse very fetching fun, roughly felicitous burlesque, and pantomimic characterization [Hapgood 1900, p.550].

226

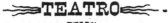

Ill. 28
Theatre in Little Italy (from *The Bookman*, August 1900)

Pasquale Rapone's and Agostino Balletto's farces and brilliant comedies thus created a world of fancy that still had a direct link with the immigrants' everyday life in America, and through laughter and irony helped audiences in their adaptation to the New World. "Il Caffè Chantant", originally by Italian author Eduardo Scarpetta but adapted first to French and finally to American situations, was for instance a humorous piece of metatheatre. It showed a couple of good actors unable to secure engagements in legitimate theatre. With their wives, they barely survive in a garret, but stubbornly refuse to yield to the lures of *café chantant*, which they consider a low form of theatre. Finally, they have to surrender, and the last act presents a complete performance at the *café chantant*, in which their value as actors clearly stands out against the ineptness and fakery of the great majority of the company.

But it was mainly in the saloon backrooms that a popular theatre thrived and attracted an enthusiastic audience. Here, farce and skits were *impromptu* affairs, often full of *double entendres*, performed *a braccio*, loosely structured, and based upon a direct communication between performers and audience, without props nor realistic effects. Here, the Bowery was even nearer, with its pantomimes, its Moses, and its improvised actors. But the *caffè concerto*, either in the small saloon backrooms or in the more renowned places, added a peculiar dimension: that of the immigrant character wrestling with a foreign world and of his adaptation strategies, the most important one, charged with tragi-comical effects, being "Italglish". It was out of these places that a peculiar Italian-American contribution really evolved, something that, while it was undoubtedly rooted in an age-old tradition, now tried to operate with the materials of a new experience. This contribution was represented by the *macchiette coloniali*, compositions in verse and prose, originally dialectal but largely "cleaned up" so as to speak to Italian immigrants from different regions. The *macchiette* gave birth to crucial characters such as Eduardo Migliaccio's Neapolitan Farfariello and Giovanni De Rosalia's Sicilian Nofrio, and were often published in the Italian-American newspapers. Together with Carlo Ferrazzano's 'Rabelaisian trifles' [Mencken 1923, p.419][10], Farfariello and Nofrio not only enlarged the scope of the Lower East Side's ethnic theatre, but possibly also influenced Charlie Chaplin's *little man* and represented an early form of urban "stand-up comedy". Unfortunately, the rather fluid features of the *colonia* and its being mainly made up of "birds of passage" militated against a steady and stable theatrical activity. Although often published in *La follia di New York* and other well-known magazines, the *macchiette* never really reached beyond Little Italy's borders and were also unable to mix fruitfully with the burgeoning multi-ethnic vaudeville. Neither did melodrama and farce develop real Italian-American materials, and so almost only puppets remained to represent Italian theatre in New York for a few decades, before radio and the movies killed them too.

V.

The golden age of Yiddish theatre in America lasted some five decades and, not surprisingly, coincided with the golden age of the Lower East Side. As with the Italian and Chinese one, Yiddish theatre too had its antecedents in folk traditions and religious rituals. The solemn reading of the Torah, the cantorial singing, the precise protocol of Sabbath, Succoth, and Passover, the intricate gesturing which accompanied *pilpul* or *Gemarah* reading — all contained a high degree of theatricality. Most of all, it was the *purim-shpil* (the Purim festival) and the figure of the *badchen* that opened the doors to Yiddish theatre[11].

By the mid-1870s, especially in Jassy (Roumania) and Odessa (Ukraine), several groups of wandering actors, musicians, and wedding bards came into prominence, like Zunser, song-writer Abraham Goldfaden, and the wine-cellar entertainers known as the Singers of Brod. Goldfaden himself is credited with making the decisive step towards the creation of a Yiddish theatre. In 1876, at the Pommel Verde, a wine cellar and summer garden in Jassy, Goldfaden linked his songs with a short dialogue in the form of a playlet. Other groups soon elaborated upon this early accomplishment, till a veritable professional theatre began to emerge, which mixed together coffee-house entertainment and serious plays and soon had to face the Orthodox Jews' hostility. Worse than that, the Czarist regime immediately saw in this kind of cultural awakening (surely stimulated by *Haskalah*) a possible instrument of political propaganda. Yiddish theatre was thus prohibited, and a theatrical diaspora began, which closely paralleled the social one, with a difference. While, in fact, most Jewish emigrants directly headed for the United States, the great majority of Yiddish comedians first called at several Western European cities. London proved to be the most important port of call — a veritable decompression chamber, where these "vagabond stars" could familiarize themselves with the English language and (via both the legitimate theatre, Shakespeare in particular, and the early British music-hall) with Western culture and theatrical forms [Sandrow 1977; L. Rosenfeld 1977].

Three dates in particular (1882, 1891, 1915) can serve as a useful thread in order to synthesize the otherwise rather complex history of Yiddish theatre in America. By 1882, several actors and playwrights began to arrive in New York. Among these was the 15-year old Baruch (Boris) Thomashefsky, who, in August 1882, made the first attempt to stage a Yiddish play in America. After several rehearsals at Frank Wolfe's beer saloon Friend of the Working Man (7 Hester Street), the Hebrew Opera and Dramatic Company performed Avrom Goldfaden's "The Sorceress" at the Turnhalle. The play told the story of an old Jewish woman and of a Jewish peddler, who turned out to be, respectively, a sorceress and a thief. For this reason, and for its being performed in Yiddish, it was violently opposed by the German Jewish community, which considered it insulting and dangerous for the Jewish image in New York. Due to inexperience and poor organization, this early foray was a disaster. The leading lady didn't show up, the orchestra left before the start, the audience hissed and shouted. Still, the first step had been taken, and Thomashefsky went on acting and singing at the Bowery Garden, a very popular and low resort. His repertoire was mainly made up of Goldfaden's comedies, but a hit was also Israel Barsky's "The Madwoman", the first play to be written in America with an American locale. It told the story of a girl who loves an artist, while her father wants to marry her to a rich and cruel man. The clash is violent, and the girl goes mad. The artist leaves to become very successful, and when he comes back he marries the girl, now recovered. Meanwhile, the father, after losing all his money, has become a blind beggar. As such, he sings in the streets and is finally recognized by the daughter, who cures him [L. Rosenfeld 1977, p.220]. In this, as well as in the other comedies he staged, Thomashefsky began to work on character types that were similar in a way to *commedia dell'arte* types. He also experimented with music and songs, mixing hymns, synagogue prayers, marches and waltzes and, in order to offer Yiddish materials to his audience, accepted to squeeze his acts and short plays between vaudeville skits ('[l]et it be vaudeville, as long as it is theatre') [quoted in L. Rosenfeld 1977, p.221; also see Lifson 1975; Slobin, in S. B. Cohen, ed., 1986]. He thus worked from the very beginning on a basis of continuous *contaminatio* that would remain typical of Yiddish (and more generally Lower East Side) theatre [Howe 1976, pp.462-463].

In May 1884, the Russian Jewish Opera Company arrived in New York, and performed at the Turnhalle before appearing at the Oriental Theatre, the old Bowery Garden so renamed by its American manager in the hope of attracting the increasing population of near-by

Chinatown. Two years later, the Jewish Operetta Company of Rumania also came and took quarters at the National Theatre, renaming it the Rumania Opera House. In 1887, Goldfaden himself arrived, and the Rumania became the Goldfaden Opera House. The same year, a new theatre was added to this budding theatrical scene, Poole's, at the corner of East 8th Street and Fourth Avenue. Other actors came too — the great comic star Zelig (Sigmund) Mogulesco, David Kessler, Bertha Kalish, Kenni Liptzen, and possibly the greatest of them all, Jacob Adler, popularly known as *Nesher Hagodel* (Hebrew for "the great eagle", *Adler* meaning "eagle" in Yiddish). For the next decade, the New-York Yiddish theatre struggled to survive and finally took root along the Bowery, inheriting those theatres that the German uptown shift and the momentary stasis in the world of American popular entertainment made avaiable — a complex history of constant interaction with other groups and of births and deaths of companies, with violent arguments, betrayals and desertions, and even long strikes.

Two names in particular seemed to dominate the scene during that decade — those of Moshe Isaac Hurwitz (Horowitz) and Joseph Lateiner. They were prolific and unscrupulous playwrights (altogether they wrote some two hundred plays) who knew how "to bake" a play: they took whatever material they could lay hands upon, slightly changed characters and plot, gave a new Yiddish title and new Yiddish names, and set it either in a East European *shtetl* or in old Palestine, or in New York's Lower East Side. Or else, they picked up a sensational news item and quickly dramatized it, often robbing each other of the idea and trying to reach the stage first. Lateiner's works ("Ezra; or, The Eternal Jew", "Blumele; or, The Pearl of Warsaw", "Mishke and Moshke; or, Europeans in America; or, the Greenhorns", "Tisza Eslar", the celebrated "The Jewish Heart") and Hurwitz's ("Monte Cristo", "Rashi; or, The Persecution of the Jews in France", "Judah the Galilean; or, The Prince of Bethlehem", "Elijah the Prophet; or, Millionaire and Beggar") came to be known as *shund* (=trash), "onion plays", "one-, two-, three-handkerchief plays" — a cheap theatre exploiting the audience's naïveté and propension for strong and immediate emotions [Sandrow 1977, p.116]. In "Rabbi Shabshi's Daughter" and "Zirele, the Rabbi's Daughter; or, The Beauty of Krakow", for instance, two Yiddish girls are forced to abandon their community. One becomes an adopted princess in Bohemia, the other is led astray by a Christian student and becomes a prostitute. But fate '[hales] the wanderers back, humbled and suppliant, to the people and the religion of their childhood, with its sweet and sacred rites, its homeliness and severity. "Ein Yid bleibt ewig ein Yid!" exclaims Rabbi

Shabshi's daughter at the last, and the sentiment rouses boundless enthusiasm' [Corbin 1898, p.38]. "The Jewish Heart" tells of a Rumanian Jewish student who discovers that his mother (who deserted the family long before) is also mother to his arch-enemy, a Christian student. The play develops with many contrasts and *coups de scène*, till in a fight between the Jewish and the Christian students, a revolver goes off, and the latter falls dead. The griefstricken mother confesses to the murder and is imprisoned. Under arrest, she attends the wedding of her Jewish son and then dies, while he sings a song whose refrain goes: 'Always remember your mother's song' [Sandrow 1977, pp.116-122]. "Annie the Finisher" is about a young sweatshop worker in New York, and in "The Aristocracy of a Province"

> a humble serving-man in Bessarabia is bequeathed a fortune of two million dollars by a relative who had become rich in America. His landlord — the provincial aristocrat — finds this out, steals the vital documents, comes to America, impersonates his old servant, and enjoys the stolen millions. The action takes place in New York, where the thief is marrying his son to the daughter of a Broadway merchant, while the true heir lives in poverty as an East Side coal-man. On the one hand is shown the life of the struggling Yiddish people — tenement life, street life, the brutality of the New York police; while on the other is shown the life of a prosperous resident of Fifth Avenue [Corbin 1898, pp.39-40].

A "high *shund*" also developed, with the so-called "melodrama operettas" by Meyer Shaikevitch "Shomer", Moyshe Zeifert, Zalman Libin, and of course by the greatest of them all, Goldfaden. It made large use of romance and bombast, sensation and rhetoric, in a veritable rush to a *kitsch* which resorted to a solemn and pompous language known as *Deitchmerish*, neither German nor Yiddish. Finally, there was a widely appreciated form called *Tsaybilder*, or "scenes of the times", which elaborated upon sensational news from the American contemporary scene, a sort of theatrical *feuilleton*/newsreel, based upon murders and trials, accidents and front-page news. All were complex forms, which included comic subplots when the main action was tragic (and vice versa), and were invariably accompanied by music and songs which became real favourites, like "Rumania, Rumania" ('Once there was a country, sweet and beautiful'), "A Brivele der Mamen" ("A Letter to Mother"), "Mayn Shtetele Belz" ("My Beloved Little Village"), and that veritable hymn of the Jewish diaspora, "Eli Eli".

232

Much was false and superficial, sentimental and pathetic, in *shund* and high *shund*, the well-spring of much later *schmaltz* in Jewish-American culture. Still, as Thomashefsky put it, "there were no moving pictures yet" [quoted in L. Rosenfeld 1977, p.244], and the decade, however dominated by *shund*, was a fundamental one: for the first time, the Jewish emigrants began to think of a theatre of their own. Actors and playwrights became central figures in the ghetto, with a rôle that transcended the purely theatrical[12]. Mogulesco soon specialized in comic interpretations and became a beloved jester and clown capable of making audiences laugh at their own idiosincracies with warmth and self-pity. Thomashefsky remained a popular leading man in romantic comedies and "onion plays". His wife Bessie, Bertha Kalisch, and Kenni Liptzen were great stars, soon to be followed by the women in the Adler clan (Sara, Celia, Stella). Jacob Adler topped them all, with an intelligence and energy, a character and versatility that allowed him to play downtown and uptown, on the Bowery and on Broadway (after the first Yiddish production of "The Merchant of Venice" at the People's Theatre, he was a marvellous Yiddish-speaking Shylock in an all-English production, in 1901). However poor in materials and substance, this early phase of Yiddish theatre was marked by great vitality and a capacity to make theatre out of everything, and by an easy and direct approach to the issues of an immigrant community. It expressed that raw energy that was necessary to survive, and helped to create — in a never-ending process of self-critical elaboration — a magnificent school of actors.

And, by 1892 (the second key-date), it fostered a reaction to *shund* itself. In that year, the polemic for a better theatre — till then waged almost solitarily by Abraham Cahan on the pages of the *Arbeiter Tsaytung* — gained its most important spearhead in the person of Jacob Gordin, a Russian Jewish journalist and actor of major charisma. His play "Siberia", written almost upon arrival in New York, was the dramatic story of an innocent man exiled to Siberia, who manages to escape and join his family, moving to another part of Russia and there becoming a successful member of the community. But a jealous competitor betrays him, and once more he is forced into exile. The play had no sensational scene, no *kitsch* backdrop, no solemn speech in *Deitchmerish*, and from the beginning left the cast (made up of such not so easy personalities as Kessler, Adler, and Mogulesco) quite perplexed and even annoyed. What struck them, and the audience, was above all its plain speech, its sombre atmosphere, so far from the bombastic tone of *shund*.

Ill. 29
Yiddish Playwrights in a Café (Drawing by Jacob Epstein, from Hutchins Hapgood's
The Spirit of the Ghetto, 1902)

For nearly two decades, Cahan, Gordin and Adler were the undisputed protagonists of a battle for realism on stage that literally split the Lower East Side audience and cultural scene. They proposed a cosmopolitan and socially aware theatre that, drawing materials and inspiration from the greenhorn experience, followed the lesson of Tolstoy and of the great European naturalists and reworked the classics of the past, Shakespeare and Goethe *in primis* — a theatre of issues and introspection, but also of passions and emotional raptures, that would not simply *amuse* its audience but oblige it to *rethink* its own life, its relationship with past and present, and, last but not least, that would celebrate the Yiddish word by definitely abandoning linguistic spuriousness [Gordin 1901; Rischin 1962, 1977; R. Sanders 1969; Howe 1976]. It was a courageous step to take, that meant a drastic cut with a short-lived but already deeply rooted set of habits, and could only be accomplished by the coming together of determined personalities. The playwright's talent was in fact inseparable from that of Adler, Kessler, Mogulesco, Kalisch, Liptzen (and from Cahan's as well, before a rift was opened between the two upon ideological grounds). Thanks to Gordin, to the actors of his plays, and to Cahan's polemical reviews, in those two scant decades a radically new repertoire

234

emerged, which was geared to the immigrant experience in America and able to transfigure age-old themes, folk characters, and traditional issues, and to reflect upon theatre itself and its capacity to show and shape reality and feelings.

So, in "The Yiddish King Lear" (one of Adler's triumphs), Shakespeare's plot was reworked into the contemporary story of an old Jew, who is betrayed and abandoned by his selfish and ungrateful daughters and whom, in a marvellous *coup de métathéâtre*, a friend vainly tries to warn by retelling the story of King Lear. In "The Wild Man" (another acclaimed *tour de force* of Adler's, full of grotesque mimicry and of an emotional atmosphere that directly brought to mind the immediacy of the Elizabethan stage), an idiot is witness to his step-mother's adulteries, which slowly rip apart the family nucleus. But, as a result of his madness, he is incapable of telling coherently what he has been exposed to, and so that very same condition which enabled him to discover the sin keeps him from solving the family's tragic bind. "God, Man, and Devil" was a reworking of the Faust theme, while "Mirele Efros; or, The Yiddish Queen Lear" was another variation on the Shakespearean plot. "The Russian Jew in America" explored the split between past and present, memories and realities, in the story of an old Jewish immigrant who relives his whole life, and quietly dies singing 'Moscow, my Moscow, city of cities, streets of gold'. In "The Homeless" — another powerful exploration of the central theme of the clash of past and present resulting into madness —, a greenhorn wife is deserted by her husband in favor of a cultured woman, breaks down, and spends several years in a mental institution. When she comes back, she discovers that her husband has remarried and her son does not remember her. She has no home any more. Madness slowly takes hold of her, while she thinks back on Russia and a time in which she was the center of a house and family. The neighbors call for an ambulance, and when it arrives, she is dancing around like a child, whispering 'I am going home! I am going home!'. 'Yes, lady! I'll take you home', the young American doctor can but tell her. "Dementia Americana", which Gordin wrote in 1908, the year before dying, told a story of real estate speculation in Brooklyn and East New York and was a scathing satire of the American myth of success and of its powerful hold on immigrants, ready to shed their past and their traditions to kneel before "the Dollar".

Gordin's years saw a real explosion of the Yiddish theatre. In 1896, the first Yiddish Frei Folk's Buehne was founded, a veritable nucleus of workers' theatre. In 1900, a bitter actors' strike gave rise to the Hebrew Actors' Union, affiliated with the AFL. In the same year, *The Theatre*

Ill. 30
The Musical Score for Jacob Gordin's "The Jewish King Lear" (YIVO Institute for Jewish Research, New York)

236

Journal appeared, followed in 1907 by Thomashefsky's 8-page sheet *The Yiddish Stage*. In 1901, Adler had his great Bowery-and-Broadway success. In 1903, the new Grand Theatre was opened on Grand Street. Ibsen and Tolstoy were being produced in Yiddish on the Bowery and vicinity, often before any English production in America. And a new generation of dramatists emerged, perhaps not so powerful nor so charismatic as Gordin, but gifted and lively. Leon Kobrin closely followed Gordin's steps as an artist and cultural leading spirit. He wrote plays in which the Lower East Side locale was minutely recreated as the background for new explorations mingling realism and introspection ("Sonya of East Broadway", "East Side Ghetto", "Nature, Man and Animal", "Broken Chains", "Riverside Drive"), and in 1912 founded the Jewish Playwrights Association. David Pinsky ("Isaac Sheftel", "The Zwie Family", "Yankel the Smith") and Zalman Libin ("The Belated Wedding", "A Vain Sacrifice") were two other interesting authors, while H. Leivick's "Rags" was universally considered one of the best theatrical representation of working-class life in the Ghetto [Hapgood 1903, 1962; Lifson 1975; Howe 1976]. Younger authors followed, like Osip Dymov, and soon were joined by the new great names in Yiddish writing, Sholem Asch and Sholem Aleichem.

Tenements, sweatshops, roofs, stoops, streets were the usual settings of plots which repeatedly dealt with the relationship between greenhorns and settlement workers, Jews and America, Jews and other ethnic groups, and old and young generations facing the New World. Language received particular attention, not only in the painstaking and often humourous representation of malapropisms, but in the effort to reach a standard Yiddish out of the great variety of dialects spoken in New York, until, by 1919, a Volhyinian dialect was finally chosen, to the exclusion of the Litvak, Polish and Galitzian ones — a turning point of great importance for the effects it had on the homogenization of spoken Yiddish as well [Lifson, in Seller, ed., 1983, p.574]. Yiddish theatre thus thrived on the Lower East Side and came very near to become a *national* theatre, capable at the same time of attracting a cosmopolitan audience[13]. Its repertory system was a novelty to an American audience accustomed to long runs; its star system (with all its shortcomings) was the element that cemented the stage and the neighborhood; its thematic realism was accompanied by an often turgid acting, directly stemming from the central rôle these great actors played on the stage and in the neighborhood — what Harold Clurman termed "realism with a little extra" [quoted in Howe 1976, p.472] and would often remain typical of this tradition.

David Kessler's decision, in 1912, to open a new theatre on Second

Ill. 31
The Musical Score for Leo Tolstoi's "The Living Corpse" (YIVO Institute for Jewish Research, New York)

238

Avenue, leaving behind a Bowery by now too given over to urban decay, signalled the coming of age of the Yiddish theatre — the end of its more pioneer and popular phase and the beginning of a new era. Not only did Second Avenue become "the other Broadway" — it also became (and with it, more generally, the Lower East Side) a veritable crossroads of international theatrical exchange and experimentation. Foreign troupes like the Vilna Troupe, the Moscow Art Theatre, the Habima, the Orleneff Troupe repeatedly came to the quarter, and performed Chekhov, Ibsen, Hauptman, Andreyev, their arrival invariably sparking mass enthusiasm. Such ferment also came to touch the wide and lively archipelago of small amateurish companies and dramatic clubs, which in 1915 came together in the new Freie Yiddish Folksbuhne, an organisation sponsored by the Workmen's Circle, from which many of the great names of the Yiddish theatre's third period would emerge and which would remain, up to the late 1970s, the only Yiddish theatre in New York [Lifson, in Seller, ed., 1983, pp.568-569; Wolitz 1988]. The influence of the international theatrical world (German and Russian *in primis*) soon made itself felt, and the shift was apparent when Maurice Schwartz took over the Irving Place Theatre, and there opened the new Yiddish Art Theatre. With a cast which could count upon such personalities as actor-director Jacob Ben Ami (soon to split from the group, to found the Jewish Art Theatre), actor Muni Weisenfeld (soon to leave for Hollywood, where he took the name of Paul Muni) and playwright Peretz Hirschbein, Schwartz's theatre became a veritable conduit of national and international energies. It staged Asch's and Aleichem's works, as well as Leivick's and Goldfaden's and adaptations from I. J. Singer's novels ("Yoshe Kalb", "The Brothers Ashkenazi").

By now, however, Yiddish theatre was clearly projecting itself beyond the borders of the Lower East Side, but the quarter's rôle continued to be central — roots were there, and this was Yiddish theatre's great force and at the same time its great weakness. It is true that, during the Great Depression, other important experiences took place in its streets. For instance, that was the great season of the Artef (Arbeiter Teater Farband), founded in 1925 after a meeting of 2,000 representing some 100,000 workers interested in a workers' theatre — a remarkable contribution to the period's agit-prop theatre, almost exclusively supported by and made up of sweatshop workers and directed by Benno Schneider, who had worked with Stanislavsky[14]. But, at the same time, a more subterranean phenomenon was taking place. Another diaspora was pushing the new, American-born generations of Jews out of the area, while their gradual Americanization meant that

Yiddish was slowly being abandoned and more and more came to distinguish old-timers alone, that hard core of Jewish immigrants who, out of choice or necessity, would not leave the old neighborhood and remained at the margins of America's social and cultural mainstream. As soon as *that* language — so vigourously and passionately fought for in the past — began to be abandoned, Yiddish theatre too began to lose ground. When Schwartz disbanded his Yiddish Art Theatre in 1950, it already was a survivor of the past. Other groups had meanwhile disappeared, like Ben Ami's Jewish Art Theatre, considered possibly the best of this second flowering; and many promising actors, playwrights and directors — or, more generally, many energies — had left theatre for the new, promising industry of moving pictures.

At the same time, however, that never-ending process, so typical of the Lower East Side, went on. The products of its laboratory reached out of it and subtly and decisively influenced mainstream culture itself. If (from the point of view of an appreciable influence) the spring of Yiddish theatre was clearly drying up, nonetheless it did not disappear. It took on new forms: Hollywood was one, the "*borscht* circuit" (the many hotels and resorts in the Catskills mountains, not far from New York, where a mainly Jewish audience was entertained by Yiddish actors and comedians) and show-business were two others. That strong power of *contaminatio* — the ability, out of necessity, to work with and upon different materials and to bring them together in new forms — thus presided upon new phases of transformation and creation[15].

VI.

But on the Lower East Side there was more than just ethnic theatre. Late-nineteenth-century New York was in itself a spectacular city, well beyond the appointed places of leisure and entertainment (Broadway, the Bowery, Coney Island). Elevated railroads, skyscrapers, billboards, bridges, electric illumination gave the new metropolis a special theatricality that was further enhanced by the large bodies of people constantly moving along the grid of its streets. To this already feverish set, the neighborhood contributed in very specific ways[16].

By the turn of the century, the reappropriation/reinvention of such public spaces as streets, sidewalks, stoops, halls, rooftops, and backyards, to serve as new stages for Old-World rituals and customs, was a *fait accompli* and as such recorded by scores of journalists and sociologists, writers and artists. In the streets and on the sidewalks, collective experiences took place that contained a high degree of spectacularity. The frequent, huge trade-union and political

240

demonstrations accompanied by banners, bands, and chants; the solemn and mournful funeral processions (or the joyous and colorful religious and patriotic processions); the tense atmosphere of early-morning picketing; the street-corner speeches of soapbox orators with their effective use of voice and gestures to capture passers-by; the hurlyburly of street life and street markets; the cries and antics of peddlers, vendors, newsboys; the dancing of children in the trail of the hurdy-gurdy man; the complex rituals of street-games and the toughness of gang battles — all this was a never-ending pageant, which denied fixed rôles for actors and spectators and, by exalting interaction and reciprocity, stimulated that circularity (of materials, ideas, experiences, emotions, images) which was emerging as peculiar to the neighborhood[17]. Stoops, hallways, rooftops, and backyards provided other possible stages, perhaps less collective than streets and sidewalks, but still quite public. They became polysemic places for gossiping and courting, memories and nostalgia, quarrels and exchanges of informations. And all around the inner yard, where religious processions often ended after parading through the streets, tenement windows and fire-escapes easily functioned as theatre balconies. Such enclosed spaces as dancing halls and sweatshops, candy stores, drugstores and cafés offered still other outlets, while flats (the kitchen, the parlor) became more intimate sets for a private theatre made up of story-telling, religious rituals, family reunions, marriage and birthday parties, Old-World recollections, generational rifts [Reich 1899; Cahan July 8, 1899; Minsky and Machlin 1986, p.15; Gold 1930, 1984, pp.82-83; Catapano 1988, p.20][18].

Above all, the tempo and variety of city experience and the Lower East Side's diffuse theatricality found expression in a specific theatrical form, which was born when American popular culture (the humorists of the frontier, the comic lecturers, the folk heroes, the drama and melodrama spoofers) met with the new materials springing from urbanization and immigration. This new form was called "variety" or "vaudeville"[19] and, already by mid-century, on New York's Bowery, many were the dime museums, the "drop-in" places, the concert saloons that offered a (mainly) male audience a succession of "olios" (acts), in which the speed and fragmentation, the novelty and aggressiveness of modern city life were turned into mass entertainment[20]. Blackface minstrel shows, acrobatics, animal acts, freaks, curios, Irish, Italian and Dutch (=German) songs, comedy skits, melodrama spoofs, magicians, monologists, clog-, sand-, rope-, and egg-dancers, banjo players, bone soloists and knife-throwers, hat-spinners and quick-change specialists — all came together to form a

241

loose, racy and often bawdy show, which attracted and blended the most varied elements[21]. In this way, vaudeville and the Bowery really functioned as crossroads of cultures past and present, native and immigrant. Ethnic stereotypes surely abounded, but possibly no other contemporary cultural form was so effective in crossing boundaries. To its decline in the 1920s, vaudeville thus continued to function as a sympathetic mirror to an ever-changing immigrant population, the cradle of so much later show business, and often provided an important although neglected (or despised) basis for ethnic theatre's early steps[22]. Above all, by '[putting] together what does not fit' [Hapgood 1910, p.86], vaudeville proved an extraordinary tool for the reappropriation of a complex, ever-shifting, and often confusing reality. To the Lower East Side audience, it was a way to come to terms with the rhythms of a city that contained them and yet repelled them, fascinated them and yet crushed them[23].

In time, powerful ethnic comedians emerged. After Weber and Field and a whole series of pathfinders, it was the turn of the Italian Migliaccio and De Rosalia, who somehow never really managed to break through Little Italy's confines, while Harrigan and Hart occupied a fertile middle ground between vaudeville and musical comedy, which had the important function of helping vaudeville to develop into more complex and better structured forms. In the clubs and restaurants, dives and bars of Chinatown and vicinity, the figure of the singing waiter was also acquiring ever more prominence. His art was

> in a class by itself. It consists of carrying a song over a multitude of busy doings, remarks, orders, servings, making change and cleaning tables, all done during the song. Occasionally you interrupt the song to sing out the order, and then you must immediately take up the last word and note you left off. [...] During the heartrending moments of the piece you may have to make change for a two-dollar bill and reckon up the amount due, put down the change, receive your tip, move to the next table, mop its surface dry, remove empty glasses on a tray, call at the little door for your ordered drinks, pass out the right brass tags to the checker, show people to the tables, smile to known frequenters, laugh at a friendly gibe and stoop to pick up a coin thrown as a compliment to your vocal efforts [Ornitz 1923, pp.139-140].

It is thus no surprise that at this school — as well as at the school of the streets and at that other decisive one represented by the "Amateur Nights" at Miner's Theatre — such great names in vaudeville and later

242

in show business graduated as Irving Berlin, Jimmy Durante, Eddie Cantor, George Burns, Jimmy Cagney...Pretty soon, vaudeville also stopped being a matter of mainly male audiences and artists. Great female performers emerged from (or found their early success in) the immigrant quarters, and the Lower East Side in particular, vaudeville providing them a new and till then rather unusual channel to economic, social and cultural independence. In the early decades of the twentieth century, Fanny Brice, Belle Baker, and the most loved of them all, Sophie Tucker (who could alternate the tenderness and nostalgia of such songs as "My Yiddische Mamme" to the spicy *double-entendres* of "Some of These Days" and the four-letter vocabulary of her perfomances), were clear examples of the changes vaudeville had recorded and helped to bring about in the fields of entertainment, mass culture, and city experience [Cantor 1928; Tucker and Giles 1945; Cagney 1976; Burns 1980; S. B. Cohen, in S. B. Cohen, ed., 1986; Sochen, in S. B. Cohen, ed., 1986; Snyder 1989].

***

By the early 1880s, show business had discovered vaudeville as an enormous economic potential and had set about to clean it up. From his original Opera House at 201 Bowery, Tony Pastor moved first to 585-587 Broadway and, in 1881, to the Tammany Hall building at the corner of Union Square and East 14th Street. As Pastor slowly moved uptown, the acts he presented became more refined, till middle-class ladies and whole families were mainstays in the audience. The decisive step was then taken by Benjamin F. Keith, who not only built a veritable "vaudeville trust" after the example of what was happening in other fields of the nation's economic life (it was the era of the "robber barons"), but also gave strict and precise rules to avoid any kind of vulgarity in his circuit's shows [Royle 1901]. At the same time, Keith was responsible for a central change in the still fluid structure of vaudeville, a change that even more signalled its strict adherence to city-life rhythms — the introduction of the continuous performance. By offering an uninterrupted sequence of acts from 10 A.M. to 11 P.M., Keith recognized the centrality of new habits and ways of life, the economic rôle of such new urban types as female shoppers or newsboys, the transformation of an audience which, due to the labor market's needs, divided its day differently than in the past.

While this turn was to have important effects on the patterns of urban culture and on the entertainment industry's future developments, Keith & Co.'s "moralizing" drive could reach only to a certain point.

Vaudeville's inner core was organically transgressive and irreverent, even licentious, and this could be toned down, but not completely eradicated without killing vaudeville itself. In the years following 1900, while Keith & Co. proudly commented upon the accomplished clean-up, vaudeville's racy aggressiveness surfaced time and again, as the cases of "scandalous" Eva Tanguay and Sophie Tucker easily show. And, when moving pictures dealt vaudeville a first deadly blow (the second one was dealt by radio), those peculiar features went over to influence Griffith, Sennett, Chaplin (and, later on, the Marx Brothers or, more recently, *Hellzapoppin'* and Abbott and Costello), with their anarchistic and surrealist humour, their sexual charge and innuendo, their assault on genteel values and common sense. Or the long line of humourists, monologists, and stand-up comedians, who connect vaudeville to Lenny Bruce, Mort Sahl, Woody Allen, the "Saturday Night Live Show", "The Blues Brothers", Eric Bogosian [Sandrow, in S. B. Cohen, ed., 1986; Slobin, in S. B. Cohen, ed., 1986].

VII.

But, once more, the theatrical scene on the Lower East Side did not dry up with (and after) these forms. In the Depression decade, it flourished again, by treasuring and bringing to a head all past experiences and by establishing a fruitful relationship with what was happening outside the neighborhood (the "little theatre" movement) and outside America (the German expressionist theatre, or the Soviet revolutionary theatre). Such crucial companies as the Theatre Guild or the Group Theatre were thus, at least in part, still rooted in the Lower East Side — if only because some of their members (Lee Strasberg, Stella Adler, Luther Adler) came from it and some of their poetics and techniques had already been explored and practiced by small Lower East Side groups [Clurman 1945; Himelstein 1963; Strasberg 1989]. The political and cultural effervescence of the 1930s inevitably turned to the neighborhood's rich and complex experience, although overt references to it were not so common. By then, in fact, the Lower East Side theatrical production had rendered familiar such sets as tenements, streets, roofs, sweatshops, or such themes as the confrontation with America, the needs of daily survival, the generation gap, the desire to move uptown and the subsequent loss of self-identity — all elements that can be easily found in the theatre of the 1930s, in the works of the period's more representative authors, Elmer Rice, Clifford Odets, Sidney Kingsley.

Elmer Rice's "Street Scene" (1929), for instance, although not located in the neighborhood, still undoubtedly draws upon Lower East

Side materials from its very title. In the play's microcosm, all ethnic enclaves are presented, along with the most usual and exemplary city experiences: the noise of the city, the heat wave, the different dialects, the elements of leisure and of work, the settlement worker, and so on. We don't see the actual acts of coming to birth and of dying. But we do see, hear, and witness all the rest, the in-between which takes place in the street, on the sidewalk, on the stoop — the gossiping, talking, courting, arguing, fancying...Sidney Kingsley's "Dead End" (1936), on the contrary, makes it explicit that its location is *not* the Lower East Side, *but* what will become the rich Upper East Side, shown in a transitional period — tenements side by side with plush condos. Again, however, the Lower East Side materials are there: the street gang kids (that would give birth to a long tradition of "Dead End Kids", soon to be exploited by movies), the Babel of languages, the murky waters of the East River, the strong, obscure desire to come up for air, the sense of being frustrated in the search and achievement of one's potential. An element in particular would also become common: that of the character who comes back to the old neighborhood and in so doing opens up painful, and deeply buried, contradictions under the smoothness of its everyday surface.

But, above all, the 1930s will be the decade of agit-prop theatre, and here again, as we have seen with the Artef, the Lower East Side had a lot to teach and to show — something that, given the extremely volatile character of this kind of theatre, is rather difficult to reconstruct exhaustively. Without doubt, agit-prop groups drew upon the widespread theatricality which the quarter had never ceased to express and which conferred so much intensity to all things political in the turn-of-the-century years. The Workers' Laboratory Theatre (later the Theatre of Action), the Theatre Collective, the already quoted *Proletbuhne*, the Red Vaudeville — all of them more or less linked to the Communist Party and thus variously reflecting its often tortuous history — staged their short, aggressive, elementary pieces of political theatre in the streets and parks of New York, in front of factory gates, in halls or at the Labour Temple ("Miners Are Striking", "We Demand", "Can You Hear Their Voices?", "15 Minute Red Revue", and — perhaps the most accomplished one — "Newsboy") [Samuel, MacColl, Cosgrove 1985]. Benefit shows were staged to support striking dressmakers and Chinese unemployed and, in 1932, a National Workers' Theatre Spartakiade was organized — rehearsals being held on East 12th Street and shows on East 4th Street.

But by then the story was already a different one, and the political plays of the Group Theatre and of Clifford Odets or the activity of the

various agit-prop companies were something that went well beyond the
Lower East Side.

**

More than anything else, perhaps, it is thus theatre, in its many forms,
that gives the most graphic account of the way in which the Lower East
Side laboratory functioned — of its enormous capacity of elaboration
and fusion, creation and dispersion of finished and unfinished products,
so highly charged with cultural voltage as to modify, in time, even what
lay beyond its borders. And also of its great capacity of attraction.
Because this constant centrifugal flux was always accompanied by a
corresponding centripetal one — the magnetic fascination which the
outside (what lay beyond those borders) felt for the Lower East Side.

Notes

1. The kind of theatrical activity going on in the area is best exemplified by
the history and repertoire of two of the Bowery's most celebrated theatres. In
1858, the German actor Otto Von Hoym opened Hoym's Theatre at 199-201
Bowery. It offered a ballet corps and vaudeville acts, minstrel companies and
Shakespearean bills ("Macbeth", "King Henry IV"), mainly addressed to a German
audience. In 1865, the theatre passed over to future "show-biz king" Tony Pastor
and till 1875, as the Tony Pastor's Opera House, met with enormous success:
Bedouin Arabs, clog dancers, infant gymnasts, fire kings, bone soloists,
contortionists, animal acts, minstrel shows, "Dutch" (German) and Irish singers,
and Harrigan and Hart's ethnic musical comedies (four different ones in a month)
filled its bills. In 1883, the new manager, Harry Miner, rebuilt the theatre and
called it People's Theatre (or Miner's), and the repertoire became extremely
varied. The usual fare of minstrel shows, "Dutch" and Irish singers, freaks and
entertainers, alternated with some of the era's most important companies (Augustin
Daly's and Lester Wallack's) and celebrated actors (Frank Mayo in "Davy
Crockett", Robert McWade in "Rip Van Winkle", James O'Neill — Eugene's
father — in "Monte Cristo", Thomas Keene in an impressive Shakespearean bill,
W. S. Hart in "The Man with the Iron Mask"). It also had Buffalo Bill in "The
Prairie Waif", Dion Boucicault in "The Shaughraun", the heavyweight boxing
champion James J. Corbett in "After Dark" and "Gentleman Jack", the famous
Bowery saloonkeeper Steve Brodie in "On the Bowery", Edward Harrigan in "Old
Lavender"; and such nationally and internationally acclaimed successes as "The
Pirates of Penzance", "Fedora", "Across the Continent", "The Mikado", "Wide,
Wide World", "Uncle Tom's Cabin", "Dr.Jekyll and Mr.Hyde", "Tom Sawyer",
"Bleak House", "Lady Windermere's Fan", "Kidnapped", "Mme. Croesus". It
presented melodramas, both of the sensational urban kind ("A Night in New
York", "A Bowery Girl", "A Trip to Chinatown", "Dangers of a Great City",

246

"Sidewalks of New York", "Waifs of New York", "Outcasts of a Great City") and of the "ethnic" one ("The Shadchen", "Darkest Russia", "The Nihilists", "The Vendetta", "Coon Hollow"), "tenement comedies" ("McSorley's Twins", "McFadden's Row of Flats", "Hogan's Alley"), and, at the time of the Spanish-American War, a patriotic bill comprising "A Spy of Spain", "The Cuban's Vendetta", "A Daughter of Cuba", "Cuba's Vow", "Remember the Maine". In 1899, management changed hands once more, and the theatre went Yiddish under the direction of Jacob Adler. Also the Neue Stadttheater (at 43-47 Bowery), built in 1864, initially catered to a mostly German audience. Otto Von Hoym's "Othello" (in German) was followed by "Richard III", "The Merchant of Venice", "Faust", "William Tell", "The Robbers", by the usual vaudeville bills, and by several seasons of German opera ("Fidelio", "Don Juan", "Egmont", and, for the first time in America, "Lohengrin"). The fact that the theatre also offered "Il Trovatore" and a play called "Moses Abraham, the Old Clothes Dealer" was a sign of its audience's growing ethnic complexity. In 1878, it changed name to Windsor Theatre, and presented Buffalo Bill in "The Scout of the Plains", "The Prairie Waif", "Twenty Days, or Buffalo Bill's Pledge", Frank Mayo in "The Streets of New York", James O'Neill in "A Celebrated Case" and "The Danicheffs". The usual popular successes (from "Across the Continent" to "Uncle Tom's Cabin", from "Shenandoah" to "Under the Gaslight", from "Little Lord Fauntleroy" to "Oliver Twist") and the usual Shakespearean bill ("Hamlet", "Romeo and Juliet") alternated with musicians and troubadours, and with Chinese drama companies — another sign of increasing ethnic diversity. Finally, in 1893, Sigmund Mogulesco took over the Windsor and turned it into another great Yiddish theatre [Brown 1903, 1964; Odell 1945].

2. Part of this fascination with theatre was undoubtedly due to the fact that it offered the possibility to identify with a variety of characters and rôles — a vital experience for immigrants who often, from their very names, had been forced to leave their own identities at Ellis Island, soon to find themselves buried in the grooves of city anonimity and drudgery.

3. Not by chance the author of the frequently staged "McFadden's Row of Flat" was Edward Townsend, "slumming novelist" and creator of the "Chimmie Fadden" character, probably inspired by the real Chuck Connors, "mayor of Chinatown". For this tradition in the field of fiction, see below, Chapter Six.

4. A noted production of Hauptmann's "The Weavers" was given at the Irving Place in 1896, some twenty years before its first English production (the play was a popular one on the Lower East Side: a remarkable interpretation was given in 1904, at the Thalia Theatre, by famous Anarchist leader Johann Most) [Goldman 1934, p.380]. In its turn, the Irving Place Theatre was relieved in 1926 by Jewish actor, director, and producer Maurice Schwartz, which signalled still another social and cultural shift [Leuchs 1928; Nadel 1981; Carvajal, in Seller, ed., 1983].

5. 'A distillery on the ground floor, Hogan, McGreevy, and Donnizetti [sic] families on the second floor, the tailor Lowasky and the Cuban cigar maker with Burns the lamplighter and four other Scandinavian families on the third floor. On the fourth the German dying with consumption and the Negro family's christening party' (set notes in *Investigations*, 1884, quoted in Moody 1980, p.140-141).

6. A few examples from "The Mulligan Guard Ball": '*Cordelia*: [...] Dan is

247

not home from the Gas House yet. *Mrs. Dublin*: Poor man, he must be tired shovelling gas all day. *Cordelia*: The poor man works hard wheeling smoke and weighing coke [...]. *Cordelia*: My husband is a vegetarian. *Mrs. Dublin*: I thought he was a corkonian. *Cordelia*: No, he's from Tipperary [...]. *Cordelia*: Now, get me two bunches of Thyme. Hurry, hurry. *Mrs.Dublin*: You can't hurry Time. There's only one man can do that and that man's a judge. [...] (Dan sits on the sausages left by Lochmuller on the chair) *Daniel*: Heavens! I've sat on the Bow wow puddings[...]. *Lochmuller*: Oh dots nothing. Dem is second hand bolognas. I sell dem to Italiens' (pp.2-3, 6-7, 25-26. Harrigan's holographs are in The New York Public Library, but the handwriting is often so bad as to render many of them almost illegible).

7. It also had an important social function. While female rôles were originally played by men, Chinese actresses were the first professional women to enter the United States after the 1882 Exclusion Act. The fact that they often played women warriors, and presented themselves as heroines of a new order, gave a considerable stimulus to the emancipation of women in the male-dominated society of Chinatown — one of the first results being the end of their segregated seating in theatres [*Pear Garden* 1987].

8. On Harpo Marx, see *Pear Garden* 1987. Very little is known, to this day, about theatre in Chinatown: even such a thorough study as Seller 1983 carries just a few lines on the subject. The Chinatown History Museum is however engaged in an important research work, with the aim of rediscovering and reappraising the community's theatrical past, even recent.

9. An anecdote about this last play ("The Executed Man", in English) helps to show the kind of emotional rapture these melodramas stimulated in the audience. Originally, it ended with the execution of the main character, unjustly accused of murder. But at the première the audience protested so vehemently that author Ricciardi had to introduce significant changes four times in the same evening: the condemned man was pardoned by the governor (American justice prevailing), mother and son could embrace joyfully (commotion sweeping the audience), the former condemned man was reunited with his fiancée (love winning at last), and a wedding took place on stage (family values being finally sanctified). Other plots can be read in Corbin 1898, Hapgood 1900, Cautela 1927, and Sogliuzzo 1973. It is interesting to note that the Italian-American melodrama also influenced American authors: see, for instance, Horace B. Fry's play "Little Italy" (1899).

10. In his seminal work, Mencken devotes a few pages to the rôle of the *macchiette* in the formation of "Italglish" and quotes some passages from one of them. As a key study, he mentions Arthur Livingstone's "La Merica Sanemagogna" (*Romanic Review*, Vol.IX, No.2) and refers to one of Migliaccio's most significant *macchiette*, "'A lingua 'nglese'". As to Nofrio, see Giovanni De Rosalia, *Nofrio al Telefono* (New York: Italian Book Co., 1918). Also see Cautela 1927 and Sogliuzzo 1973.

11. The holiday of Purim, in the Hebrew month of Adar (February/March), celebrated the deliverance of the Jewish people from the hands of Haman as narrated in the Book of Esther. The holiday was one of joyous transgression, during which intoxication and unruly behavior were tolerated, and had at its center the *purim-shpil*, a ritual play enacted by a group of disguised jesters. These "Purim

players" went from door to door and entertained the families and their relatives by telling Biblical stories or improvising a short sketch or humorous dialogue made up of references to their guests, verbal puns and obscene hints, pranks and imitations of the families already visited. For an interesting description of the *purim-shpil*, complete with two texts, see Kershenblatt-Gimblett 1980, besides Sandrow 1977 and Lifson, in Seller, ed., 1983. As to the *badchen*, he was the wedding bard and jester who improvised long, moving and joyful, speech-songs in honor of the newly-married couple. The influence of this figure, so central to Jewish culture and folk-ways, can still be felt today in stand-up comedy (from Lenny Bruce to Eric Bogosian, *via* Woody Allen), with its close relationship between performer and audience, its improvisations and *impromptu* character, and its peculiar mirroring quality. The best-known *badchen* was Eliakum Zunser, who emigrated to the Lower East Side at the end of the nineteenth century and became popular both for his wedding monologues and for his songs [Cahan 1928; Hapgood 1903, 1962; Zunser 1952; Slobin 1982; Lewis, in S. B. Cohen, ed., 1986].

12. The kind of emotional rapture involved in Yiddish theatre is tellingly described by a few episodes. During the performances of "The Yiddish King Lear", for several consecutive nights, when the main character (played by Jacob Adler) finally discovers his daughters' betrayal, an old man stepped down the aisle and invited Adler to come home with him, that he would take care of him. Also, when Emma, Boris Thomashevsky's sister, seemed determined to join another company and perhaps even marry its main actor, Boris brought the matter up between acts, before the curtain, in front of the audience, and with the houselights on. He finally asked Emma to swear not to join the other company and called the audience as a witness to the oath [L. Rosenfeld 1977, p.336, 296]. When Goldfaden died in 1908, some 50 thousand mourners followed his hearse; when Adler died in 1926, the *New York Times* called the cortège "a demonstration on the Lower East Side seldom equaled in the history of New York" [quoted in L. Rosenberg 1977, p.352].

13. The *New York Times* compared the "intellectual renaissance" taking place on the Lower East Side to that of 16th-century London [Lifson, in Seller, ed., 1983, p.552], and Isadora Duncan recalled that at many of her School's performances the audience 'consisted mostly of people from the East Side who, by the way, are among the real lovers of Art in America to-day. The appreciation of the East Side so touched me that I went there with my entire School and an orchestra, and gave a free performance in the Yiddish Theatre, and, if I had had the means, I would have remained there dancing for these people whose very soul is made for music and poetry' [Duncan 1927, p.317]. On her part, wrote the celebrated Russian actress Alla Nazimova, who in the early years of the new century spent some time on the Lower East Side with the Orleneff troupe: 'The intellect of New York you will find on the East Side. [...] They may lack, for the present, the material things of life, but the future is theirs!' [quoted in L. Rosenfeld 1977, p.340].

14. On theatre in the 1930s, see Clurman 1945; Himelstein 1963; Lifson, in Seller, ed., 1983; Howe 1976; Samuel, MacColl, Cosgrove 1985.

15. At least two works must here be referred to, which, although they don't specifically fall within the category of "Yiddish theatre", nonetheless had a relevance of their own and drew upon Yiddish materials — Israel Zangwill's "The

Melting-Pot" (1908) and Samuel Raphaelson's "The Jazz Singer" (adapted from one of his short-stories in 1922). Both of them are significant in that they elaborate upon familiar Lower East Side themes: acculturation and Americanization, the contrast between Old World and New World, the allegiance to traditional mores and the attraction to new ways of life, in addition to making use of typically Lower East Side elements (courting on the rooftops, synagogue atmosphere, street culture, the developing of vaudeville and show-business, etc). Zangwill's play is credited for introducing the complex (and often ambiguous) metaphor and concept of "melting pot" — an issue which is discussed at length in Werner Sollors 1986 —, while Raphaelson's supplied the basis for Al Jolson's movie, the first sound motion picture.

16. Among the several events which, at the turn of the century, consciously exploited the spectacular dimension of New York as Metropolis, the 1913 Paterson Pageant — organized by the IWW and a committee of radical activists and intellectuals to support the silk-workers' strike in Paterson, N.J. — was surely among the most important ones [Green 1988]. On New York's modernism (the reference to Walter Benjamin and Siegfried Kracauer is here *de rigueur*), also see Barth 1980; Trachtenberg 1982; Berman 1982; Conrad 1984.

17. Beautiful examples of this spontaneous street-theatre rooted in the necessities of everyday survival are recorded in Ornitz 1923, pp.35, 116; Yezierska 1925, 1975, pp.189-190; Cantor 1928, pp.22, 48; Burns 1980, pp.33, 39.

18. Cahan's, Yezierska's, Roth's works are crucial in order to catch the theatrical dimension implicit in the Jewish religious rituals. It must also be remembered that halls and theatres were often used for purposes other than theatrical (political meetings, wedding parties, benefits, etc.) and that, in turn, these occasions often took on exquisitely theatrical dimensions. A good example is offered by Lillian Wald's description of a "Spoken Newspaper" at the Thalia Theatre as a way to raise funds for the *Jewish Daily Forward* — something that can really be taken as a forerunner of many subsequent experimentations [Wald 1971, pp.263-264; also see Vacha 1986; Samuel, MacColl, Cosgrove 1985].

19. Traditional etymology refers to the French *val de Vire* — the valley of a Normandy river from which several *chansonniers* and balladeers came. But Snyder 1989 convincingly argues for a more intriguing *voix de ville* (voice of the city).

20. Not by chance, in the process of formation of a turn-of-the-century mass culture, vaudeville was inseparable from ragtime — the swift, mechanical, syncopated musical rendition of the new urban rhythms. In ragtime, and more generally in the new music stemming from city experience, *contaminatio* was again efficaciously ruling. In the works of East Sider George Gershwin, this *contaminatio* would reach a high level of sophistication, with a skilful weaving of traditional Jewish themes, Black songs, ragtime elements and American folk tunes [Ornitz 1923, pp.116-148; Blesch and Janis 1971; Howe 1976; Berlin 1980].

21. 'A standard bill opened with a sketch. This was followed by a single — a song and dance man or woman, or instrumentalist — any act that could be done in one to give the stagehands opportunity to reset. The next act, in full stage, was usually an alley oop. Then back to a single, say a seriocomic in one, which was followed by another sketch, generally a blackface comedy in full stage. For the rest of the show an average bill would run like this: a female song and dance single in

one; a double specialty, usually a musical, in full stage; a pedestal or straight clog, or sand jig in one; a blackface song and dance team, full stage; a protean man or woman or costume change act in one; a juggler, full stage (the eighties audiences took their juggling seriously); then an afterpiece, musical extravaganza, or drama, with full company' [Gilbert 1940, 1963, p.38].

22. A good turn-of-the-century example of vaudeville's mirroring function is the show described by Hapgod 1910: 'Some time ago "Chuck Connors and Co." played for a few weeks at a Bowery vaudeville theater. Chuck's associates were all genuine Bowery characters. There was no "fake" about it. They all enacted themselves, talked Bowery slang, gave Bowery songs and dances, and reproduced the life with great fidelity. "It's de real t'ing. We don't act, we just play ourselves — see? We're a bunch of blokes and bundles from de Lane [the Bowery]. The scene of our play is in Barney Flynn's saloon. Dere ain't no plot in me play, fer it's de real t'ing. Dere ain't no plot in life, is dere? De rest of de bunch has been rehearsed every day. But I never rehearse. I go on the stage and talk what I want — see? I do me best, I do meself. [...] I's de real t'ing we play, see? Wat's de good of acting when we play de real t'ing!". The "play" now began and was realistic to a degree. The Bowery girls and "blokes" sat about the bar, and Chuck talked in the middle of the stage, just as he does in real life. His coming down "de lane" was announced by the "bunch" in the saloon. He entered with his small derby hat, his Bowery walk, his black cigar held tightly between his teeth, and as soon as he arrived the regular Bowery "chimming" began. They all leveled carefully prepared witticisms at the Mayor of Chinatown, who is also the King of the Tough and the leader and arbiter of Bowery taste. Chuck turned them with his habitual success, talking in his slow, jerky way, always seeking — and finding — just the word to express his meaning. None of the actors exaggerated for the sake of stage effect. It was all in the low relief of life, admirably true and admirably indicative of that intense if ragged culture always attending the uncompromising living out of any set of conditions. [...] After "de bunch" had talked a bit, they sang a bit — "In the Bowery" and other songs, and danced a bit — the real Bowery hearty dances. It was a genuine slice of life — no "fake" about it, and full of unpretentious art' [pp.34-36; for other telling decriptions of Bowery vaudeville houses, see of course Stephen Crane's *Maggie*, possibly the best literary treatment of such a socio-cultural phenomenon]. It is easy to find, in Connors's character, a mixture of types coming from different traditions: the comic frontier lecturer, the master of ceremonies, the ethnic monologist, the Jewish *badchen*, and so on. One important example of vaudeville's crossroad function was its use of diverse languages. Ever since ethnic characters appeared on its stage (Burt and Leon, Watson and Ellis, Moore and Lessinger, Weber and Fields, Farfariello, Nofrio), their intentional or fortuitous malapropisms and linguistic puns remained a key element of vaudeville. 'Was hast gesachta? Zu klein gemachta,/ A gang of suckers, around the town. The kleine kinder, looks in the winder.../Dot was sung by the Widow Rosenbaum': so went, for instance, the refrain in "The Widow Rosenbaum", a parody on the popular Irish song "The Widow Dunn" [quoted in Gilbert 1940, 1963, p.73]. While entertaining the audience, these puns and linguistic operations familiarized it with the metropolis's many languages and contributed to their dissemination across ethnic and cultural boundaries, finally

reaching out to mainstream culture [Mencken 1923; Wittke 1952; Slobin 1980].

23. Its relevance to the new urban and technological reality, in the eye of an immigrant and working-class audience, is particularly clear in such acts as the famous "Speed Mechanics", which consisted in disassembling and reassembling a Ford car on stage, in eight minutes. Also, the rapid succession of some thirty different acts and the necessity of facing an often rowdy audience required perfect timing and a great resourcefulness on the part of actors and stage-hands, and this was not without socio-cultural implications [Cantor 1928; Burns 1980].

CHAPTER SIX: MORE THAN BROADWAY AND FIFTH AVENUE

Often when I have been rather tired of the New York that everyone sees, I have gone down on the East Side to the theatres, clubs, cafés, and felt that I was in a universe that was young and full of hope.

Norman Hapgood, 1916

I.

While generation after generation of immigrants discovered America (and themselves *within* America) on the Lower East Side, another dimension opened up in the neighborhood experience — that of its discovery from the outside. Since the 1880s and even before, the neighborhood was not only creating a specific culture out of its working-class character and the encounter/conflict among its many ethnic groups and between these and the New World. It was also stimulating a complex and important set of reactions from the outside. Haunted by recurring crises both structural and superstructural, American culture often turned to it as a fertile terrain of socio-cultural mythopoeia and *metaphorein*, projecting onto it its own anxieties and yearnings and also, in so doing, exalting its cross-cultural, laboratory-like character. To be sure, some of these reactions, at least initially, were of a rather mistifying nature — ideological attempts to circumscribe and control an alien world of bodies, words, and mores, or to invest it with a set of assumptions and expectations that had little to do with its reality. But others would reach deeper into the experience of the Lower East Side and, in a fruitful relationship with its life and culture, attain decisive transformations. All of them reacted in a stupefied way to what was taking place below East 14th Street, setting a pattern that would repeat itself over and over in the following decades.

The first attitude was decidedly one of anxiety, even of fear. Since mid 19th century, the attention of journalists, novelists, lay and religious reformers had focused on the city as part of the more general problem of a transition from a predominantly agricultural society to an increasingly industrial one. The dark forebodings variously expressed by Thomas Jefferson, Edgar Allan Poe, Herman Melville — that

American cities would soon approach European cities in terms of social chaos — seemed to be confirmed. American cities *were* growing, and at a rate that would soon place them well beyond the stage reached by their European counterparts. They had come to mean conflicting interests, ever-shifting landscapes, socio-cultural heterogeneity, widespread poverty, riots, epidemics, and a nervous frenzy born of new rhythms. In a way, perhaps in the most disquieting way, they *already* were European cities — New York had as many Italian immigrants as half the population of Naples, as many German immigrants as the population of Hamburg, as many Jews as those living in Warsaw, and twice the Irish living in Dublin [Rosenwaike 1972, Chapter 4]. At the same time, to thousands of young Americans from the countryside, the new metropolis was 'like a lighted candle to the moth. It attracts them in swarms that come year after year with the vague idea that they can get along here if anywhere; that something is bound to turn up among so many...' [Riis 1890, 1971, p.69].

The threats of urban poverty, vice and violence, in particular, called for a reorganization of theoretical concepts. Traditional Puritan or Jacksonian values seemed to be of little help and also had to face competition from other religious faiths (Catholic, Jewish) and from secular theories (darwinism, socialism)[1]. The generalized discovery of slums thus answered many needs. Partly, it was the result of a typically Victorian mixture of social anxiety, morbid curiosity, and moralistic attitude (the slum as a dangerous *terra incognita* to be explored, charted, and finally controlled) [Keating, ed., 1976]. Partly, it was the reflection of the early sociological involvement of middle-class reformers in what would soon become the "settlement movement" (the slum as a field of social practice and experiment). And partly, it was the expression of a wider cultural trend coincident with the development of realist writing (the slum as yet another region to be added to the American literary map). Whatever the motive, the very condition of "outsiders" of these journalists, reformers, artists, and writers generally (but with a few significant exceptions) implied a set of values reaffirming and reinforcing separateness — those of mainstream America, with its genteel preoccupations, moralities, and stereotypes.

This was already apparent in a series of works which, in their development from crude "city investigations" to more ambitious surveys, can be viewed as veritable path-finders in the field of American sociology. From the end of the Civil War, a real *genre* developed, that could boast several works specifically devoted to New York[2]. Although built on the contrast of light and shadow, wealth and poverty, virtue and vice, in most of them the Lower East Side did not yet emerge as a clearly defined area, with an identity by itself. It was simply Gotham Court, Bayard, Mott and Mulberry streets, the Five Points — abysses of dejection to be contrasted with the splendors of Broadway and Fifth Avenue, within a metropolis that contained "two cities", the beautiful *and* the ugly. The function of contrast ascribed to these still undefined areas inevitably conditioned the image the reader made of them[3].

A more systematic view began to take shape in those writings which tried to focus exclusively on the city's poorer areas. In Edward Crapsey's *The Nether Side of New York; or, The Vice, Crime, and Poverty of the Great Metropolis* [Crapsey 1872, 1969], for instance, although the contrast technique has not yet completely disappeared[4], the city's hidden face is investigated in full. But the author's view is biased. To him, the "nether side" basically coincides with the petty or not so petty criminal underworld. This receives extensive coverage through fifteen chapters, accurately portraying the deeds and dens of professional and casual criminals, harbor thieves, "circular" swindlers, "skinners", "fences", gamblers of all sorts, prostitutes, and even abortionists. Only three chapters ("Tenement Life", "Outcast Children", "Pauperism") are devoted to a description of slum life, with the result of practically relating it to vice and crime. Crapsey describes Gotham Court and the area of Madison, Grand, Corlears, Monroe, and Jackson streets. He offers estimates, data, and figures on poverty and overcrowding, with particular attention to the condition of thousands of children abandoned in the streets and to the physical and moral implications of pauperism. But, to him, these evils are simply the *expression* of crime and vice[5]. New York's masses become *tout court* 'our criminal, disorderly, and pauper classes' (p.24). Immigration, ignorance, party chicanery and the lack of a resident middle class ('that invaluable balance-wheel to political action', p.8) have turned the city into 'a camping ground [...], a collection of Bedouins' (p.7). And so, albeit devoid of morbidity and sensationalism, the book has no description of workplaces, community life, leisure-time activities, no hint of the complex cultural texture laboriously woven by these "aliens". The "nether side" is just dejection, poverty, and crime.

A similar picture, but wider in scope, emerges from Charles Loring Brace's *The Dangerous Classes of New York, and Twenty Years' Work Among Them* [Brace 1872]. From the title itself, the book betrays the same social anxiety as Crapsey's. The recurring use of the term *prolétaires* reminds the reader of the quite recent Paris Commune, and Brace also refers several times to the 1863 New York Draft Riots[6]. While the equation "proletarians=criminals" holds true to Brace as well, his interest is mainly drawn to a *certain* layer of the population, viewed as the biggest threat to the city's and the nation's social stability — the waifs, the urchins, the gamins, the ragamuffins, the street arabs, 'the outcast street-children grown up to be voters, to be the implements of demagogues, the "feeders" of the criminals, and the sources of domestic outbreaks and violations of law' (p.ii). In Brace's voyage of discovery, supplemented by twenty years' work as preacher and reformer, the Lower East Side appears once more as a series of notorious places rather than as a well-defined area. But the author has a sharp eye for the different sections of the neighborhood. He describes 'the infamous German "Rag-pickers' Den", in Pitt and Willett Streets — double rows of houses, flaunting with dirty banners, and the yards heaped up with bones and refuse' (p.93), or 'the murderous blocks in Cherry and Water Streets, where so many dark crimes were continually committed, and where the little girls who flitted about with baskets and wrapped up in old shawls became familiar with vice before they were out of childhood' (pp.93-94), or 'the Italian quarter of the "Five Points" [where], in large tenement-houses, were packed hundreds of poor Italians mostly engaged in carrying through the city and country "the everlasting hand-organ", or selling statuettes' (p.194).

But the initial equation dominates the book, constraining the whole neighborhood within its frame of reference and forcing everything under the banner of brutishness. Amid descriptions of miserable living conditions, quotations from records and reports, moral considerations on poverty and vice, heredity and environment, plans for "industrial schools" and proposals for the creation of jobs, only once does Brace open a window on the slums' culture, just to close it quickly again:

> The great amusement of this multitude of street vagabonds is the cheap theatre. Like most boys, they have a passion for the drama. But to them the pictures of kings and queens, the processions of courtiers and soldiers on the stage, and the wealthy gentlemen aiding and rescuing distressed peasant-girls, are the only glimpses they ever get of the great world of history and society above them, and they are naturally entranced by them. Many a lad will pass a night in a box, and spend his last sixpence, rather than lose this show. Unfortunately, these low theatres seem the rendezvous for all the disreputable characters; and here the "bummers" make the acquaintance of the higher class whom they so much admire, that of "flashmen", thieves, pickpockets, and rogues. We have taken the pains at different times to see some of the pieces represented in these places and have never witnessed anything improper or

immoral. On the contrary, the popular plays were always of a heroic and moral cast (p.345).

The picture gets clearer in 1890, with Jacob A. Riis's *How the Other Half Lives* [Riis 1890, 1971], the first systematic study of New York's tenements — a reality by then practically (if not completely) synonimous with the Lower East Side. Himself an immigrant from Denmark, Riis leads his readers where the 'whole district is a maze of narrow, often unsuspected passage-ways' (p.49) — to the German, Irish, Italian, Black, Chinese, Jewish quarters, to the sweatshops of the garment and cigar industries, to the dives on the waterfront, to the dens of beggars and thieves. He gives first-hand accounts and official statistics about population density, death rate, cost of living, rents, wages, and work hours. He carefully explains the mechanisms at the core of the "sweating system" and accurately describes the work of basters and finishers, cutters and cigar-makers. He shows why and how tenements developed in New York and the appalling conditions in which their dwellers are compelled to live. He devotes whole chapters to female and child labor as well as to crime, pauperism and alcoholism, and draws up the first maps of the neighborhood's ethnic enclaves, sketching their daily life and reciprocal relationships:

Bayard Street is the high road to Jewtown across the Bowery, picketed from end to end with outposts of Israel. Hebrew faces, Hebrew signs, and incessant chatter in the queer lingo that passes for Hebrew on the East Side attend the curious wanderer to the very corner of Mulberry Street. But the moment he turns the corner the scene changes abruptly. Before him lies spread out what might better be the market-place in some town in Southern Italy than a street in New York — all but the houses; they are still the same old tenements of the unromantic type. But for once they do not make the fore-ground in a slum picture from the American metropolis. The interest centres not in them, but in the crowd they shelter only when the street is not preferable, and that with the Italian is only when it rains or he is sick. When the sun shines the entire population seeks the street, carrying on its household work, its bargaining, its love-making on street or sidewalk, or idling there when it has nothing better to do, with the reverse of the impulse that makes the Polish Jew coop himself up in his den with the thermometer at stewing heat...(pp.49-50)[7].

Even such a pioneer work has severe limits. Riis's quest for an integrated and homogeneous American society implied an urge to dismiss immigrant cultures, which are thus approached, experienced, and described as undifferentiated wholes without inner shades and contradictions. At worst, they are seen as sources of dangerous social and cultural diversity[8]. As in the cases of Crapsey and Brace, this attitude is not simply the result of personal biases or of inadequate investigative work. Neither is it the result of the complexity of the author's central purpose (be it the rescue of street arabs or the battle against the slum), leaving little space for other concerns. Rather, it is the expression of the search for a social and cultural *cordon sanitaire* [Fried 1979; Hales 1984]. At the same time, the sharp critique of New York's tenements and their *raison d'être* (profits) is accompanied by rather modest proposals (the elimination of a particularly shameful block, the closing of subhuman lodging-houses, the opening of a park), or by naive appeals to the humanity of landlords and employers which in the end voice a pervasive and frustrating sense of helplessness: 'there is no way out; [...] the "system" that was the evil offspring of public neglect and private greed has come to stay, a storm-centre for ever of our civilization. [...] the tenements will exist in New York forever' (p.1, 14). A threat thus hangs over the stability of both metropolis and country, in the form of 'a proletariat ready and able to avenge the wrongs of their crowds' (p.13). Should the days of "mob-rule" return, asks Riis, should 'the vast army of workers, held captive by poverty, [rise up in rage,] what will the harvest be?' (p.17). The book ends with the image — so common in Victorian social literature and rather disturbing for an American reader living in the turbulent 1890s — of a 'mighty population' that, like a sea about to rise in storm and to sweep away everything before itself, 'heaves uneasily in the tenements' (p.229). And the closing words seem to sum up the book's peculiar mixture of intuition and naivety:

Once already our city, to which have come the duties and responsibilities of metropolitan greatness before it was able to fairly measure its task, has felt the swell of its resistless flood. If it rise once more, no human power may avail to check it. The gap between the classes in which it surges, unseen, unsuspected by the thoughtless, is widening day by day. No tardy enactment of law, no political expedient, can close it. Against all other dangers our system of government may offer defence and shelter; against this not. I know of but one bridge that will carry us over safe, a bridge founded upon justice and built of human hearts. I believe that the

danger of such conditions as are fast growing up around us is greater for the very freedom which they mock. The words of the poet, with whose lines I prefaced this book, are truer to-day, have far deeper meaning to us, than when they were penned forty years ago:
"Think ye that building shall endure
Which shelters the noble and crushes the poor?" (p.229).

II.

But Brace and Riis were no simple journalists or slummers, who ventured into the depths of the metropolis to emerge with titillating and moralistic reports on a dark and vicious underworld. In different periods and with different rôles, both were active in the wide reform movement, made up of tract societies, temperance and evangelical missionaries, sanitary reformers, that had begun to develop in order to face the serious problems of industrialization, urbanization, and immigration. In 1843, Robert M. Hartley had founded the Association for Improving the Conditions of the Poor (A.I.C.P.). Ten years later, Brace himself had founded the Children's Aid Society (C.A.S.). Then, in the second half of the century, the Young Men's Christian Association (Y.M.C.A.), the Salvation Army, the Charity Organization Society (C.O.S.) were born [Bremner 1956, 1972; P. Boyer 1978]. Common to all of them, notwithstanding differences in programs and expectations, was a twofold aim: to control socially and culturally the new "alien" masses and to reassure an isolated and bewildered middle class by offering it a chance of concrete action. The slum population had to be "reformed" and, in the typical Puritan and Victorian contention that given conditions are the result of moral fault and character weakness, "moral uplift" was to be essentially a matter of personal change.

So, the C.O.S. operated a network of "friendly visitors" who kept careful files of individuals and families, suggested the most fitting type of assistance, and more generally proposed themselves as models of behavior[9]. For its part, the C.A.S. directed its efforts towards youths adrift in the streets, trying to envisage credible alternatives to their vagrancy. It also endeavoured to give a unique direction to already existing programs and to increase the number of institutions able to welcome kids and stamp out harmful street influences, while safeguarding 'the best quality of this class — their sturdy independence' [Brace 1872, p.100]. Places were thus inaugurated such as the

Newsboys' Lodging House in Park Place, the Shakespeare Hotel (a permanent lodging-house for homeless boys at the corner of Duane and Chambers streets), the Wilson Industrial School on Avenue D, the various Boys' Meetings on East 8th Street and Avenue D, the lodging house and industrial school for homeless boys at 630 East 6th Street, and so on. The high point of the C.A.S.'s activity was then the dispatch of many of these boys and girls to the West, where they could live and work with new families in a supposedly regenerating contact with the land[10]. A substantial continuity linked these reform agencies, both those based on voluntary work and the more "scientific" ones. Above all, they shared a deep concern about the ever widening gulf between social classes and the project of a "middle-classification" of the poor, which inevitably implied the break up of the immigrant communities into a shere sum of individuals to be isolated first and uplifted later.

The last decade of the century was experiencing a deep economic, social, and cultural crisis, in the shift from *laissez-faire* to monopoly capitalism, from Social Darwinism to pragmatism and environmentalism, and from a purely individualistic and paternalistic view of what had to be done in the slums to a more complex perspective which involved both government and the propertied classes [Hofstadter 1955; Wiebe 1967]. In this new context, such historical organizations as the A.I.C.P., the C.A.S., the C.O.S., began a steady decline. While still maintaining the basic purposes of control and reassurance, the reformist approach had to change, and of this transitional phase Riis was undoubtedly a central figure. With his multifaceted activity as a journalist, writer, photographer, and reformer, Riis — an intimate friend and collaborator of Theodore Roosevelt when the latter was president of New York City's Police Board — seemed to embody that transition and to anticipate future developments [Riis 1901, 1966; Lane 1974].

It was during this period that the first "settlement houses" — modelled on London's Toynbee Hall — were established. They were community centers managed by social workers who, unlike the earlier "friendly *visitors*", actually *lived and operated* in the slums. The most famous were Jane Addams's Hull House in Chicago and, in New York, in the very heart of the Lower East Side, Stanton Coit's Neighborhood Guild (later renamed University Settlement), Lillian Wald's Henry Street Settlement, the Educational Alliance, the College Settlement, and, later on, the Christodora House, the Grand Street Settlement, and several others[11]. The settlements organized kindergartens and evening schools, held parties and holiday celebrations, sponsored theatre groups and art classes, promoted investigations into living and working conditions, exposed irregularities and misuses on part of landlords and employers, helped in the organization of non-unionized workers and in the propaganda for women's vote, and — in a broader sense — attended to the Americanization of the immigrants. They were veritable outposts of an enlightened middle class which had come to believe less in the individual nature of misery and more in the rôle of environment in causing it, and was persuaded of the possibility of a concerted action in close touch with "the other half". In its purpose 'to bring men and women of education into closer relations with the laboring classes for their mutual benefit' [quoted in Bremner 1956, 1972, p.62], the University Settlement seemed determined to put into practice the final image of *How the Other Half Lives*: that of a bridge between the classes as the only remedy against the threat posed by a sea swelling in the slums.

But the world of the settlement movement was a rather composite one. Within the general framework of an Americanization drive, different positions coexisted. Some social workers were genuinely interested in a deeper *knowledge* of the immigrants' ways and mores as a first step to a concerted action. Others were more biased by middle-class views and fears, and thus objected to any kind of manifestation of social and cultural separateness on part of the various communities. Last but not least, the "melting-pot theory", with its rethorical (and contradictory) updating of old democratic ideals, was also attracting some attention [Gleason 1964; Sollors 1986]. So, while a great part of the settlement movement still expressed a paternalistic attitude, a sort of cultural "trickle down" theory, some "houses" became a fruitful terrain of conflict and negotiation and a venue for the social and cultural creativity of the Lower East Side masses.

The variety of these positions (the genuine interest as well as the stereotyped prejudice) can be clearly read in the articles and essays of the settlement workers, in the pages of important organs such as *The Charities Review* (which in 1901 changed its name to *Charities*, in 1905 to *Charities and the Commons*, and in 1909 to *The Survey*), in the reports of the Henry Street Settlement, of the University Settlement, of the College Settlement, of the Greenwich House, and in the memoirs of activists like Lillian Wald and Mary Simkhovitch[12]. Whatever their theoretical or cultural limits, these writings, even the most hostile to the immigrants' ways of life, contain a wealth of material that cannot be slighted. The Lower East Side now really comes to the surface with an identity of its own, in all its physical, cultural, social traits.

But the reformers were not the only ones interested in it. The growth in importance and diffusion of newspapers and magazines was one of the most striking phenomena of the post-Civil War period. A more pragmatic attitude and the need to win a larger readership led editors and journalists to pay a keener attention to contemporary society. Life in the immigrant slums soon became a subject of great appeal. Not so strait-jacketed by reformist preoccupations, the journalists of the *Harper's Weekly* and *Monthly*, *Frank Leslie's Illustrated Newspaper*, *Scribner's Magazine*, *The Bookman*, *The Cosmopolitan*, *The Outlook*, the *New York Commercial Advertiser*, and of several others, were thus ready to depict certain panoramas with an attention and an immediacy that were often lacking in the settlements' reports and made up for the excess of local color and sensationalism such newspapers and magazines were often prone to. In this context of progressive discovery — albeit contradictory and incomplete —, a remarkable book appeared in 1902, Hutchins Hapgood's *The Spirit of the Ghetto*.

Its author was neither a reformer in the mold of Brace or Riis, nor a sociologist involved in settlement work[13]. He belonged to the growing number of turn-of-the-century "new journalists", uprooted intellectuals attracted by the "other America" who would later turn to naturalistic fiction, to muckraking, or to a radicalism often tinged with *bohème* — Stephen Crane, Frank Norris, Theodore Dreiser, Jack London, Upton Sinclair, Josiah Flynt, Ernest Poole, Charlotte Perkins Gilman, Mabel Dodge Luhan, Lincoln Steffens, John Reed, and many others. Quite different as authors, they were united by a strong desire for a new kind of relationship with American reality — or, better, with *those* American realities that did not agree with ruling values. Coming to the big metropolis from smalltown America, Hapgood found a job at the *New York Commercial Advertiser*, where Lincoln Steffens had just been made editor. Under the guiding hand of Abraham Cahan, who was also on the staff, he discovered the Lower East Side's ethnic and cultural complexity and became fascinated with it. He approached the neighborhood with a curiosity that was not morbid and with a receptivity that was free of biases (much in the same way in which John Reed would approach the striking Paterson silkworkers in 1912 and thus discover the "other America"): 'I was led to spend much time in certain poor resorts of Yiddish New York not through motives either philanthropic or sociological, but simply by virtue of the charm I felt in men and things there. East Canal and the Bowery have interested me more than Broadway and Fifth Avenue' [Hapgood 1902, 1967, p.5].

Hapgood does not conceal or gloss over the miseries and hardships of life in the Lower East Side. But he understands that something else is also occurring south of East 14th Street — something which, although rooted in misery and hardship, represents a phenomenon of great promise for the future. In fact, '[n]o part of New York has a more intense and varied life than the colony of Russian and Galician Jews who live on the East Side and who form the largest Jewish city in the world. The old and the new come here into close contact and throw each other into high relief' (p.9). Precisely this 'contact' of old and new Hapgood singles out as one of the most creative aspects of a reality too often dismissed as ugly and brutalizing. It is not — or, at least, it is not so much — a sort of romantic attraction for an outcast world that draws Hapgood to the area, but rather the understanding that there, out of this 'contact', a composite, almost unknown, culture is being born. In order to eradicate indifference and refusal, Hapgood probes this anonimity, reaches beyond it, and the articles he writes between 1898 and 1902 offer what was so often missing in earlier surveys — a view of daily life in all its aspects (work and leisure, jealously guarded traditions and surfacing new cultural expressions, the rôle of old and young, men and women, the tensions unleashed in the new American context) and the picture of an evolving culture, in which it is already possible to catch the signs of its future major contributions[14].

There emerges a text made up of scenarios and atmospheres, and at the same time of individuals. Precious because so rare, the portraits stand out of Morris Rosenfeld, Jacob Gordin, Abraham Cahan, Jacob Epstein, Bernard Gussow, Abraham Wald, of writers, artists, journalists, theatre folk and religious people, some to return to the anonimity of the ghetto, others to become famous far beyond its borders.

One of his friends called the poet [Abraham Wald] on one occasion an intellectual *débauché*. It was in a Canal Street café, where Wald was talking in an excited tone to several other intellectuals. He is a short, stocky man, with a suggestion of physical power. His eyes are brilliant, and there seems to be going on in him a sort of intellectual consumption. He is restlessly intent in manner, speaks in images, and is always passionately convinced of the truth of what he sees so clearly but seldom expresses in cold logic. His fevered idealism meets you in his frank, quick gaze and impulsive and rapid speech (pp.107-108).

To *this* "nether side of New York", Hapgood would return in 1910 with *Types from City Streets*, this time crossing the boundaries of the Jewish ghetto and exploring the world of the Bowery. In its dives and saloons, so despised by reformers, Hapgood thinks he can find the cultural antidotes to a widespread and passive acceptance of middle-class values, one of his favorite targets: 'It is not rare to meet a "tough" in the unsavory resorts of the Bowery who is much more nearly related to the chosen aristocrat than to the clean and ordinary citizen of the comfortable middle-class. [...] A general air of distinction sometimes prevails even amidst the extravagances of the ragtime' [Hapgood 1910, p.28]. To a certain extent, this frame of reference also constitutes the book's limitation. But whenever it is left aside we have Hapgood at his best, skilful at alternating collective scenes and individual portraits, sharp analyses and quick sketches of a world so little explored and so full of surprises and stimula, between vaudeville and farce, ragtime and melodrama, crime and prostitution, sport and *bohème*.

Memorable thus remain the pages devoted to popular entertainment, the interviews with famous prize-fighters, the tales of such key-characters of the area as "Chuck" Connors, the gallery of Bowery "types" (the "tough", the "spieler", the "cruiser" so similar to Stephen Crane's Maggie), the confessions of the celebrated prize-fighter John L. Sullivan, ever ready to take off the boxing gloves to tread the boards of small, smoke-filled theatres, because '"acting is better than fighting"'(p.339), their rough-hewn, vivid speech, and the sense of a continuous search for "de real thing": because '"de real thing", "on de level" are two phrases which best express the canons of Bowery morality. Be frank and direct, and care not for frills, but for "the real thing" — these are the two great Bowery commandments' (p.33).

III.

The same pattern — from Crapsey to Hapgood — can be detected in the fictional discovery of the Lower East Side. Sensational writing — the form it most immediately took — had its antecedents in George Lippard and E. Z. C. Judson (whose popular romances freely mixed gothic elements, *feuilleton* themes, and melodramatic situations) and got much of its inspiration and material from the abundant production of "city *éxposés*", often reproducing that school's conceptual clichés. It resorted to the central and reassuring conventions of depicting slums and slum-life as mysteries to be unveiled and brought to light by proxy, before being abandoned again to their own destiny, and of using the "descent-to-Hell" trope with a policeman or detective as a Virgilian guide. Rather than giving birth to a specific genre, however, the sensational approach — with its melodramatic overtones and Victorian moralism — influenced a wide range of different works, often tempting ethnic writers as well [Bremner 1956; Fine 1977; Giamo 1989; Sante 1991]. Some of its features can be found, for instance, in Edward Smith King's *Joseph Zalmonah* (1893), which dramatized Joseph Barondess's life and struggles in the Lower East Side's garment industry, or in Roy McCardell's *Wage Slaves of New York* (1899) — a manicheistic division between "good" and "bad" fellows, a nativist accent in describing foreign political activists, the common stereotype of the "dark" woman as a symbol of passion and seduction, the presence of veritable "spirits of evil" as the true perpetrators of social injustice...

Romantic fascination was the other most immediate reaction, well exemplified by "Sidney Luska"'s Jewish novels — *As It Was Written: A Jewish Musician's Story* (1885), *Mrs. Peixada* (1886) and *The Yoke of the Torah* (1887)[15]. But even this reaction was the expression of the tendency to isolate the neighborhood. In William Dean Howells's *A Hazard of New Fortunes* (1890), the novel that marks a turning point in the author's career and in the development of realistic city fiction, the distance between the Lower East Side and the rest of the city is graphically pictured through the device of having the main character Basil March discover the immigrant quarter during his rambles about the city — a device that brought together Dickensian tradition and contemporary social exploration. March's attitude towards the downtown area is initially patronizing, as he considers 'the picturesque raggedness of Southern Europe with the old kindly illusion that it existed for [his] appreciation and that it found adequate compensation for poverty in this' [Howells 1890, II, p.67]. Only after meeting Berthold Lindau, a German immigrant and Socialist whom he calls to work for the new magazine he is editing, does March's attitude towards the Lower East Side become a more intimate one, and fascination for picturesque exteriority gives way to an embryonic understanding of its life's complexity. It is at this point that Howells gives his readers some of the very earliest pictures of the neighborhood, in which neither sensationalism nor mawkishness are present. But — and this contradiction is at the heart of Howells's social and cultural credo and more generally can be taken as emblematic of much "outside" writing — March is simply a "foreigner in the land", an honest and even sympathetic, but always external, observer who consciously keeps his distance from the human material he is discovering, in a way always by proxy, *through* Lindau. So, when Lindau dies during a confrontation between police and strikers, the connecting link is definitively broken, and separation between the two worlds becomes once more insuperable.

Social and cultural distance was also implicit in the sentimental and picturesque school, that "tenement tale tradition" which was more directly influenced by "local color". In the works of Luigi Donato Ventura (*Peppino*, 1885)[16], Brander Matthews (*Vignettes of Manhattan*, 1894), Edward Townsend (*"Chimmie Fadden"; Major Max; and Other Stories*, 1895; *A Daughter of the Tenements*, 1895), Richard Harding Davis (*Gallagher and Other Stories*, 1891; *Van Bibber and Others*, 1892), James Sullivan (*Tenement Tales of New York*, 1895), Julian Ralph (*People We Pass*, 1896), Henry C. Bunner (*Jersey Street and Jersey Lane: Urban and Suburban Sketches*, 1896), Jacob A. Riis (*Out of Mulberry Street*, 1897; *Children of the Tenements*, 1903) — in these and many other works, classes are still unrelated and a provisional connecting link is necessary. A "slumming" novelist or journalist is generally invested with the function, the result being that the work has rather the form of the sketch limited to one episode, character, or place. Mystery is reduced and picturesqueness enhanced, or replaced with a condescending irony. In keeping with the "local color" tenets, more attention is also devoted to slum language, customs, and folkways, and this gives a realistic cast to the portraits of people, places and situations. Unrelatedness, while undoubtedly present, is less definitive or absolute than in the sensational fiction. Some kind of relationship is looked for, although generally in the form of a superimposition of mainstream cultural stereotypes on the Lower East Side world — almost an attempt to assimilate culturally and socially the lower classes to the higher ones.

With the partial exception of Sullivan and Ralph, who tended to work more from *within* a given locale, almost completely avoiding the connecting link and thus reducing the "distance effect"[17], these works present the usual stereotypes of poverty ennobled and virtue rewarded, female purity and family sacredness, and such ethnic *déjà-vus* as greedy Jews, mysterious Orientals, stiletto-armed Italians, drunken Irish, gloomy Germans, and wild-eyed Anarchists. And, while some of them have undeniable documentary importance, pathetic sentimentalism generally prevails. The case of Jacob A. Riis is telling. While his photographic work has nothing mawkish in it, his literary sketches abound precisely in a sort of second-rate Dickensianism and Bret-Harteism that drastically undercuts his material's potentiality (not by chance, so many of his stories — "The Rent Baby", "The Kid Hangs Up His Stocking", "The Slipper-Maker's Fast", "Little Will's Message", in *Children of the Tenement* — take place on Christmas Eve, or on what the author apparently considers its Jewish counterpart, Yom Kippur).

266

The real turning point comes in 1893. In that year, Stephen Crane publishes in fact, under the pseudonym of Johnstone Smith, *Maggie. A Girl of the Streets*, and three years later follows it up with *George's Mother*. He is the first author who convincingly manages to cross the borders, both socially and culturally. Not only, in fact, are both his short novels located in the Bowery area, but the point of view, the approach, the intimate assumptions are radically different from all previous slum literature. On one hand, Crane does away with the fictional *trait d'union*, the Virgilian guide who up to then had seemed an unavoidable convention in this kind of writing. Readers are thus immediately plunged into the middle of the Lower East Side and of its culture (and, as a matter of fact, of a very specific part of it, such as the Bowery world), now seen through the eyes of its inhabitants, without shields nor mediations. This reversal of a common point of view is not simply a structural change. It is a serious conceptual turn, because, in so doing, Crane presents the quarter no more as the *separate* (mysterious, abysmal) world of slum novelists and "tenement tale" local colourists, or of Howells himself. In his eyes, the Bowery, the Lower East Side, are *organically* linked to the rest of the city, in a geographical, cultural, and social continuity that the new point of view makes clear.

The world of Maggie and George *is* a jungle and as such Crane describes it, with a warm irony that implies emotional participation. He thus avoids the traps of sentimentalism with its poverty ennobled, femininity sanctified, family extolled, suffering rewarded. Individuals fight each other, because the task of each of them, in the city, is to stay alive, notwithstanding the tremendous toll exacted by the environment. But, as toil, overcrowding, misery, ignorance turn Crane's characters into jungle beasts, we also come to realize that there is more than pure dejection. The Bowery *has* a culture of its own — the saloons, the cafés, the small theatres, where the borderline between entertainment, lawlessness, and prostitution is surely blurred, are filled with an ever-flowing life energy. And now the author's target becomes clear. Because it is here that a subtler enemy than simply environment or social injustice hides itself. It is the set of received beliefs, concepts, and ideas, which form a thick net and entrap those individuals who are incapable to harden themselves against them. This is what really crushes Maggie — the weight of social and cultural conventions that she inherits from the missionary tracts distributed along the Bowery, from the sentimental novels forming the neighborhood's reading fare, from the outside values and the "transcendental realism" filling the popular melodramas. In this also consists the social and cultural continuity that

267

Crane stresses in *Maggie* and, perhaps less successfully, in *George's Mother*.

In both novels, Crane thus gives us a masterful picture of a budding modern entertainment, at a time when the dialectical relationship between uptown and downtown, immigrant worlds and mainstream culture, was most acute. Ragtime, vaudeville, Bowery theatres are shown from the inside, in their great variety and in the ways in which they contribute to the Americanization of the immigrants and speak an alternative and often transgressive language [Crane 1893, 1984, Chapter VII. Also see Fine 1977; Gullason 1978; Giamo 1989]. That the author's view is still bleak and pessimistic — notwithstanding the courage with which he did away with shields, *traits d'union*, and conventions — cannot be blamed entirely upon him, so arduous (even to insiders) was the road away from a one-dimensional view of the Lower East Side.

Things began to change significantly by the turn of the century. Crane's and Cahan's books had showed *what* slum-life really amounted to and *how* it could be described, the new generation of city journalists (Steffens, Hapgood, Poole) had helped to bring about a better understanding of that experience, the Lower East Side itself had begun to speak its own voice, new ideas of realism had emerged, and some readers had thus increasingly come to judge by their standards. Social distance was, if not canceled, reduced and, above all, the ideological concept of the unrelatedness of the classes gave way to a more critical acknowledgement of the bond tightly linking them and of the complexity of such a relationship. Theodore Dreiser's *Sister Carrie* (1900) — although dealing with the Bowery only at the end, and notwithstanding its gloomy portrait of that world — is exemplary. His Bowery is invested by exactly that metaphorical function that the Lower East Side was more and more acquiring in American letters. It is *the* social bottom, but rather than being something separate from society, it is organically a part of it — the city's drain that gathers and disposes human waste (and from this point of view the novel should be read together with some of Dreiser's later sketches, particularly "The River of the Nameless Dead", collected in 1923 in the beautiful and too often forgotten *The Color of a Great City*). It *is* a sad picture, but, as in Crane, it makes a clean sweep of the sentimental and hypocritical approach of so much earlier "outside" fiction.

In the following years, even the element most missing in this literature — a rightful acknowledgement of the neighborhood's cultural texture — becomes more explicit. "Bruno Lessing" (pseud. of Rudolph Block), with *Children of Man* (1903) and *Lapidowitz the Schnorrer:*

"With the Best Intention" (1914), and Myra Kelly, with *Little Citizens* (1904), *Wards of Liberty* (1907) and *Little Aliens* (1910), offered more balanced portraits of the Lower East Side's world. And finally, in James Oppenheim's *Dr.Rast* (1909) and *The Nine-Tenth* (1911), Theresa Malkiel's *Diary of a Shirt-Waist Striker* (1910), Florence Converse's *The Children of Light* (1912), *"Albert Edwards"* (Arthur Bullard)'s *Comrade Yetta* (1913), and Zoe Beckley's *A Chance to Live* (1918), the neighborhood really began to speak its own voice through the voice of outsiders. Mostly written by settlement workers or trade union activists, these minor novels managed to show its social and cultural complexity, the variety of experiences and languages, the dramatic texture of dejection and creativity, and generally introduced an eloquent new trope — that of the evolution of an American character suddenly and deeply exposed to such an alien world (and above all to its struggles for personal dignity and social justice) and thoroughly remolded by this encounter.

With John Dos Passos's *Manhattan Transfer* (1925), the process reaches its apex. Here, the Lower East Side becomes an integral part of the city kaleidoscope, no longer a mysterious or sensational place. More than that, it has by now attained that kind of metaphorical and mythopoeic dimension. It is the place where much America comes from, individually and collectively — the place of the past, of history, of one's own roots. But it is also the place of otherness, of contrast and antagonism, where the reversal of codes and lifestyles is experienced *per force* rather than *by choice*. And the place from where inspiration can flow perhaps more vividly and impressively than from elsewhere. And, in this, the artists of the word were now in complete agreement with the artists of the image.

IV.

The force of such books as *How the Other Half Lives* and *The Spirit of the Ghetto* did not lie, in fact, in the written word only. It came from the images as well, which directly or indirectly accompanied them. Besides being a journalist and reformer, Jacob A. Riis was a veritable pioneer of American social photography. The first edition of *How the Other Half Lives* contained only seventeen imperfect halftones and eighteen line drawings from photos [Madison 1971, p.viii; Alland, Sr., 1974, p.30]. But in those years, Riis had already begun to use lantern slides as visual aids in lectures and debates about the urban problem, and in later editions (and in such other books as *Children of the Poor* and *The Battle with the Slum*) photographs became ever more important.

As to *The Spirit of the Ghetto*, Jacob Epstein contributed forty-eight sketches and Bernard Gussow three. Another chapter was thus being written in turn-of-the-century New York's complex cultural history, which again had the Lower East Side at its center. Once more, its rôle wasn't simply the passive one of making available materials and situations till then unknown or ignored. It also was the active one of encouraging artists to a deeper expressive research, and almost made certain styles or technical choices inevitable. In the end, it helped create iconic images that would interact with America in a strongly evocative way.

The question of how to present reality was central to nineteenth-century American culture. The need to know and document a process of discovery and colonization at first, of settlement and development afterwards — and at the same time to give birth to a national art —, had fueled discussions and arguments not only in the field of visual arts. Writers and painters, and later photographers, had accompanied scientific and military expeditions, and drawn and narrated a new world quite literally opening up before their eyes. Distinct American styles were slowly taking form in painting, in a relationship with European developments that was both of conflict and of mediation. The Hudson River School, the genre and *trompe-l'oeil* painters, the still-lifers and the artist-naturalists, all were variously manifesting a need for realism. But, while not indifferent to European trends and schools, these artists' indigenous realism expressed itself in forms and contents that were often stifled by the temptations of a celebratory and mannerist academism and classicism [Novak 1969; Mendelowitz 1970]. A fascinating response to the problem of attaining a high level of realism in representation seemed to come from photography. The dramatic photographs of the Civil War, the *réportages* on the various military and scientific expeditions and on the laying of the intercontinental railroads, the portraits of famous and common men and women had a tremendous effect on collective imaginary [Taft 1938, 1964; Jensen, Kerr, Belsky, eds., 1970; Welling 1978]. To the American artist, that still imperfect medium was a source of stimula as well as of threats, and, from that moment on, photography and painting would pursue each other without pause, sometimes influencing each other, sometimes claiming autonomy, separation, superiority.

As large cities developed, the need to document and represent them became even more urgent, as the debate on realism in fiction clearly shows [Berthoff 1965; Pizer 1966; Ziff 1966; Trachtenberg 1982]. In photography, while the so-called "grand style" seemed to derive from the urban experience the thrust towards a celebration of the Gilded Age

270

(above all in the photographs of the "White City", at the 1893 World's Columbian Exposition in Chicago) [Hales 1984], the reform movement was quick in finding out how to use the new medium in order to translate into practice the Victorian and "enlightened" expectations that characterized it — to reveal the living conditions hidden behind the facade and thus to mobilize public opinion around the issue. Some years later, in what can be viewed both as an apt definition of much late-19th-century reform movement and as a telling intuition on the rôle photography played in it, Lillian D. Wald would write: 'To my inexperience it seemed certain that conditions such as [the ones that could be found in the Lower East Side] were allowed because people did not *know*, and for me there was a challenge *to know and to tell*. [...] my naive conviction remained that, if people *knew* things, [...] such horrors would cease to exist...' [Wald 1915, 1971, p.8, my italics].

In the final analysis, the Gilded Age's movement for realism represented precisely the attempt to answer to a widespread need for security, in the belief that "to know and to tell" (and thus "to name", as it suits an authentic "map" of the real) means "to control", or perhaps "to exorcise". But, in an American context in which the visual dimension was becoming increasingly more central, merely "to tell" risked being not enough, if limited to words alone. Towards the end of the century, in particular, the complexity of city life, the recent architectural and urbanistic developments (skyscrapers, imposing stations and department stores, elevated railways, tenements, and bridges), and the mass arrival of immigrants from very different cultures necessitated means able to integrate — if not, indeed, to substitute — the written word in the representation of such a new and hectic reality. In the pages of countless city *exposés*, novels and short stories, the need *visually* to show what was being unveiled frequently resulted in a rather unique dramatic tension, almost as if photography — or even cinema — were already present *in nuce*, as a more or less conscious yearning for a more effective and expressive instrument of representation[18]. For their own part, turn-of-the-century reformers felt necessary to accompany the written or spoken word with images that were no mere ornaments, but possessed an apodictic eloquence and an intrinsic capacity to tell audiences "how things are". Initially, the image was still conceived as a vicarious surrogate for first-hand experience[19]. In time, the power of the images came to serve another logic. This was the era of a growing pragmatism, of a fascination for Jack London's 'irrefragable facts'. Photography was able to capture these "facts" and irrefragably to show them, because '[it] has an added realism of its own

271

[...], the average person believes implicitly that the photograph cannot falsify...' [Hine 1909; also see Bogardus and Szasz 1986]. This operation of reality capturing and reality taming also possessed clear reassuring purposes. By means of photography, it was possible to freeze the magmatic flow of contemporary reality, and thereby (perhaps) know it better, while simultaneously keeping the necessary, soothing distance. Fragmentary, vicarious, momentary as it was, this "knowledge" was of fundamental importance precisely for that middle class shocked by the 'non-rationality of reality' [Amoruso 1976, p.10], from which so many social reformers came.

Of this world, in which photography and reforms fed each other, Jacob A. Riis and Lewis W. Hine were undoubtedly the most famous protagonists. The birth of American social photography is due exactly to Riis's dissatisfaction with available media ('A drawing might have done it, but I cannot draw, never could. [...] I wrote, but it seemed to make no impression') [Riis 1901, 1966, pp.266-267]. The period was a favorable one, as technical innovations quickly followed one another. Dry plate and albumin printing paper were being introduced, George Eastman had perfected the film that could be rolled and launched the celebrated Kodak instantaneous camera, the easy-to-carry "detective" camera was put on the market, newspapers and magazines were experimenting with half-tone facsimile reproduction on newsprint, stereographs and lantern-slide shows were ever more commonly used as teaching aids or ways of entertainment, and new, still adventurous, lightning processes were being advertised in newspapers.

Riis was immediately fascinated by the possibility — so charged with symbolical and metaphorical valences — of bringing to light the darkest corners of the city scene. He began taking photoes almost by chance [Riis 1888], but slowly his night explorations became more systematic. First as a member of the New York Society of Amateur Photography, then with other colleagues detached at the Mulberry Street police headquarters or with representatives of various city boards (Dr. John Nagle, for example, Chief of the Bureau of Vital Statistics in the City Health Department), later on with the short-lived help of professional photographers, and lastly by himself, Riis put together a large documentation that triggered a series of chain reactions and influenced many later photographers. His experience was a pioneering one, but Riis never was a naive photographer, neither was his camera so candid. The construction of his photos was only *seemingly* haphazardous. The journalist-photographer painstakingly pursued the effect he wanted to reach, his aim being 'to terrify his audience with a vision of the most apocalyptic sort of chaos, threaten their worldview, then offer them a logic which replaced their lost fantasy but demanded activism in return' [Hales 1984, p.202].

Of Riis's activity, the Lower East Side was the central, albeit not exclusive, focus. The crowded streets and interiors, the contiguity of bodies, the constant feeling of claustrophobia and precariousness, the lack of light in flats and alleys, the reversal of middle-class living and working habits, the diversity of clothes, features, and postures — this was what Riis captured with his photoes and this in turn was what deeply affected his photographing. When projected on a screen, in front of an audience made up of citizens often unaware of (and in any case physically and mentally distant from) these realities, Riis's pictures were genuine "shock shots". Right from its title, for instance, "Bandits' Roost" (taken for Riis by Dr. Henry G. Piffard or by Richard Hoe Lawrence) conjures up a sense of impending danger, even though, at close examination, what we are struck by is the filth in the alley, the suffocating closeness of the houses, the absolute lack of privacy, the scarcity of light made worse by the festooning laundry, the instability of the brick and wood buildings (Table 3). "Mullen's Alley, Cherry Hill" or "Gotham Court" (both by Riis), with their gangs of boys who fill up the narrow, dark alleys, almost barring them from intruders, appear as additional versions of the same theme — future "bandits" caught in an apprenticeship that has in environment its chief element (Table 2).

Some of the indoor photos push the disorder, poverty, and precariousness of living to the foreground, thanks to the intelligent organization of spaces and bodies and to the perspective adopted by the photographer. Others possess the striking power of authentic candid shots, suspended as they are between the surprise of those caught by the camera and the shocked dismay of the person who uncovers such conditions. The documentation on the sweatshops is particularly important. Amid windows that block out daylight, crowded and unealthy rooms, floors littered with discards and remnants, piles of clothes heaped in corners, dirty and cluttered workbenches, bent and contorted bodies, feverish looks and gestures, the work of basters, finishers, cigarmakers, tiecutters is frozen for an instant, with results far more eloquent than many word descriptions (Table 4). In the street scenes, we perceive an initial sense of liberation — the impression of being able to breathe again, the anticipation of movements that can be given full vent after the constriction of the oppressive indoors and the merciless pace of work. But then the photographs tell us that here too congestion rules, and the street appears to us as a swirling river of bodies and objects compressed together, a series of frantic gestures of necessity, of daily errands without pose (Table 5).

273

In overt contrast with the "grand style"'s picturesque and celebratory tendencies, Riis's work represented a turning point in the current city photography. After him, the interest for the urban scene — even disengaged from reform aims — became more lively and sensitive to the signs and languages, human types and collective rhythms. In her cameos of street people — perhaps a little affected, but sympathetic and attentive to the smallest details of metropolitan reality —, E. Alice Austen managed for instance to steer clear of banal portraiture forever fluttering between anonymous little pictures and sentimental, romantic scenes. Somewhat later, Jessie Tarbox Beals did the same with her portraits of children in the streets and apartment interiors. In their photos, as in those of Warren Dickerson, Joseph and Percy Byron, John James McCook, and of so many unknown photographers, the Lower East Side again became the favourite physical and human laboratory, with its ant-like crowdedness, its gallery of faces and trades, its maze and tangle of cultures forming a paradigm of modern metropolis [Szasz and Bogardus 1974; Hales 1984] (Tables 6, 8, 10)[20]. Even in photography, however, the face of the quarter will continue to be a rather peculiar one — almost always the face of misery, very rarely the face of a composite culture modeled out of materials past and present. Surely, Riis took some shots of dive interiors, of San Gennaro and San Rocco altars, of street games, but that was all. In a way, his pictures confirm his social writings, and vice versa. His aim was to expose and compel to action. All that could possibly reveal a *separate* social and cultural *identity*, no matter how embryonic or fragmented, was of no great interest to him. Indeed, it became an embarrassing, menacing proof of the impossibility of control, of the final impracticability of that 'bridge founded upon justice and built of human hearts' he cherished so much.

The photographic work of Riis, Dickerson, Austin, and others would soon open the way for the great American photography. From the very beginning of the 20th century, two distinct trends delineated, which would run parallel in the following years, not without reciprocal influences. With Lewis W. Hine, social photography was to follow in Riis's steps and reach its peak during the Depression years, with Walker Evans, Dorothea Lange, Ben Shahn, Berenice Abbott, and so on. At the same time, Alfred Stieglitz's and Edward Steichen's Photo-Secession and then Charles Sheeler's and Paul Strand's early work would develop a more artistically oriented photography in which the medium's technical and pictorial possibilities become more important than mere subject matter, almost in competition with the European avant-garde, in quasi-constructivist, precisionist, or abstract compositions[21].

In the brief span of years separating Riis from Hine, many things changed in social photography. Hine worked in a context in which photography had become a central part of dailies and magazines, a fundamental ingredient of the articles in *Charities and the Commons* and *The Survey* (as well as of such radical publications as *The International Socialist Review*). For its part, social work had decidedly taken the road of the settlement houses, in a more scientific, and at the same time bureaucratic, approach. In harmony with the "age of reform"'s corporate idea of society, it was no longer a matter of the greatest urgency to *reveal* the existence of immigrant, working-class quarters. It was now more important to *document and catalogue* urban and national realities in all their aspects. Agencies multiplied, such as the National Civic Federation or the National Child Labor Commission, and so did production houses and picture agencies, such as Underwood and Underwood, the Byron Company, the Bain News Service, the Brown Bros., with their systematized catalogues of facts, persons, elements of city life.

For these reasons, Hine could no longer be a "pathfinder" like Riis, but, rather, a social-conscious artist working side by side with sociologists, demographers, physicians, in a kind of collective project of analysis of American society. He thus collaborated with the University of Chicago school of sociology, with the National Child Labor Commission, with several reform magazines and insitutions. As a consequence of this involvement, as well as out of a different personal sensibility, his point of view as a photographer changed too, and this change can easily be seen in the Ellis Island photos (which document the immigrants' dramatic impact with the new American reality), in the Lower East Side portraits (a veritable catalogue of human types, cultures, and nationalities), in the contribution to *The Survey*'s inquiry in the living and working conditions of Pennsylvania's industrial areas, and in the photographic essay *Men At Work* (1932), where a sort of Whitmanesque and even rhetorical praise of the "American worker" can already be felt, together with a growing interest for formal composition. In all this, Hine seems to be more attracted by and to the individual. Almost in a synthesis of Riis and Austen, he is drawn to the human element, more than he is interested in the environment's shock value. Which is not to say that the context is forgotten. Certainly, it acquires importance *because* the individual is there and is approached with a different spirit and aim. Such pictures as "Climbing into the Land of Promise" (1905), "Madonna of Ellis Island" (1905), or "East Side, New York" (c.1910), are able to capture the existential and ethnic complexity of their subjects, in a setting that has by now become part

275

both of the collective imaginary and of the medium's specific taxonomy [N. and W. Rosenblum, eds., 1977; Seixas 1987].

During the Depression years, public attention would focus even more sharply on "the other half", social photography tending more and more towards that 'profound and sober chronicling of the external world' [Elizabeth McCausland, quoted in Rosenblum 1985, p.130] that would become its own distinctive character. Once more, the Lower East Side was crucial — no more as a neighborhood to discover, but as a workers' neighborhood *par excellence*. The unemployed's demonstrations, the rent strikes, the tenants' movements, the living conditions in an area that was undergoing rapid transformations but still maintained its basic character and traditions — all these aspects caught the attention of the artists of the Works Projects Administration (such as Arnold Eagle, with his 1932-1938 *réportages* on the tenements) and of the leftist Photo League (with the Feature Groups series dedicated to certain neighborhoods of New York — e.g., the Pitt Street Document by Walter Rosenblum, or the photos by Leo Seltzer, Morris Engel, and many others).

V.

But, until the half-tone process for reproducing photographs on print was perfected, images in newspapers, magazines, and books had been limited to line drawings and engravings. For the 1890 edition of *How the Other Half Lives*, artists Kenyon Cox, Otto H. Bacher, Clifton H. Johnson, and W. C. Fitler redrew Riis's and his collaborators' photos. Other artists did the same with the photos by Riis, O. G. Mason, Frederick Vilmar, and E. Warrin, Jr., in Helen Campbell's *Darkness and Daylight: Or, Lights and Shadows of New York Life* (1897). In these same years, books and articles on slum life, illustrated by artist-reporters, became more and more frequent (it is the case of *Sketches of Lowly Life in a Great City*, 1899, entirely made up of drawings by Michael Angelo Woolf).

By comparing Riis's photos with these illustrations, it is easy to gauge the greater effectiveness of the former over the latter. First of all, the drawings followed nineteenth-century stylistic conventions. Wretched living conditions were somewhat ennobled by the Madonna-like expressions of the women and by the cherubin-like faces of the children. Interiors were sort of "cleaned up", and if it was really necessary to communicate a sense of misery and anguish, it was merely hinted at in single individuals, in a naively stereotyped way. Reality told in words could even be morbidly obscene, but its visual rendering had

276

to respect traditional canons of good taste and decency, thus implicitly recognizing the image's potential superiority as compared to the word. Canons and conventions apart, there were technical problems too. In order to be more understandable, drawings had to be cleared of many details that otherwise risked to clutter the scene. In so doing, the claustrophobic sense of darkness and congestion that made the photos so shocking was often lost, notwithstanding the artists' efforts to adhere to the original. Elsewhere, the difficulty — or technical impossibility — of rendering certain cavern-like atmospheres destroyed the efficacy of the original, flattening everything as in a stage backdrop.

The problem was a bit different for illustrations in *Harper's Weekly* or *Frank Leslie's Illustrated Magazine*, often entrusted to such fine artists as Charles Graham and Sol Eytinge, and, above all, to W. A. Rogers and E. W. Kemble (this last was also the illustrator of Mark Twain's *Adventures of Huckleberry Finn* and of Edward Townsend's *Daughter of the Tenements*). Here, the need to narrate visually slum life to a far removed public compelled the artist to create large street scenes, full of movement, figures, and details — but the results were often ambiguous. While a significant departure from the style and stereotypes of other illustrators' works, such drawings as, for instamce, "A Wedding in the Chinese Quarter — Mott Street, N.Y.", "In the Italian Quarter — Mulberry Street on a Winter Evening", "The Slaves of the Sweaters" (all by W. A. Rogers for *Harper's*) had other drawbacks (Illustrations 17, 18, 22). Their viewpoint and organization are such that the observer's eye is drawn to too many details (almost a *summa* of slum life) and, being unable to linger on them, slides along the retreating line of perspective — quite the opposite to the effect sought by Riis, of capturing the attention by focusing it on a few elements full of shock value.

Although somewhat artistically limited, it was however partly from newspaper and magazine illustrators that a decisive change came to American art at the turn of the century. Increasingly displaced by photography, many of these artist-reporters went back to painting and carried with them the treasures of technical skill and subject-matter gained in earlier profession. The history of this shift began in Philadelphia, where, at the Pennsylvania Academy, Thomas Eakins was Professor of Drawing and Painting and later Director. Along with Winslow Homer, Eakins was one of the great names of American painting in the second half of the 19th century. Both reacted against the era's sterile academic approach, with its neo-classical propensities and subordination to European models, and championed instead a robust realism in polemical response to squeamishness and timidity. While

277

Homer increasingly sought an almost exclusive relationship with nature (a sort of extreme evolution, full of tragic pathos, of the Hudson River School), Eakins continued to concentrate on the human figure, which he studied, painted, and taught with an intensity that would place him in open contrast with the ultra-conservative Academy [Goodrich 1933 and 1969]. There was much Whitman in Eakins, to the point that the poet's conception of an "athletic Democracy" seemed to pour into the canvases and teaching of the painter, convinced that 'respectability in art is appalling' [quoted in Perlman 1979, p.20][22] and that task of the artist was to peer deeply into the heart of American life and to portray its scenes and types.

Among Eakins's students was Robert Henri, who became a faculty member at the Academy and gathered around himself, first in Philadelphia and later in New York, a group of younger artists — John Sloan, George Luks, Everett Shinn, William Glackens, Maurice Prendergast, Ernest Lawson, Arthur Davies, and — somewhat at a distance — George Bellows. Coming from different backgrounds, they shared interests and experiences — the discovery of the Impressionists, the work as artist-reporters for important newspapers, a profound dissatisfaction with the contemporary American art and social scene, and an instinctive, perhaps romantic, attraction for the "other America". The job as artist-reporters, in particular, not only put them in direct contact with the full complexity of city life. It also forced them to learn technical skills that would prove precious for their development as realist painters[23]. This apprenticeship inevitably ended up refining photographic memory and attention to detail, and developed an ability to draw rapidly, to get at the heart of the matter, to express the emotional core of certain scenes. Above all, it enabled a new relationship with the city and its elements. When the group gathered again in New York around Henri, at the beginning of the century, the big metropolis seemed to boast all these characteristics and to stimulate personal approaches, orientations, and styles, out of a common nucleus [Sloan 1965; Negri 1989].

For Sloan, Bellows, Luks, and Shinn, the discovery of the Lower East Side was decisive. It was not a casual encounter, nor was it the fruit of sentimental or morbid curiosity[24]. It was born of a conscious search for contexts in which American life expressed itself with greater genuineness, pathos, and humour. In previous years, other artists had tried to approach pictorially America's other realities[25]. But they were isolated and somewhat ignored episodes. Things changed with this new group of young artists, who soon came to be known as the Eight, or Ash Can School. Their realism never was the photographic reproduction

278

of reality, nor the dark representation of misery. In their best works, we can perceive a profound closeness to the "human comedy" — a closeness able to catch its tragedy and its humour, its drama and its fun, and that for some of these artists also meant a personal political commitment[26]. Taken together, with their obvious differences in style and quality, the works of this group compose an extraordinary city pageant, a fascinating visual comment on the American metropolis and on the culture that was being born there, a catalogue of characters, situations, and sequences evoked with care and warm curiosity — the bars and the dives, the shows and the boxing matches, the crowd on the Bowery, the lighted shopwindows south of East 14th Street, the organ grinder and its small audience, the coffee-lines at night, the groups of girls leaving work, the street urchins, the parade of the Italian Bersaglieri in Little Italy, the Chinese restaurant and the McSorley's saloon, people sleeping or embracing on rooftops, laundry hung in the backyard, the crowded entrance of theatres or nickelodeons, the swim in the East River [Tables 15, 16, 17].

Above all, the human body catches the eye — the Whitmanesque body that, through Eakins and Henri, showed itself again in Sloan and Luks, in Shinn and Bellows — the '[c]rowds of men and women attired in the usual costumes' (Walt Whitman, "Crossing Brooklyn Ferry"), the flesh-and-blood persons who live in the city and in its misery, but are not crushed or annihilated by it. Denied and exorcised by a diehard prudery, compressed in the tenement flat and contorted in the sweatshop, the body sensuously though dramatically reasserted itself in the street, in the cheap museum, in the dancing hall, in the boxing match. The Ash Can artists were quick to grasp this aspect — so inequivocably Lower-East-Side — and to translate it on canvases and in etchings, a vital gain for American painting and culture.

But their contribution was not only in terms of subject matter. The urban context deeply influenced their style and technique. Their palette used chiaroscuro colors, their brushstrokes turned thicker and larger, their backdrops became darker and more uniform. In a sense, the group ended up claiming with pride the adjective critics often used to characterize them negatively — subjects, colors, and technique were *dirty*, their paintings didn't have the same bright and polished surfaces of so much contemporary art, but the clots and spots, the thickness and irregularity of modern life and environment. From subjet matter, the city panorama and the Lower East Side in particular became pictorial technique. The streets, the rooftops, the fire-escapes, the stoops, the backyards, the signs, the El, the tenements, the chimneys, the color blotches lighting up the night darkness, all this left deep traces on the canvases, a complex hieroglyph of signs which the Ash Can School's sometimes naive realism paradoxically bequeathed to the avant-garde's future experimentations.

As to Jerome Myers, if he wasn't a real member of the Ash Can School, he shared many of its tenets and, what is more, came to be a kind of Lower East Side's adopted child[27]. To the neighborhood, he constantly turned as the first source of inspiration for his 'ashcans and the little people around them, [...] visions of the slums clothed in dignity, never to me mere slums but the habitations of a people who were rich in spirit and effort' [J. Myers 1940, pp.35, 48]. Myers too was fascinated by the quarter's "human comedy", by the great variety and vitality of its street life, and, until his death in 1941, never ceased to paint it. The spell was so strong on him that his painting often became exceedingly sentimental, almost suspended in a smiling, dreamlike atmosphere:

> Curiously enough, my contemplation of these humble lives opened to me the doors of fancy. The factory clothes, the anxious faces disappeared; they came to me in gorgeous raiment of another world — a decorative world of fancy, like an abstract vision. I was led to paint pictures in which these East Side scenes are lost in a tapestry of romance. Reality faded in a vault of dreams...[J. Myers 1940, p.49].

In "The End of the Walk", "Seward Park", "Life on the East Side" [Table 18], "The Tambourine", the ever present children, the women with handkerchiefs on their heads, the bearded old men, the organ grinders compose a humanity that seems to retain the past in the present, the *shtetl* under the tenements, the *paesello* under the imposing but faraway skyscrapers — up to the point that, at times, it is instinctive to look for a figure lightly hovering above the roofs: as in a dream, or in a painting by Chagall. But in his mellower colours and softer and fable-like touch, the distance from the Ash-Can School was apparent; nor was Myers — a fine teacher at the Educational Alliance, a promoter of various artistic enterprises, and a dedicated supporter of the new realism in American art — able to grasp the new trends arriving from Europe[28].

But the season of the Eight was brief too. The 1913 Armory Show — which the group had wanted and organized along with Myers and other artists, in order to assert the "new" American art and to have it meet the latest European artistic trends — was more or less its swan song [J. Myers 1940; M. Green 1988; Negri 1989]. After an event that was to leave a mark in the 20th-century American culture, the group began to dissolve. For a while, Sloan continued to paint city scenes and above all, in years of growing national and international tensions, gave himself to political satire for *The Masses* and other radical magazines, establishing — together with Bellows, Robert Minor, Maurice Becker, John Balfour Ker, Art Young — a fertile school of radical cartoonists. Then, he discovered a new source of inspiration in the region around Santa Fe (New Mexico). The others too continued to paint, but almost aloof. Some (Davies above all, but not Luks nor Shinn) came under the spell of the European avant-garde, while Bellows — in the few years before his early death in 1925 — tried to couple his beloved themes with a greater attention to formal research. A true group of realist urban painters ceased to exist. The artists' New York was increasingly becoming a "modernist city" — the "pictorial city" of John Marin, Alfred Stieglitz, and Edward Steichen, or the abstract, cubist, futurist city of Abraham Walkowitz, Louis Lozowick [Table 19], Joseph Stella, Charles Demuth, Georgia O'Keefe, Stuart Davis, or the alienated, empty city of Edward Hopper [Conrad 1984]. In a certain way, *this* city too was rooted in the Lower East Side, where the Babel of languages could so easily become a Babel of signs almost devoid of content and reduced to pure form, in the forced physical contiguity of disparate cultures — Chinese ideograms intertwined with letters from Hebrew and Arab alphabets, side by side with Italian and German writings and with the by-now ever present advertising billboards.

Urban realism certainly was not dead in New York. Throughout the 1920s, 1930s, and 1940s, in a highly personal style, Reginald Marsh recorded the Lower East Side scene, its borders and its extensions — the Bowery of the derelicts, the East 14th Street of the burlesques and nickelodeons, the Coney Island of the beaches and "tunnels of love". A student of Sloan, Marsh entertained a rather original relationship with the Eight. His realism related to the crowded compositions of Michelangelo and Rubens rather than to the portraits of Rembrandt and Franz Hals so favored by Sloan, Myers, and Epstein. His canvases were characterised by an almost morbidly hyperbolic, grotesque, and fantastic vein [Conrad 1984, pp.95-101]. Like the Eight, for his subjects Marsh went to the streets and subways, and to the world of show-business, so popular in the 1920's and 1930s. He painted men and women trapped between a bleak desperation and a gushing will to live, between lights and shadows, movement and convulsion, human wreckage and dreams of happiness, erotic hints and explicit provocations, unsatiable voyeurism and barely controlled tensions. In "Ten Cents a Dance", "Coney Island Beach", "Twenty Cent Movie",

281

"In Fourteenth Street", "Chatham Square", "Eyes Examined", "Striptease at New Gotham", "10 Shots, 10 Cents", "Star Burlesk", the Whitmanesque body reappears within a city that becomes a tangle of limbs and a trail of footprints, the grand spectacle of the *comédie humaine* which now, in agreement with an era so far from the turn-of-the-century one, Marsh catches with the disenchanted eye of a *sui generis* chronicler — one who is attracted by the warts he is drawing and fascinated by whatever coarse, rough, and vulgar (but at the same time, extremely vital) could be found in the mass culture of a metropolis by now triumphant on the American scene [M. Cohen 1983]. Marsh's city thus becomes a "continuous performance", a hectic interlacing of individuals that carry with them yearnings and frustrations, a pageant without pause in which, next to the sensuality of "Merry-Go-Round" or "Pip & Flip", lies in wait the mirror-like, nightmarish anguish of such later works as "Smokehounds" or "The Bowery — Strokey's Bar" [Table 20]. A representation of the city that in a way already foretold the activity of photographers like Weegee and Diane Arbus.

VI.

The 'cinematic vision of the city' [M. Cohen 1983, p.12] that we find in Marsh's paintings also constitutes a fascinating comment on the relationship between urban scene and movies in those days. The circumstances related to cinema's early years, to its gradual conquest of the city, surely form one of the most interesting chapters in the American cultural history, and, once more, a large portion of this chapter was written in the Lower East Side[29]. After the more or less contemporary experiments of Eadweard Muybridge and Etienne Marey, of Edison, Méliès and the Lumière brothers, the last decade of the 19th century saw the rise, in America, of the kinetoscope peep-shows and of the large-screen motion-picture projection, and the birth of real production houses such as Edison's Vitascope and W. K. L. Dickson's Biograph. When cinema made its debut in New York, in the spring of 1896, on the screen of the Koster and Bial's Music Hall on 23rd Street near Sixth Avenue, a particular phase in the new art's infancy opened [Sklar 1975; Musser 1991]. For about twenty years, more or less till the end of World War I, these imperfect but fascinating one- or two-reel shows called nickelodeons were the main attraction of penny arcades, storefront theatres, vaudeville houses — the places of a vital and heterogeneous popular entertainment. At first, they were simple "vaudeville 'chasers'", new attractions inserted at the end of the program. But soon they were able to stand on their own, and it was then that the "nickel madness" exploded.

The bond linking early cinema and immigrant neighborhoods was also a physical and geographical one. The places where nickelodeons could be seen were to be found in the heart of the tenement district or on its borders, along East Houston Street, East 14th Street, the Bowery, Third Avenue, Grand Street, First Avenue and Avenue A. They catered to an audience largely made up of recent immigrants, who spoke little or no English and thus found in this silent form of entertainment an easier way to employ their leisure-time. Here, the movies 'will stay as long as the slums stay. For in the slums they are the fittest, and must survive' [Patterson 1907]. And as a hand-book for the entrepreneurs in the field recommended, the 'ideal location is a densely populated workingmen's residence section, with a frontage on a much-traveled business street' [quoted in Sklar 1975, p.16; also see Currie 1907; Vorse 1911][30]. Audiences were primarily fascinated by the magic of movement and by the mastery of time, both implicit in the new medium. At the beginning, most popular were the "trick films" inspired by Méliès, but by 1900 bawdy and risqué reels were even greater successes — movies that titillated and forewarned by telling a "low-life" story and thus updating the never-ending 'morality tale of urban dangers' [Sklar 1975, p.41].

The golden age of nickelodeons lasted only twenty years. But for a long time the cinema's original mark — immigrant and working-class — remained apparent. Movies directly inspired by slum life were relatively rare, and the silents were almost always of a sentimental and stereotyped character, probably inspired more by Riis's edifying stories and by the "tenement tale" local colorists than by the events narrated by Cahan and the urban realists: *Cohen's Advertising Scheme* (1903), *The Life of a Bootblack* (1907), *Mixed Babies* (1908), *The Black Hand* (1908), *Smuggling Chinese into the USA* (1908), *The Eviction* (1908), *The Story of Rosa in Little Italy* (1908), *The Little Match Girl* (1908), *The Rag-Picker's Christmas* (1908), *Old Isaacs, the Pawnbroker* (1908), *The Child of the Ghetto. Rivington Street: The Strugglers* (1910), *The Heart of a Jewess* (1910), *Levi and McGinnis Running for Office* (1914), *The Italian* (1915)...[Lindsay 1915, pp.39-42; Cripps 1975; Merritt, in Balio, ed., 1976]. Nonetheless, some of these films managed to present friendly and warmly humorous depictions of immigrant life, in the polyethnic and cross-cultural tradition of vaudeville. What is even more important, the silent movies adapted from popular fiction and melodrama a range of *topoi*, situations, and characters which were to have a long life in American cinema: the mistaken babies of different ethnic families, the good and the bad immigrant, the arguments between families, the mixed marriages, the rôle of environment, the competition between Irish and Jews, Italians and Germans, the sexual inuendos and the light social commentary. And, above all, the ever changing street-life. Sifted from the Lower East Side's everyday reality, the street accident, the chase through the maze of alleys and rows, the villainous gang and the innocent female victim, the simple but good hero and the orphaned kid became stock elements in films, soon to be reshaped into higher forms by artists like Charles Chaplin and Buster Keaton (who, not by chance, had their apprenticeship in ethnic vaudeville). As an anonymous journalist wrote: 'The showman goes much farther than the composer can go by throwing upon the screen the very ideas supplied him by the crowd in the streets' [*The Nation*, July 28, 1913, quoted in Cripps 1975, p.194; also see Lindsay 1915].

These aspects became even more apparent when David Wark Griffith came on the scene. From 1908 to 1912, just before switching to feature production with *Birth of the Nation* (1915), Griffith directed four hundred and fifty one-reelers for Biograph. A good portion of them were made up of stories about the Lower East Side and its immigrant and working-class people, 'endowed with a humanity that set them apart from stock caricatures. Often minority figures were heroes of his films, exhibiting moral strength superior to their white antagonists' [Sklar 1975, p.72]. In *The Romance of a Jewess* (1908), *The Cord of Life* (1909), *In Little Italy* (1909), *The Italian Barber* (1911), and above all in *The Musketeers of Pig Alley* (1912), what really fascinates the audience and leaves a deep mark on cinematic imagery is this sense of the street as a limitless theatre of fortuitous incidents, of the Lower East Side territory as marvelously suitable to chases and hiding-places, to chance meetings and sudden plot resolutions [Kracauer 1960, Chapter 4] — something that would remain deeply embedded in the relationship between cinema and the neighborhood, up to our days (Susan Seidelman's *Smithereens* and *Desperately Seeking Susan* and Jonathan Demme's *Married to the Mob* being good examples).

After 1915, the world of American movies changed radically. Attracted by its enormous economic potential, big business took over. A moralizing campaign was launched with the aim to cleanse films of everything that was not acceptable to middle-class values. Vaudeville houses and storefront theatres were closed, and the original working-class character of most nickelodeon parlors was slowly but thoroughly eliminated, while the first movie palaces appeared and audiences became a cross-section of American population. Besides, film industry moved from New York and the East Coast to California and

Hollywood, opening a completely new chapter. But, even in this move and in the rise of Hollywood, the Lower East Side played a specific rôle. The driving thrust behind the new film industry was in fact represented by a handful of recent immigrants, such as Samuel Goldwyn, Louis B. Mayer, Marcus Loew, Irving Thalberg, Myron Selznick. Till a few years before, many of them had been contractors and then successful "sweaters" in a Lower East Side garment industry that, in terms of organization and division of labour and above all of work processes ("cutting and stitching"), closely resembled film industry [Ramsaye 1926, 1986, p.823; May and May 1983; Schulberg 1941, 1978].

And so, even in Hollywood's silent era, the multi-faceted life of the quarter, with its texture of lives, dreams, and illusions, was a constant feature. *Hungry Hearts* (1922, from Yezierska's book), *Potash and Perlmutter* (1923), *Salome of the Tenements* (1925, also from Yezierska's book), *Broken Hearts* (1926), *Izzie and Lizzie* (1926), *Rose of the Tenements* (1927), *Abie's Irish Rose* (1927), or *The Madonna of Avenue A* (1928, by Michael Curtiz), were dramatic or melodramatic, romantic or sentimental stories, centered around poverty and mixed marriages, misunderstandings and stereotypes. Above all, the assimilation theme ruled, a clear sign that a process that had lasted a full half century was — at least for those concerned — about to end.

***

This discovery from the outside (American culture's coming to terms with the Lower East Side) surely was a complex phenomenon. At one extreme, guardians of "high culture" values felt the need to control, subjugate, or at least exorcise, a diversity which was felt all the more explicit and menacing. At the other, upon a small but growing minority within American art, literature and journalism, the Lower East Side had the power of attraction of a mental and physical territory, experienced as radically alternative to mainstream normalcy and conformity. It was a complex phenomenon also because its different expressions and attitudes, far from being separate or opposite, were on the contrary dialectically related, and because it would leave deep traces *both* on American culture *and* on the neighborhood itself. And it was a never-ending phenomenon, complex for its dimensions and implications, *and for its duration*. Starting in the 1880s, the battle for an inner and outer identity, in a delicate balance and interplay between forces and representations both inner and outer, was to go on for a century. It still goes on today.

Notes

1. See Bremner 1956, 1972; Lubove 1962; A. Davis 1967; P. Boyer 1978; Trachtenberg 1982; Glaab and Brown 1983. For an interesting, contemporary analysis of urban violence, see Headley 1873, 1971. Also see Cook 1974.

2. Among the most famous and important were George G. Foster's *New York by Gas-Light* (1850), James D. McCabe's *The Secrets of the Great City: A Work Descriptive of the Virtues and the Vices, the Mysteries, Miseries, and Crimes of New York City* (1868), Matthew Hale Smith's *Sunshine and Shadow in New York* (1868), Junius Henri Browne's *The Great Metropolis. A Mirror of New York* (1869), Edward Crapsey's *The Nether Side of New York; or, The Vice, Crime, and Poverty of the Great Metropolis* (1872), Charles Loring Brace's *The Dangerous Classes of New York, and Twenty Years' Work Among Them* (1872), Thomas De Witt Talmage's *The Night Side of New York* (1878), James D. McCabe, Jr.'s *New York by Sunlight and Gaslight. A Work Descriptive of the Great American Metropolis* (1882), James William Buel's *Mysteries and Miseries of America's Great Cities* (1883), Jacob A. Riis's *How the Other Half Lives. Studies Among the Tenements of New York* (1890), Ballington Booth's *New York's Inferno Explored. Scenes Full of Pathos Powerfully Portrayed* (1891), Benjamin O. Flower's *Civilization's Inferno; or, Studies in the Social Cellar* (1893), Helen Campbell's *Darkness and Daylight; or, Lights and Shadows of New York* (1895).

3. Some works were also meant to be true "guides to the metropolis", written in order to admonish the youth, possible preys to the city's vice and temptations. Horatio Alger, Jr.'s novels easily fit in this category [Maffi 1982-83]. Then there were surveys of other kinds, more scientific and less sensational: the medical reports, for instance, like John H. Griscom's *The Sanitary Condition of the Laboring Population of New York, with Suggestions for its Improvement: A Discourse* (1845), or the *Report of the Council of Hygiene and Public Health upon the Sanitary Condition of the City* (1865), or the evidences of police officers, like William H. Bell's 1850-51 diary [Wilentz 1979]. But surely the circle of their readers was infinitely less wide than that of the "city explorations", specifically aimed at a large audience. On the implications of the persisting image of the "two cities" in American culture, see Sharpe and Wallock, in Campbell and Rollins, eds., 1989.

4. 'This is a city of princes and paupers. Great wealth and extreme poverty are found elbow to elbow almost everywhere from the Battery to Spuyten Duyvel. Here is the stately mansion, there the tumbling tenement...' (p.128).

5. '[A] total of 4,038,991 aliens landed at this port in these twenty-two years [...]. Of these millions nothing, with few exceptions, but the dregs settled in the metropolis where they landed. All the rest, representing nearly all that was valuable in this avalanche of humanity, was poured upon the untilled lands of the West, where a mighty empire sprang from their loins with the amazing swiftness of necromancy. The thrifty emigrants who came to us forehanded and determined to wring competence from the new republic, merely made New York their stepping stone to fortune; the emigrants who exhausted their stores in securing their passage, and landed penniless perforce, staid [sic] with us to add to the dissonance of this mixture of peoples. In time many of these became self-sustaining, and they

286

or their children pushed forward into the ranks of our most substantial citizens, but a large proportion, as was inevitable, became public burdens, and permanent additions to the vice, crime, or pauperism of the metropolis' (p.6).

6. 'It has been common, since the recent terrible Communistic outbreak in Paris, to assume that France alone is exposed to such horrors; but, in the judgment of one who has been familiar with our "dangerous classes" for twenty years, there are just the same explosive social elements beneath the surface of New York as of Paris. [...If] the opportunity offered, we should see an explosion from this class which might leave this city in ashes and blood. [...In fact, who] will ever forget the marvelous rapidity with which [during the Draft Riots] the better streets were filled with a ruffianly and desperate multitude, such as in ordinary times we seldom see — creatures who seemed to have crept from their burrows and dens to join in the plunder of the city?' (pp.29, 30). On the pervasive fear of the mob among reformers like Brace, see Sproat 1968, Chapter 8.

7. A police reporter at the Mulberry Street Headquarters for the New York *Tribune*, the Associated Press Bureau, and the *Evening Sun*, and an active member of the Tenement House Commission in 1884, Riis was a true walker in the city, 'a kind of war correspondent' (p.61) who combed all corners of the Lower East Side, by day and by night, alone or with colleagues and policemen, during police raids or investigations of the New York Health Board. In his autobiography, he recalls that '[e]xcept in the short winter days it was always broad daylight when I came home from work. My route from the office lay through the Fourth and the Sixth wards, the worst in the city, and for years I walked every morning betwee two and four o'clock the whole length of Mulberry Street, through the Bend and across the Five Points down to Fulton Ferry. There were cars on the Bowery, but I liked to walk, for so I saw the slum when off its guard. [...] I went poking around among the foul alleys and fouler tenements of the Bend when they slept in their filth, sometimes with the policeman on the beat, more often alone, sounding the misery and depravity of it to their depth' [Riis 1901, 1966, pp.235-236]. The narrations of his night wanderings in the Lower East Side maze are not devoid of a certain literary quality, their atmospheres and scenarios reminding those of a by then familiar urban fiction (from Poe and Lippard to Crane and Cahan): 'Evening has worn into night as we take up our homeward journey through the streets, now no longer silent. The thousands of lighted windows in the tenements glow like dull red eyes in a huge stone wall. From every door multitudes of tired men and women pour forth for a half-hour's rest in the open air before sleep closes the eyes weary with incessant working. Crowds of half-naked children tumble in the street and on the sidewalk, or doze fretfully on the stone steps. As we stop in front of a tenement to watch one of these groups, a dirty baby in a single brief garment — yet a sweet, human little baby despite its dirt and tatters — tumbles off the lowest step, rolls over once, clutches my leg with unconscious grip, and goes to sleep on the flagstones, its curly head pillowed on my boot' [Riis 1890, 1971, p.107]. This difference in perspective also accounts for a significant difference in rhethoric. As compared to Brace's *preaching* and *moralizing* tone, Riis's is rather more the aggressive reformer's, ready to mobilize *economic* and *social* forces around the issue of tenements and sweatshops.

8. Stereotypes abound in Riis' pages, and his tone, generally paternalistic, is not immune from racist and chauvinist accents. Writing of Chinatown, for instance, Riis almost blatantly evokes the spectres of miscegenation and "Yellow Peril" and calls for the 'harshest repressive measures' (p.83) against its inhabitants.

9. By mid-1890s, the C.O.S. headquarters in New York had gathered accurate information on approximately 170,000 families and individuals [Boyer 1978, p.150].

10. By the mid-1890s, the C.A.S. had sent West some 90,000 boys: the process was really one of getting rid of bothersome boys and girls, who were given away to any taker [Boyer 1978, p.98. Also see Brace 1872].

11. On the "settlement-house movement", see Addams 1910, 1981; Wald 1915, 1971; "A New Centre" 1928; also see Lubove 1962; A. Davis 1967; Scheuer 1985; *The Landmarked Buildings*, n.d.; Shustko n.d. To these settlement houses, Cooper Union should also be added, although different in character: a professional school founded by Peter Cooper in 1859, with its art courses, lectures on science, huge library, and a Great Hall which hosted Abraham Lincoln and Mark Twain as well as women's suffrage activists and striking sweatshop workers, it too had a crucial function on the Lower East Side.

12. For an analysis of the settlement workers' attitude that also takes in account their gender approach, see Ewen 1985, especially Chapter 5. Also see Siegel 1983.

13. Indeed, he was rather critical about such undertakings: 'One result of a strong interest in low life is to tend to put a man out of sympathy with "reform" and with setlement work among the poor. I do not desire to minimize the good which is undoubtedly accomplished in detail by settlement workers; but the elements of charity, of condescension, and of "reform", which enter so largely into these enterprises, take, in my opinion, from their value. [...] The East Side does not like charity, and everybody, no matter how poor he may be, prefers to pay for what he receives' [Hapgood 1910, pp.25-26].

14. Hutchins Hapgood's view is well echoed by his brother Norman, one of the first and more attentive scholars of the American Yiddish theatre: see N. Hapgood 1916. It is also rather interesting to contrast Hutchins Hapgood's book with Henry James's *The American Scene* (1907), where social and cultural distance is on the contrary continuously reaffirmed.

15. "Sidney Luska" was the pen-name of none other than Henry Harland, the writer who soon fled the United States and became famous as the editor of the celebrated *fin de siècle* magazine, *The Yellow Book* [Fiedler 1958].

16. Ventura's case is a complex one. While his name surely is Italian (and in the "Preface", he mentions teaching Italian in Burlington, Vermont), his novelette is written in French and was published by William R. Jenkins, *"Éditeur et Libraire Français"*, in a series called *"Contes Choisis"* and listing "the very best French fiction" (Edmond About, Alphonse Daudet, George Sand, Guy De Maupassant). Sollors [1988, p.497] seems to be more convinced of Ventura's Italian citizenship, but, for want of further information, I chose to put Ventura among the "outsider" writers.

17. Sullivan's *Tenement Tales* only partially deals with the Lower East Side, while Ralph's *People We Pass* limits its scope to a few blocks, what will become a common device in much later city fiction [Gelfant 1954].

18. Such a tension can be easily felt where certain *topoi* occur: the "descent", the change in places as one drifts farther from the familiar areas and approaches unknown ones, the journey through the slums, the darkness of the night scenes in alleys, basements, and rookeries peopled by an "alien" crowd [Crapsey 1872, 1979, pp.110-114; Brace 1872]. In particular, Crane's *Maggie* is surely the most cinematic text of the American *fin de siècle*.

19. When, for example, New York's A.I.C.P. decided to use W. H. Drake's illustrations for its 1884 *Annual Report*, 'the secretary [...] explained that Drake's pictures were designed to show members "how and where the poor of New York live" and thereby to "obviate the necessity of [...] personal exploration of these unwholesome depths"' [A.I.C.P.'s *Forty-First Annual Report*, 1884, quoted in Bremner 1956, 1972, p.116].

20. Good reproductions are in Schoener, ed., 1967, and in Jensen, Kerr, Belsky, eds., 1970. The Jacob Riis Collection and the Byron Collection are at the Museum of the City of New York, the Alice Austen Collection is at the Staten Island Historical Collection, Jessie Tarbox Beals's photographs are at the Community Service Society of New York, Warren Dickerson's are at the Los Angeles County Museum of Natural History, John James McCook's Lower East Side photos are in *The Social Reform Papers of John James McCook* [microfilms by the Antiquarian and Landmarks Society, Inc., of Connecticut (Roll 11, Folder E)], and a large number of Lewis W. Hine's photos are at the George Eastman House (Rochester). The Brown Brothers agency in Sterling (Pa.) also has a valuable collection of unknown photographers, as do the Museum of the City of New York, the New-York Historical Society, the New York Public Library, the Tenement Museum, the Chinatown History Museum, the Amalgamated Clothing Workers of America, the International Ladies' Garment Workers' Union, and the Library of Congress.

21. On "social photography", see Hurley 1972; Stryker and Wood 1973; Von Blum 1982; Foner and Schultz, eds., 1985. On Stieglitz and the Photo-Secession, see Homer 1977; Doty 1978.

22. Lewis Mumford [1931, 1971, p.97] quoted Walt Whitman as saying: 'I never knew but one artist, and that's Tom Eakins, who could resist the temptation to see what they think they ought to rather than what is'.

23. 'Sketches were made hurriedly on the scene, and the newspaper artists carried envelops, menu cards, and laundry checks for just such a purpose. Any scrap of paper which might contain even a small working surface was suitable. Such on-the-spot sketches usually consisted of a myriad of markings with numerals shot off at tangents, a sort of artistic shorthand developed through trial and error' [Perlman 1979, p.52]. Also see Negri 1989.

24. 'I have never gone slumming to get subject matter' [Sloan 1978, caption to illustration number 33].

25. See for instance John Ferguson Weir ("Gun Foundry", 1866; "Forging the Shaft", 1866), Winslow Homer ("Cotton Pickers", 1876), John George Brown ("The Longshoremen's Noon", 1879), Thomas P. Anshutz ("Ironworkers —

Noontime", 1881), F. Hopkinson Smith ("Under the Towers", 1882), Louis Maurer ("Forty-third Street West of Ninth Avenue", 1883), Charles F. Ulrich ("In the Land of Promise — Castle Garden", 1884), Robert Koehler ("The Strike", 1886), W. Louis Sonntag, Jr. ("The Bowery at Night", 1895).

26. Sloan was a member of the Socialist Party and artistic director of the radical magazine *The Masses*, for which he drew some of his finest cartoons [Zurier 1988].

27. Myers came from a large and poor family in Virginia, and moved to New York in 1886, but only in 1916 did he go to live on the Lower East Side, on East 10th Street, near St.Mark's Church [Holcomb 1977].

28. Life in the slums, and in the Lower East Side in particular, influenced turn-of-the-entury sculpture as well. See for instance the works by Charles Haag ("Organized Labor", "The Strike") and Abastenia St.Leger Eberle ("Charring of the Day", "Avenue A").

29. As already noted, the ripeness of American culture for a cinematic interpretation of reality was shown by much contemporary fiction. At a certain point in Howells's novel *A Hazard of New Fortunes*, the main characters, Basil and Mabel March, watch the city in awe from an El train and see a sort of uninterrupted frame sequence: 'a family party of work-folk at a late tea, some of the men in their shirt sleeves; a woman sewing by a lamp; a mother laying her child in its cradle; a man with his head fallen on his hands upon a table; a girl and her lover leaning over the window-sill together. [...Basil] said it was better than the theatre, of which it reminded him' [Howells, 1890, I, p. 95]. The frequency with which such images occur in contemporary works — even in non-fictional ones ('Take the Second Avenue Elevated Railroad at Chatham Square and ride up half a mile through the sweater's district. Every open window of the big tenements, that stand like a continuous brick wall on both sides of the way, gives you a glimpse of one of these shops as the train speeds by. Men and women bending over their machines, or ironing clothes at the windows, half-naked...' [Riis 1890, 1971, p. 100]) — leads one to venture that this situation (the reader/audience moving in front of still frames) is a sort of "inverted" anticipation of movie techniques. By the time John Dos Passos wrote *Manhattan Transfer*, movie techniques had clearly influenced literary ones.

30. A 1911 survey revealed that 78 per cent of the New York audience (with a weekly attendance of between 1.2 and 1.6 million people — about 25 per cent of the city's population) came from the slums [Merritt, in Balio, ed., 1976, p.63]. Also see Lindsay 1915. For an important gender analysis on the subject, see Ewen 1980.

AFTERWORD

Chi Lai/ Arriba/ Rise Up!
                    (title of the mural on Madison and Pike streets)

The walker in the city who returns to the Lower East Side of today, after such a long trip across time and space, is confronted with a bleak scenario, a reality which is more dramatic than yesterday's one, because it is even more ruled by fragmentation and disintegration. Since the turn of the century (when they were about half million), the neighborhood's inhabitants have now dropped to little more than 160.000[1]. But such a drop, far from allowing better living conditions, is really another sign of displacement and abandonment. The advance of gentrification, despite a slowdown after the 1987 Wall Street collapse, is still inexorable, as the blocks east and west of Avenue C, between East 10th and 4th streets, clearly show [see Map 3]. The vast empty lots and burnt out tenements, the incidence of drugs and the growth of violence are sufficient evidence of the collapse of community. The same is partially true farther south, in Chinatown: here, physical waste is perhaps less apparent, but the massive inflow of capital from Hong Kong and Taiwan (in view of the 1997 end of the British Rule) has lacerated the social texture, giving rise, by the early 1980s, to a powerful Chinese mafia and a related, serious youth gang phenomenon [Kleinfield 1986; Kwong 1987][2].

But the effects of gentrification are even subtler and deeper than that. Throughout the last decade, many groups have waged an unflinching, daily battle to maintain a level of cultural and social unity/identity and to save the neighborhood for its working-class, immigrant residents — a difficult and demanding task, which has taken its toll of energies and lives and becomes ever more arduous today, as the country enters a new period of economic recession and new cuts affect city and federal budgets. The variegated front represented by the Cooper Square Committee, Pueblo Nuevo, the East 6th Street Community Center, Adopt-A-Building, R.A.I.N., the homesteaders and the squatters, the Asian Americans for Equality, the Chinatown History Workshop, the Chinese Staff and Workers Associations, Charas, the Taller Latino-Americano, the Nuyorican Poets' Café, the Worker's Center on East 3rd Street, many settlements and local groups, theatres and bookstores, all walk on the razor's edge. Both on the grassroots level and

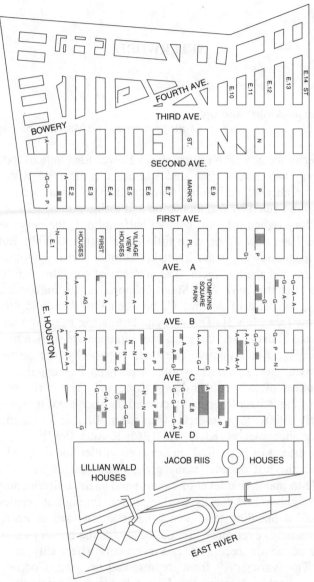

Ill. 32

Map 3: The Advance of Gentrification in the Lower East Side's Northern Section (early 1992)

Legenda:　A　= Abandoned buildings
　　　　　　P　= Parking lots
　　　　　　G　= Gardens
　　　　　　N　= New buildings
　　　　　　▨　= Empty lots

on a more institutional one, the neighborhood still expresses a high level of antagonism to redevelopment and displacement — a daily resistance rooted in the specific conditions of life and work in its streets, tenements, and sweatshops, *and* in a long tradition of community mobilization[3].

At the same time, however, fragmentation and isolation are growing in the neighborhood, as they are in the wider metropolitan area. The difficulty of sustaining a continuous and concerted effort without a larger strategy and wider battle front and the pressures thus brought to bear on agencies and individuals engaged in local struggles inevitably foster inner divisions and disagreement, individualistic temptations and disillusionment, with a severe haemorrhage of energies[4]. What Pedro Pietri had written in 1970 may thus appear even truer today: 'Juan/ died hating Miguel because Miguel's/ used car was in better running condition/ than his used car/ Miguel/ died hating Milagros because Milagros/ had a color television set/ and he could not afford one yet/ Milagros/ died hating Olga because Olga/ made five dollars more on the same job/ Olga/ died hating Manuel because Manuel/ had hit the numbers more times/ than she had hit the numbers/ Manuel/ died hating all of them/ Juan/ Miguel/ Milagros/ and Olga/ because they all spoke broken english/ more fluently than he did' ["Puerto Rican Obituary", in Pietri 1973, pp.8-9].

And yet '[the] people the buildings & whatnot/ People out there, life/ Goes on in [this] everyday/ Disaster area' [Holman 1987, p.33]. "Refuse and Resist" (as was called a radical group once active in the area) thus seems the aptest password, the punning description of a situation — a further testimony of the Lower East Side's stubborn vitality as an integrated neighborhood. And in fact forces social and cultural, collective and individual have never ceased to be at work in the quarter's laboratory. The geodesic domes built by the Charas people, Adam Purple's Garden of Eden (with its huge yin-yan symbol drawn with city detritus), the several windmills erected on the rooftops as a short way to energetic self-sufficiency, the *casitas* of wood and cardboard mushrooming in the empty lots as *impromptu* meeting places, the gardens and the murals — all this and much more attest to a visionary and transgressive, utopian and pragmatic creativity, born of (and in response to) the very material conditions of disarray and abandonment that have always characterized the area. Along a tenuous but resistant *thread of time*, present realities are thus linked to past accomplishments, and it is this ever renewing continuity that makes the Lower East Side a living metaphor of socio-cultural resistance and envisioning — the great laboratory offering precious insights on the way culture (in a very wide, anthropological and political, meaning) is produced and circulated ["Editorial" 1993].

Out of this long history, two elements in particular stand out, which, if ever a "Lower East Side aesthetics" can be spoken of, might be considered as its main components. One is the direct relationship with the street always entertained by this community. A physical sense of the city runs through all social and cultural expressions stemming from the neighborhood — the compressed bodies, the congested life, the 'smell of raw concrete' [Willem de Kooning, quoted in Hess 1988, p.9], the words and noises, the drama and comedy, the way in which change (and decay) is visually revealed, creation (and survival) ever renewed. In this Abraham Cahan's and Henry Roth's language was rooted (or, more recently, Gregory Corso's, or Allen Ginsberg's, or Miguel Piñero's), as was the language of such performers as Eddie Cantor, Sophie Tucker, George Burns (or is now that of Ann Magnuson and Eric Bogosian), and the phrasing of such musicians as George Gershwin and Irving Berlin (or Archie Shepp, John Cage, Laurie Anderson, LaMonte Young). In this, the Ash Can School's dirty brush work or Reginald Marsh's fascination for popular culture join, well beyond formal boundaries, the New York School with its storefront galleries or the early pop artists: because a 'walk down 14th Street is more amazing than any masterpiece of art' [Allan Kaprow, quoted in Ashton 1988, p.149].

Israel Levitan's and Louise Nevelson's sculptures, Robert Rauschenberg's paintings, Jasper John's works, Red Grooms's and Claes Oldenburg's happenings, all relied upon the city's street treasures, the *objets trouvés* of a recycling that never ceased to be a distinctive feature in the quarter — a strategy of survival as well as an artistic technique [Lloyd 1987]. Bread & Puppet Theatre's founder and director, Peter Schumann, recalls how their early puppets were made of objects found in the streets, broom-sticks providing one of the most crucial contributions [Schumann, interview, 1990], while artist David Finn created his intriguing and disquieting "Masked Figures" (which he then hid in the branches of the Tompkins Square Park's trees, from where they gradually appeared when the leaves began to fall), out of 'the actual physical debris of the Lower East Side' [Finn, letter to the author, 1987]. So, the fantastic architecture of the Gas Station (corner of East 2nd Street and Avenue B), created by Ruben Garcia, Domi Piturro and other artists out of discarded objects, the tall "May Pole" in the garden on Avenue B and East 6th Street, or the scrap metal foundry on Forsyth and Rivington, are further celebrations of this creativity bred by city life, the necessary recycling of what is found in the street[5].

294

No More Cuts / No More Evictions

We call on all community organizations as well as individuals to rally together at City Hall; the time has come to bring all of the forces of social concern together and demand JUSTICE!

The time and place: **Friday, January 25 at 3 pm on the steps of City Hall,** where we will demand of Mayor Dinkins a pledge of **NO MORE CUTS** and **NO MORE EVICTIONS.**

The people of this city are being robbed not only of their present but of their *future* by this administration. Cuts in fire stations will lead to a new wave of arson and homelessness. Cuts in education doom our youth. Evictions tear apart communities and destroy lives. **The Mayor must stop listening to Wall Street and start hearing the voices of the people.**

If we do not obtain a pledge of **NO MORE CUTS** and **NO MORE EVICTIONS** from Mayor Dinkins, we will come back to City Hall again and again and we will bring with us the people from Housing Court who are facing evictions, the homeless from the streets, the families of those who have died in building fires, those who cannot get decent healthcare or an education, the unemployed, the squatters who have created housing and whom the city now wants to evict and all of the other victims of present policies--**to demand JUSTICE from this administration and this system!**

WE WON'T TAKE ANYMORE!
We demand a JUST distribution of the public wealth to meet the needs of the people!

The time and place: **Friday, January 25 at 3 pm on the steps of City Hall.**

Fight the Class War at Home!

Housing Solidarity
Bring your own banners. For more information about this rally and/or to reserve a place on the speakers' list, please call 292-6443.

Ill. 33
An Anti-Gentrification Leaflet with Drawings by Seth Tobocman

Ill. 34
A Drawing by Eric Drooker for *Squatter Comics*

The second element relates to the deep changes ethnic communities are bringing about in the cultural texture of America — something which is particularly clear in such historical immigrant neighborhoods as the Lower East Side. Here, in fact, the use and reuse of the city's fragmented objects (what has by now become — and the change *is* significant — 'the wretched refuse of [*America*'s] teeming shore') goes together with a strong tendency, mainly expressed by minority artists, towards a kind of recomposition, a dialectical synthesis founded upon past and present, ethnicity and America, that is, perhaps, still unresolved (and such will remain for long), but is also clearly growing and writing new chapters in an old book. The ethnic artist — outsider out of necessity — thus directly plays the rôle Benjamin and Kracauer ascribed to the cultural outsider in the early years of the 20th century, engaged in picking the rags and fragments, the second-hand goods and the forgotten objects of the experience of modernity, in order to reassemble its deep and current meaning [Berman 1982; Frisby 1985].

In a New York which is 'the capital of the 20th century' as, to Benjamin, Paris was of the 19th century (and which more and more asserts itself, in this *fin de siècle*, as the epitome of a modernity and of a modernism vainly proclaimed dead by the ideological constructions about 'post-modernism') — in a Lower East Side which is more and more a merging of past and present and an exemplification of that socio-cultural dialectics, of that process of alchemic hybridization which (too often we forget) from the beginning founded the American experience lending it such an evocative specificity [Sollors 1986; L. Lippard 1990] — in *this* reality, the ethnic artist is thus a magnet able to attract different experiences, interpretations, approaches and, thanks to this position, to reassemble the mosaic of the city. Hybridization still seems to be the key cultural reality of the Lower East Side. The world of the "Nuyorican poets" thus contains an already mixed, cross-cultural dimension, in which Africa meets Taíno meets Spain meets United States meets Black America meets Chicano Aztlan meets Chinese America, while Fay Chiang and The Basement (or, more recently, the New York Chinatown History Museum) have shown that their aim is not *simply* the jealous safeguard of tradition, but the cross-cultural search for an identity transcending boundaries.

That is why the Lower East Side has become a living metaphor. It is (has always been) a middle ground, a stable field of forces, without which immigrants would be condemned ever to wave between sterile ghettoization in an impossible dream of 'descent' (the past, the Old World, the ethnic roots) and supine assimilation in the mainstream of 'consent' (assimilation, the present, America). It is 'a terrain of

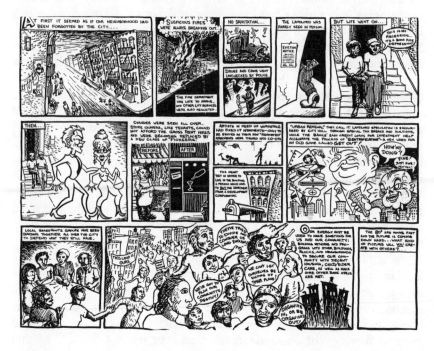

Ill. 35
An Anti-Gentrification Cartoon

negotiation and confrontation' [Denning 1987, p.136], a socio-cultural laboratory where identities and territories can be reshaped, the relationship with one's own past and present can be reconsidered, and cultural hybridization, working *both inward and outward*, can take place. In proclaiming her decision to 'stay in the city' because it contains the *real* master plot of identity, Fay Chiang clearly sketches this middle ground, identifying it with a community of inner-city artists and activists ["A Poem for Richard", in Chiang 1979, p.55]. Here, 'consent' and 'descent' can fruitfully clash together, the result being something different from both — socio-cultural products which can even result raw and unfinished, but are always charged with a kind of high voltage and thus deeply affect and remould what lies *within and without* the margins, the boundaries.

This dimension, which is linguistic and psychological, cultural and political, is beautifully captured by Sandra María Esteves (and her own reading makes the alchemic process even more fascinating):

298

Being Puertorriqueña Americana
Born in the Bronx, not really jíbara
Not really hablando bien
But yet, no Gringa either
Pero ni portorra, pero sí portorra too
Pero ni qué what am I?
Y que son, pero con what voice do my lips move?
["Not Neither", in Esteves 1984, p.26][6].

Or by Tato Laviera:

we gave birth to a new generation,
AmeRícan salutes all folklores,
european, indian, black, spanish,
and anything else compatible:
[...]
AmeRícan, across forth and across back
        back across and forth back
        forth across and back and forth
        our trips are walking bridges!
AmeRícan, speaking new words in spanglish tenements,
        fast tongue moving street corner "que
        corta" talk being invented at the insistence
        of a smile!
AmeRícan, abounding inside so many ethnic english
        people, and out of humanity, we blend
        and mix all that is good!
["AmeRícan", in Laviera 1985, pp.94, 95].

***

More than a hundred years have passed since the Lower East Side laboratory began to operate, and the end of another century is now approaching. Misery, displacement, dejection are still there. But so is the laboratory, 'its last words still to be lived' [Zukofsky 1967, p.3]. From the outside, the lights may appear dim — as dim as the small, solitary lamp gleaming outside the Nuyorican Poets' Café, in the darkness of East 3rd Street. But, inside, the fires are still burning brightly.

Notes

1. According to the 1990 Census, the Lower East Side is inhabited by 14.790 non-Hispanic Blacks, 49.023 non-Hispanic Whites, 47.733 Asian Americans, and 52.586 Hispanics, with a density of 148 persons per acre [United States Department of Commerce 1991]. Compared to the 1980 Census, while the number of non-Hispanic Blacks and of non-Hispanic Whites has remained more or less stable, the number of Asian-Americans has increased and that of Hispanics has slightly decreased [Department of City Planning 1984]. It must be remembered that, to the term "Hispanic" adopted in all official documents, the Puerto Rican (and *chicana*) community prefer that of "Latino/a".

2. 'Crack' in particular is responsible for a further, tragic fragmentation in the neighborhood. As a highly addictive drug likely to be taken in conditions of (and conducive to) extreme isolation, it has been instrumental not only in the creation of a powerful and pityless drug market, mostly ruled by a Dominican and Colombian underworld, but even in the destruction of that minimal cohesive factor to the ghetto youth represented in the past by the street gang. Whatever street gang activity exists on the Lower East Side nowadays (both in Chinatown and in Loisaida), it tends to be ruled by that market rather than being the expression of an unfulfilled need of aggregation [personal conversations with Chino Garcia and Bimbo Rivas]. On its part, the diffusion of heroin in the quarter is one of the reasons for the high level of reported AIDS cases — a devastating reality, to which great attention is devoted both by local magazines and community centers and by the Lower East Side Aids Service Center [Schwarz 1988, with statistics and projections about the epidemic in the quarter].

3. It is no surprise, for instance, that one of the most pugnacious and organized groups demonstrating against the U.S. military intervention in the Gulf in January-February 1991 was the Lower East Siders Against War, a name that voiced an implicit pride for a long heritage of anti-war battles (the Lower East Side Mobilization for Peace-Action, L.E.M.P.A., was one of the main anti-Vietnam War groups active in the mid-1960s).

4. The intensity of the controversy raging in the community (even before the dismantling of the homeless' tent-colony in Tompkins Square Park) is apparent in Vincent 1990, who criticizes the strategies currently adopted in the area and is considered highly biased by the concerned agencies. But disagreement is often strong also within the Joint Planning Council, or between such groups as the Cooper Square Committee and the homesteaders, or between the squatters and most of the organized groups.

5. This is something that has also to do with homesteaders' and squatters' strategies [Boyle, interview, 1991], and of course updates many concepts already elaborated by the early-20th-century avant-gardes.

6. Esteves has recently changed the first line to: "Being Puertorriqueña Dominicana" (letter to the author, July 25, 1991).

300

BIBLIOGRAPHY

A.

Daniel Aaron, *Writers on the Left* (New York: Harcourt, Brace & World, Inc., 1961)

Paul Abelson, "The East Side Home", *Report* (New York: University Settlement Society, 1897)

Edward A. Abramson, *The Immigrant Experience in American Literature* (Durham: The BAAS Pamphlets in American Studies, 1982)

Janet Abu-Lughod, ed., *From Urban Village to "East Village". The Struggle for the Lower East Side* (London: Blackwell, 1994)

Kathy Acker, *Blood and Guts in High School* (New York: Grove Press, 1986)

---, *Literal Madness: Kathy Goes to Haiti, My Death My Life By Pier Paolo Pasolini, Florida* (New York: Grove Press, 1988)

Charlotte Adams, "Italian Life in New York", *Harper's New Monthly Magazine*, Vol. LXII (April 1881), No.CCCLXXI

Jessie B. Adams, "The Working Girl from the Elementary School in New York", *Charities and the Commons*, 19 (February 22, 1908)

Jane Addams, *Twenty Years at Hull-House* (1910; New York: New American Library, 1981)

Edward Adler, *Notes from a Dark Street* (New York: A. A. Knopf, 1962)

"Advisory. Lower East Side Demographic Information", Community Service Society of New York, n.d.

Emelise Aleandri, "Women in the Italian-American Theatre of the Nineteenth Century", in Betty Boyd Caroli, Robert F. Harney, Lydio F. Tomasi, eds., *The Italian Immigrant Woman in North America* (Toronto: The Multicultural History Society of Ontario, 1978)

--- and Maxine Schwartz Seller, "Italian-American Theatre", in Maxine Schwartz Seller, ed., *Ethnic Theatre in the United States* (Westport, Conn.: Greenwood Press, 1983)

Miguel Algarín and Miguel Piñero, eds., *Nuyorican Poetry. An Anthology of Puerto Rican Words and Feelings* (New York: William Morrow & Co., 1975)

Miguel Algarín, "Introduction: Nuyorican Language", in Miguel Algarín and Miguel Piñero, eds., *Nuyorican Poetry. An Anthology of Puerto Rican Words and Feeling* (New York: William Morrow & Co., 1975)

---, *Mongo Affair* (New York: Nuyorican Poets' Café, Inc., 1978)

---, *On Call* (Houston: Arte Público Press, 1980)

---, *Body Bee Calling (From the 21st Century)* (Houston: Arte Público Press, 1982)

---, *Time's Now. Ya Es Tiempo* (Houston: Arte Público Press, 1985)

---, "Nuyorican Aesthetics", in Asela Rodríguez de Laguna, ed., *Images and Identities. The Puerto Rican in Two World Contexts* (New Brunswick, N.J.: Transaction Books, 1987)

Horatio Alger, Jr., *Julius, the Street Boy* (New York: A.L.Burt, 1904)
Alexander Alland, Sr., *Jacob A. Riis. Photographer & Citizen* (Millerton, N.Y.: Aperture, Inc., 1974)
Vito Amoruso, *Letteratura e società in America. 1890-1900. Dialettica di un'integrazione* (Bari: De Donato Editore, 1976)
John B. Andrews, "History of Women in Trade Unions. Report on Conditions of Women and Child Wage-earners in the United States", Vol.X (Washington: 61st Congress, 2nd Session, Senate Document No.645, 1911)
Anon., "Another Centre on the East Side", *The New York Times* (Dec. 30, 1928)
Anon., "Diamond Dan O'Rourke Ready To Revive Famed Bowery Bar", *New York Herald Tribune* (June 25, 1935)
Anon., *History of Coney Island. Lists and Photographs of Main Attractions* (New York: Burroughs and Co., 1904)
Anon., "The Rent Strike Grows", *Charities and the Commons*, XIX (Jan.11, 1908)
Anthology ABC No Rio Open Mike (New York: ABC No Rio, 1987)
Frances R. Aparicio, "La Vida Es un Spanglish Disparatero: Bilingualism in Nuyorican Poetry", in Geneviève Fabre, ed., *European Perspectives on Hispanic Literature of the United States* (Houston: Arte Público Press, 1988)
Stanley Appelbaum, ed., *Show Songs from "The Black Crook" to "The Red Mill"* (New York: Dover Publications, Inc., 1974)
Carol Aronovici, "Italian Immigration", *University Settlement Studies Quarterly*, Vol.II (October 1906), No.3
Herbert Asbury, *The Gangs of New York. An Informal History of the Underworld* (1927; New York: Paragon House, 1990)
Sholem Asch, *Uncle Moses* (1918), in S. Asch, *Three Novels: Uncle Moses. Chaim Lederer's Return. Judge Not* (New York: G. P. Putnam's Sons, 1938)
Dore Ashton, "The City and the Visual Arts", in Leonard Wallock, ed., *New York. Culture Capital of the World, 1940-1965* (New York: Rizzoli International Publications, Inc., 1988)
"A Souvenir History of the Strike of the Ladies Waist Makers' Union" (New York: ILGWU, 1910)
W. H. Auden, "I'll Be Seeing You Again, I Hope", *The New York Times* (March 18, 1972)
Autobiography of Emanuel Carnevali (New York: Horizon Press, 1967)
Edward B. Aveling and Eleanor Marx Aveling, *The Working-Class Movement in America* (1891; New York: Arno Press, 1969)

B.
Charles V. Bagli, "Child Labor and Sweatshops — Growing Problems in the City", *The New York Observer* (Oct. 3, 1988)
Hans Bak, ed., *Multiculturalism and the Canon of American Culture* (Amsterdam: Vu University Press 1993)
Joseph Barondess, "How the New York Cloak Union Started", *Souvenir Journal* (ILGWU Convention, 1903), now in Leon Stein, ed., *Out of the Sweatshop*, (New York: Quadrangle/The New York Times Book Co., 1977)

302

Efraín Barradas and Rafael Rodríguez, *Herejes y mitificadores. Muestra de poesía puertorriqueña en los Estados Unidos* (Río Piedras, Puerto Rico: Ediciones Huracán, Inc., 1980)

Gunther Barth, *City People. The Rise of Modern City Culture in Nineteenth-Century America* (New York: Oxford University Press, 1980)

Françoise Basch, "Introduction. Histoire d'un grève de femmes à New York en 1909", in Theresa Serber Malkiel, *Journal d'une gréviste* (Paris: Payot, 1980)

Mo Bates, "Communising Community Art", *Circa. Art Magazine*, 27 (March/April 1986)

Ellen Baxter & Kim Hopper, *Private Lives/Public Spaces. Homeless Adults on the Streets of New York City* (New York: Community Service Society, 1981)

Louis Beck, *New York's Chinatown. An Historical Presentation of Its People and Places* (New York: Bohemia Publishing Company, 1898)

Zoe Beckley, *A Chance to Live* (New York: Macmillan, 1918)

Vincent Van Marter Beede, "Italians in America", *Chautauquan*, XXIV (1901-1902)

Peter Belsito, ed., *Notes from the Pop Underground* (Berkeley, Cal.: The Last Gasp of San Francisco, 1985)

Rina Benmayor, "'Getting Home Alive': The Politics of Multiple Identity", *The Americas Review*, Vol.17 (Fall-Winter 1989), Nos.3-4

Carol Bergé, "An Informal Timetable of Coffee-house Activities in New York", *Magazine-2* (New York: Crank Books, 1965)

Edward A. Berlin, *Ragtime: A Musical and Cultural History* (Berkeley: University of California Press 1980)

Marshall Berman, *All That Is Solid Melts Into Air* (New York: Simon & Schuster, 1982)

Franca Bernabei, "The Novels of Bernardino Ciambelli: Little Italy's Eugene Sue", *In Their Own Words*, III (Spring 1986), No.1

Charles S. Bernheimer, "High Rents on New York's East Side", *Charities and the Commons*, 19 (January 18, 1908)

---, "Lower East Side Dwellers", *University Settlement Studies*, Vol.IV (March 1908), No.1

---, "The Social Settlements on New York's Lower East Side", *Charities and the Commons*, 20 (Sept.26, 1908)

Dennis Bernstein, "Did Lincoln Swados Have To Die?", *The Village Voice*, Vol.33 (April 25, 1989), No.17

Herman Bernstein, *In The Gates of Israel: Stories of the Jews* (New York: J.F.Taylor, 1902)

---, *Contrite Hearts* (New York: A. Wessels, 1905)

---, "The Old East Side Gives Way to the New", *The New York Times* (April 3, 1910)

Misha Berson, ed., *Between Worlds. Contemporary Asian-American Plays* (New York: Theatre Communications Group, 1990)

Warner Berthoff, *The Ferment of Realism. American Literature, 1884-1919* (New York: The Free Press, 1965)

Lillian W. Betts, "Tenement-House Life and Recreation", *Outlook*, 61 (Febr.11, 1899)

Between Wars. An Oral History, ed. by Arthur Tobier (New York: Community Documentation Workshop at St.Mark's Church-in-the-Bowery, 1980)

"The Bimbo Rivas Issue", *The Quality of Life in Loisaida*, XV (August 1992), No.3

Wolfgang Binder, "Die Nordwanderung der Puertoricaner und ihre Literatur", in Berndt Ostendorf, ed., *Amerikanische Gettoliteratur. Zur Literatur ethnischer, marginaler und unterdrückter Gruppen in Amerika* (Darmstadt: Wissenschaftliche Buchgesellschaft, 1983)

Mary Black, ed., *Old New York in Early Photographs* (New York: Dover Publications, Inc., 1973)

"The Black Hand Manacled at Last", *The New York Times* (April 3, 1910)

David Blaustein, "The Inherent Cultural Forces of the Lower East Side", *Report* (New York: University Settlement Society, 1901)

---, "Cockroach Landlords", *New Era*, 6 (May 1904)

---, "The People of the East Side before Emigration and after Immigration", *University Settlement Studies*, I (July 1905), No.2

Rudi Blesh and Harriet Janis, *They All Played Ragtime* (New York: Oak Publications, 1971)

Roberto A. Bobbio, *L'ultima città dell'Occidente. Il fenomeno urbano negli Stati Uniti* (Roma: Edizioni Lavoro, 1988)

William Boelhower, *Through a Glass Darkly: Ethnic Semiosis in American Literature* (New York: Oxford University Press, 1987)

---, ed., *The Future of American Modernism: Ethnic Writing Between the Wars* (Amsterdam: VU University Press, 1990)

Ralph F. Bogardus and Ferenc M. Szasz, "Reality Captured, Reality Tamed: John James Cook and the Uses of Documentary Photography in *Fin-de-Siècle* America", *History of Photography*, Vol.10 (April-June 1986), No.2.

Elizabeth Bogen, *Immigration in New York* (New York: Praeger, 1987)

Dion Boucicault, "The Poor of New York", in Daniel C. Gerould, ed., *American Melodrama* (New York: Performing Arts Journal Publications, 1983)

Verne M. Bovie, "The Public Dance Halls of the Lower East Side", *Report* (New York: University Settlement Society, 1901)

Paul Boyer, *Urban Masses and Moral Order in America, 1820-1920* (Cambridge, Mass.: Harvard University Press, 1978)

Richard O. Boyer and Herbert M. Morais, *Labor's Untold Story* (New York: United Electrical, Radio & Machine Workers of America, 1955)

Charles Loring Brace, *The Dangerous Classes of New York, and Twenty Years' Work Among Them* (New York: Wynkoop & Hallenbeck, Publishers, 1872)

Cyrus Townsend Brady, "A Vaudeville Turn", *Scribner's Magazine*, 30 (Sept.1901)

Howard Brandstein, "Is Homesteading for You?", *The Quality of Life in Loisaida*, Vol.VII (March-August 1984), No.2

---, "Participate in Your Own Land Trust", *The Quality of Life in Loisaida*, Vol.VIII (January-February 1985), No.1

---, "Changes: A Homesteading Perspective", *The Quality of Life in Loisaida*, Vol.X (January-February, 1987), No.1

---, "310 East 4th Street A Decade Later", in *The Consumer-Farmer Cooperator*, No.55 (Spring 1990)

Robert H. Bremner, *From the Depths. The Discovery of Poverty in the United States* (1956; New York: New York University Press, 1972)

---, "The Big Flat: History of a New York Tenement House", *American Historical Review*, Vol.64 (October 1958)

T. Allston Brown, *A History of the New York Stage. From the First Performance in 1732 to 1901* (1903; New York: Benjamin Blom, Inc., 1964)

Joseph Bruchac, ed., *Breaking Silence. An Anthology of Contemporary Asian American Poets* (Greenfield Center, N.Y.: The Greenfield Review Press, 1983)

Ezra Brudno, *The Fugitive* (New York: Doubleday, Page, 1904)

Gert Buelens, "Coping with the Promised Land. History and Ethnicity in Jewish-American Narrative, 1892-1934" (University of Sussex: Ph.D. Dissertation, 1990)

Henry C. Bunner, "Jersey and Mulberry", 13 (May 1893), No.5

---, "The Bowery and Bohemia", *Scribner's Magazine*, 15 (April, 1894), No.4

---, *Jersey Street and Jersey Lane: Urban and Suburban Sketches* (New York: Scribner's, 1896)

Rudy Burckhardt and Vincent Katz, *New York Hello!* (Chicago: Cosmos Press, 1989)

George Burns, *The Third Time Around* (New York: G.P. Putnam's Sons, 1980)

Janet Burstein, "Jewish-American Women's Literature: The Long Quarrel With God", *Studies in American Jewish Literature*, 8 (1989), No.1

Valerie Chow Bush, "Division Street. East Meets West, and the Poor Loose", *The Village Voice* (July 23, 1991)

Joseph Byron, *Photographs of New York Interiors at the Turn of the Century* (New York: Dover Publications, Inc., 1976)

---, *New York Life at the Turn of the Century* (New York: Dover Publications, Inc., 1985)

C.

James Cagney, *Cagney on Cagney* (New York: Doubleday, 1976)

Abraham Cahan, *Yekl. A Tale of the New York Ghetto* (New York: D. Appleton Co., 1896)

---, *The Imported Bridegroom, and Other Stories of the New York Ghetto* (New York: Houghton, Mifflin, and Co., 1898)

---, *Yekl and The Imported Bridegroom, and Other Stories of the New York Ghetto* (1896, 1898; New York: Dover Publications, Inc., 1970)

---, "Tailors at Peace", *New York Commercial Advertiser* (August 13, 1898), now in Moses Rischin, ed., *Grandma Never Lived in America. The New Journalism of Abraham Cahan* (Bloomington: Indiana University Press, 1985)

---, "Fish, Fish, Living, Floundering, Jumping, Dancing Fish", *New York Commercial Advertiser* (Sept.24, 1898), now in Moses Rischin, ed. *Grandma Never Lived in America. The New Journalism of Abraham Cahan* (Bloomington: Indiana University Press, 1985)

---, "The Bolt of Israel", *New York Commercial Advertiser* (Nov. 11, 1898), now in Moses Rischin, ed., *Grandma Never Lived in America. The New Journalism of Abraham Cahan* (Bloomington: Indiana University Press, 1985)

---, "Strikes Naturalized", *New York Commercial Advertiser* (February 13, 1899), now in Moses Rischin, ed., *Grandma Never Lived in America. The New Journalism of Abraham Cahan* (Bloomington: Indiana University Press, 1985)

---, "When Bauer Laughed", *New York Commercial Advertiser* (July 8, 1899), now in Moses Rischin, ed., *Grandma Never Lived in America. The New Journalism of Abraham Cahan* (Bloomington: Indiana University Press, 1985)

---, "Rabbi Eliezer's Christmas", *Scribner's Magazine*, XXVI (December 1899), now in Moses Rischin, ed., *Grandma Never Lived in America. The New Journalism of Abraham Cahan* (Bloomington: Indiana University Press, 1985)

---, "Let's Dance", *New York Commercial Advertiser* (June 30, 1900), now in Moses Rischin, ed., *Grandma Never Lived in America. The New Journalism of Abraham Cahan* (Bloomington: Indiana University Press, 1985)

---, "The Scholarly Waistmakers", *New York Commercial Advertiser* (August 24, 1900), now in Moses Rischin, ed., *Grandma Never Lived in America. The New Journalism of Abraham Cahan* (Bloomington: Indiana University Press, 1985)

---, "Summer Complaint: The Annual Strike", *New York Commercial Advertiser* (August 25, 1900), now in Moses Rischin, ed., *Grandma Never Lived in America. The New Journalism of Abraham Cahan* (Bloomington: Indiana University Press, 1985)

---, "If You Join the Strikers, I'll Marry You", *New York Commercial Advertiser* (September 8, 1900), now in Moses Rischin, ed., *Grandma Never Lived in America. The New Journalism of Abraham Cahan* (Bloomington: Indiana University Press, 1985)

---, "Those for Cleanliness and Self-Respect, Follow Me!", *New York Commercial Advertiser* (January 12, 1901), now in Moses Rischin, ed., *Grandma Never Lived in America. The New Journalism of Abraham Cahan* (Bloomington: Indiana University Press, 1985)

---, "Cockroach Pharaohs", *New York Commercial Advertiser* (July 15, 1901), now in Moses Rischin, ed., *Grandma Never Lived in America. The New Journalism of Abraham Cahan* (Bloomington: Indiana University Press, 1985)

---, "Tragedies and Comedies of Rent Day", *New York Commercial Advertiser* (April 5, 1902), now in Moses Rischin, ed., *Grandma Never Lived in America. The New Journalism of Abraham Cahan* (Bloomington: Indiana University Press, 1985)

---, "Women of Valor", *New York Commercial Adviser* (June 29, 1902), now in Moses Rischin, ed., *Grandma Never Lived in America. The New Journalism of Abraham Cahan* (Bloomington: Indiana University Press, 1985)

---, *The Rise of David Levinsky* (1917; New York: Harper & Row, Publishers, 1960)

---, "Foreword", in *Selected Songs of Eliakum Zunser* (New York: Zunser Publishing Co., 1928)

---, *Bleter fun Mein Leben* (New York: The Forward Association, 1926-1931). English edition: *The Education of Abraham Cahan* (Philadelphia: Jewish Publication Society of America, 1969)

Claudio Canal, *Tutti mi chiamano Ziamele. Musiche yiddish* (Firenze: Giuntina, 1990)

Eddie Cantor, *My Life Is in Your Hands* (New York and London: Harper & Bros, Publishers, 1928)

Emanuel Carnevali, *Il primo dio* (Milano: Adelphi, 1978)

C. Carr, "Night Clubbing. Reports from Tompkins Square", *The Village Voice* (Aug.16, 1988)

---, "When the Rainbow Is Not Enough. People's Park: Round Two", *The Village Voice* (Aug.23, 1988)

Bruno Cartosio, "Italian Workers and Their Press in the United States, 1900-1920", in Christiane Harzig and Dirk Hoerder, eds., *The Press of Labor Migrants in Europe and North America. 1880s to 1930s* (Bremen: Publications of the Labor Newspaper Preservation Projekt, Universität Bremen, 1985)

---, *Lavoratori negli Stati Uniti* (Milano: Arcipelago, 1989)

---, *Anni inquieti. Società, media, ideologie negli Stati Uniti da Truman a Kennedy* (Roma: Editori Riuniti, 1992)

Christa Carvajal, "German-American Theatre", in Maxine Schwartz Seller, ed., *Ethnic Theatre in the United States* (Westport, Conn.: Greenwood Press, 1983)

Herbert N. Casson, "The Story of the Slocum Disaster", *Munsey's Magazine* (December, 1904)

Milton Catapano, *46 Eldridge/P.S.65. A Memoir* (Chicago: Milton Catapano, 1988)

Giuseppe Cautela, "The Bowery", *The American Mercury*, XI (Nov. 1926), No.35

---, "The Italian Theatre in New York", *The American Mercury*, XII (Sept. 1927), No.45

Celebrating 25 Years of Cooper Square. 1959-1984 (New York: The Cooper Square Committee, 1984)

Luisa Cetti, *Donne, lavoro e politica negli Stati Uniti. 1900-1930* (Milano: UNICOPLI, 1983)

---, "Work Experience Among Italian Women in New York, 1900-1930", *RSA. Rivista di Studi Anglo-Americani*, III (1984-85), n.4-5

Jules Chametzky, *From the Ghetto. The Fiction of Abraham Cahan* (Amherst: The University of Massachusetts Press, 1977)

Lenora Champagne, ed., *Out from Under. Texts by Women Performance Artists* (New York: Theatre Communications Group, 1990)

Paul Charosh and Robert A. Fremont, eds., *Song Hits from the Turn of the Century* (New York: Dover Publications, Inc., 1975)

Jerome Charyn, *The Isaac Quartet (Marilyn the Wild. Blue Eyes. The Education of Patrick Silver. Secret Isaac)* (London: Zomba Books, 1984)

---, *Metropolis. New York As Myth, Marketplace, and Magical Land* (New York: Avon Books, 1986)

---, *War Cries Over Avenue C* (1985; New York: Viking Penguin, 1986)

Jack Chen, *The Chinese of America. From the Beginnings to the Present* (San Francisco: Harper & Row, Publishers, 1981)

Fay Chiang, *In the City of Contradictions* (New York: Sunbury Press, 1979)

---, *Miwa's Song* (New York: Sunbury Press, 1982)

---, "Looking Back", in *Basement Yearbook 1986* (New York: Basement Workshop, 1986)

---, "Our Stories: The Importance of Remembering", *Bu Gao Ban*, No.6 (Summer/Fall 1987)

---, "Asian American Cultural Identity: Two Voices", *Upfront*, No.14-15 (Winter/Spring 1987-88)

---, "Chinatown. A work in progress" (typescript, New York, 1987)

Frank Chin, Jeffery Paul Chan, Lawson Fusao Inada, Shawn Hsu Wong, eds., *Aiiieeeee! An Anthology of Asian-American Writers* (Washington, D.C.: Howard University Press, 1974)

---, *The Big Aiiieeeee. An Anthology of Chinese American and Japanese American Literature* (New York: Meridian Book, 1991)

Chinatown. Map & Historical Guide. A New York Chinatown History Project Production (New York: Center for Community Studies, Inc., 1988)

Samuel Chotzinoff, *A Lost Paradise. Early Reminiscences* (London: Hamish Hamilton, 1956)

Louis Chu, *Eat a Bowl of Tea* (1961; Seattle and London: University of Washington Press, 1979)

Bernardino Ciambelli, *I misteri di Mulberry Street* (New York: Frugone & Balletto, 1893)

Camillo Cianfarra, *Diario di un emigrante* (New York: L'Araldo taliano, 1900)

"City Wilderness", *Charities. The Official Organ of the Charity Organization Society of the City of New York*, Vol.IV (February 24, 1900), No.13

Kate Holliday Claghorn, "Foreign Immigration and the Tenement House in New York City", in Robert W. DeForest and Lawrence Veiller, eds., *The Tenement House Problem* (New York: Macmillan, 1903)

Sue A. Clark and Edith Wyatt, "Working Girls' Budgets", *McClure's Magazine* (November 1910)

Harold Clurman, *The Fervent Years* (New York: Alfred A. Knopf, Inc., 1945)

Eva Cockcroft, "*La Lucha Continua*: Murals on the Lower East Side", *Upfront*, 9 (Fall 1984)

Barbara Cohen, ed., *New York Observed. Artists and Writers Look at the City* (New York: Harry N. Abrams, Inc., Publishers, 1987)

Marilyn Cohen, *Reginald Marsh's New York. Paintings, Drawings, Prints, and Photographs* (New York: Whitney Museum of Modern Art and Dover Publications, Inc., 1983)

Rose Cohen, *Out of the Shadow* (New York: George H. Doran, 1918)

Sarah Blacher Cohen, ed. *From Hester Street to Hollywood. The Jewish-American Stage and Screen* (Bloomington: Indiana University Press, 1986)

---, "Yiddish Origins and Jewish-American Transformations", in Sarah Blacher Cohen, ed. *From Hester Street to Hollywood. The Jewish-American Stage and Screen* (Bloomington: Indiana University Press, 1986)

Terry Coleman, *Passage to America. A History of Emigrants from Great Britain and Ireland to America in the Mid-Nineteenth Century* (1972; London: Penguin Books, 1974)

John Collier, "Cheap Amusements", *Charities and the Commons*, 20 (April 1908)

Jesus Colon, *A Puerto Rican in New York and Other Sketches* (1961; New York: International Publishers, 1982)

"*Community Histories*: Community Documentation Workshop — Lower East Side, Manhattan. An Interview with Arthur Tobier", *Action Image*, Vol.1 (Autumn 1984), No.1

Sarah Comstock, "In the Strikers' Hall", *Colliers* (December 25, 1909)

Chuck Connors, *Bowery Life* (New York: Richard K. Fox Publishing Co., 1904)

Peter Conrad, *The Art of the City. Views and Versions of New York* (New York and Oxford: Oxford University Press, 1984)

Florence Converse, *The Children of Light* (Boston: Houghton Mifflin, 1912)

Adrian Cook, *The Armies of the Streets. The New York City Draft Riots of 1863* (Lexington: The University Press of Kentucky, 1974)

Paulette Cooper, ed., *Growing Up Puerto Rican* (New York: New American Library, 1972)

John Corbin, "How the Other Half Laughs", *Harper's New Monthly Magazine*, Vol.XCVIII (Dec.1898), No.DLXXXIII

Francesco Cordasco and Eugene Bucchioni, eds., *The Puerto Rican Experience. A Sociological Sourcebook* (Totowa, N.J.: Rowman and Littlefield, 1973)

Edward Corsi, "My Neighborhood", *Outlook* (Sept.16, 1925)

Stephen Crane, *Maggie: A Girl of the Streets. A Story of New York* (1893; New York: D. Appleton and Company, 1896)

---, *George's Mother* (London: Edward Arnold, 1896)

---, *Prose and Poetry* (New York: The Library of America, 1984)

Edward Crapsey, *The Nether Side of New York; or, the Vice, Crime and Poverty of the Great Metropolis* (1872; Montclair, N.J.: Patterson Smith, 1969)

Thomas Cripps, "The Movie Jew as an Image of Assimilationism, 1903-1927", *Journal of Popular Film*, IV (1975), No.3

Barton Currie, "The Nickel Madness", *Harper's Weekly*, 51 (Aug. 24, 1907)

D.

Agustin Daly, "Under the Gaslight", in Daniel C. Gerould, ed., *American Melodrama* (New York: Performing Arts Journal Publications, 1983)

Stephen Daly, "The Shape of Its Future Splits East Village", *The New York Times* (March 20, 1983)

Cus D'Amato, *Making Neighborhood Heroes*, ed. by Arthur Tobier (New York: Community Documentation Workshop at St.Mark's Church-in-the-Bowery, 1982)

Daniela Daniele, "Il prisma delle identità: memoria etnica e sottoculture nell'East Village di New York", *Nuova Corrente*, XL (Gennaio-Giugno 1993), No. 111.

Roger Daniels, *Asian Americans: Emerging Minorities* (New York: Prentice Hall, 1988)

---, *Coming to America. A History of Immigration and Ethnicity in American Life* (New York: Harper Collins, 1990)

Sarah Sidney Davidge, "Working-Girls' Clubs", *Scribner's Magazine*, 15 (May 1894), No.5

Marshall B. Davidson, *New York. A Pictorial History* (New York: Charles Scribner's Sons, 1977)

Philip Davies, *The Metropolitan Mosaic. Problems of the Contemporary City* (Durham: BAAS Pamphlets in American Studies, 1980)

Allen F. Davis, *Spearheads for Reform. The Social Settlements and the Progressive Movement, 1890-1914* (New York: Oxford University Press, 1967)

Phil Davis, "The Kosher Meat Strike", *The Survey*, 39 (1918)

Richard Harding Davis, *Van Bibber and Others* (New York: Harper & Bros., 1892)

Mary V. Dearborn, *Love in the Promised Land. The Story of Anzia Yezierska and John Dewey* (New York: The Free Press, 1988)

Mario De Ciampis, "Note sul movimento socialista tra gli emigrati italiani negli U.S.A. (1890-1921)", *Cronache meridionali*, VI (aprile 1959)

Robert W. DeForest and Lawrence Veiller, eds., *The Tenement House Problem* (New York: Macmillan, 1903)

Frank F. DeGiovanni, *Displacement Pressures in the Lower East Side* (New York: Community Service Society, 1987)

Román de la Campa, "En la Utopía Redentora del Lenguaje: Pedro Pietri y Miguel Algarín", *The Americas Review*, Vol.16 (Summer 1988), No.2

Asela Rodríguez de Laguna, ed., *Images and Identities. The Puerto Rican in Two World Contexts* (New Brunswick: Transaction Books, 1987)

Allen De Loach, "Introduction", in Allen De Loach, ed., *The East Side Scene. American Poetry, 1960-1965* (Garden City, N.Y.: Doubleday & Company, Inc., 1972)

Lindsay Denison, "The Black Hand", *Everybody's Magazine*, XIX (1908)

Michael Denning, *Mechanic Accents. Dime Novels and Working-Class Culture in America* (London: Verso, 1987)

Department of City Planning, *District Atlas 84. Manhattan Community District 3* (City of New York, January 1984)

Rosalyn Deutsche and Cara Gendel Ryan, "The Fine Art of Gentrification", *October*, 31 (Winter 1984), now also in *The Portable Lower East Side*, Vol.4, No.1 (Spring 1987)

"Diamond Dan O'Rourke Ready to Revive Famed Bowery Bar", *New York Herald Tribune* (June 25, 1935)

Charles Dickens, *American Notes for General Circulation* (1842; Harmondsworth, Middlesex: Penguin Books, 1972)

Pietro Di Donato, *Naked Author* (New York: Phaedra, 1970)

Emily Wayland Dinwiddie, "The Rent Strike in New York", *Charities and the Commons* (January 4, 1908)

---, "The New-Law Tenement and What It Means", *Charities and the Commons*, 19 (February 15, 1908)

Robert J. Di Pietro and Edward Ifkovic, eds. *Ethnic Perspectives in American Literature* (New York: The Modern Language Association of America, 1983)

Diane Di Prima, *Memoirs of a Beatnik* (1969; San Francisco: Last Gasp, 1988)

Elèna Mortara Di Veroli, "Da Babele al silenzio: Il romanzo sinfonico di Henry Roth", *Letterature d'America*, V (autunno 1984), nn.24-25

---, "Scrivere con il carbone d'angelo: l'arte di Henry Roth", in Mario Materassi, a cura di, *Rothiana. Henry Roth nella critica italiana* (Firenze: Giuntina, 1985)

Farrell Dobbs, *Revolutionary Continuity. The Early Years, 1848-1917* (New York: Monad Press 1980)

Alfred Döblin, *Die beiden Freundinnen und ihr Giftmord* (1924; Reinbek bei Hamburg: Rowohlt Taschenbuch Verlag GmbH, 1978)

Michael Donohue, *Starting off from Dead End. An Oral History*, ed. by Arthur Tobier (New York: Community Documentation Workshop at St.Mark's Church-in-the-Bowery, 1980)

Richard M. Dorson, "Mose the Far-Famed and World Renowned", *American Literature*, 15 (March 1943-Jan.1944)

John Dos Passos, *Manhattan Transfer* (Boston: Houghton Mifflin Co., 1925)

Robert Doty, *Photo-Secession: Stieglitz and the Fine Art Movement in America* (New York: Dover Publications, Inc., 1978)

Theodore Dreiser, *Sister Carrie* (New York: Doubleday, Page, 1900)

---, *The Color of a Great City* (New York: Boni and Liveright, Publishers, 1923)

Eric Drooker, *Flood! A Novel in Pictures* (New York: Four Walls Eight Windows, 1992)

Melvin Dubofsky, *When Workers Organize. New York City in the Progressive Era* (Amherst: University of Massachusetts Press, 1968)

Isadora Duncan, *My Life* (Garden City, N.Y.: Doubleday and Co., 1927)

George Arthur Dunlap, *The City in the American Novel. 1789-1900* (Philadelphia: Dissertation, University of Pennsylvania, 1934)

Kenneth Holcomb Dunshee, *As You Pass By* (New York: Hastings House Publishers, 1952)

Kellogg Durland and Louis Sessa, "The Italian Invasion of the Ghetto", *University Settlement Studies*, 1 (1905-1906), nos.3-4

Elizabeth Dutcher, "Budgets of the Triangle Fire Victims", *Life and Labor* (Sept. 1912)

Nancy Dye, "The Women's Trade Union League of New York, 1903- 1920" (Ph.D., University of Wisconsin, 1974)

---, "Creating a Feminist Alliance: Sisterhood and Class Conflict in the New York's W.T.U.L., 1903-1914", in Milton Cantor and Bruce Laurie, eds., *Class, Sex, and the Woman Worker* (Westport, Conn.: Greenwood Press, 1977)

Deborah Dwork, "Health Conditions of Immigrant Jews on the Lower East Side of New York: 1880-1914", *Medical History*, Vol.25 (Jan.1981), No.1

E.

East Village 85. A Guide. A Documentary (New York: Pelham Press 1985)

East Village 86. A Guide. A Documentary (New York: Pelham Press, 1986)

"East Village Performance Issue", *The Drama Review*, Vol.29, (Spring 1985), No.1

"Editorial. A New Beginning", *The Quality of Life in Loisaida*, XVI (Spring 1993), No.1

Susan Edmiston and Linda D. Cirino, *Literary New York: A History and Guide* (Boston: Houghton Mifflin, 1976)

"Albert Edwards", *Comrade Yetta* (New York: Macmillan, 1913)

Jacob Epstein, *Autobiography* (London: Hulton Press, 1965)

Melech Epstein, *Jewish Labor in U.S.A. An Industrial, Political, and Cultural History of the Jewish Labor Movement, 1882-1914* (New York: Trade Union Sponsoring Committee, 1950-53)

Robert Ernst, *Immigrant Life in New York City. 1825-1863* (New York: Columbia University Press, 1949)

Sandra María Esteves, *Yerba Buena* (Greenfield Center, N.Y.: Greenfield Review, 1981)

---, *Tropical Rains: A Bilingual Downpour* (Bronx, N.Y.: African Caribbean Poetry Theatre, 1984)

---, "Ambivalence or Activism from the Nuyorican Perspective in Poetry", in Asela Rodríguez de Laguna, ed., *Images and Identities. The Puerto Rican in Two World Contexts* (New Brunswick, N.J.: Transaction Books, 1987)

---, *Bluestown Mockingbird Mambo* (Houston: Arte Público Press, 1990)

Nilda Estrada, "The Hispanic Community", *The Quality of Life in Loisaida*, XV (March-April 1982), No.1

Elizabeth Ewen, "City Lights: Immigrant Women and the Rise of the Movies", *Signs*, Vol.5 (Spring 1980), No.3, Supplement

---, *Immigrant Women in the Land of Dollars. Life and Culture on the Lower East Side, 1890-1925* (New York: Monthly Review Press, 1985)

F.

Geneviève Fabre, ed., *European Perspectives on Hispanic Literature of the United States* (Houston: Arte Público Press, 1988)

Edwin Fenton, *Immigrants and Unions. A Case Study: Italians and American Labor, 1870-1920* (1957; New York: Arno Press, Inc., 1975)

Sarah Ferguson, "How To Unify a Neighborhood. Five-day Police Occupation of Loisaida Backfires", *The Village Voice* (May 16, 1989)

---, "Tompkins Squares Everywhere", *The Village Voice* (Spet. 24, 1991)

Loren W. Fessler and China Institute in America, Inc., eds., *Chinese in America. Stereotyped Past, Changing Present* (New York: Vantage Press, Inc., 1983)

Leslie A. Fiedler, "Genesis: The American-Jewish Novel Through the Twenties", *Midstream*, IV (Summer 1958)

---, "Henry Roth's Neglected Masterpiece", *Commentary*, 30 (Aug.1960).

Ronald L. Filippelli, *Labor in the U.S.A. A History* (New York: Alfred A. Knopf, 1984)

---, ed., *Labor Conflict in the United States. An Encyclopedia* (New York: Garland Publishing, Inc., 1990)

David M. Fine, *The City, the Immigrant and American Fiction, 1880-1920* (Metuchen, N.J.: The Scarecrow Press, Inc., 1977)

Guido Fink e Gabriella Morisco, a cura di, *Il recupero del testo. Aspetti della letteratura ebraico-americana* (Bologna: CLUEB, 1988)

---, M. Maffi, F. Minganti, B. Tarozzi, *Storia della letteratura americana* (Firenze: Sansoni, 1991)

Karen Finley, *Shock Treatment* (San Francisco: City Lights, 1990)

First Report of the Tenement House Department of the City of New York, 1902-1903 (New York: Martin B. Brown Press, 1904)

Minnie Fisher, *Born One Year Before the Century. An Oral History*, ed. by A.Tobier (New York: Community Documentation Workshop at St.Mark's Church-in-the-Bowery, 1976)

Ernest Flagg, "The New York Tenement-House Evil and Its Cure", *Scribner's Magazine*, Vol.XVI (July 1894), No.1

Eleanor Flexner, *Century of Struggle. The Woman's Rights Movement in the United States* (New York: Atheneum, 1968)

Juan Flores, *Divided Borders. Essays on Puerto Rican Identity* (Houston, TX: Arte Público Press, 1993)

Elizabeth Gurley Flynn, *The Rebel Girl. An Autobiography. My First Life (1906-1926)* (New York: International Publishers, 1973)

Lisa W. Foderaro, "Will It Be Loisaida or Alphabet City. Two Visions Vie in the East Village", *The New York Times* (May 17, 1987)

Michael Folsom, ed., *Mike Gold: A Literary Anthology* (New York: International Publshers, 1972)

Nancy Foner, ed., *New Immigrants in New York* (New York: Columbia University Press, 1987)

Philip S. Foner, ed., *Mother Jones Speaks: Collected Writings and Speeches* (New York: Monad Press, 1983)

--- and Reinhard Schultz, eds., *The Other America. Art and the Labour Movement in the United States* (London: The Journeyman Press, 1985)

"Foreign Population in New York", *Charities*, Vol.I (Aug., 1898), No.9

George G. Foster, *New York by Gas-Light: With Here and There a Streak of Sunshine* (1850; Berkeley: University of California Press, 1990)

A. H. Frankel, *In Gold We Trust* (Philadelphia: W. Piles' Sons, 1898)

Lee K. Frankel, "The Cost of Living in New York", *Charities and the Commons*, 19 (November 16, 1907)

William Freiburger, "War Prosperity and Hunger: The New York Food Riots of 1917", *Labor History*, 25(Spring 1984), No.2

Robert A. Fremont, ed., *Favorite Songs of the Nineties* (New York: Dover Publications, Inc., 1973)

Lewis Fried, "Jacob Riis and the Jews: The Ambivalent Quest for Community", *American Studies*, Vol.20 (Spring 1979), No.1

---, "Jacob Riis and the Making of His Self", *In Their Own Words. Essays on American Ethnic Literature*, III (Spring 1986), No.1

Israel Friedlander, "The Americanization of the Jewish Immigrant", *The Survey*, 38 (1917)

David Frisby, *Fragments of Modernity. Theories of Modernity in the Work of Simmel, Kracauer and Benjamin* (Cambridge: Polity Press, 1985)

Michael H. Frisch and Daniel J. Walkowitz, eds., *Working-Class America. Essays on Labor, Community, and American Society* (Urbana, Ill.: University of Illinois Press, 1983)

Sadie Frowne, "The Story of a Sweatshop Girl", *The Independent* (September 25, 1902), now in Leon Stein and Philip Taft, eds., *Workers Speak. Self Portraits* (New York: Arno & The New York Times, 1971)

Norman Fruchter, *Coat Upon a Stick* (1963; New York: The Jewish Publication Society, 1987)

Horace B. Fry, *Little Italy. A Tragedy in One Act* (New York: R.H.Russell, 1902)

Colomba M. Furio, "The Cultural Background of the Italian Immigrant Woman and Its Impact on Her Unionization in the New York City Garment Industry, 1880-1919", in George E. Pozzetta, ed., *Pane e lavoro: The Italian American Working Class* (Toronto: The Multicultural History Society of Ontario, 1980)

G.

Donna R. Gabaccia, *From Sicily to Elizabeth Street. Housing and Social Change Among Italian Immigrants, 1880-1930* (Albany: State University of New York Press, 1984)

Lesia Gajdycz, *Learning American. An Oral History*, ed. by Arthur Tobier (New York: Community Documentation Workshop at St.Mark's Church-in-the-Bowery, 1984)

Leonardo Gandini, "L'immagine della città nel cinema hollywoodiano, 1927-1932" (Bologna: Università degli Studi, Dottorato di Ricerca in Discipline dello Spettacolo, 1990)

Marie Ganz, *Rebels. Into Anarchy — And Out Again* (New York: Dodd, Mead and Company, 1919)

Hamlin Garland, *Crumbling Idols. Twelve Essays on Art Dealing Chiefly With Literature, Painting and Drama* (1894; Cambridge, Mass.: The Belknap Press of Harvard University Press, 1960)

Michael V. Gazzo, *A Hatful of Rain* (New York: Random House, Inc., 1956)

William Geist, "The Lower East Side Learns How to See In the New Year", *International Herald Tribune* (Oct.6, 1986)

Blanche H. Gelfant, *The American City Novel* (Norman: The University of Oklahoma Press, 1954)

J. W. Gerard, "Impress of Nationalities on New York City", *Magazine of American History* (Jan. 1890)

Daniel C. Gerould, ed., *American Melodrama* (New York: Performing Arts Journal Publications, 1983)

Leslie Gevirtz, "Cops in Crisis. Police Riot in Tompkins Square Was No Accident", *The Village Voice* (Aug.23, 1988)

Benedict Giamo, *On the Bowery. Confronting Homelessness in American Society* (Iowa City: University of Iowa Press, 1989)

Douglas Gilbert, *American Vaudeville. Its Life and Times* (1940; New York: Dover Publications, Inc., 1963)

Timothy J. Gilfoyle, "The Urban Geography of Commercial Sex: Prostitution in New York City, 1790-1860", *Journal of Urban History*, 13 (August 1987)

Lucy P. Gillman, "Coney Island", *New York History*, XXXVI (July, 1955), No.3

Ray Ginger, *Eugene V. Debs: A Biography. The Making of an American Radical* (1949; New York: Collier Books, 1962)

Allen Ginsberg, *Howl* (San Francisco: City Lights Books, 1957)

---, "Preface" in Ann Waldman, ed., *Out of This World* (New York: Crown Publishers, 1992)

Charles N. Glaab and A. Theodore Brown, *A History of Urban America* (New York: Macmillan, 1983)

Nathan Glazer and Daniel P. Moynihan, *Beyond the Melting Pot. The Negroes, Puerto Ricans, Jews, Italians, and Irish of New York City* (Cambridge, Mass.: The M.I.T. Press, 1963)

Philip Gleason, "The Melting-Pot: Symbol of Fusion or Confusion?", *American Quarterly*, XVI (1964)

Toby & Gene Glickman, *The New York Red Pages. A Radical Tourist Guide* (New York: Praeger Publishers, 1984)

Michael Gold, "Birth. A Prologue to a Tentative East Side Novel", *The Masses*, Nov.-Dec. 1917, now in Michael Folsom, ed., *Mike Gold: A Literary Anthology* (New York: International Publishers, 1972)

---, *Jews Without Money* (1930; New York: Carroll & Graf, 1984)

---, "A Jewish Childhood in the New York Slums", *People's World*, April 11, 25; May 9, 23; June 20; July 4, 18; August 1, 15, 29; Sept. 26; Oct. 17, 1959, now in Michael Folsom, ed., *Mike Gold: A Literary Anthology* (New York: International Publishers, 1972)

Harry Golden, "Buying a Suit on the East Side", in Harry Golden, *Only in America* (Cleveland and New York: The World Publishing Co., 1944, 1958)

Emma Goldman, *Living My Life* (New York: Alfred A. Knopf, 1931)

Richard Goldstein, "The Gentry Comes to the East Village", *The Village Voice*, Vol.XXV (May 19, 1980), No.20

Robert J. Goldstein, "The Anarchist Scare of 1908: A Sign of Tensions in the Progressive Era", *American Studies*, XV (Fall 1974), No.2

Samuel Gompers, *Seventy-five Years of Life and Labor* (New York: E. P. Dutton, 1925)

Cary Goodman, *Choosing Sides. Playgrounds and Street Life on the Lower East Side* (New York: Schocken Books, 1979)

---, "(Re)creating Americans at the Educational Alliance", *The Journal of Ethnic Studies*, Vol.6 (winter 1979), No.4

Pearl Goodman and Elsa Ueland, "The Shirtwaist Trade", *Journal of Political Economy*, 18 (December 1910)

Lloyd Goodrich, *Thomas Eakins. His Life and Work* (New York: Whitney Museum, 1933)

---, *Winslow Homer's America* (New York: Tudor, 1969)

Jacob Gordin, "The Yiddish Stage", *Report* (New York: University Settlement Society, 1901)

Diana R. Gordon, *City Limits. Barriers to Change in Urban Government* (New York: Charterhouse, 1973)

Josh Gosciak and Alan Moore, eds., *A Day in the Life. Tales from the Lower East. An Anthology of Writings from the Lower East Side, 1940-1990* (New York: Evil Eye Books, 1990)

Martin Gottlieb, "Space Invaders. Land Grab on the Lower East Side", *The Village Voice*, Vol.XXVII (December 14, 1982), No.50

John Grafton, *New York in the Nineteenth Century. 317 Engravings from "Harper's Weekly" and Other Contemporary Sources* (New York: Dover Publications, Inc., 1977)

Percy Stickney Grant, "Children's Street Games", *The Survey*, 23 (Nov.13, 1909)

Lois S. Gray, "The Jobs Puerto Ricans Hold in New York City", *Monthly Labor Review*, Vol. 98 (Oct. 1975), No.10

Leo Grebler, *Housing Market Behavior in a Declining Area. Long-Term Changes in Inventory and Utilization of Housing on New York's Lower East Side* (New York: Columbia University Press, 1952)

Martin Green, *New York 1913. The Armory Show and the Paterson Strike Pageant* (New York: Charles Scribner's Sons, 1988)

Rose Basile Green, *The Italian-American Novel. A Document of the Interaction of Two Cultures* (Rutherford: Fairleigh Dickinson University Press, 1974)

Clement Greenberg, *Art and Culture: Critical Essays* (Boston: Beacon Press, 1961)

Mabel Greene, "This Show a Family Affair", *New York Sun* (Febr. 14, 1933)

Judith Greenfield, "The Rôle of the Jews in the Development of the Clothing Industry in the United States", *YIVO. Annual of Jewish Social Science*, II, III (1947-48)

William R. Greer, "The Fortunes of the Lower East Side Are Rising", *The New York Times* (Aug.4, 1985)

David Grimstead, *Melodrama Unveiled: American Theater and Culture, 1800-1850* (Chicago: University of Chicago Press, 1968)

Emmett Grogan, *Ringolevio. A Life Played for Keeps* (1972; New York: Citadel Press Books, 1990)

Carol Groneman, "Working-Class Immigrant Women in Mid-Nineteenth-Century New York. The Irish Woman's Experience", *Journal of Urban History*, 4 (May 1978), No.3

Barbara W. Grossman, *Funny Woman. The Life and Times of Fanny Brice* (Bloomington, IN: Indiana University Press, 1992)

John Gruen, *The New Bohemia. The Combine Generation* (New York: Grosset & Dunlap, 1966)

Thomas A. Gullason, "The Prophetic City in Stephen Crane's 1893 *Maggie*", *Modern Fiction Studies*, XXIV (Spring 1978)

Herbert G. Gutman, "Class Composition and the Development of the American Working Class, 1840-1890", in Herbert G. Gutman, *Power and Culture: Essays on the American Working Class*, ed. by Ira Berlin (New York: Pantheon, 1987)

Allen Guttman, *The Jewish Writer in America. Assimilation and the Crisis of Identity* (New York: Oxford University Press, 1971)

H.

Jessica Hagedorn, *Dangerous Music* (San Francisco: Momo's Press, 1975)

---, "Loft Living", *The Portable Lower East Side*, Vol.4 (Spring 1987), No.1

---, "Tenement Lover: no palm trees/in new york city", in Misha Berson, ed., *Between Worlds. Contemporary Asian-American Plays* (New York: Theatre Communications Group, 1990)

---, Laurie Carlos, Robbie McCauley, "Teenytown", in Lenora Champagne, ed., *Out from Under. Texts by Women Performance Artists* (New York: Theatre Communications Group, 1990)

---, *Dogeaters* (Harmondsworth, Middlesex: Penguin Books 1990)

Steven Hager, *Art After Midnight. The East Village Scene* (New York: St. Martin's Press, 1986)

Peter Bacon Hales, *Silver Cities. The Photography of American Urbanization, 1839-1915* (Philadelphia: Temple University Press, 1984)

Albert Halper, "Notes on Jewish-American Fiction", *Menorah Journal*, 20 (Spring 1932)

---, *Union Square* (1931; New York: Belmont Books, 1962)

Oscar Handlin, *The Uprooted. The Epic Story of Great Migrations That Made the American People* (New York: Grosset & Dunlap, Publishers, 1951)

Hutchins Hapgood, "The Foreign Stage in New York. The Italian Theater of New York", *The Bookman*, XI (Aug.1900)

---, *The Spirit of the Ghetto* (1902; Cambridge, Mass.: The Belknap Press of Harvard University Press, 1967)

---, *Types from City Streets* (New York: Funk & Wagnalls Co., 1910)

Norman Hapgood, "The Jew and American Democracy", *Menorah Journal*, 2 (1916)

Jack Hardy, *The Clothing Workers. A Study of the Conditions and Struggles in the Needle Trades* (New York: International Publishers, 1935)

Alvin F. Harlow, *Old Bowery Days* (New York: D. Appleton & Co., 1931)

Steve Harney, "Ethnos and the Beat Poets", *Journal of American Studies*, Vol. 21 (December 1991), No. 3

Michael Harrington, *The Other America. Poverty in the United States* (New York: The Macmillan Company, 1962)

Benjamin and Barbara Harshav, eds., *American Yiddish Poetry. A Bilingual Anthology* (Berkeley and Los Angeles, Cal.: University of California Press, 1986)

G. H. Hartman and S. Budick, eds., *Midrash and Literature* (New Haven: Yale University Press, 1986)

Christiane Harzig, "The Rôle of German Women in the German-American Working-Class Movement in Late Nineteenth-Century New York", *The Journal of American Ethnic History*, Vol.8 (Spring 1989), No.2

Joel Tyler Headley, *The Great Riots of New York, 1712 to 1873* (1873; New York: Dover Publications, Inc., 1971)

Louise Levitas Henriksen, *Anzia Yezierska. A Writer's Life* (New Brunswick, N.J.: Rutgers University Press, 1988)

Ad Hereijgers and Yvon van der Steen, "Squeezing the Lower East Side. Patterns and Processes of Neighborhood Change in a Dollar-driven Land Use Market" (Final Thesis for the Dutch Doctoral Degree in Human Geography, University of Amsterdam and City University of New York, December 1986)

Freddy Hernandez, "The History of a Name: Loisaida", in *The Quality of Life in Loisaida*, X (July-August 1987), 4

David Herreshoff, *American Disciples of Marx* (Detroit: Wayne State University Press, 1967)

Thomas B. Hess, "Introduction", in Fred W. McDarrah and Gloria S. McDarrah, *The Artist's World In Pictures* (1961; New York: Shapolsky's Publishers, Inc., 1988)

Granville Hicks, Michael Gold, et al., eds., *Proletarian Literature in the United States. An Anthology* (New York: International Publishers, 1935)

John Higham, *Send These To Me. Immigrants in Urban America* (Baltimore: Johns Hopkins University Press, 1984)

Archibald Hill, "Rental Agitation on the Lower East Side", *Charities* (April 16, 1904)

Morris Hillquit, *History of Socialism in the United States* (1903, 1910; New York: Dover Publications, Inc., 1971)

Morgan Y. Himelstein, *Drama Was a Weapon. The Left-Wing Theatre in New York, 1929-1941* (New Brunswick, N. J.: Rutgers University Press, 1963)

Milton Hindus, ed., *The Old East Side. An Anthology* (Philadelphia: The Jewish Publication of America, 1971)

Lewis W. Hine, "Social Photography; How the Camera Can Help in the Social Uplift", *Proceedings of the National Conference of Charities and Corrections* (June 1909), now in Alan Trachtenberg, *Classic Essays on Photography* (New Haven: Leete's Island Books, 1980)

Charles Hirschman and Morrison G. Wong, "Socio-Economic Gains of Asian Americans, Blacks, and Hispanics, 1960-1976", *American Journal of Sociology*, Vol.90 (November 1984), No.3

Dirk Hoerder, ed., *"Struggle a Hard Battle".* Essays on Working-Class Immigrants (De Kalb, Il.: Northern Illinois University Press, 1986)

Abbie Hoffman, *Soon To Be A Major Motion Picture* (New York: G. Putnam & Sons, 1980)

Richard Hofstadter, *The Age of Reform* (New York: A.A. Knopf, 1955))

Grant Holcomb, "The Forgotten Legacy of Jerome Myers (1867-1940): Painter of New York's Lower East Side", *The American Art Journal* (May 1977)

Bob Holman, "'Zooin' in Alphabet City", in Bob Holman, *PANic* DJ. Performance Text Poems, Raps, Songs* (New York: Larry Qualls and Associates, University Arts Resources, 1987)

Marlon Hom, "The Chinatown Literary Movement: 1940s", *Bu Gao Ban* (New York Chinatown History Museum), no.7 (Fall 1988)

Eric Homberger, *American Writers and Radical Politics, 1900-1939: Equivocal Commitments* (London: Macmillan, 1986)

William Innes Homer, *Alfred Stieglitz and the American Avant-Garde* (Boston: New York Graphic Society, 1977)

Kim Hopper, Ellen Baxter, Stuart Cox, Laurence Klein, *One Year Later. The Homeless Poor in New York City, 1982* (New York: Community Service Society, 1982)

Isaac A. Hourwich, *Immigration and Labor* (1912; New York: Arno Press, 1969)

"How New York Lives", *The New York Times* (June 2, 1859)

Irving Howe and Eliezer Greenberg, eds., *A Treasury of Yiddish Stories* (New York: The Viking Press, Inc., 1953)

Irving Howe, "Life Never Let Up", *The New York Times Book Review* (Oct.25, 1964)

--- (with the assistance of Kenneth Libo), *World of Our Fathers* (New York: Harcourt, Brace, Jovanovich, 1976)

--- and Eliezer Greenberg, eds., *A Treasury of Yiddish Poetry* (New York: Schocken Books, 1976)

John Howell, "Jenny Holzer. The Message Is the Medium", *ArtNews*, Vol.87 (Summer 1988), No.6

William Dean Howells, "Editor's Study", *Harper's New Monthly Magazine*, LXXIII (July 1886)

---, *A Hazard of New Fortunes* (New York: Harper & Bros., 1890)

---, "An East Side Ramble", in W.D.Howells, *Impressions and Experiences* (New York: Harper & Bros., 1896)

318

I. W. Howerth, "Are the Italians a Dangerous Class?", *The Charities Review*, IV (1894)

F. Jack Hurley, *Portrait of a Decade: Roy Stryker and the Development of Documentary Photography in the Thirties* (Baton Rouge: Louisiana State Uniersity, 1972)

Paula E. Hyman, "Immigrant Women and Consumer Protest: The New York City Kosher Meat Boycott of 1902", *American Jewish History*, 70 (September 1980), No.1

I.
César Andreu Iglesias, ed., *Memoirs of Bernardo Vega. A Contribution to the History of the Puerto Rican Community in New York* (New York: Monthly Review Press, 1984)

"An Introduction to Squat-Homesteading" (New York: 537 E. 13th Street Collective, n.d.)

Donna Ippolito, *The Uprising of the 20,000* (Pittsburgh: Motheroot Publications, 1979)

Oscar Israelowitz, *The Lower East Side Guide* (New York: Israelowitz Publishing, 1988)

Belle L. Israels, "The Way of the Girl", *The Survey*, 22 (1909)

"Italian Plays for a Nickel", *The New York World* (May 5, 1895)

The Italians of New York. A Survey Prepared by the Workers of the Federal Writers' Project, Works Progress Administration in the City of New York (New York: Random House, 1938)

J.
Jane Jacobs, *The Death and Life of Great American Cities. The Failure of Town Planning* (New York: Random House, 1961)

Henry James, *The American Scene* (1907; London: Granville Publishing, 1987)

Thomas A. Janvier, "The Evolution of New York", *Harper's New Monthly Magazine*, Vol.LXXXVI (May and June 1893), Nos. DXVI and DXVII

Edith Jarolim, "'The World'", *Project Papers*, Vol.1 (1987), No.6

Michael C. Jaye and Ann Chalmers Watts, eds., *Literature and the Urban Experience. Essays on the City and Literature* (New Brunswick, N.J.: Rutgers University Press, 1981)

Oliver Jensen, Joan Paterson Kerr, Murray Belsky, eds., *American Album* (New York: American Heritage and Ballantine Books, 1970)

Leroi Jones/Amiri Baraka, *Autobiography of Leroi Jones/Amiri Baraka* (New York: Freundlich Books, 1984)

Marvin Jones and Chris Huestis, "Jack Levine. An Interview", *The New Common Good* (September 1986; October 1986)

Jenna Weissman Joselit, *Our Gang. Jewish Crime and the New York Jewish Community, 1900-1940* (Bloomington: Indiana University Press, 1983)

---, "The Landlord as Czar. Pre-World War I Tenant Activity", in Ronald Lawson, ed., *The Tenant Movement in New York City, 1904-1984* (New Brunswick, N.J.: Rutgers University Press, 1986)

Garth S. Jowett, "The First Motion Picture Audiences", *Journal of Popular Film*, 3 (1974)

JWG, "The Bachelor Society in Chinese American History", *Bu Gao Ban* (New York Chinatown History Museum), Summer 1985

K.

E. J. Kahn, *The Merry Partners* (New York: Random House, 1955)

Lisa Kaplan, "The Housing Struggle: These Ten Years", *The Quality of Life in Loisaida*, Vol.XI (March-April 1988), No.2

---, "The Community Struggle for a Fair Housing Plan", *The Quality of Life in Loisaida*, Vol.XII (September-October 1989), No.5

Yuri Kapralov, *Once There Was a Village* (New York: St. Martin's Press, 1974)

---, "The House That Jack Built" (paper read at New York Public Library, Tompkins Square Branch, May 3, 1980, courtesy of Yuri Kapralov and the Seward Park Branch of the New York Public Library)

Janet Kardon, *The East Village Scene* (Philadelphia: Institute of Contemporary Art and University of Pennsylvania, 1984)

John F. Kasson, *Amusing the Million. Coney Island at the Turn of the Century* (New York: Hill & Wang, 1978)

Stuart Kaufman et al., eds., *The Samuel Gompers Papers, Vol.I: The Making of a Union Leader 1850-86)* (Urbana and Chicago: University of Illinois Press, 1963)

Alfred Kazin, "Neglected Books", *The American Scholar*, 25 (Fall 1956)

Peter Keating, ed., *Into Unknown England, 1866-1913. Selections from the City Explorers* (London: Fontana, 1976)

Myra Kelly, *Little Citizens* (New York: McClure, Phillips, 1904)

---, *Wards of Liberty* (New York: McClure, 1907)

---, *Little Aliens* (New York: Scribner's, 1910)

Barbara Kershenblatt-Gimblett, "*Contraband*: Performance, Text and Analysis of a *Purim-shpil*", *The Drama Review*, Vol.24 (Sept. 1980), No.3

Robert Kerstein, "Stage Models of Gentrification", *Urban Affairs Quarterly*, Vol. 25 (June 1990), No.4

Alice Kessler-Harris, "Organizing the Unorganizable: Three Jewish Women and Their Union", *Labor History*, 17 (Winter 1976), No.1

---, "Introduction", in A.Yezierska, *Bread Givers* (1925; New York: Persea Books, 1975)

Thomas Kessner, *The Golden Door. Italian and Jewish Immigrant Mobility in New York City, 1880-1915* (New York: Oxford University Press, 1977)

--- and Betty Boyd Caroli, "New Immigrant Women at Work: Italians and Jews in New York City, 1880-1950", *Journal of Ethnic Studies*, IV (Winter 1978), No.4

--- and Betty Boyd Caroli, *Today's Immigrants. Their Stories* (New York: Oxford University Press, 1982)

Charlotte Kimball, "An Outline of Amusements Among Italians in New York", *Charities*, Vol.V (August 18, 1900), No.12

Edward S. King, *Joseph Zalmonah* (New York: Lee and Shepard, 1893)

Frederick A. King, "Influences in Street Life", *Report* (New York: University Settlement Society, 1900)

John M. Kingsdale, "The 'Poor Man's Club': Social Functions of the Urban Working Class Saloon", *American Quarterly*, 25 (Oct.1973)

S. C. Kingsley, "Penny Arcade and the Cheap Theater", *Charity and the Commons*, 18 (June 8, 1907)

Walter J. Kingsley, "Thirty Years of Vaudeville", *New York Dramatic Mirror* (Nov.26, 1913)

Galway Kinnell, *The Avenue Bearing the Initial of Christ into the New World. Poems 1946-64* (Boston: Houghton Mifflin Co., 1974)

Edward C. Kirkland, *A History of American Economic Life* (New York: Appleton-Century-Crofts, 1969)

Paul Klapper, "The Yiddish Music Hall", *University Settlement Society*, 2 (1905), no.4

Norman L. Kleeblatt and Susan Chevlowe, eds., *Painting a Place in America. Jewish Artist in New York, 1900-1945* (Bloomington, IN.: Indiana University Press, 1992)

N. R. Kleinfield, "Mining Chinatown's 'Mountain of Gold'", *The New York Times* (June 1, 1986)

Yuri Kochiyama, *Fishermerchant's Daughter. An Oral History. Vol.1 & Vol.2*, ed. by Arthur Tobier (New York: Community Documentation Workshop at St.Mark's Church-in-the-Bowery, 1981)

Ron Kolm, *The Plastic Factory* (New York: Red Dust, 1989)

---, *Suburban Ambush* (New York: Appearances, 1991)

John Koren, "The Padrone System and the Padrone Bank", *Special Bulletin* (U.S. Bureau of Labor), 9 (March 1897)

Virginia E. Sánchez Korrol, *From Colonia to Community. The History of Puerto Ricans in New York City, 1917-1948* (Westport, Conn.: Greenwood Press, 1983)

John A. Kouwenhoven, *The Columbia Historical Portrait of New York. An Essay in Graphic History* (1953; New York: Harper & Row Publishers, 1972)

Roman Kozak, *This Ain't No Disco. The Story of CBGB* (Boston-London: Faber and Faber, 1988)

Siegfried Kracauer, *Theory of Film* (New York: Oxford University Press, 1960)

Aaron Kramer, ed., *A Century of Yiddish Poetry* (New York: Cornwall Books, 1989)

Alan M. Kraut, *The Huddled Masses: The Immigrant in American Society, 1880-1921* (Arlington Heights, Ill.: Harlan Davidson, Inc. 1982)

Rob Kroes, ed., *American Immigration. Its Variety and Lasting Imprint* (Amsterdam: VU University Press, 1979)

Riva Krut, "Introduction", in A. Yezierska, *Hungry Hearts and Other Stories* (1920; London: Virago Press, 1987)

Nathan Kussy, *The Abyss* (New York: Macmillan, 1916)

Peter Kwong, *Chinatown, N.Y. Labor & Politics, 1930-1950* (New York: Monthly Review Press, 1979)

---, *The New Chinatown* (New York: Hill and Wang, 1987)

--- and Joann Lum, "Chinatown: Rousing a Political Giant. A Chance To Build Coalitions", *The Village Voice* (April 12, 1988)

L.
Walter E. Lagerquist, "Social Geography of the East Side", *The New York Times* (April 3, 1910)
Charlie Lai and John Kuo Wei Tchen, "How We Began", *Bu Gao Ban* (New York Chinatown History Museum), Summer 1984
The Landmarked Buildings of Henry Street Settlement (New York: Henry Street Settlement, n.d.)
James B. Lane, *Jacob A. Riis and the American City* (Port Washington, N.Y.: Kennikat Press, 1974)
Richard H. Lane, "East Side Benefit Societies", *Report* (New York: University Settlement Society, 1899)
Bruno Lasker, "The Food Riots", *The Survey*, 37 (March 3, 1917)
Michael La Sorte, *La Merica. Images of Italian Greenhorn Experience* (Philadelphia: Temple University Press, 1985)
"Latin Americans in NYC Issue", *The Portable Lower East Side*, Vol.V (1988), nos.1 and 2
Joe Laurie, Jr., "The Early Days of Vaudeville", *American Mercury*, LXII (Febr. 1946)
Maria Laurino, "In a Great Big Room, That's the Way We Live. Loisaida Housing Groups Battle over Tactics", *The Village Voice* (Sept.6, 1988)
Tato Laviera, *La Carreta Made a U-Turn* (Houston: Arte Público Press, 1981)
---, *Enclave* (Houston: Arte Público Press, 1981)
---, *AmeRícan* (Houston: Arte Público Press, 1985)
---, *Mainstream Ethics. Ética corriente* (Houston: Arte Público Press, 1988)
Ronald Lawson, "A Pictorial History", in Ronald Lawson, ed., *The Tenant Movement in New York City, 1904-1984* (New Brunswick, N.J.: Rutgers University Press, 1986)
---, ed., *The Tenant Movement in New York City, 1904-1984* (New Brunswick, N.J.: Rutgers University Press, 1986)
Emma Lazarus, *The Poems of Emma Lazarus* (Boston: Houghton Mifflin Company, 1889)
Charles Leinenweber, "Socialists in the Streets: The New York City Socialist Party in Working Class Neighborhoods, 1908-1918", *Science and Society*, 41(Summer 1977), No.2
---, "The Class and Ethnic Bases of New York City Socialism, 1904-1915", *Labor History*, 22 (Winter 1981), No.1
Clara Lemlich, "Life in the Shop", *New York Evening Journal* (November 28, 1909), now in Leon Stein, ed., *Out of the Sweatshop* (New York: Quadrangle/The New York Times Book Co., 1977)
"Bruno Lessing", *Children of Man* (New York: McClure, Phillips, 1903)
---, *"Lapidowitz the Schnorrer": With the Best Intentions* (New York: Heart's International Library, 1914)

Jacob Lestschinsky, "Jewish Migrations, 1840-1956", in Louis Finkelstein, ed., *The Jews*, Vol.II (New York: Harper & Row, 1960)

Fritz A.H. Leuchs, *The Early German Theatre in New York, 1840-1872* (New York: Columbia University Press, 1928)

Constance D. Leupp, "The Shirtwaist Makers' Strike" (December 18, 1909)

David Leviatin, ed., *Followers of the Trail. Jewish Working-Class Radicals in America* (New Haven, Connecticut: Yale University Press, 1989)

Anthony Lewis, "The Jew in Stand-Up Comedy", in Sarah Blacher Cohen, ed. *From Hester Street to Hollywood. The Jewish-American Stage and Screen* (Bloomington: Indiana University Press, 1986)

Gordon K. Lewis, *Puerto Rico. Freedom and Power in the Caribbean* (New York: Monthly Review Press, 1963)

Oscar Lewis, *La Vida. A Puerto Rican Family in the Culture of Poverty — San Juan and New York* (New York: Random House, 1965)

W. T. Lhamon, Jr., "Horatio Alger and American Modernism: The One-Dimensional Social Formula", *American Studies*, XVII (Autumn 1976), No.2

David S. Lifson, *The Yiddish Theatre in America* (New York: Thomas Yoseloff, 1965)

---, ed., *Epic and Folk Plays of the Yiddish Theatre* (Cranbury, N.J.: Associated University Presses, Inc., 1975)

---, "Yiddish Theatre", in Maxine Schwartz Seller, ed., *Ethnic Theatre in the United States* (Westport, Conn.: Greenwood Press, 1983)

Frederick S. Lightfoot, ed., *Nineteenth-Century New York in Rare Photographic Views* (New York: Dover Publications, Inc., 1981)

Shirley Geok-lin Lim, Mayumi Tsutakawa, Margarita Donnelly, eds., *The Forbidden Stitch. An Asian American Women's Anthology* (Corvallis, OR: Calyx Books, 1989)

Vachel Lindsay, *The Art of the Moving Picture* (New York: Macmillan, 1915)

George Lippard, *New York. Its Upper Ten and Lower Million* (Cincinnati: H. R. Rulison, 1858)

Lucy R. Lippard, "Asian and Hispanic Artists", *Upfront*, 9 (Fall 1984)

---*Mixed Blessings. New Art in a Multicultural America* (New York: Pantheon Books, 1990)

Richard Lloyd, "The Eternal Recurrence: Recycling East Village Style", *East Villager* (October 1987)

Pierpaolo Loffreda, ed., *New York New Wave* (Pesaro: Editrice Flaminia, 1989)

"Loisaida: Continent of Seven Colors" (New York: Taller Latinoamericano, 1990)

Loisaida/New York City. Voci, immagini, suoni dal Lower East Side (Milano: Lo Zibetto, 1983)

Stephen Longstreet, *City on Two Rivers. Profiles of New York — Yesterday and Today* (New York: Hawthorn Books, Inc., 1975)

Pedro López-Adorno, ed., *Papiros de Babel. Antología de la poesía puertorriqueña en Nueva York* (Río Piedras, PR: Editorial de la Universidad de Puerto Rico, 1991)

Lewis Lorwin (Louis Levine), *The Women's Garment Workers. A History of the International Ladies' Garment Workers Union* (New York: B.W.Huebsch, 1924)

Roy Lubove, *The Progressives and the Slums: Tenement House Reform in New York City, 1890-1917* (Pittsburgh: University of Pittsburgh Press, 1962)

Mabel Dodge Luhan, *Movers and Shakers* (New York: Harcourt, Brace, 1936)

Mary Lui, "Grocers, Letters, and Community. The Local Store in Chinatown's 'Bachelor Society'", *Bu Gao Ban* (New York Chinatown History Museum), Winter 1991

Judith Wing siu Luk, "What Was Her Life Like?", *Bu Gao Ban* (New York Chinatown History Museum), Winter/Spring 1985

"Sidney Luska", *As It Was Written: A Jewish Musician's Story* (New York: Cassell, 1885)

---, *Mrs.Peixada* (New York: Cassell, 1886)

---, *The Yoke of the Thorah* (New York: Cassell, 1887)

Bonnie Lyons, *Henry Roth. The Man and His Work* (New York: Cooper Square Publishers, 1976)

M.

Agnes M., "The True Life Story of a Nurse Girl", *The Independent* (September 24, 1903), now in Leon Stein and Philip Taft, eds., *Workers Speak. Self Portraits* (New York: Arno & The New York Times, 1971)

James D. McCabe, Jr., *New York by Sunlight and Gaslight* (1882; New York: Greenwich House, 1984)

Roy McCardell, *Wage Slaves of New York* (New York: Dillingham, 1899)

Fred W. McDarrah and Gloria S. McDarrah, *The Artist's World In Pictures* (1961; New York: Shapolsky's Publishers, Inc., 1988)

Evelyn McDonnell, "Café Society. The New Guerrilla Poets Act Out at the Nuyorican Poets' Café", *The Village Voice* (April 9, 1991)

Catherine MacKenzie, "Memory of Bowery Dims", *The New York Times* (August 25, 1935)

F. H. McLean, "Bowery Amusements", *Report* (New York: University Settlement Society, 1899)

Tom McNamara, "The Latin Crowns Go Social", *East Village Other*, Vol.I (May 15-31, June 1-15, June 15-30, July 1-15, 1966), Nos.12, 13, 14, 15

David Madden, ed., *Proletarian Writers of the Thirties* (Carbondale and Edwardsville: Southern Illinois Press, 1968)

Charles A. Madison, "Preface", in Jacob A. Riis, *How the Other Half Lives. Studies Among the Tenements* (1890; New York: Dover Publications, Inc., 1971)

Mario Maffi, "Horatio Alger, Jr., la tradizione puritana e i codici di comportamento nella città industriale", *Rivista di Studi Anglo-Americani*, II, Nos.2-3 (1982-83)

---, "Architecture in the City, Architecture in the Novel: William Dean Howells's *A Hazard of New Fortunes*", *Studies in the Literary Imagination*, Vol. XVI (Fall 1983), No.2

---, "Prefazione", in A. Cahan, *Perduti in America. Una storia del ghetto di New York* (Milano: SugarCo Edizioni, 1985)

---, "Prefazione", in A. Cahan, *Lo sposo importato* (Milano: SugarCo Edizioni, 1987)

---, "Fay Chiang. Temporale pomeridiano", *Linea d'ombra*, 29 (luglio-agosto 1988)

---, "The Nuyorican Experience in the Plays of Pedro Pietri and Miguel Piñero", in Mirko Jurak, ed., *Cross-Cultural Studies. American, Canadian and European Literatures: 1945-1985* (Ljubljana, Yugoslavia: Edvard Kardelj University of Ljubljana, 1988)

---, "Introduzione", in T.Howe, A.Innaurato, M.Piñero, D.Rabe, *Nuovo teatro d'America* (Genova: Costa & Nolan, 1988)

---, "Nuyorican. Il teatro di Pietri e Piñero", *Linea d'ombra*, VII (gennaio 1989), 34

---, "Da Buffalo Bill a Coney Island: Due forme di spettacolo popolare tra Otto e Novecento", *Rivista di Studi Anglo-Americani*, V (1989), No. 7

--- e Franco Minganti, "City Maps and City Alphabets", *Rivista di Studi Anglo-Americani*, V (1990), No.8

---, "New York City Newsboys' Strike of 1899", in Ronald L. Filippelli, ed., *Labor Conflict in the United States. An Encyclopedia* (New York: Garland Publishing, Inc., 1990)

---, *Nel mosaico della città. Differenze etniche e nuove culture in un quartiere di New York* (Milano: Feltrinelli, 1992)

---, "'Chi Lai! Arriba! Rise Up!'. Some Remarks on Ethnic Writing in New York City", in Hans Bak, ed., *Multiculturalism and the Canon of American Culture* (Amsterdam: Vu University Press 1993)

---, "Ritratto dell'autore da scarafaggio", in P. Pietri, *Scarafaggi metropolitani, e altre poesie* (Milano: Baldini & Castoldi, 1993).

William Mailly, "The Working Girls' Strike", *The Independent*, 67 (December 23, 1909)

Manuel Maldonado-Denis, *The Emigration Dialectic. Puerto Rico and the USA* (1976; New York: International Publishers, 1980)

Theresa Serber Malkiel, *The Diary of a Shirtwaist Striker. A Story of the Shirtwaist Makers' Strike in New York* (New York: The Co-operative Press, 1910)

Antonio Mangano, "The Associated Life of the Italians in New York City", *Charities*, Vol.XII (May 7, 1904), No.18

George J. Manson, "The Foreign Element in New York City: the Germans", *Harper's Weekly* (Aug.4, 1888)

Maxwell F. Marcuse, *This Was New York! A Nostalgic Picture of Gotham in the Gaslight Era* (New York: LIM Press, 1965)

Edwin Markham, "60,000 Children in Sweatshops", *Cosmopolitan Magazine* (Jan. 1907), now in Allon Schoener, ed., *Portal to America: The Lower East Side, 1870-1925* (New York: Holt, Rinehart and Winston, 1967)

Sanford E. Marowitz and Lewis Fried, "Abraham Cahan (1860-1951): An Annotated Bibliography", *American Literary Realism 1870-1910*, Vol. III (Summer 1970), No.3

René Marqués, *La Carreta. Drama en tres actos* (1952; Río Piedras, PR: Editorial Cultural, 1983)

Howard R. Marraro, "Italians in New York During the First Half of the Nineteenth Century", *New York History*, XXVI (July 1945)

E. S. Martin,"East Side Considerations", *Harper's New Monthly Magazine*, Vol.XCVI (May 1898), No. DLXXVI

John W. Martin, "Social Life in the Street", *Year Book of the University Settlement Society of New York*, 1899

Mario Materassi, a cura di, *Rothiana. Henry Roth nella critica italiana* (Firenze: Giuntina, 1985)

---, a cura di, *Scrittori ebrei americani* (Milano: Bompiani, 1989)

---, "Postfazione", in H. Roth, *Alla mercé di una brutale corrente* (Milano: Garzanti, 1990)

Brander Matthews, *Vignettes of Manhattan* (New York: Harper and Bros., 1894)

Lary L. May and Elaine Tyler May, "Why Jewish Movie Moguls: An Exploration in American Culture", *American Jewish History* (September 1982)

Belle L. Mead, "The Social Pleasure of the East Side Jews" (M.A. Thesis, Columbia University, New York 1904)

William Brown Meloney, "Slumming in New York's Chinatown", *Munsey's Magazine*, XLI (Sept. 1909), No.VI

H.L. Mencken, *The American Language. An Inquiry into the Development of English in the United States* (New York: Alfred A. Knopf, 1923)

Daniel M. Mendelowitz, *A History of American Art* (New York: Holt, Rinehart and Winston, Inc., 1970)

Saverio Merlino, "Italian Immigrants and their Enslavement", *Forum*, 15 (April 1893)

Russell Merritt, "Nickelodeons Theaters 1905-1914: Building an Audience for the Movies", in Tino Balio, ed., *The American Film Industry* (Madison: The University of Wisconsin Press, 1976)

H. C. Merwin, "Irish in American Life", *Atlantic Monthly* (March 1896)

Isaac Metzker, ed., *A Bintel Brief. Sixty Years of Letters from the Lower East Side to the "Jewish Daily Forward"* (Garden City, NY: Doubleday & Company, Inc.: 1971)

John Anderson Miller, *Fares, Please! A Popular History of Trolleys, Horse-Cars, Street-Cars, Buses, Elevateds and Subways* (1941; New York: Dover Publications, Inc., 1960)

John C. Miller, "The Emigrant and New York City: A Consideration of Four Puerto Rican Writers", *MELUS*, 5 (Fall 1978)

Morton Minsky and Milt Machlin, *Minsky's Burlesque* (New York: Arbor House, 1986)

Joseph Mitchell, *McSorley's Wonderful Saloon* (New York: Penguin Books, 1945)

Emelicia Mizio and Clara Valiente-Barksdale, *Hispanic Community-Based Organizations: Issues of Survival and Non-Survival* (New York: Community Service Society, 1985)

Eugene V. Mohr, *The Nuyorican Experience. Literature of the Puerto Rican Minority* (Westport, Conn.: Greenwood Press, 1982)

Nicholasa Mohr, *In Nueva York* (1977; Houston: Arte Público Press, 1988)

---, *Rituals of Survival. A Woman's Portfolio* (Houston: Arte Público Press, 1985)

---, *Nilda* (Houston: Arte Público Press, 1986)

---, "Puerto Rican Writers in the United States, Puerto Rican Writers in Puerto Rico: A Separation Beyond Language", *The Americas Review*, Vol.15 (Summer 1987), No.2

---, "Puerto Ricans in New York: Cultural Evolution and Identity", in Asela Rodríguez de Laguna, ed., *Images and Identities. The Puerto Rican in Two World Contexts* (New Brunswick, N.J.: Transaction Books, 1987)

Marlis Momber, "A Culture Called Loisaida", *The Quality of Life in Loisaida*, Vol.VII (May-June 1984), No.3

Francesco Moncada, "New York's 'Little Italy' in 1850", *Atlantica* (April 1937)

Richard Moody, *Ned Harrigan. From Corlear's Hook to Herald Square* (Chicago: Nelson-Hall, 1980)

Alan Moore and Marc Miller, eds., *ABC No Rio Dinero. The Story of a Lower East Side Art Gallery* (New York: ABC No Rio with Collaborative Projects, 1985)

Wayne Moquin and Charles Van Doren, eds., *A Documentary History of Italian Americans* (New York: Praeger Publishers, Inc., 1974)

Ed Morales, "East Side Story", *The Village Voice* (Aug. 20, 1991)

Julio Morales, *Puerto Rican Poverty and Migration. We Just Had to Try Elsewhere* (New York: Praeger, 1986)

Thomas Morgan, "New York City Bulldozes Squatters' Shantytowns", *The New York Times* (Oct. 16, 1991)

Lloyd Morris, *Incredible New York. High Life and Low Life of the Last Hundred Years* (New York: Random House, 1951)

Toni Morrison, "City Limits, Village Values: Concepts of the Neighborhood in Black Fiction", in Michael C. Jaye and Ann Chalmers Watts, eds., *Literature and the Urban Experience. Essays on the City and Literature* (New Brunswick, N.J.: Rutgers University Press, 1981)

Henry Moskowitz, "A Study of the East Side Cheder", *Report* (New York: University Settlement Society, 1898)

Frank Moss, *The Great Metropolis* (New York: Peter Fenelon Collier, 1897)

Syeus Mottel, *Charas. The Improbable Dome Builders* (New York: Drake Publishers, Inc. 1973)

Nicolas Moufarrege, "Another Wave, Still More Savagely than the First: The Lower East Side", *Arts Magazine*, Vol.57 (July 1982), No.1

Ozier Muhammad, "Pioneers in a Tenement", *Newsday* (May 7, 1989)

Lewis Mumford, *The Brown Decades. A Study of the Arts in America. 1865-1895* (1931; New York: Dover Publications, Inc., 1971)

Maureen Murphy, "Irish-American Theatre", in Maxine Schwartz Seller, ed., *Ethnic Theatre in the United States* (Westport, Conn.: Greenwood Press, 1983)

Charles Musser, *Before the Nickelodeon. Edwin S. Porter and the Edison Manufacturing Company* (Berkeley: University of California Press, 1991)

Michael Musto, *Downtown* (New York: Vintage Books, 1986)

Jerome Myers, *Artist in Manhattan* (New York: American Artists Group, Inc., 1940)

C. Kilmer Myers, *Light the Dark Streets* (1957; Garden City, N. Y.: Doubleday & Co., Inc., 1961)

N.

Laurence Nachtgeist, "A Kinder, Gentler Gentrification. The Death of Lincoln Swados", *East Villager* (April 1989)

---, "Squat or/then Rot", *East Villager* (May 1989)

Stanley Nadel, "Kleindeutschland: New York City's Germans, 1845-1880" (Doctoral dissertation, Columbia University, New York 1981)

Mark Naison, "From Eviction Resistance to Rent Control. Tenant Activism during the Great Depression", in Ronald Lawson, ed., *The Tenant Movement in New York City, 1904-1984* (New Brunswick, N.J.: Rutgers University Press, 1986)

David Nasaw, *Children of the City. At Work & At Play* (New York: Oxford University Press, 1985)

The National Poetry Magazine of the Lower East Side (New York)

Antonello Negri, *Il realismo. Da Courbet agli Anni Venti* (Bari: Laterza, 1989)

---, *Il realismo. Volume II* (forthcoming)

Humbert S. Nelli, "The Italian Padrone System in the United States", *Labor History*, V (Spring 1964)

---, *From Immigrants to Ethnics. The Italian Americans* (New York: Oxford University Press, 1983)

"New Asia Issue", *The Portable Lower East Side*, Vol.7 (1990), No.2

New York Bureau of Labor Statistics, *Reports* (1896)

New York Department of City Planning, *1990 Census* (New York: Population Division, March 25, 1991)

New York Panorama (1938; New York: Pantheon Books, 1984)

"The Nickelodeon", *Moving Picture World*, 1 (May 4, 1907)

Hugh Nissenson, *My Own Ground* (New York: Farrar, Straus, and Giroux, 1976)

Kenneth B. Noble, "Sweatshops Are Found Resurging and Spreading", *The New York Times* (Sept.4, 1988)

"'Not For Sale': The East Village Scene and the Lower East Side", *Upfront*, 9 (Fall 1984)

Barbara Novack, *American Painting of the Nineteenth Century* (New York: Praeger, 1969)

O.

George C. D. Odell, *Annals of the New York Stage* (New York: Columbia University Press, 1945)

Louise C. Odencrantz, *Italian Women in Industry: A Study of Conditions in New York City* (New York: Russell Sage Foundation, 1919)

William L. O'Neill, ed., *Echoes of Revolt. "The Masses"*, *1911-17* (Chicago: Ivan R. Dee, Inc., 1989)

Frank Oppel, ed., *Tales of Gaslight New York* (Secaucus, N.J.: Castle, 1985)

James Oppenheim, *Dr. Rast* (New York: Sturgis and Walton, 1909)

---, *The Nine-Tenths* (New York: Harper Bros., 1911)

[Samuel Ornitz], *Haunch, Paunch, and Jowl. An Anonymous Autobiography* (New York: Boni and Liveright, 1923)

Marina Orsini, "Abraham Cahan: la diaspora come traduzione incessante", in Guido Fink e Gabriella Morisco, a cura di, *Il recupero del testo. Aspetti della letteratura ebraico-americana* (Bologna: CLUEB, 1988)

M. Oskison, "Public Halls of the East Side", *Year Book of the University Settlement Society of New York*, 1899

Jane Osmers, "How the Other Half Still Lives", *East Villager* (February 1-14, 1983)

Berndt Ostendorf, ed., *Amerikanische Gettoliteratur. Zur Literatur ethnischer, marginaler und unterdrückter Gruppen in Amerika* (Darmstadt: Wissenschaftliche Buchgesellschaft, 1983)

Manuel Ramos Otero, "The Point Blank Page", *The Portable Lower East Side* (1991)

P.

Elena Padilla, *Up from Puerto Rico* (New York: Columbia University Press, 1958)

Albert B. Paine, "The New Coney Island", *The Century Magazine* (August 1904)

J. John Palen and Bruce London, eds., *Gentrification, Displacement and Neighborhood Revitalization* (Albany, N.Y.: State University of New York Press, 1984)

Lewis E. Palmer, "The World in Motion", *The Survey*, 22 (1909)

Jon Pareles, "Lower East Side a Mainstay for Music", *The New York Times* (Febr. 6, 1987)

Robert Patrick, *Kennedy's Children. A Play in Two Acts* (New York: Samuel French, Inc., n.d.)

Joseph M. Patterson, "The Nickelodeons: The Poor Man's Elementary Course in the Drama", *Saturday Evening Post*, 180 (Nov. 23, 1907)

Pear Garden in the West. America's Chinese Theater, 1853-1983 (New York: New York Chinatown History Project, 1987)

Kathy Peiss, *Cheap Amusements. Working Women and Leisure in Turn-of-the-Century New York* (Philadelphia: Temple University Press, 1986)

David Perez, *Long Road from Lares*, ed. by Arthur Tobier (New York: Community Documentation Workshop at St.Mark's Church-in-the-Bowery, 1979)

Bennard B. Perlman, *The Immortal Eight. American Painting from Eakins to the Armory Show (1870-1913)* (Cincinnati: North Light Publishers, 1979)

Hubert Perrier, "The Socialists and the Working Class in New York: 1890-1896", *Labor History*, 22 (Fall 1981), No.4

Elizabeth Israels Perry, "Industrial Reform in New York City: Belle Moskowitz and the Protocol of Peace, 1913-1916", *Labor History*, 23 (Winter 1982), No.1

Lucy F. Pierce, "The Nickelodeon", *Nickelodeon*, 1 (Jan. 1909)

Marge Piercy, *Woman on the Edge of Time* (1978; London: The Woman's Press, Ltd., 1979)

Pedro Pietri, *Puerto Rican Obituary* (New York: Monthly Review Press, 1973)

---, "LewLulu" (typescript, 1975)

---, "The Livingroom" (typescript, 1975)

---, "Sell the Bell, or Go Straight to Hell" (typescript, 1980)

---, "No More Bingo at the Wake" (typescript, 1982)

---, "Getting the Message Across" (typscript, 1983)

---, *Traffic Violations* (Maplewood, N.J.: Waterfront Press, 1983)

---, *The Masses Are Asses* (Maplewood, N.J.: Waterfront Press, 1984)

---, "Happy Birthday, MF" (typescript, 1990)

---, *Illusions of a Revolving Door. Plays. Teatro* (Río Piedras, PR: Editorial de la Universidad de Puerto Rico, 1992)

Miguel Piñero, *Short Eyes* (New York: Hill and Wang, 1974)
---, *La Bodega Sold Dreams* (Houston: Arte Público Press, 1980)
---, *Plays* (Houston: Arte Público Press, 1984)
---, *Outrageous. One-Act Plays* (Houston: Arte Público Press, 1986)
Steven I. Piott, "The Lesson of the Immigrant: Views of Immigrants in Muckraking Magazines, 1900-1909", *American Studies*, XIX (Spring 1978), No.1
Donald Pizer, *Realism and Naturalism in Nineteenth-Century American Literature* (Carbondale, Ill.: Southern Illinois University Press, 1966)
"Places of Interest on the Lower East Side", Box 19, General Subjects — Community Councils (Lillian D. Wald Collection, Rare Book and Manuscript Library, Columbia University Library, New York)
Roger S. Platizky, "Humane Vision in Miguel Piñero's 'Short Eyes'", *The Americas Review*, Vol.19 (Spring 1991), No.1
Ann-Byrd Platt, "The Art Scene Moves to the East Vilage", *The Wall Street Journal* (May 2, 1984)
Sara Plotkin, *Full-Time Active. An Oral History*, ed. by Arthur Tobier (New York: Community Documentation Workshop at St. Mark's Church-in-the-Bowery, 1980)
Phyllis Plous and Mary Looker, eds., *Neo York. Report on a Phenomenon* (Santa Barbara, Cal.: University Art Museum, 1984)
Philip Pocock and Gregory Battcock, *The Obvious Illusion: Murals from the Lower East Side* (New York: George Braziller, 1980)
"Police Club Strikers", *The New York Times* (October 12, 1894)
Ernest Poole, *The Plague in Its Stronghold* (New York: Committee on the Prevention of Tuberculosis of the New York Charity Organization Society, 1903)
Alessandro Portelli, a cura di, *Canzoni e poesie proletarie americane* (Roma: Savelli, 1976)
---, *The Text and the Voice. Writing, Speaking and Democracy in American Literature* (New York: Columbia University Press, 1994)
Reinaldo Povod, *Cuba and His Teddy Bear* (New York: Samuel French, Inc., 1986)
George E. Pozzetta, "The Italians of New York City, 1890-1914" (Dissertation, University of North Carolina, Chapel Hill, 1971)
---, "The Italian Immigrant Press of New York City: The Early Years, 1880-1915", *The Journal of Ethnic Studies*, I (Fall 1973), No.3
---, ed., *Pane e lavoro: The Italian American Working Class* (Toronto: The Multicultural History Society of Ontario, 1980)
---, "The Mulberry District of New York City: The Years before World War One", in Robert F. Harney and J. Vincenza Scarpaci, eds., *Little Italies in North America* (Toronto: The Multicultural History Society of Ontario, 1981)
George M. Price, "Factory Introspection [*sic*]. The Shop Survey Carried Out by the Board of Sanitary Control of the Cloak and Suit Trade of New York", *The Survey*, 26 (May 6, 1911)

Q.
The Quality of Life in Loisaida (Retrospective Issue), Vol.XIV (Sept.-Oct. 1991), No.5

R.

Julian Ralph, *People We Pass: Stories of Life Among the Masses of New York City* (New York: Harper and Bros., 1896)

Terry Ramsaye, *A Million and One Nights. A History of the Motion Picture* (1926; New York: Simon & Schuster, Inc., 1986)

Marcus Eli Ravage, *An American in the Making. The Life Story of an Immigrant* (1917; New York: Dover Publications, Inc., 1971)

Vivien Raynor, "Art: Gathering of the Avant-Garde", *The New York Times* (May 31, 1985)

Real Estate and Builders Guide, I (June 10, 1893)

"Real Great Society", *East Village Other*, Vol.2 (April 1- 15, 1967), No.9

Benjamin Reich, "A New Social Center. The Candy Store as a Social Influence", *Year Book of the University Settlement Society of New York*, 1899

Andrew Reinhardt, "Hoopla over Housing", *Streets. The Magazine of the Lower East Side*, Vol.1 (Spring 1988), No.1

Sheldon Renan, *The Underground Film. An Introduction to Its Development in America* (1967; London: Studio Vista, Ltd., 1968)

"The Rent Strike Grows", *Charities and the Commons*, XIX (Jan.11, 1908)

Report (New York: University Settlement Society, 1897)

Charles Reznikoff, *By the Waters of Manhattan* (1933; New York: Markus Wiener Publishing, 1986)

Walter B. Rideout, *The Radical Novel in the United States, 1900- 1954* (Cambridge, Mass.: Harvard University Press, 1956)

Jacob A. Riis, "Flashes from the Slums: Some of the Results of a Journey through the City with an Instantaneous Camera — the Poor, the Idle, the Vicious", *The New York Sun* (Febr.12, 1888)

---, *How the Other Half Lives. Studies Among the Tenements* (1890; New York: Dover Publications, Inc., 1971)

---, *Out of Mulberry Street: Stories of Tenement Life in New York City* (New York: Century, 1898)

---, "Feast Days in Little Italy", *The Century Magazine*, LVIII (August 1899), No.4

---, *The Making of an American* (1901; New York: Harper & Row, Publishers, 1966)

David L. Rinear, "F. S. Chanfrau's Mose: The Rise and Fall of an Urban Folk-Hero", *Theatre Journal*, Vol. 33, No. 2 (May 1981)

Moses Rischin, *The Promised City. New York's Jews, 1870-1914* (1962; Cambridge, Mass.: Harvard University Press, 1977)

---, "Introduction", in Hutchins Hapgood, *The Spirit of the Ghetto* (1902; Cambridge, Mass.: The Belknap Press of Harvard University Press, 1967)

---, ed., *Grandma Never Lived in America. The New Journalism of Abraham Cahan* (Bloomington: Indiana University Press, 1985)

Bimbo Rivas, "El Piraguero de Loisaida" (typescript, New York, 1972)

---, "The Winos" (typescript, New York, 1982)

---, "Coco Balé" (typescript, New York, 1985)

---, "Benito Vasconpique" (typescript, New York, 1987)

Edward G. Robinson (with Leonard Spigelgass), *All My Yesterdays. An Autobiography* (New York: Hawthorn Books, Inc., Publishers, 1973)

Walter Robinson and Carlo McCormick, "Slouching Toward Avenue D", *Art in America*, Vol.72 (Summer 1984), No.6

Robert A. Rockaway, "The Rise of the Jewish Gangster in America", *The Journal of Ethnic Studies*, Vol.8 (Summer 1980), No.2

Clara E. Rodríguez, "Puerto Ricans in the Melting Pot", *The Journal of Ethnic Studies*, Vol.1 (Winter 1974), No.4

---, Virginia Sánchez Korrol, José Oscar Alers, eds., *The Puerto Rican Struggle: Essays on Survival in the U.S.* (New York: Puerto Rican Migration Research Consortium, 1980)

---, *Puerto Ricans. Born in the U.S.A.* (Boston: Unwin Hyman, 1989)

William Rosa, "Visión humorística del espacio en la poesía de Pedro Pietri", *The Americas Review*, Vol.19 (Spring 1991), No.1

Joel Rose and Catherine Texier, eds., *Between C & D. New Writing from the Lower East Side Fiction Magazine* (New York: Penguin, 1988)

Joel Rose, *Kill the Poor* (New York: The Atlantic Monthly Press, 1988)

---, "Lower East Side. Directors Love It To a Fault", *The New York Times* (May 7, 1989)

Viola Roseboro, "The Italians of New York", *Cosmopolitan*, IV (January 1888), No.5

Harold Rosenberg, "Tenth Street. A Geography of Modern Art", *Art News Annual* (1958-59)

---, *The Tradition of the New* (New York: Horizon Press, 1959)

---, *Discovering the Present. Three Decades in Art, Culture, and Politics* (Chicago: University of Chicago Press, 1973)

Naomi and Walter Rosenblum, eds., *America and Lewis Hine* (Millerton, N.Y.: Aperture, Inc., 1977)

---, "Camera Images of Labor", in Philip S. Foner and Reinhard Schultz, eds., *The Other America. Art and the Labour Movement in the United States* (London: The Journeyman Press, 1985)

Lulla Rosenfeld, *Bright Star of Exile. Jacob Adler and the Yiddish Theatre* (New York: Thomas Y. Crowell Co., 1977)

Max Rosenfeld, ed., *Pushcarts and Dreamers. Stories of Jewish Life in America* (New York: Thomas Yoseloff, 1967)

Ira Rosenwaike, *Population History of New York City* (Syracuse, N.Y.: Syracuse University Press, 1972)

Henry Roskolenko, *The Time That Was Then. The Lower East Side, 1900-1914. An Intimate Chronicle* (New York: The Dial Press, 1971)

Henry Roth, *Call It Sleep* (1934; Harmondsworth, Middlesex: Penguin Books Ltd., 1979)

---, *Alla mercé di una rude corrente* (Milano: Garzanti, 1989)

---, "Trolley Car Runs", *RSA Journal. Rivista di Studi Nord-Americani*, 1 (1990)

---, *Mercy of a Rude Stream. Vol. I: A Star Rose over Mt. Morris Park* (New York: St. Martin's Press, 1994)

Jerome Rothenberg, "The History/Pre-History of the Poetry Project", *Project Papers*, Vol.1 (1987), No.2

Edwin Milton Royle, "The Vaudeville Theatre", *Scribner's Magazine*, 30 (September 1901)

RSA-Rivista di Studi Anglo-Americani, III (1984-85), nn.4-5
David Rubel, "Little Russia on the East Side", *Lower East Side Voice* (March 1983)
Emily Rubin-Luis Guzman, "We Don't Want Cheese, We Want Apartments, Please" (typescript, New York, 1982)
Joe Rubin, "Housing and Gardens in New York", *The Quality of Life in Loisaida*, Vol.XII (Sept.-Oct. 1989), No.5
Pat M. Ryan, "The Hibernian Experience: John Brougham's Irish-American Plays", *MELUS*, 10 (Summer 1983), No.2

S.
M. Sakolski, "The Small Industries of the Lower East Side', *University Settlement Studies* (Oct.1906)
Raphael Samuel, Ewan MacColl, Stuart Cosgrove, *Theatres of the Left, 1880-1935. Workers' Theatre Movements in Britain and America* (London: Routledge & Kegan Paul, 1985)
Ed Sanders, "Yiddish Speaking Socialists of the Lower East Side (a work with music)", *The Portable Lower East Side*, Vol.1, (Winter 1984), No.2
---, *Tales of Beatnik Glory. Volumes I and II* (1975; New York: Citadel Press, 1990)
Ronald Sanders, *The Downtown Jews. Portrait of an Immigrant Generation* (New York: Harper & Row, Publishers, 1969)
---/Edmund V. Gillon, Jr., *The Lower East Side. A Guide to Its Jewish Past in 99 New Photographs* (New York: Dover Publications, Inc., 1979)
Nahma Sandrow, *Vagabond Stars. A World History of Yiddish Theatre* (New York: Harper & Row, Publishers, 1977)
Luc Sante, *Low Life. Lures and Snares of Old New York* (New York: Farrar, Straus, Giroux, 1991)
Jonathan D. Sarna, ed., *The American Jewish Experience* (New York: Holmes & Meier, Publishers, Inc., 1986)
Sophie Saroff, *Stealing the State. An Oral History*, ed. by Arthur Tobier (New York: Community Documentation Workshop at St. Mark's Church-in-the-Bowery, 1983)
Geraldine Sartain, "Old World in New York — Russia", *New York World-Telegram* (May 23, 1934)
Richard Schechner, *La cavità teatrale* (Bari: De Donato 1968)
J. W. Schereschewsky, "Stress and Strain", *U.S. Public Health Service Bulletin*, 71 (Washington: 1915), now in Leon Stein, ed., *Out of the Sweatshop* (New York: Quadrangle/The New York Times Book Co., 1977)
Jeffrey Scheuer, *Legacy of Light: University Settlement's First Century* (New York: University Settlement Society, 1985)
Dorothee Schneider, "The New York Cigar Makers Strike of 1877", *Labor History*, 26 (Summer 1985), No.3
Rose Schneiderman, "A Cap Maker's Story", *The Independent* (April 27, 1905), now in Leon Stein and Philip Taft, eds., *Workers Speak. Self Portraits* (New York: Arno & The New York Times, 1971)
---, *All for One* (New York: P. S. Erikson, 1967)

Allon Schoener, ed., *Portal to America: The Lower East Side, 1870-1925* (New York: Holt, Rinehart and Winston, 1967)
---, *The Italian Americans...Per terre assai lontane* (Milano: Alinari e Rizzoli, 1988)
Budd Schulberg, *What Makes Sammy Run?* (1941; Harmondsworth, Middlesex: Penguin Books, 1978)
Katherine Schwarz, "The Threat of AIDS", *The Quality of Life in Loisaida*, XI (March-April, 1988), No.2,
Joseph Sciorra and Martha Cooper, "'I Feel Like I'm in My Country': Puerto Rican Casitas in New York City", *TDR. The Drama Review*, 34 (Winter 1990), No.4
Virginia Scott, ed., *American Born and Foreign. An Anthology of Asian American Poetry* (New York: The Sunbury Press, 1979)
Joel Seidman, *The Needle Trades* (New York: Farrar & Rinehart, Inc., 1942)
Peter Seixas, "Lewis Hine: From 'Social' to 'Interpretive' Photographer", in *American Quarterly*, Vol.39 (Fall 1987), No.3
Maxine S. Seller, "Beyond the Stereotype: A New Look at the Immigrant Woman", *The Journal of Ethnic Studies* (Spring 1975)
---, *To Seek America. A History of Ethnic Life in the United States* (Englewood, N.J.: Jerome S. Ozer, Publisher, 1977)
---, ed., *Ethnic Theatre in the United States* (Westport, Conn.: Greenwood Press, 1983)
Laurence Senelick, "George L. Fox and Bowery Pantomime", in Myron Matlaw, ed., *American Popular Entertainment. Papers and Proceedings of the Conference on the History of American Popular Entertainment* (Westport, Conn.: Greenwood Press, 1979)
Clarence Senior, *The Puerto Ricans. Strangers — Then Neighbors* (Chicago: Quadrangle Books, 1965)
Theodore Shank, Jr., "The Bowery Theatre, 1826-1836" (Ph.D. Dissertation, Stanford University, 1956)
David Shapiro, ed., *Social Realism. Art As a Weapon. Critical Studies in American Art* (New York: Frederick Ungar Publishing Co., 1973)
Susan Shapiro-Kiok, "CityArts Workshop: Out of the Gallery and into the Streets", in Eva Cockcroft, John Weber, James Cockcroft, eds., *Toward a People's Art* (New York: E. P. Dutton, 1977)
William Sharpe and Leonard Wallock, eds., *Visions of the Modern City. Essays in History, Art, and Literature* (New York: Heyman Center for the Humanities, Columbia University, 1983)
---, "Tales of Two Cities: Gentrification and Displacement in Contemporary New York", in Mary B. Campbell and Mark Rollins, eds., *Begetting Images. Studies in the Art and Science of Symbol Production* (New York: Peter Lang, 1989)
James Sheehan, "Here Comes the Neighborhood: Midtown Meets Melting Pot on Tompkins Square", *The Villager* (March 7, 1985)
Isaiah Sheffer, *The Rise of David Levinsky* (New York: Samuel French, Inc., n.d.)
Richard F. Shepard, "Visit to a Small Republic on the Lower East Side", *The New York Times* (Dec. 22, 1979)
William G. Shepherd, "Eyewitness at Triangle", *Milwaukee Journal* (March 27, 1911), now in Leon Stein, ed., *Out of the Sweatshop* (New York: Quadrangle/The New York Times Book Co., 1977)

Beatrice Shustko, *The Educational Alliance. "The Edgies" Then and Now* (New York: The Educational Alliance, n.d.)

Adrienne Siegel, *The Image of the American City in Popular Literature. 1820-1870* (Port Washington, N.Y.: Kennikat Press, 1981)

Beatrice Siegel, *Lillian Wald of Henry Street* (New York: Macmillan Publishing Co., Inc., 1983)

Robert Siegle, *Suburban Ambush. Downtown Writing and the Fiction of Insurgency* (Baltimore and London: The Johns Hopkins University Press, 1989)

"Silent Parade for the Triangle Dead", *The Survey*, 26 (April 15, 1911)

Isaac Bashevis Singer, *Enemies. A Love Story* (1972; New York: Signet Books, 1989)

Amritjit Singh and Joseph T. Skerrett, eds., *The Uses of Memory in Multi-Ethnic Literature* (forthcoming)

Paul C.P. Siu, "A Sojourner's Monologue", *Bu Gao Ban* (New York Chinatown History Museum) (Summer 1985)

Robert Sklar, *Movie-Made America: A Cultural History of American Movies* (New York: Vintage Books, 1975)

"In Search of New York (Special Issue)", *Dissent* (Fall 1987)

John Sloan, *John Sloan's New York Scene: From the Diaries, Notes, and Correspondence, 1906-1913* (New York: Harper, 1965)

---, *New York Etchings (1905-1949)* (New York: Dover Publications, Inc., 1978)

Mark Slobin, "From Vilna to Vaudeville: Minikes and 'Among the Indians' (1895)", *The Drama Review*, Vol.24 (Sept.1980), No.3

---, *Tenement Songs. The Popular Music of the Jewish Immigrants* (Urbana, Ill.: University of Illinois Press, 1982)

---, "Some Intersections of Jews, Music, and Theater", in Sarah Blacher Cohen, ed., *From Hester Street to Hollywood. The Jewish-American Stage and Screen* (Bloomington: Indiana University Press, 1986)

Helen Smindak, "The Lower East Side Ukrainians", *The Quality of Life in Loisaida*, X (July-August, 1987), No.4

Neil Smith and Peter Williams, eds., *Gentrification of the City* (Boston: Allen & Unwin, 1986)

R.J.Smith, "Message in a Bottle. Homesteaders Rock the Lower East Side", *The Village Voice* (Aug.23, 1988)

Robert E. Snow and David E. Wright, "Coney Island: A Case Study in Popular Culture and Technical Change", *Journal of Popular Culture*, 9 (Spring 1976)

Robert W. Snyder, *The Voice of the City. Vaudeville and Popular Culture in New York* (New York: Oxford University Press, 1989)

June Sochen, *The New Woman in Greenwich Village, 1910-1920* (New York: Quadrangle/The New York Times Book Co., 1972)

---, "Fanny Brice and Sophie Tucker: Blending the Particular with the Universal", in Sarah Blacher Cohen, ed. *From Hester Street to Hollywood. The Jewish-American Stage and Screen* (Bloomington: Indiana University Press, 1986)

A. Richard Sogliuzzo, "Notes for a History of the Italian-American Theatre of New York", *Theatre Survey*, XIV (November 1973), No.2

Werner Sollors, *Beyond Ethnicity. Consent and Descent in American Culture* (New York: Oxford University Press, 1986)

---, "Immigrants and Other Americans", in Emory Elliott, ed., *Columbia Literary History of the United States* (New York: Columbia University Press, 1988)

---, "'Of Plymouth Rock and Jamestown and Ellis Island' — Or, Ethnic Literature and Some Redefinitions of 'America'", in Hans Bak, ed., *Multiculturalism and the Canon of American Culture* (Amsterdam: VU University Press, 1993)

Friedrich A. Sorge, *Labor Movement in the United States. A History of the American Working Class from Colonial Times to 1890*, Philip S. Foner and Brewster Chamberlin, eds. (1891; Westport, Conn.: Greenwood Press, 1977)

Pedro Juan Soto, *Spiks* (1970; New York: Monthly Review Press, 1973)

Souvenir Journal. The Quality of Life in Loisaida, 1988

Daniel Soyer, "*Landsmanshaftn* and the Jewish Labor Movement: Cooperation, Conflict, and the Building of Community", *Journal of American Ethnic History*, Vol.7 (Spring 1988), No.2

Adriana Spadoni, "The Italian Working Women of New York", *Collier's*, (March 23, 1912)

Edward K. Spann, *The New Metropolis. New York City, 1840-1857* (New York: Columbia University Press, 1981)

Raymond C. Spaulding, "Saloons of the District", *Year Book of the University Settlement Society of New York, 1899* (New York: University Settlement Society, 1899)

Gino C. Speranza, "The Italians in the United States", *Chautauquan*, IX (1888-1889)

---, "Italian Foreman as a Social Agent", *Charities*, Vol.XI (1903)

---, "The Italians in Congested Districts", *Charities*, Vol.XX (April 4, 1908)

John G. Sproat, *'The Best Men': Liberal Reformers in the Gilded Age* (London: Oxford University Press, 1968)

Christine Stansell, "The Origins of the Sweatshop: Women and Early Industrialization in New York City", in Michael H. Frisch and Daniel J. Walkowitz, eds., *Working-Class America. Essays on Labor, Community, and American Society* (Urbana, Ill.: University of Illinois Press, 1983)

---, *City of Women: Sex and Class in New York, 1789-1860* (New York: Alfred A. Knopf, 1986)

Shirley Staples, *Male-Female Comedy Teams in American Vaudeville. 1865-1932* (Ann Arbor, Mich.: Umi Research Press, 1984)

Lincoln Steffens, *The Autobiography of Lincoln Steffens* (New York: Harcourt, Brace and World, Inc., 1931)

Michael A. Stegman, ed., *Housing and Vacancy Report* (New York: City of New York, 1987)

Charles W. Stein, ed., *American Vaudeville As Seen by Its Contemporaries* (New York: A.A.Knopf, 1984)

Leon Stein, *The Triangle Fire* (Philadelphia: J.B.Lippincott, 1962)

--- and Philip Taft, eds., *Workers Speak. Self Portraits* (New York: Arno & The New York Times, 1971)

Leon Stein, ed., *Out of the Sweatshop* (New York: Quadrangle/The New York Times Book Co., 1977)

Edward Steiner, *The Mediator* (New York: F.H.Revell, 1907)

Stan Steiner, *The Islands. The Worlds of Puerto Ricans* (New York: Harper & Row, 1974)

Merle Steir, *Making Mud. An Oral History*, ed. by Arthur Tobier (New York: Community Documentation Workshop at St. Mark's Church-in-the-Bowery, 1979)

Antonio Stella, "Tuberculosis and the Italians in the United States", *Charities*, Vol.XII (May 7, 1904), No.18

Micheal Stewart, *Harrigan 'n Hart* (New York: Samuel French, Inc., n.d.)

Lee Strasberg, *A Dream of Passion. The Development of the Method* (London: Methuen Drama, 1989)

Roy E. Stryker and Nancy Wood, *In This Proud Land: America 1935-1943 As Seen in the FSA Photographs* (Greenwich, Conn.: New York Graphic Society, 1973)

Herbert Sturz, "The Fire Tender and the Hungry", *The New York Times* (Dec. 22, 1987)

Ronald Sukenick, *Down and In. Life in the Underground* (New York: William Morrow and Company, Inc., 1987)

James Sullivan, *Tenement Tales of New York* (New York: Henry Holt, 1895)

Mary Brown Sumner, "The Spirit of the Strikers", *The Survey*, 23 (January 22, 1910)

---, "A Strike for Clean Bread", *The Survey*, 24 (June 18, 1910)

Barry E. Supple, "A Business Elite: German-Jewish Financiers in Nineteenth-Century New York", *Business History Review*, 31 (Summer 1957)

Constance R. Sutton and Elsa Chaney, eds., *Caribbean Life in New York City: Sociocultural Dimensions* (Staten Island, New York: Center for Migration Studies, 1987)

Sweat Equity Urban Homesteading. A How To Manual (Westport, CT: Save the Children, n.d.)

Ferenc M. Szasz e Ralph Bogardus, "The Camera and the American Social Conscience: The Documentary Photography of Jacob A. Riis", *New York History*, 55 (1974)

T.

"Table on Children Found at Work in New York City Tenements (Oct. 1906-April 1907)", in Mary Van Kleeck, "Child Labor in New York City Tenements", *Charities and the Commons*, 19 (Jan.18, 1908)

Robert Taft, *Photography and the American Scene, 1839-1889* (1938; New York: Dover Publications, Inc., 1964)

A.J. Tamburri, P.A. Giordano, F.L. Gardaphé, eds., *From the Margin. Writings in Italian American* (West Lafayette, Ind.: Purdue University Press, 1991)

Meredith Tax, *Rivington Street* (New York: Avon Books, 1982)

---, *Union Square* (New York: William Morrow, Inc., 1988)

John Kuo Wei Tchen, "The *China Daily News*: Pioneers of the Chinatown Literary Movement", *Bu Gao Ban* (New York Chinatown History Museum), no.7, Fall 1988

"The Italian Population in New York", *Charities*, Vol.XII (May 7, 1904), No.18

"The Tenement House Exhibition", *Charities*, Vol.IV (February 17, 1900), No.12

"The Tenement-House Problem. Extract from the Report of the New York Tenement-House Commission of 1900", *The Charities Review*, VI (March 2, 1901), No.9

Catherine Texier, *Love Me Tender* (New York: Penguin, 1987)

---, *Panic Blood* (New York: Viking, 1990)

"Three Ethnic Groups Disputing Plans for Lower East Side", *The New York Times* (March 12, 1980)

"13,000 Tailors on Strike", *The New York Times* (July 29, 1895)

Norman Thomas, ed., *The Collected Poems of Arturo Giovannitti* (New York: Arno Press, 1975)

Piri Thomas, *Down These Mean Streets* (1967; New York: Vintage Books, 1974)

Craig Thompson and Allen Raymond, *Gang Rule in New York. The Story of a Lawless Era* (New York: The Dial Press, 1940)

Richard Thompson, "How City's First Yuppies Built the East Village", *The Villager* (March 17, 1988)

Arthur Tobier, ed., *Working at St.Mark's. Preservation Youth Project. An Oral History* (New York: Community Documentation Workshop at St. Mark's Church-in-the-Bowery, 1978)

Seth Tobocman, *You Don't Have To Fuck People Over To Survive* (San Francisco: Pressure Drop Press, 1990)

Lydio F. Tomasi, ed., *The Italian in America: The Progressive View, 1891-1914* (New York: Center for Migration Stdies, 1972)

Edward Townsend, *A Daughter of the Tenements* (New York: Lovell, Coryell, 1895)

---, *Chimmie Fadden; Major Max; and Other Stories* (New York: Lovell, Coryell, 1895)

Alan Trachtenberg, *The Incorporation of America. Culture & Society in the Gilded Age* (New York: Hill and Wang, 1982)

Carlo Tresca, "Autobiography" (University of Minnesota, Immigration History Research Center)

"The Triangle Fire", *New York World* (March 26, 1911), now in Allon Schoener, ed., *Portal to America: The Lower East Side, 1870-1925* (New York: Holt, Rinehart and Winston, 1967)

Leon Trotzky, *History of the Russian Revolution* (1930; New York: Pathfinder, 1980)

"True Pictures Among the Poor", *Scribner's Magazine*, Vol.XVI (November, 1894), No.5

Evelyn Tseng, "Changes at 32 Mott Street", *Bu Gao Ban* (New York Chinatown History Museum), Summer 1985

Sophie Tucker and Dorothy Giles, *Some of These Days. The Autobiography of Sophie Tucker* (Garden City, N.Y.: Doubleday, Doran and Co., 1945)

Anthony Turano, "The Speech of Little Italy ", *American Mercury*, 26 (1932)

Faythe Turner, ed., *Puerto Rican Writers at Home in the USA. An Anthology* (Seattle, Washington: Open Hand Publishing Inc., 1991)

"Two Voices from Chinatown's Basement Workshop. Fay Chiang: A Place in Art/History; Margo Machida: An Artist's Perspective", *Upfront*, 14-15 (Winter-Spring 1987-88)

U.
United States Census Office, *Manufactures* (Washington, D.C.: Government Printing Office, 1900), Part III
United States Department of Commerce, Bureau of the Census, *Statistical Abstract of the United States* (Washington, D.C.: Government Printing Office, 1971)
United States Department of Commerce, Bureau of Census, *1990 Census of Population and Housing. Summary Population and Housing Characterstics. New York* (August 1991)
United States Industrial Commission, *Reports of the Industrial Commission on Immigration: Including Testimony with Review and Digest. And on Education, Including Testimony, with Review and Digest*, Vol.XV (Washington, D.C.: Government Printing Office, 1901)
Upfront. Special Issue on Displacement, No.11 (Winter 1985-86)
William J. Urchs, "St. Mark's Place, Manhattan", in Henry Collins Brown, ed., *Valentine's Manual of Old New York*, No.7, New Series (1923)
Ross Urquhart, "Martin Wong...Richard Roberts...And Others", *The New Common Good* (February, 1988)

V.
John E. Vacha, "The Federal Theatre's Living Newspapers: New York's Docudramas of the Thirties", *New York History*, 67 (Jan.1986), No.1
Mary Van Kleeck, "Child Labor in New York City Tenements", *Charities and the Commons*, 19 (Jan.18, 1908)
--- and Alice P. Barrows, "How Girls Learn the Millinery Trade", *The Survey*, 24 (April 16, 1910)
---, *Artificial Flower Makers* (New York: Survey Associates, Inc., 1913)
Roger Vaughan, "The Real Great Society", *Life*, Vol.63 (September 15th, 1967), No.11
Ed Vega, *Mendoza's Dreams* (Houston: Arte Público Press, 1987)
---, *Casualty Report* (Houston: Arte Público Press, 1991)
L. D. Ventura, *Peppino* (New York: William R. Jenkins, 1885)
Elisabetta Vezzosi, "La Federazione Socialista Italiana del Nord America tra autonomia e scioglimento nel sindacato industriale, 1911-1921", *Studi emigrazione. Rivista Trimestrale del Centro Studi Emigrazione*, XXI (marzo 1984), n.73
---, "Italian Immigrant Women", *RSA. Rivista di Studi Anglo-Americani*, III (1984-85), n.4-5
Steven Vincent, "Samson and the Temple of Poverty", *Lower East Side News*, Vol.I (November 1990), No.7
Paul Von Blum, *The Critical Vision. A History of Social & Political Art in the U.S.* (Boston: South End Press, 1982)

Mary H. Vorse, "Some Picture Show Audiences", *Outlook*, 97 (June 24, 1911)

W.

Kal Wagenheim, *A Survey of Puerto Ricans on the US Mainland in the 1970s* (New York: Praeger, 1975)
---, *Puerto Ricans in the U.S.* (New York: Minority Rights Group, 1983)
Dan Wakefield, "New York's Lower East Side Today. Notes and Impressions", *Commentary*, 27 (June 1959)
---, *Island in the City. Puerto Ricans in New York* (Boston: Houghton Mifflin, 1959)
---, *New York in the Fifties* (New York: Houghton Mifflin, 1992)
Lillian Wald, *The House on Henry Street* (1915; New York: Dover Publications, Inc., 1971)
Roger D. Waldinger, *Through the Eye of the Needle: Immigrants and Enterprise in New York's Garment Trades* (New York: New York University Press, 1986)
Ann Waldman, "An Introduction into 'The World'", in Ann Waldman, ed., *The World Anthology. Poems from the St. Mark's Poetry Project* (Indianapolis and New York: The Bobbs-Merrill Co., 1969)
---, ed., *Out of This World* (New York: Crown Publishers, 1992)
William E. Walling, "What the People of the East Side Do", *University Settlement Studies*, Vol.I (July 1905), No.2
Leonard Wallock, ed., *New York. Culture Capital of the World, 1940-1965* (New York: Rizzoli International Publications, Inc., 1988)
David Warfield/Margherita Hamm, *Ghetto Silhouettes* (New York: James Pott, 1907)
Paul Wasserman, "Life Cycles of a Multicultural Center", *Upfront*, 14-15 (Winter-Spring 1987-88)
Robert Watchorn, "The Black Hand and the Immigrant", *Outlook*, XCII (1909)
Elizabeth C. Watson, "Home Work in the Tenements", *The Survey*, 25 (Febr.4, 1911)
Jerome Weidman, *Fourth Street East. A Novel of How It Was* (New York: Random House, Inc., 1970)
Bill Weinberg, "Gentrification Is Breeding Death: The Changing Face of New York City", *Downtown* (May 10, 1989)
Bernard Weinstein, "Cahan's David Levinsky: An Inner Profile", *MELUS*, 10 (Fall 1983), No.3
Susan Weinstein, "The Legacy of St.Mark's in the Bowery", *East Villager* (March 1987)
Michael R. Weisser, *A Brotherhood of Memory. Jewish Landsmanshaftn in the New World* (Ithaca, N.Y.: Cornell University Press, 1989)
Frank Weitenkampf, *Manhattan Kaleidoscope* (New York: C. Scribner's Sons, 1947)
Phillip Weitzman, *Worlds Apart. Housing, Race/Ethnicity and Income in New York City, 1978-1987* (New York: Community Service Society Working Papers, 1989)
William Welling, *Photography in America: The Formative Years, 1839-1900* (New York: Thomas Y. Crowell, 1978)

Christopher Wellisz, "A Festival of Festivals, Starting with the Venerable Feast of San Gennaro", *The New York Times* (Sept. 9, 1983)
Janet Wickenhaver, "Radical Recollections — Robert Collier", *Streets. The Magazine of the Lower East Side* (May 1989)
Robert H. Wiebe, *The Search of Order, 1877-1920* (New York: Hill and Wang, 1967)
Sean Wilentz, "Crime, Poverty and the Streets of New York City: The Diary of William H. Bell, 1850-51", in *History Workshop*, no.7 (Spring 1979)
---, *Chants Democratic. New York City and the Rise of the American Working Class, 1788-1850* (New York: Oxford University Press, 1984)
Bud Wirtschafter, "7th Street Environment", *TDR. The Drama Review*, Vol.12 (Spring 1968), No.3
Carl Wittke, "The Immigrant Theme on the American Stage", *The Mississippi Valley Historical Review*, Vol.XXXIX (Sept.1952), No.2
---, *The Irish in America* (Baton Rouge: Louisiana State University Press, 1956)
David Wojnarowicz, *Close to the Knives. A Memoir of Disintegration* (New York: Vintage Books, 1991)
Gerard R. Wolfe, *New York. A Guide to the Metropolis* (New York: New York University Press, 1975)
--- and Jo Renée Fine, *The Synagogues of New York's Lower East Side* (New York: Washington Mews Books, 1978)
Seth L. Wolitz, "The Americanization of Tevye, or Boarding the Jewish Mayflower", *American Quarterly*, Vol.40 (December 1988), No.4
Bernard P. Wong, *Chinatown. Economic Adaptation and Ethnic Identity of the Chinese* (New York: Holt, Rinehart, and Winston, 1982)
The WPA Guide to New York City. The Federal Writers' Project Guide to 1930s New York (1939; New York: Pantheon Books, 1982)

Y.
Li Yang, "Ballad of Laundry Work", *China Daily News* (November 14, 1945), ora in *Bu Gao Ban* (New York Chinatown History Museum), no.7, Fall 1988
Virginia Yans-McLaughlin, "Immigrant Women and Work: Experience and Perception", in Milton Cantor and Bruce Laurie, eds., *Class, Sex, and the Woman Worker* (Westport, Conn.: Greenwood Press, 1977)
John Yau, *Martin Wong* (New York: Exit Art, 1988)
Anzia Yezierska, *Hungry Hearts and Other Stories* (1920; London: Virago Press, 1987)
---, *Salome of the Tenements* (New York: Boni and Liveright, 1923)
---, *Bread Givers* (1925; New York: Persea Books, 1975)
---, *Red Ribbon on a White Horse. My Story* (1950; London: Virago Press Ltd., 1987)
Judy Yung, "Chinese Women of America: 1834-1982", *Bu Gao Ban* (New York Chinatown History Museum), Winter/Spring 1985

X.
Johnny Xerox, "The Danger Is Here! What Are You Going To Do About It?", *East Villager* (September 15-30, 1984)
---, "How Do You Spell Relief? S-Q-U-*-T", *East Villager* (October 1-14, 1984)
---, "How To Stop Gentrification", *East Villager* (October 15-31, 1984)

Z.
Israel Zangwill, "The Future of Vaudeville in America", *Cosmopolitan*, XXXVIII (April 1905)
Parker R. Zellers, "The Cradle of Variety: The Concert Saloon", *Educational Theatre Journal*, 20 (Dec.1968)
Larzer Ziff, *The American 1890s. Life and Times of a Lost Generation* (New York: The Viking Press, 1966)
Louis Zukofsky, "Foreword", in L. Zukofsky, *"A". 1-12* (Garden City, N.Y.: Doubleday & Co., Inc., 1967)
Miriam Shomer Zunser, "The Jewish Literary Scene in New York at the Turn of the Century", *YIVO. Annual of Jewish Culture*, 7 (1952)
Rebecca Zurier, *Art for "The Masses". A Radical Magazine and Its Graphics, 1911-1917* (Philadelphia: Temple University Press, 1988)

Interviews:
Miguel Algarín, New York, 5/10/1987
George Barteneff, New York, 16/9/1988
Rosie Begun, New York, 3/10/1987
David Boyle, New York, 29/1/1991
Jorge Brandon, New York, 29/1/1991
Howard Brandstein, New York, 8/1/1991
Fay Chiang, New York, 17/9/1987
Peter Cramer and Jack Waters, New York, 19/9/1988
Sam and Esther Dolgoff, New York, 22/9/1988
Maria Dominguez, New York, 16/1/1991
David Finn (letter to the author, Ithaca, N.Y., 10/4/1987)
Olean For, New York, 23/1/1991
Carlos "Chino" Garcia, New York, 7/10/1984; 14/5/1986; 16/1/1991
Frances Goldin, New York, 21/9/1987
Frank Ilchuk, New York, 7/10/1987
Marvin Jones, New York, 23/9/1987
Joe Juliano, New York, 22/9/1987
Yuri Kapralov, New York, 15/9/1988
Tuli Kupferberg, New York, 2/10/1987
Charlie Lai, New York, 1/10/1987
Val Orselli, New York, 21/9/1988
Mary McCarthy, New York, 22/9/1987
Marlis Momber, New York, 18/9/1987
Bimbo Rivas, New York, 24/9/1987

Joel Rose, New York, 22/9/1987
Peter Schumann, Milano, 16/1/1990
Jack Scully, New York, 2/10/1987
Ellen Stewart, New York, 30/11/1988
Arthur Tobier, New York, 28/9/1987; New York, 21/1/1991 (unrecorded conversation)
Esther Unger, New York, 15/9/1988
Evelyn Weiner, New York, 21 e 27/9/1987